On clear days, visitors to the top of the Empire State Building can see for 80 miles. They can see four other states: New Jersey, Pennsylvania, Connecticut, and Massachusetts.

New York

HARCOURT
SOCIAL Studies

New York

Harcourt
SCHOOL PUBLISHERS

www.harcourtschool.com

HARCOURT SOCIAL Studies New York

Series Authors

Dr. Michael J. Berson
Associate Professor
Social Science Education
University of South Florida
Tampa, Florida

Dr. Tyrone C. Howard
Associate Professor
UCLA Graduate School of Education &
    Information Studies
University of California at Los Angeles
Los Angeles, California

Dr. Cinthia Salinas
Assistant Professor
Department of Curriculum and Instruction
College of Education
The University of Texas at Austin
Austin, Texas

Series Consultants

Dr. Marsha Alibrandi
Assistant Professor of Social Studies
Curriculum and Instruction Department
North Carolina State University
Chapel Hill, North Carolina

Dr. Patricia G. Avery
Professor
College of Education and Human
    Development
University of Minnesota
Minneapolis/St. Paul, Minnesota

Dr. Linda Bennett
Associate Professor
College of Educaton
University of Missouri—Columbia
Columbia, Missouri

Dr. Walter C. Fleming
Department Head and Professor
Native American Studies
Montana State University
Bozeman, Montana

Dr. S. G. Grant
Associate Professor
University at Buffalo
Buffalo, New York

C.C. Herbison
Lecturer
African and African-American Studies
University of Kansas
Lawrence, Kansas

Dr. Eric Johnson
Assistant Professor
Director, Urban Education Program
School of Education
Drake University
Des Moines, Iowa

Dr. Bruce E. Larson
Associate Professor
Social Studies Education
Secondary Education
Woodring College of Education
Western Washington University
Bellingham, Washington

Dr. Merry M. Merryfield
Professor
Social Studies and Global Education
College of Education
The Ohio State University
Columbus, Ohio

Dr. Peter Rees
Associate Professor
Department of Geography
University of Delaware
Wilmington, Delaware

Dr. Phillip J. VanFossen
James F. Ackerman Professor of
    Social Studies Education
Associate Director, Purdue Center for
    Economic Education
Purdue University
West Lafayette, Indiana

Dr. Myra Zarnowski
Professor
Elementary and Early Childhood Education
Queens College
The City University of New York
Flushing, New York

Content Reviewers

New York Geography

Dr. Ines Miyares
Associate Professor of Geography
Department of Geography
Hunter College
New York, New York

New York History

Dr. Laura Dull
Assistant Professor
Department of Secondary Education
    Social Studies Education Program
State University of New York at New Paltz
New Paltz, New York

Dr. David Gerber
Professor
Department of History
State University of New York at Buffalo
Buffalo, New York

Susan Goodier
Assistant Professor of History
Division of Social and
    Behavioral Sciences
Cazenovia College
Cazenovia, New York

Dr. Richard L. Haan
Professor of History
Department of History
Hartwick College
Oneonta, New York

Dr. Larry E. Hudson, Jr.
Associate Professor
Department of History
University of Rochester
Rochester, New York

Kathleen Hulser
Public Historian
New–York Historical Society
New York, New York

Classroom Reviewers

Marilyn Barr
Director of Social Studies
Rush-Henrietta Central School District
Henrietta, New York

Cal Baxter
Director of Humanities
Buffalo Public Schools
Buffalo, New York

Herbert Brodsky
Social Studies District Coordinator
Freeport School District
Freeport, New York

Laurie Kay Burger
Teacher
D'Youville Porter C.S. #3
Buffalo, New York

Steven A. Goldberg
Social Studies Department Chairman
City School District of New Rochelle
New Rochelle, New York

Dr. Joseph Nwabueze
Coordinator for Core Knowledge/
   Social Studies
Community School District #23
Brooklyn, New York

Kim O'Neil
Teacher
Liverpool Elementary School
Liverpool, New York

Linda Hughson Pacelli
Teacher
Willow Field Elementary School
Liverpool, New York

Francine Scaraggi
Teacher
P.S. 17 Henry David Thoreau School
Long Island City, New York

Rose Ann Terrance
Teacher
Monica B. Leary Elementary School
Rush, New York

ISBN-13: 978-0-15-360541-3
ISBN-10: 0-15-360541-3

3 4 5 6 7 8 9 10 0914 15 14 13 12 11 10 09

Unit 1

The Land and Early People

Unit 2

Newcomers Arrive

Unit 3

A New Nation and State

Unit 4

Becoming the Empire State

Unit 5

New York in the Modern World

Discover Your Community's History

Features

Time Lines

Illustrations

Reading Your Textbook

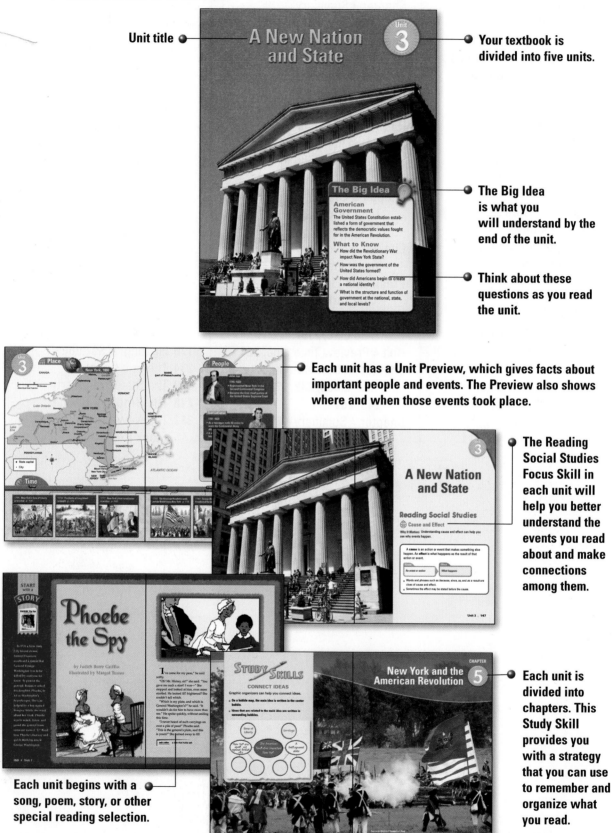

Unit title

Your textbook is divided into five units.

The Big Idea is what you will understand by the end of the unit.

Think about these questions as you read the unit.

Each unit has a Unit Preview, which gives facts about important people and events. The Preview also shows where and when those events took place.

The Reading Social Studies Focus Skill in each unit will help you better understand the events you read about and make connections among them.

Each unit is divided into chapters. This Study Skill provides you with a strategy that you can use to remember and organize what you read.

Each unit begins with a song, poem, story, or other special reading selection.

READING A LESSON

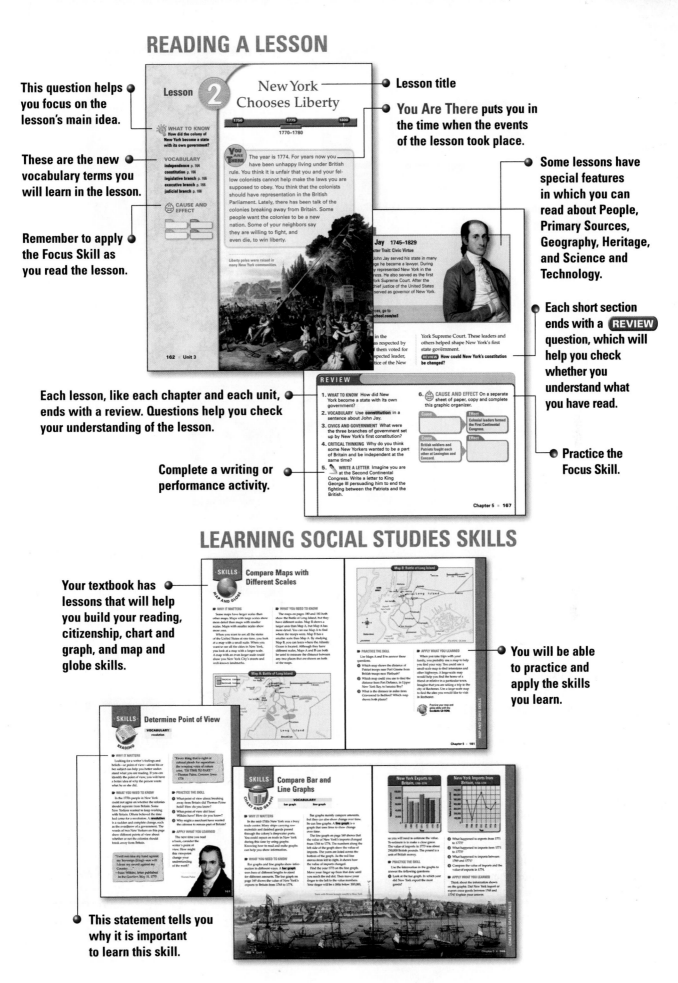

This question helps you focus on the lesson's main idea.

These are the new vocabulary terms you will learn in the lesson.

Remember to apply the Focus Skill as you read the lesson.

Lesson title

You Are There puts you in the time when the events of the lesson took place.

Some lessons have special features in which you can read about People, Primary Sources, Geography, Heritage, and Science and Technology.

Each short section ends with a REVIEW question, which will help you check whether you understand what you have read.

Each lesson, like each chapter and each unit, ends with a review. Questions help you check your understanding of the lesson.

Complete a writing or performance activity.

Practice the Focus Skill.

LEARNING SOCIAL STUDIES SKILLS

Your textbook has lessons that will help you build your reading, citizenship, chart and graph, and map and globe skills.

You will be able to practice and apply the skills you learn.

This statement tells you why it is important to learn this skill.

SPECIAL FEATURES

The feature called ● Primary Sources shows you ways to learn about different kinds of objects and documents.

The Field Trip ● feature lets you "visit" many interesting places.

ATLAS

● The Atlas provides maps and a list of geography terms with illustrations.

FOR YOUR REFERENCE

At the back of your textbook, ● you will find the reference tools listed below.

- Almanac
- Biographical Dictionary
- Gazetteer
- Glossary
- Index

You can use these tools to look up words and to find information about people, places, and other topics.

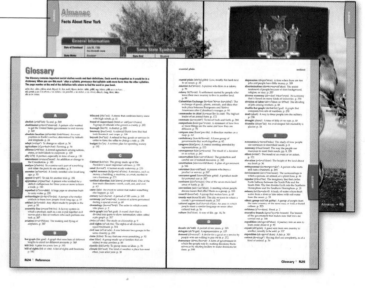

Atlas

Read a Map

VOCABULARY		
grid	locator	cardinal direction
map title	inset map	intermediate direction
map key	compass rose	map scale

▶ WHY IT MATTERS

Maps help you see where places are located in the world. They show the position of cities, states, and countries. They also identify where mountains, valleys, rivers, and lakes are found. Knowing how to read a map is an important skill for learning social studies.

▶ WHAT YOU NEED TO KNOW

A map is a drawing that shows some or all of Earth on a flat surface. Mapmakers often include features to help people use maps more easily.

Mapmakers sometimes draw grids on their maps. A **grid** is made up of lines that cross to form a pattern of squares. You can use a grid to locate places on a map. Look at the grid on the map of New York. Around the grid are letters

- A **map title** tells the subject of the map. The title may also help you know what kind of map it is.

  - Political maps show cities, states, and countries.

  - Physical maps show kinds of land and bodies of water.

  - Historical maps show parts of the world as they were in the past.

- A **map key**, or legend, explains the symbols used on a map. Symbols may be colors, patterns, lines, or other special marks.

- A **locator** is a small map or picture of a globe that shows where the place shown on the main map is located.

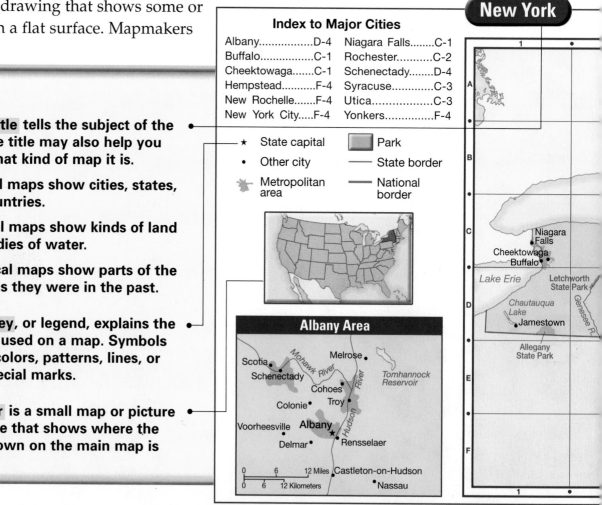

Index to Major Cities

Albany...............D-4	Niagara Falls........C-1
Buffalo................C-1	Rochester...........C-2
Cheektowaga.......C-1	Schenectady........D-4
Hempstead..........F-4	Syracuse.............C-3
New Rochelle.......F-4	Utica..................C-3
New York City.....F-4	Yonkers...............F-4

★ State capital
• Other city
Metropolitan area
Park
State border
National border

New York

Albany Area

Scotia Mohawk River Melrose
Schenectady Tomhannock Reservoir
Cohoes Hudson River
Colonie Troy
Voorheesville Albany ★
Delmar Rensselaer
0   6   12 Miles Castleton-on-Hudson
0   6   12 Kilometers • Nassau

Niagara Falls
Cheektowaga
Buffalo
Lake Erie Letchworth State Park
Chautauqua Lake
• Jamestown
Allegany State Park
Genesee R.

and numbers. The letters label the rows, which run left and right. The numbers label the columns, which run up and down. Each of the squares on the map below can be identified by its letter and number. For example, the top row of squares in the map includes squares A-1 through A-5.

Mapmakers may also include smaller maps called **inset maps**. Inset maps show a larger view of a smaller area on the main map. Look at the map of New York. The inset map allows you to see the Albany area more clearly than you can on the main map. Some inset maps may also show areas not shown on the main map.

▶ PRACTICE THE SKILL

Use the map of New York to answer these questions.

1 What cities are located in square C-4?

2 In what direction would you travel to go from Jamestown to Troy?

3 Find the map key. What symbol is used to show the state capital?

4 How many miles is it from Glens Falls to Kingston?

5 Look at the inset map of the Albany area. About how far is it from Schenectady to Cohoes?

▶ APPLY WHAT YOU LEARNED

Write ten questions about the New York map. You can ask questions about distance, direction, and location. Then exchange questions with a classmate.

- A **compass rose**, or direction marker, shows directions.
  - The **cardinal directions**, or main directions, are north, south, east, and west.
  - The **intermediate directions**, or directions between the cardinal directions, are northeast, northwest, southeast, and southwest.

- A **map scale** is used to compare a distance on the map to a distance in the real world. It helps you find the real distance between places. Notice that the map scale shows both miles and kilometers.

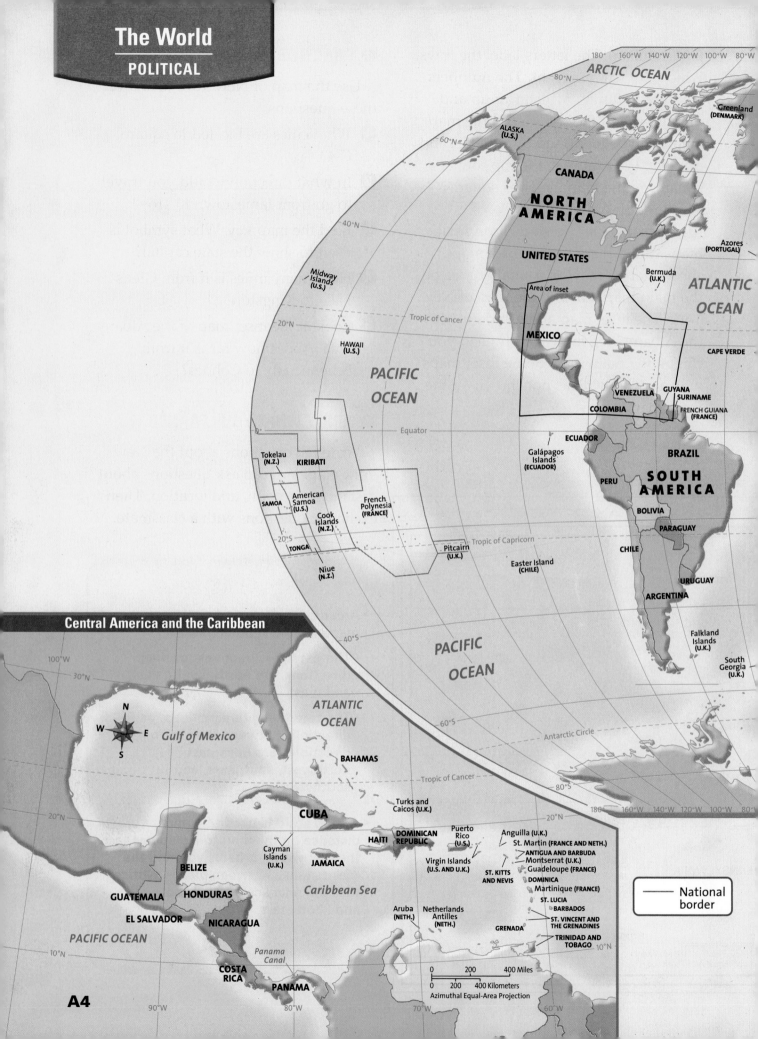

The World
POLITICAL

ARCTIC OCEAN

180° 160°W 140°W 120°W 100°W 80°W

80°N

Greenland (DENMARK)

ALASKA (U.S.)

60°N

CANADA

NORTH AMERICA

40°N

UNITED STATES

Azores (PORTUGAL)

ATLANTIC OCEAN

Bermuda (U.K.)

Area of inset

20°N

Tropic of Cancer

Midway Islands (U.S.)

MEXICO

CAPE VERDE

HAWAII (U.S.)

PACIFIC OCEAN

VENEZUELA

GUYANA
SURINAME

COLOMBIA

FRENCH GUIANA (FRANCE)

Equator

ECUADOR

Galápagos Islands (ECUADOR)

BRAZIL

Tokelau (N.Z.)

KIRIBATI

PERU

SOUTH AMERICA

SAMOA

American Samoa (U.S.)

Cook Islands (N.Z.)

French Polynesia (FRANCE)

BOLIVIA

PARAGUAY

20°S

TONGA

Niue (N.Z.)

Pitcairn (U.K.)

Tropic of Capricorn

Easter Island (CHILE)

CHILE

URUGUAY

ARGENTINA

40°S

PACIFIC OCEAN

Falkland Islands (U.K.)

South Georgia (U.K.)

60°S

Antarctic Circle

80°S

180° 160°W 140°W 120°W 100°W 80°

Central America and the Caribbean

100°W

30°N

N
W   E
S

Gulf of Mexico

ATLANTIC OCEAN

BAHAMAS

Tropic of Cancer

20°N

CUBA

Turks and Caicos (U.K.)

20°N

Cayman Islands (U.K.)

HAITI

DOMINICAN REPUBLIC

Puerto Rico (U.S.)

Anguilla (U.K.)

St. Martin (FRANCE AND NETH.)

ANTIGUA AND BARBUDA

Montserrat (U.K.)

BELIZE

JAMAICA

Virgin Islands (U.S. AND U.K.)

ST. KITTS AND NEVIS

Guadeloupe (FRANCE)

DOMINICA

GUATEMALA

HONDURAS

Caribbean Sea

Martinique (FRANCE)

ST. LUCIA

EL SALVADOR

NICARAGUA

Aruba (NETH.)

Netherlands Antilles (NETH.)

BARBADOS

ST. VINCENT AND THE GRENADINES

PACIFIC OCEAN

GRENADA

TRINIDAD AND TOBAGO

10°N

10°N

Panama Canal

COSTA RICA

PANAMA

90°W

80°W

70°W

60°W

0   200   400 Miles
0   200   400 Kilometers
Azimuthal Equal-Area Projection

——— National border

A4

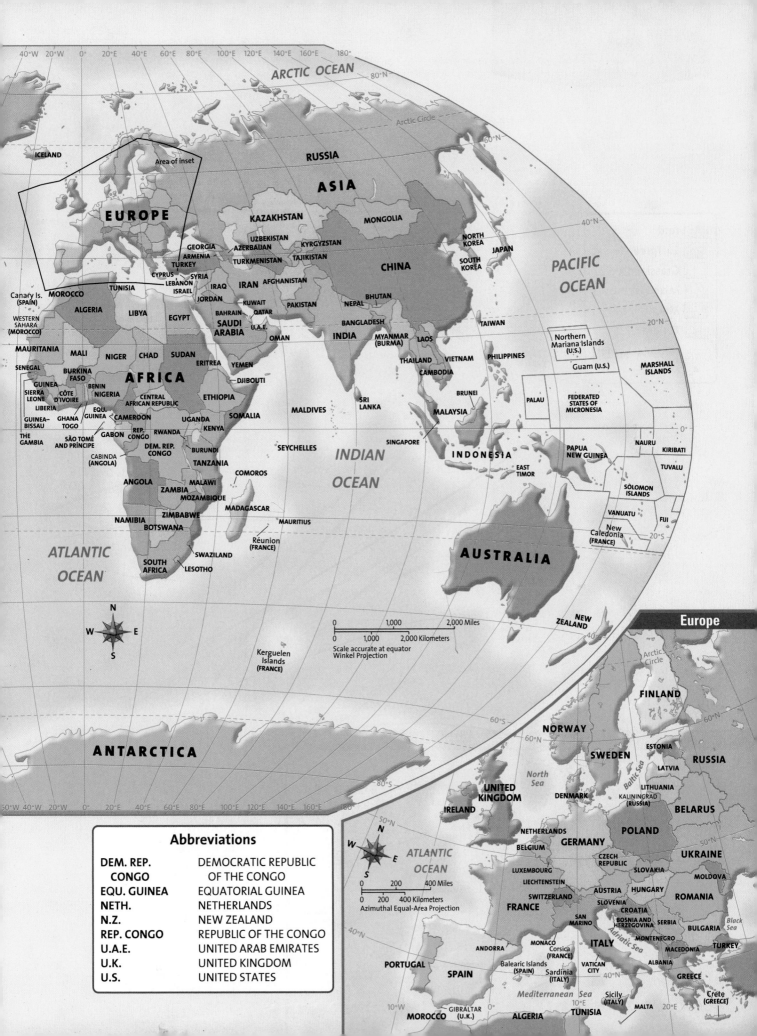

40°W 20°W 0° 20°E 40°E 60°E 80°E 100°E 120°E 140°E 160°E 180°

ARCTIC OCEAN

Arctic Circle

80°N

ICELAND

Area of inset

EUROPE

RUSSIA

ASIA

KAZAKHSTAN

MONGOLIA

60°N

GEORGIA
ARMENIA
TURKEY
AZERBAIJAN
UZBEKISTAN
KYRGYZSTAN
TURKMENISTAN
TAJIKISTAN

NORTH
KOREA
JAPAN

40°N

CYPRUS
LEBANON
ISRAEL
SYRIA
IRAQ
IRAN
AFGHANISTAN

SOUTH
KOREA

CHINA

PACIFIC
OCEAN

Canary Is.
(SPAIN)
MOROCCO
TUNISIA
JORDAN
KUWAIT
BAHRAIN
QATAR
U.A.E.
PAKISTAN
NEPAL
BHUTAN

WESTERN
SAHARA
(MOROCCO)
ALGERIA
LIBYA
EGYPT
SAUDI
ARABIA
BANGLADESH
TAIWAN
20°N

MAURITANIA
MALI
NIGER
CHAD
SUDAN
OMAN
INDIA
MYANMAR
(BURMA)
LAOS
Northern
Mariana Islands
(U.S.)

SENEGAL
BURKINA
FASO
ERITREA
YEMEN
THAILAND
VIETNAM
PHILIPPINES
Guam (U.S.)
MARSHALL
ISLANDS

GUINEA
SIERRA
LEONE
BENIN
CÔTE
D'IVOIRE
NIGERIA
AFRICA
DJIBOUTI
CAMBODIA
BRUNEI

LIBERIA
GHANA
TOGO
EQU.
GUINEA
CAMEROON
CENTRAL
AFRICAN REPUBLIC
ETHIOPIA
SRI
LANKA
FEDERATED
STATES OF
MICRONESIA
0°

GUINEA-
BISSAU
SÃO TOMÉ
AND PRÍNCIPE
GABON
UGANDA
SOMALIA
MALDIVES
PALAU

THE
GAMBIA
REP.
CONGO
RWANDA
KENYA
SINGAPORE
INDONESIA
PAPUA
NEW GUINEA
NAURU
KIRIBATI

CABINDA
(ANGOLA)
DEM. REP.
CONGO
BURUNDI
TANZANIA
SEYCHELLES
INDIAN
OCEAN
EAST
TIMOR
TUVALU

ANGOLA
ZAMBIA
MALAWI
COMOROS
SOLOMON
ISLANDS

ZIMBABWE
MOZAMBIQUE
MADAGASCAR
VANUATU
FIJI

NAMIBIA
BOTSWANA
MAURITIUS
New
Caledonia
(FRANCE)
20°S

ATLANTIC
OCEAN
SWAZILAND
Réunion
(FRANCE)
AUSTRALIA

SOUTH
AFRICA
LESOTHO

N
W E
S

0   1,000   2,000 Miles
0   1,000   2,000 Kilometers
Scale accurate at equator
Winkel Projection

NEW
ZEALAND

Kerguelen
Islands
(FRANCE)

40°S

ANTARCTICA

60°S

80°S

50°W 40°W 20°W 0° 20°E 40°E 60°E 80°E 100°E 120°E 140°E 160°E 180°

Europe

Arctic Circle

FINLAND

NORWAY

60°N

SWEDEN

ESTONIA

North
Sea

Baltic Sea

LATVIA

RUSSIA

UNITED
KINGDOM

DENMARK

LITHUANIA

KALININGRAD
(RUSSIA)

BELARUS

IRELAND

NETHERLANDS

50°N

GERMANY

POLAND

BELGIUM

N
W E
S

ATLANTIC
OCEAN

LUXEMBOURG

CZECH
REPUBLIC

UKRAINE

0   200   400 Miles
0   200   400 Kilometers
Azimuthal Equal-Area Projection

LIECHTENSTEIN

SLOVAKIA

MOLDOVA

SWITZERLAND

AUSTRIA

HUNGARY

ROMANIA

FRANCE

SLOVENIA

CROATIA

SAN
MARINO

BOSNIA AND
HERZEGOVINA

SERBIA

Adriatic Sea

Black
Sea

40°N

MONACO

Corsica
(FRANCE)

ITALY

MONTENEGRO

MACEDONIA

BULGARIA

TURKEY

ANDORRA

VATICAN
CITY

ALBANIA

PORTUGAL

SPAIN

Balearic Islands
(SPAIN)

Sardinia
(ITALY)

GREECE

Mediterranean Sea

10°E

Sicily
(ITALY)

Crete
(GREECE)

20°E

10°W

GIBRALTAR
(U.K.)

0°

MOROCCO

ALGERIA

TUNISIA

MALTA

The World
PHYSICAL

Legend:
- Arid
- Evergreen forest
- Grassland
- Mixed forest
- Mountains
- Tundra
- ⎯ National border
- ▲ Mountain peak

ARCTIC OCEAN

Beaufort Sea

Denali (Mt. McKinley) 20,320 ft. (6,194 m)

Queen Elizabeth Islands

Baffin Island

Great Bear Lake

Great Slave Lake

Hudson Bay

Bering Sea

Yukon R.

Mt. Logan 19,550 ft. (5,959 m)

ROCKY MOUNTAINS

Mackenzie R.

NORTH AMERICA

Aleutian Islands

Gulf of Alaska

Vancouver Island

Columbia R.

Missouri R.

Great Lakes

Newfoundland

GREAT PLAINS

Mississippi R.

Ohio R.

APPALACHIAN MTS.

Azores

Mt. Whitney 14,495 ft. (4,418 m)

Colorado R.

Rio Grande

Bermuda

ATLANTIC OCEAN

Gulf of California

Gulf of Mexico

Bahamas

Hawaiian Islands

Tropic of Cancer

Pico de Orizaba 18,855 ft. (5,747 m)

Yucatán Peninsula

Cuba

Hispaniola

West Indies

Caribbean Sea

PACIFIC OCEAN

Equator

Galápagos Islands

Orinoco River

Guiana Highlands

AMAZON BASIN

Amazon R.

SOUTH AMERICA

Polynesia

ANDES MOUNTAINS

Brazilian Highlands

Tropic of Capricorn

20°S

Atacama Desert

Gran Chaco

Paraná River

Mt. Aconcagua 22,834 ft. (6,960 m)

Pampa

PACIFIC OCEAN

40°S

Patagonia

Falkland Islands

Strait of Magellan

Cape Horn

Tierra del Fuego

60°S

Antarctic Circle

Antarctic Peninsula

80°S

Ross Sea

Northern Polar Region

Sea of Okhotsk

ASIA

Novaya Zemlya

EUROPE

Severnaya Zemlya

Kamchatka Peninsula

New Siberian Is.

Barents Sea

Baltic Sea

Scale:
0   400   800 Miles
0   400   800 Kilometers
Azimuthal Equidistant Projection

Wrangel Island

ARCTIC OCEAN

NORTH POLE

Svalbard

Norwegian Sea

North Sea

Bering Sea

Bering Strait

BROOKS RANGE

Beaufort Sea

NORTH MAGNETIC POLE

Queen Elizabeth Islands

Greenland Sea

British Isles

Iceland

Greenland

Baffin Bay

ATLANTIC OCEAN

Arctic Circle

PACIFIC OCEAN

NORTH AMERICA

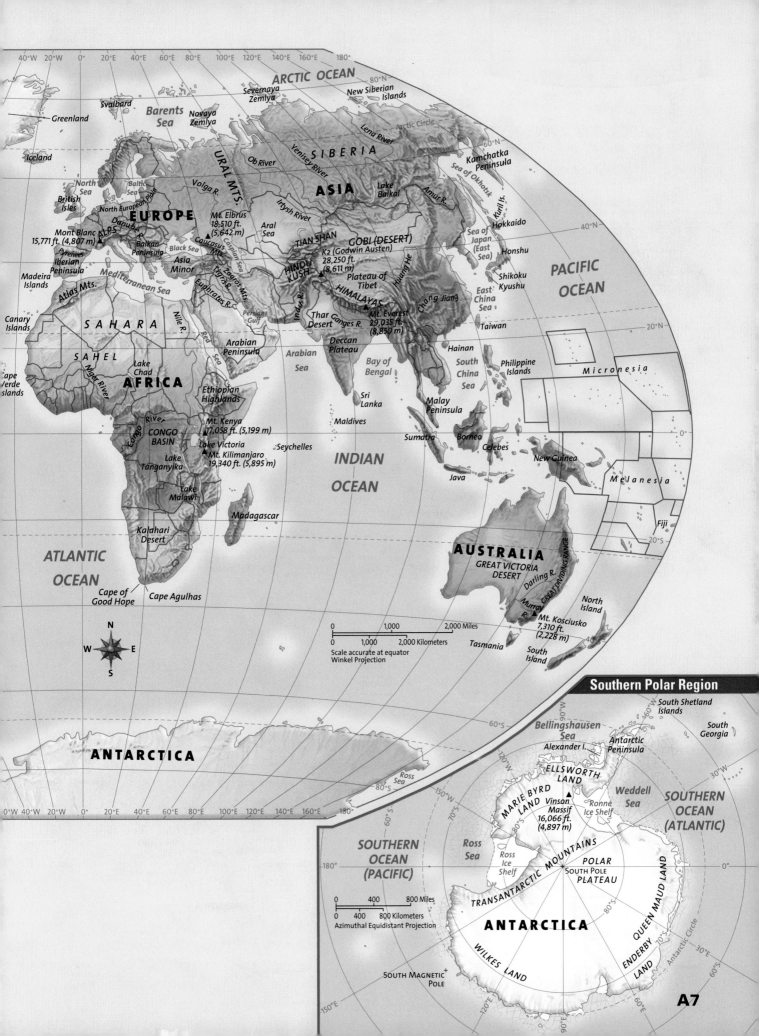

ARCTIC OCEAN

40°W   20°W   0°   20°E   40°E   60°E   80°E   100°E   120°E   140°E   160°E   180°

Greenland

Iceland

Svalbard

Barents Sea

Novaya Zemlya

Severnaya Zemlya

New Siberian Islands

80°N

Arctic Circle

60°N

SIBERIA

Ob River   Yenisey River   Lena River

Kamchatka Peninsula

Sea of Okhotsk

British Isles

North Sea   Baltic Sea

North European Plain

EUROPE

URAL MTS.

Volga R.

Mt. Elbrus 18,510 ft. (5,642 m)

Aral Sea

Irtysh River

ASIA

Lake Baikal

Amur R.

Kuril Is.

Hokkaido

Sea of Japan (East Sea)

40°N

Mont Blanc 15,771 ft. (4,807 m)

ALPS

Danube R.

Balkan Peninsula

Black Sea

Caucasus Mts.

Caspian Sea

TIAN SHAN

K2 (Godwin Austen) 28,250 ft. (8,611 m)

GOBI (DESERT)

Huang He

Honshu

Shikoku   Kyushu

PACIFIC OCEAN

Pyrenees

Iberian Peninsula

Asia Minor

Zagros Mts.

Tigris R.

Euphrates R.

HINDU KUSH

Plateau of Tibet

HIMALAYAS

Chang Jiang

East China Sea

Madeira Islands

Atlas Mts.

Mediterranean Sea

Persian Gulf

Indus R.

Mt. Everest 29,035 ft. (8,850 m)

Taiwan

20°N

Canary Islands

SAHARA

Nile R.

Red Sea

Arabian Peninsula

Thar Desert   Ganges R.

Deccan Plateau

Hainan

South China Sea

Philippine Islands

Micronesia

Cape Verde Islands

SAHEL

Lake Chad

Niger River

AFRICA

Arabian Sea

Bay of Bengal

Sri Lanka

Malay Peninsula

0°

Ethiopian Highlands

Mt. Kenya 17,058 ft. (5,199 m)

Maldives

Borneo

Celebes

New Guinea

Melanesia

Congo River

CONGO BASIN

Lake Victoria   Mt. Kilimanjaro 19,340 ft. (5,895 m)

Seychelles

Sumatra

Java

Lake Tanganyika

Lake Malawi

INDIAN OCEAN

Fiji

Madagascar

Kalahari Desert

20°S

ATLANTIC OCEAN

AUSTRALIA

GREAT VICTORIA DESERT

GREAT DIVIDING RANGE

Darling R.

North Island

Cape of Good Hope   Cape Agulhas

Murray R.   Mt. Kosciusko 7,310 ft. (2,228 m)

N
W   E
S

1,000   2,000 Miles
1,000   2,000 Kilometers
Scale accurate at equator
Winkel Projection

Tasmania

South Island

40°

80°S

ANTARCTICA

60°S

Ross Sea

80°S

0°W   40°W   20°W   0°   20°E   40°E   60°E   80°E   100°E   120°E   140°E   160°E   180°

Southern Polar Region

South Shetland Islands

Bellingshausen Sea

Alexander I.

Antarctic Peninsula

South Georgia

60°S

90°W

ELLSWORTH LAND

MARIE BYRD LAND

Vinson Massif 16,066 ft. (4,897 m)

Ronne Ice Shelf

Weddell Sea

SOUTHERN OCEAN (ATLANTIC)

30°W

70°S

SOUTHERN OCEAN (PACIFIC)

180°

Ross Sea

Ross Ice Shelf

TRANSANTARCTIC MOUNTAINS

POLAR PLATEAU

South Pole

QUEEN MAUD LAND

0°

80°S

ENDERBY LAND

400   800 Miles
400   800 Kilometers
Azimuthal Equidistant Projection

WILKES LAND

ANTARCTICA

SOUTH MAGNETIC POLE

Antarctic Circle

60°S

30°E

70°S

150°E   120°E   60°E

A7

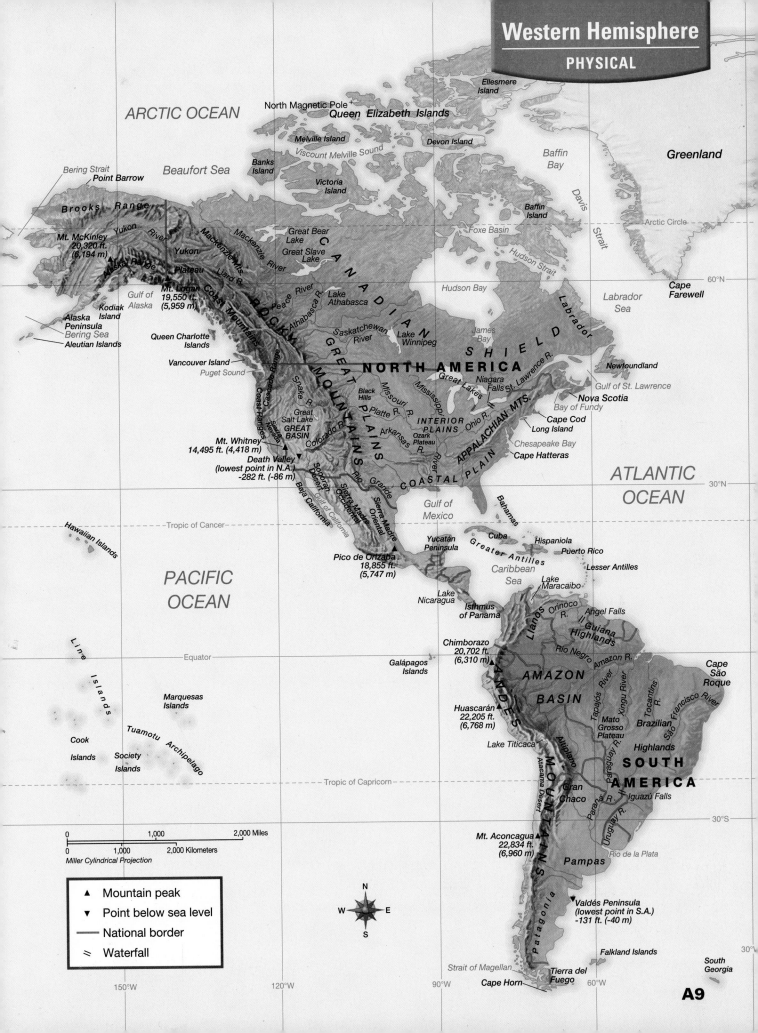

ARCTIC OCEAN

North Magnetic Pole +
Queen Elizabeth Islands

Ellesmere Island

Greenland

Melville Island

Devon Island

Baffin Bay

Viscount Melville Sound

Banks Island

Beaufort Sea

Bering Strait
Point Barrow

Brooks Range

Victoria Island

Baffin Island

Foxe Basin

Davis Strait

Arctic Circle

Mt. McKinley 20,320 ft. (6,194 m)

Yukon River

Mackenzie Mts.

Mackenzie River

Great Bear Lake

Great Slave Lake

Hudson Strait

60°N

Cape Farewell

Alaska Range

Yukon Plateau

Liard R.

Peace River

Lake Athabasca

Hudson Bay

Labrador Sea

Mt. Logan 19,550 ft. (5,959 m)

Gulf of Alaska

Coast Mountains

Athabasca R.

Saskatchewan River

James Bay

Kodiak Island

Alaska Peninsula

Bering Sea

Aleutian Islands

Queen Charlotte Islands

Lake Winnipeg

CANADIAN SHIELD

Labrador

Newfoundland

Vancouver Island

Puget Sound

ROCKY MOUNTAINS

GREAT PLAINS

NORTH AMERICA

Great Lakes

Niagara Falls St. Lawrence R.

Gulf of St. Lawrence

Nova Scotia

Cascade Range

Snake R.

Black Hills

Missouri R.

Mississippi R.

Ohio R.

APPALACHIAN MTS.

Bay of Fundy

Cape Cod

Long Island

Coast Ranges

Great Salt Lake

GREAT BASIN

Sierra Nevada

Platte R.

INTERIOR PLAINS

Arkansas R.

Ozark Plateau

Mississippi River

Chesapeake Bay

Mt. Whitney 14,495 ft. (4,418 m)

Colorado R.

Cape Hatteras

Death Valley (lowest point in N.A.) -282 ft. (-86 m)

Sonoran Desert

Rio Grande

COASTAL PLAIN

30°N

ATLANTIC OCEAN

Tropic of Cancer

Sierra Madre Occidental

Gulf of California

Baja California

Sierra Madre Oriental

Gulf of Mexico

Bahamas

Cuba

Greater Antilles

Hispaniola

Puerto Rico

Hawaiian Islands

PACIFIC OCEAN

Pico de Orizaba 18,855 ft. (5,747 m)

Yucatán Peninsula

Caribbean Sea

Lesser Antilles

Lake Maracaibo

Lake Nicaragua

Isthmus of Panama

Llanos

Orinoco R.

Angel Falls

Guiana Highlands

Line Islands

Chimborazo 20,702 ft. (6,310 m)

Galápagos Islands

Rio Negro

Amazon R.

Cape São Roque

Equator

AMAZON BASIN

A N D E S

Marquesas Islands

Huascarán 22,205 ft. (6,768 m)

Tapajós River

Xingu River

Tocantins R.

São Francisco River

Brazilian Highlands

Mato Grosso Plateau

Cook Islands

Tuamotu Archipelago

Society Islands

Lake Titicaca

Altiplano

SOUTH AMERICA

Tropic of Capricorn

M O U N T A I N S

Paraguay R.

Highlands

Gran Chaco

Iguazú Falls

Atacama Desert

Paraná R.

Uruguay R.

30°S

Mt. Aconcagua 22,834 ft. (6,960 m)

Pampas

Rio de la Plata

0   1,000   2,000 Miles

0   1,000   2,000 Kilometers

Miller Cylindrical Projection

Valdés Peninsula (lowest point in S.A.) -131 ft. (-40 m)

▲ Mountain peak

▼ Point below sea level

— National border

≈ Waterfall

Patagonia

Falkland Islands

30°

N
W   E
S

Strait of Magellan

Tierra del Fuego

Cape Horn

60°W

South Georgia

150°W

120°W

90°W

A9

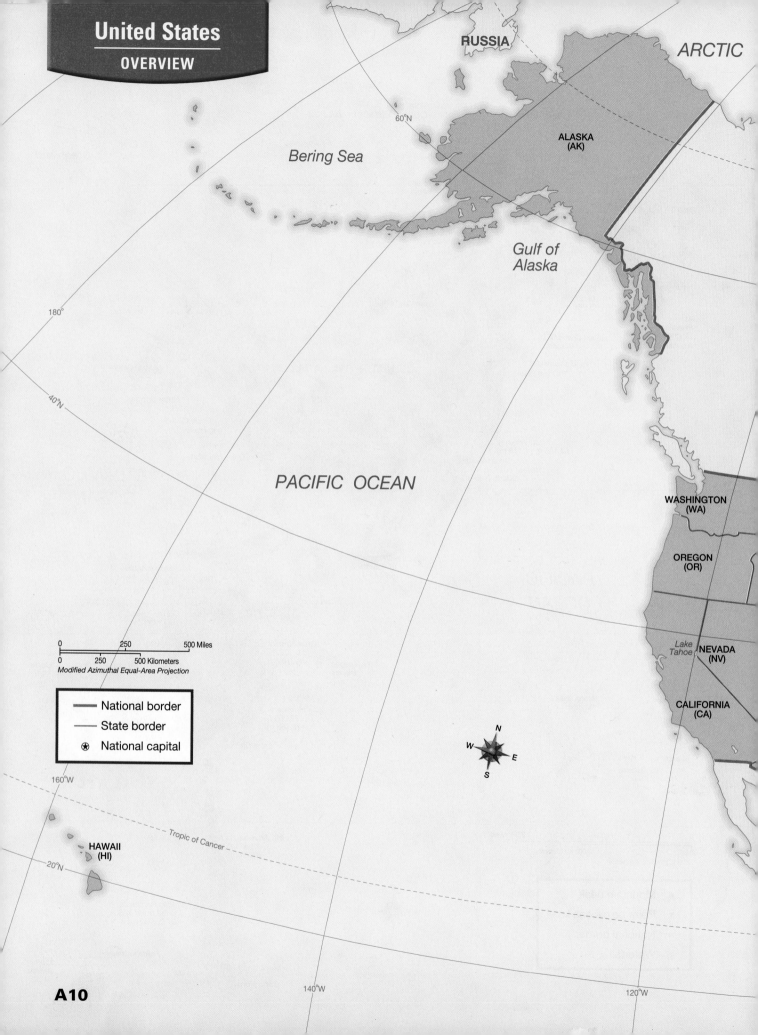

RUSSIA

ARCTIC

60°N

Bering Sea

ALASKA
(AK)

Gulf of
Alaska

180°

40°N

PACIFIC OCEAN

WASHINGTON
(WA)

OREGON
(OR)

Lake
Tahoe

NEVADA
(NV)

0   250   500 Miles
0   250   500 Kilometers
Modified Azimuthal Equal-Area Projection

CALIFORNIA
(CA)

National border
State border
⊛   National capital

160°W

N
W   E
S

Tropic of Cancer

HAWAII
(HI)

20°N

140°W

120°W

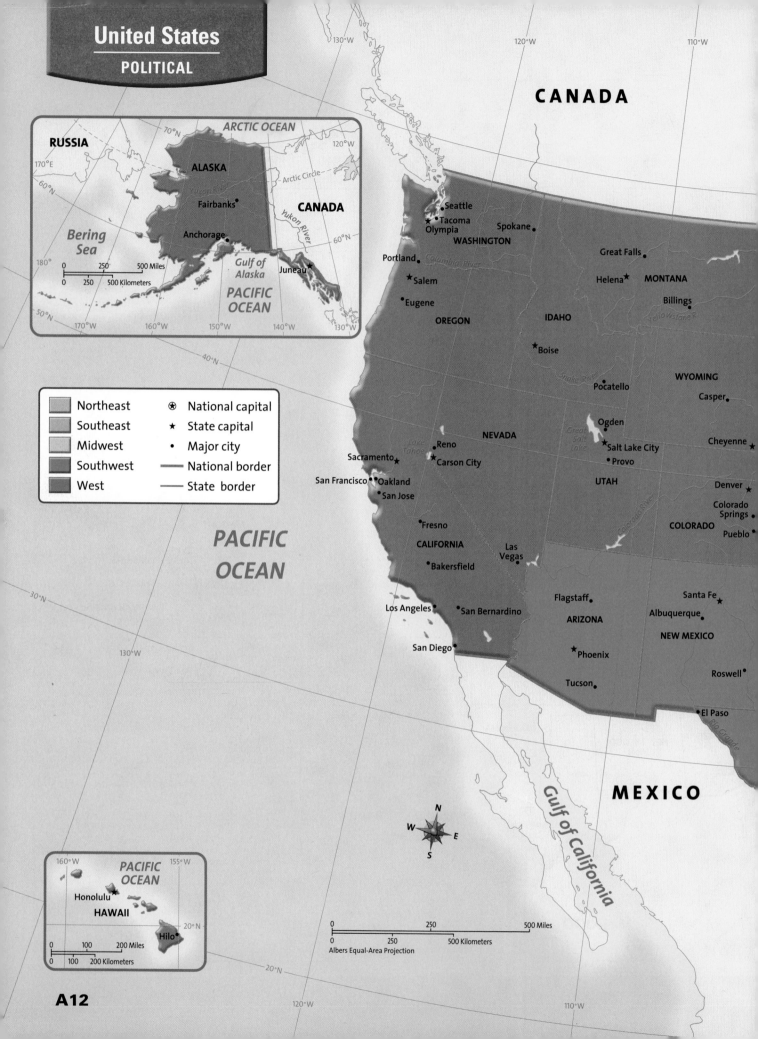

United States
POLITICAL

RUSSIA

ARCTIC OCEAN

70°N

ALASKA

Arctic Circle

Fairbanks

CANADA

Yukon River

Bering Sea

Anchorage

60°N

180°

Gulf of Alaska

Juneau

250   500 Miles

250   500 Kilometers

PACIFIC OCEAN

170°W   160°W   150°W   140°W   130°W

50°N

CANADA

40°N

Northeast	⊛	National capital
Southeast	★	State capital
Midwest	•	Major city
Southwest	—	National border
West	—	State border

PACIFIC OCEAN

30°N

130°W

Seattle
Tacoma
Olympia
Spokane
WASHINGTON

Portland
Great Falls
Columbia River
Helena ★ **MONTANA**
Salem
Billings
Eugene
Yellowstone R.
OREGON   **IDAHO**

Boise

WYOMING
Snake River
Pocatello
Casper

Lake Tahoe
Reno   **NEVADA**
Ogden
Sacramento ★
Carson City
Salt Lake City
Cheyenne
San Francisco Oakland
Provo
San Jose
UTAH
Denver ★
Fresno
Colorado Springs
CALIFORNIA
Colorado River
Pueblo
Las Vegas
COLORADO
Bakersfield

Los Angeles
San Bernardino
Flagstaff
Santa Fe ★
Albuquerque
ARIZONA
NEW MEXICO
San Diego

Phoenix ★
Roswell

Tucson
El Paso
Rio Grande

MEXICO

Gulf of California

N
W   E
S

250   500 Miles

250   500 Kilometers
Albers Equal-Area Projection

PACIFIC OCEAN

160°W   155°W

Honolulu ★
HAWAII
20°N
Hilo

100   200 Miles

100   200 Kilometers

120°W

20°N

110°W

A12

United States
PHYSICAL

CANADA

RUSSIA

ARCTIC OCEAN

Brooks Range

Seward Peninsula

ALASKA

Yukon River

Mt. McKinley 20,320 ft. (6,194 m) △

Alaska Range

Arctic Circle

CANADA

Yukon River

St. Lawrence Island

Bering Strait

Bering Sea

Gulf of Alaska

Kodiak Island

Aleutian Islands

0   250   500 Miles
0   250   500 Kilometers

Coast Ranges

Cascade Range

WA

Mt. Rainier 14,410 ft. (4,392 m)

Mt. St. Helens 8,366 ft. (2,550 m)

Columbia River

Mt. Hood 11,237 ft. (3,425 m)

OR

Columbia Plateau

Bitterroot Range

ID

Salmon River Mountains

Snake River

Fort Peck Lake

MT

Yellowstone River

ROCKY

Bighorn Mts.

Teton Range

Wind River Range

WY

Great Divide Basin

Front Range

MOUNTAINS

Cape Mendocino

Coast Ranges

Sacramento River

Sierra Nevada

Central San Joaquin Valley

CA

Pyramid Lake

Donner Pass

Lake Tahoe

NV

GREAT BASIN

Great Salt Lake

Wasatch Range

Uinta Mts.

UT

Mt. Elbert 14,433 ft. (4,399 m)

Lake Powell

Colorado River

CO

San Juan Mts.

Sangre de Cristo Mts.

Mt. Whitney 14,495 ft. (4,418 m)

Death Valley -282 ft. (-86 m)

Mojave Desert

Lake Mead

Grand Canyon

Colorado Plateau

AZ

Salton Sea

Imperial Valley

Sonoran Desert

Baldy Peak 11,403 ft. (3,476 m)

NM

Guadalupe Peak 8,749 ft. (2,667 m)

Rio Grande

PACIFIC OCEAN

Point Conception

Channel Islands

Legend:
- Arid
- Evergreen forest
- Grassland
- Mixed forest
- Mountains
- Tundra
- ——— National border
- ——— State border
- ▲ Mountain peak
- △ Highest point
- ▽ Lowest point

MEXICO

N
W   E
S

0   250   500 Miles
0   250   500 Kilometers
Albers Equal-Area Projection

Kauai   PACIFIC OCEAN

Niihau

Oahu

Molokai

HAWAII

Lanai

Kahoolawe

Maui

Hawaii

Mauna Kea 13,796 ft. (4,205 m)

0   100   200 Miles
0   100   200 Kilometers

A14

100°W 90°W 80°W 70°W

50°N

CANADA

St. Lawrence River

ME
▲ Mt. Katahdin
5,269 ft.
(1,606 m)

Moosehead
Lake

Lake of
the Woods

Isle
Royale

Lake Superior

Keweenaw
Peninsula

Upper
Red Lake

Lower
Red Lake

Mesabi
Range

ND

Lake Sakakawea

G R E A T

Lake
Oahe

SD

Black
Hills

Missouri River

Leech
Lake

Mille
Lacs
Lake

MN

WI

Wisconsin River

Mississippi River

Upper   Peninsula

Lake Huron

Lake Michigan

Lower Peninsula

Lake
Winnebago

MI

Lake
St. Clair

Lake
Champlain

VT

▲ Mt. Washington
6,288 ft.
(1,917 m)

White Mts.

NH

Cape Ann

NY

Adirondack
Mountains

Green Mts.

Finger
Lakes

MA

Cape
Cod

Niagara
Falls

Lake Ontario

Connecticut R.

Hudson R.

CT

RI

Lake Erie

PA

Long
Island

40°N

70°W

NJ

Allegheny Mts.

MD

DE

Delaware
Bay

Potomac R.

WV

VA

Cape
Charles

Chesapeake
Bay

James R.

Roanoke R.

Albemarle
Sound

Cape
Hatteras

IA

North Platte R.

Sand Hills

NE

Platte River

South Platte R.

P L A I N S

I N T E R I O R

Illinois River

IL

Wabash River

IN

OH

Ohio River

P L A I N S

CENTRAL PLAINS

Missouri River

Smoky Hills

KS

MO

Lake of
the Ozarks

Harry S. Truman
Reservoir

KY

Cumberland
Gap

Lake
Barkley

Mt. Mitchell
6,684 ft.
(2,037 m)

NC

Cape Fear River

Red Hills

Ozark Plateau

Mississippi River

Cumberland R.

TN

APPALACHIAN MOUNTAINS

P I E D M O N T

Tennessee R.

SC

Cape
Fear

**ATLANTIC
OCEAN**

OK

Arkansas
River

Canadian River

Ouachita
Mountains

AR

Lake
Texoma

Stone Mountain
1,686 ft. (514 m)

Clark
Hill Lake

Savannah River

Oconee R.

GA

C O A S T A L   P L A I N

Red River

Llano
Estacado

TX

Sabine River

LA

MS

Tombigbee R.

Alabama R.

AL

Chattahoochee R.

Ocmulgee R.

Altamaha R.

Okefenokee
Swamp

St. Johns River

Cape
Canaveral

Pecos River

Brazos River

Colorado River

Edwards
Plateau

Rio Grande

Toledo
Bend
Reservoir

Sam
Rayburn
Reservoir

Lake
Maurepas

Lake
Pontchartrain

Galveston
Bay

Mobile
Bay

Mississippi
Delta

Tampa
Bay

Lake
Okeechobee

FL

BAHAMAS

30°N

Everglades

Cape
Sable

Florida Keys

Gulf of Mexico

Straits of Florida

CUBA

100°W 90°W 80°W

A15

New York
POLITICAL

CANADA

78°W

76°W

44°N

JEFFERSON

Watertown

Lake Ontario

Oswego

OSWEGO

NIAGARA

ORLEANS

Albion

Lockport

Rochester

WAYNE

Lyons

Wampsville

GENESEE

MONROE

Syracuse

Batavia

ONONDAGA

Buffalo

Canandaigua

Auburn

ERIE

Geneseo

ONTARIO

Waterloo

CAYUGA

Warsaw

SENECA

WYOMING

YATES

LIVINGSTON

Penn Yan

CORTLAND

Cortland

Lake Erie

Ithaca

CHENANGO

SCHUYLER

TOMPKINS

Mayville

Little Valley

ALLEGANY

Bath

Watkins Glen

CHAUTAUQUA

CATTARAUGUS

Belmont

STEUBEN

TIOGA

BROOME

42°N

CHEMUNG

Owego

Binghamton

Elmira

PENNSYLVANIA

★	State capital
•	County seat
▬	National border
▬	State border
▬	County border

N
W E
S

0   25   50 Miles

0   25   50 Kilometers

Albers Equal-Area Projection

80°W

78°W

76°W

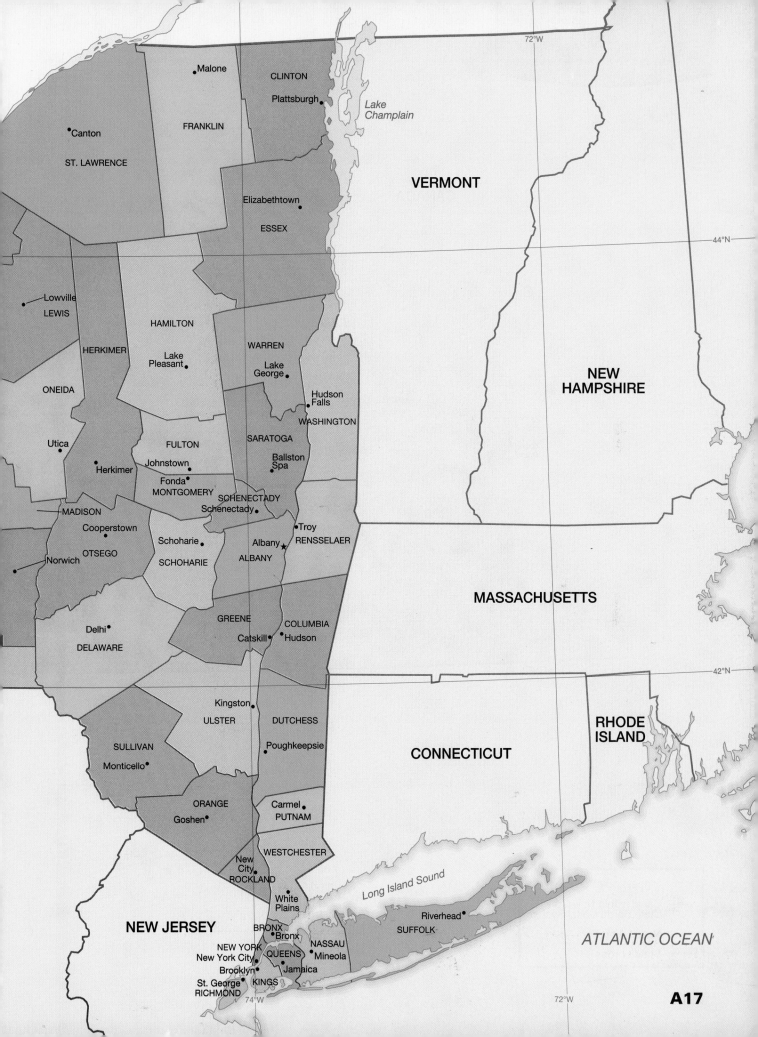

Malone

CLINTON

Plattsburgh

FRANKLIN

Lake
Champlain

Canton

ST. LAWRENCE

Elizabethtown

ESSEX

VERMONT

72°W

Lowville

LEWIS

HAMILTON

WARREN

Lake
Pleasant

Lake
George

44°N

HERKIMER

Hudson
Falls

ONEIDA

WASHINGTON

SARATOGA

Utica

FULTON

Ballston
Spa

NEW
HAMPSHIRE

Herkimer

Johnstown

Fonda
MONTGOMERY

SCHENECTADY

MADISON

Schenectady

Troy

Cooperstown

Schoharie

Albany

RENSSELAER

Norwich

OTSEGO

SCHOHARIE

ALBANY

MASSACHUSETTS

Delhi

GREENE

COLUMBIA

Catskill

Hudson

DELAWARE

42°N

Kingston

RHODE
ISLAND

ULSTER

DUTCHESS

SULLIVAN

Poughkeepsie

CONNECTICUT

Monticello

ORANGE

Carmel

PUTNAM

Goshen

WESTCHESTER

New
City

ROCKLAND

White
Plains

Long Island Sound

Riverhead

NEW JERSEY

BRONX

SUFFOLK

ATLANTIC OCEAN

Bronx

NEW YORK

NASSAU

New York City

QUEENS

Mineola

Brooklyn

Jamaica

St. George

KINGS

RICHMOND

74°W

72°W

A17

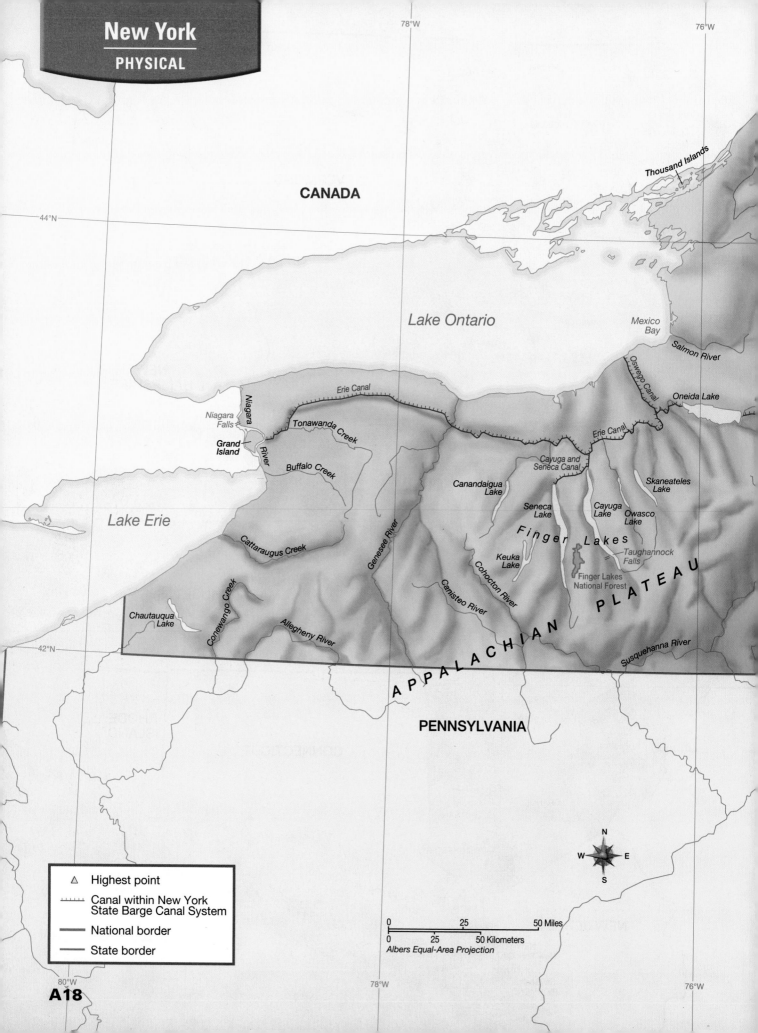

New York
PHYSICAL

CANADA

Thousand Islands

44°N

Lake Ontario

Mexico Bay

Salmon River

Oswego Canal

Oneida Lake

Erie Canal

Niagara Falls

Niagara River

Tonawanda Creek

Grand Island

Buffalo Creek

Erie Canal

Cayuga and Seneca Canal

Canandaigua Lake

Skaneateles Lake

Seneca Lake

Cayuga Lake

Owasco Lake

Lake Erie

Cattaraugus Creek

Genesee River

Keuka Lake

Finger Lakes

Taughannock Falls

Finger Lakes National Forest

Cohocton River

Canisteo River

Chautauqua Lake

Conewango Creek

Allegheny River

APPALACHIAN PLATEAU

Susquehanna River

42°N

PENNSYLVANIA

N
W E
S

Legend

△ Highest point

⊥⊥⊥⊥ Canal within New York State Barge Canal System

—— National border

—— State border

0   25   50 Miles
0   25   50 Kilometers
Albers Equal-Area Projection

80°W

78°W

76°W

A18

72°W

St. Lawrence River

Grass River

Raquette River

St. Regis River

Oswegatchie River

Saranac River

Ausable River

Saranac Lakes

Lake Placid

Lake Champlain

Cranberry Lake

Long Lake

Adirondack Mountains

Mt. Marcy
5,344 ft.
△ (1,629 m)

Schroon River

Hudson River

Lake George

44°N

VERMONT

NEW HAMPSHIRE

Black River

West Canada Creek

Great Sacandaga Lake

Erie Canal

Mohawk River

Champlain Canal

A P P A L A C H I A N   M O U N T A I N S

Taconic Range

Unadilla River

Susquehanna River

Hudson River

MASSACHUSETTS

Catskill Mountains

42°N

Delaware River

Neversink River

Shawangunk Mountains

Wallkill River

RHODE ISLAND

CONNECTICUT

NEW JERSEY

Long Island Sound

Montauk Point

Long Island

Staten Island

East River

Fire Island

ATLANTIC OCEAN

New York Bay

72°W

A19

Geography Terms

1. **basin** bowl-shaped area of land surrounded by higher land
2. **bay** an inlet of the sea or some other body of water, usually smaller than a gulf
3. **bluff** high, steep face of rock or earth
4. **canyon** deep, narrow valley with steep sides
5. **cape** point of land that extends into water
6. **cataract** large waterfall
7. **channel** deepest part of a body of water
8. **cliff** high, steep face of rock or earth
9. **coast** land along a sea or ocean
10. **coastal plain** area of flat land along a sea or ocean
11. **delta** triangle-shaped area of land at the mouth of a river
12. **desert** dry land with few plants
13. **dune** hill of sand piled up by the wind
14. **fall line** area along which rivers form waterfalls or rapids as the rivers drop to lower land
15. **floodplain** flat land that is near the edges of a river and is formed by silt deposited by floods
16. **foothills** hilly area at the base of a mountain
17. **glacier** large ice mass that moves slowly down a mountain or across land
18. **gulf** part of a sea or ocean extending into the land, usually larger than a bay
19. **hill** land that rises above the land around it
20. **inlet** any area of water extending into the land from a larger body of water
21. **island** land that has water on all sides
22. **isthmus** narrow strip of land connecting two larger areas of land
23. **lagoon** body of shallow water
24. **lake** body of water with land on all sides
25. **marsh** lowland with moist soil and tall grasses

26	**mesa**	flat-topped mountain with steep sides
27	**mountain**	highest kind of land
28	**mountain pass**	gap between mountains
29	**mountain range**	row of mountains
30	**mouth of river**	place where a river empties into another body of water
31	**oasis**	area of water and fertile land in a desert
32	**ocean**	body of salt water larger than a sea
33	**peak**	top of a mountain
34	**peninsula**	land that is almost completely surrounded by water
35	**plain**	area of flat or gently rolling low land
36	**plateau**	area of high, mostly flat land
37	**reef**	ridge of sand, rock, or coral that lies at or near the surface of a sea or ocean
38	**river**	large stream of water that flows across the land
39	**riverbank**	land along a river
40	**savanna**	area of grassland and scattered trees
41	**sea**	body of salt water smaller than an ocean
42	**sea level**	the level of the surface of an ocean or a sea
43	**slope**	side of a hill or mountain
44	**source of river**	place where a river begins
45	**strait**	narrow channel of water connecting two larger bodies of water
46	**swamp**	area of low, wet land with trees
47	**timberline**	line on a mountain above which it is too cold for trees to grow
48	**tributary**	stream or river that flows into a larger stream or river
49	**valley**	low land between hills or mountains
50	**volcano**	opening in the earth, often raised, through which lava, rock, ashes, and gases are forced out
51	**waterfall**	steep drop from a high place to a lower place in a stream or river

Introduction

> " New York is diff'rent' cause there's no place else on earth quite like New York . . . "
>
> — Steve Karmen, from the state song "I Love New York"

Learning About New York

New Yorkers are proud of their state. As you read this book, you will find out why. You will learn about the state's interesting past. You will also learn about the land, water, and climate of New York. In addition, you will find out about the many different people of the state. All of these things will help you understand why people are proud to be citizens of New York.

- Civics and Government
- Culture and Society
- **What Is Social Studies?**
- History
- Economics
- Geography

Why History Matters

The study of **history**, or what happened in the past, is very important. History teaches us how events from the past affect the present. In addition, studying history can help us prepare for future events.

History is very important to New Yorkers. In this book you will learn about the ways of life of New Yorkers long ago. You will also find out how New York has changed.

Old photographs and newspapers are examples of evidence.

Learning About Time

Understanding history requires knowing when events took place. The order in which events take place is called **chronology** (kruh•NAH•luh•jee). **Historians**, or people who study the past, look closely at the chronology of events. This helps them better understand how one event affects another and how the past and the present connect.

The New York State Museum collects and stores evidence about New York's history.

Finding Evidence

How do historians learn about the past? One way is by finding **evidence**, or proof, of when, why, where, and how things happened. Historians read books and newspapers from long ago. They study old diaries and letters. They look at paintings and photographs from the past. They also listen to oral histories. An **oral history** is a story told aloud about an event. Historians use these different kinds of evidence to piece together the history of people.

Identifying Points of View

Historians think about why different people of the past said or wrote what they did. They try to understand the different people's points of view. A person's **point of view** is how he or she sees things. A point of view is based on a person's beliefs and ideas. It can be affected by whether a person is young or old, male or female, and rich or poor. Background and experiences also affect point of view. People with different points of view may have different ideas about the same event.

To understand points of view about an event, historians learn about the people who took part in the event. They find out as much as possible about how people lived long ago. This helps them get a better idea of the actions and feelings of those people.

Drawing Conclusions

After historians have identified the facts about a historical event, they still have work to do. They need to analyze the event. To **analyze** an event is to examine each part of it and relate the parts to each other. Analyzing an event allows historians to draw conclusions about how and why it happened.

REVIEW What is history?

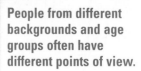

People from different backgrounds and age groups often have different points of view.

Compare Primary and Secondary Sources

VOCABULARY

primary source
secondary source

WHY IT MATTERS

People who study the past look for evidence, or proof. They want to be sure they know what really happened. They look for evidence in two different kinds of sources—primary sources and secondary sources.

WHAT YOU NEED TO KNOW

Primary sources are records made by people who saw or took part in an event. They may have written their thoughts in journals or diaries. They may have told their stories in letters, poems, or songs. They may have given speeches. They may have painted pictures or taken photographs. Objects made or used during an event can also be primary sources. All these primary sources are direct evidence from people who saw what happened.

Ⓐ These plans for the Brooklyn Bridge, Ⓑ this coin celebrating the opening day of the bridge, and Ⓒ this early photograph of the bridge are all primary sources.

Secondary sources are records of an event that were made by people who were not there. Books written by authors who only heard about or read about an event are secondary sources. So, too, are magazine articles and newspaper stories written by people who did not take part in the event. Paintings or drawings by artists who did not see the event are also secondary sources.

The sources on pages 4 and 5 tell about the Brooklyn Bridge. The bridge took 14 years to construct and was completed in 1833. At the time it was built, the 3,460-foot (1,055-m) bridge was the longest suspension bridge in the world.

➡️ **PRACTICE THE SKILL**

Look at the photographs of objects and the printed materials about the Brooklyn Bridge. Use the photographs to answer the following questions.

1 Which source was drawn by someone who was alive during the construction of the Brooklyn Bridge?

2 How are items A and E alike and different?

3 Which are primary sources? Which are secondary sources?

➡️ **APPLY WHAT YOU LEARNED**

Work with a partner to find examples of primary and secondary sources in your textbook. Discuss why you think each source is either a primary source or a secondary source.

This **D** Web site and **E** this postage stamp are secondary sources.

Why Geography Matters

VOCABULARY

geography	physical feature	region
geographer	human feature	
location	interact	

The study of Earth and the people who live on it is called **geography**. People who study geography are called **geographers**. Geographers do much more than find places on maps. They learn all they can about places and the people who live there.

Themes of Geography

Geographers sometimes divide geography into five themes, or key topics. Most of the maps in this book focus on one of the five themes. Keeping the themes in mind will help you think like a geographer.

Location
Everything on Earth has its own **location**—the place where it can be found.

Human-Environment Interactions
Humans and their surroundings **interact**, or affect each other. The actions of people change the environment. The environment also affects people.

Place
Every location on Earth has features that make it different from all other locations. Features that are formed by nature are **physical features**. Physical features include landforms, bodies of water, and plant life. Features that are created by people are **human features**. Human features include buildings, roads, and people themselves.

Movement
People, things, and ideas move every day. Each movement affects the world in some way.

Regions
Areas on Earth whose features make them different from other areas can be called **regions**. A region can be described by its physical features or by its human features.

GEOGRAPHY THEME

Essential Elements of Geography

Geographers use six other topics to help them understand Earth and its people. These topics are the six essential elements, or most important parts, of geography. Thinking about them will help you learn more about the world and your place in it.

• GEOGRAPHY •

The World in Spatial Terms

Spatial means "having to do with space." Every place on Earth has its own space, or location. Geographers want to know where places are located and why they are located where they are.

Places and Regions

Geographers often group places into regions. They do this to show that all the places in a group have a similar physical or human feature.

Physical Systems

Geographers study the physical parts of the surface of Earth. For example, they study climate, landforms, and bodies of water.

Human Systems

Geographers study where people have settled, how they earn a living, and what laws they have made.

Environment and Society

People's actions affect the environment. The environment also affects people's actions.

The Uses of Geography

Knowing how to use maps, globes, and other geographic tools helps people in their day-to-day lives.

REVIEW What is geography?

Why Economics Matters

VOCABULARY

economy
economics

Hospitals, schools, banks, and stores—these are just a few of the many places where people work. Most people work to be able to buy what they need or want and to save for the future. By working, buying, and saving, they are taking part in the economy. An **economy** is the way people use resources to meet their needs. The study of how people do this is called **economics**.

In this book you will read about how New Yorkers make, buy, sell, and trade goods to meet their needs. You will also discover how the New York economy has changed over time and how it came to be what it is today.

REVIEW What is the study of how people use resources to meet their needs?

When you earn, save, or spend money, you are taking part in the economy.

Why Civics and Government Matter

Reproduced with the permission of the New York Secretary of State.

VOCABULARY

government

civics

To live together peacefully, people form governments. A **government** is a system of leaders and laws that helps people live safely together in a community, a state, or a country. As a New Yorker, you follow the laws of your city or town, your state, and your country—the United States of America.

Harcourt Horizons: New York tells about the role of New Yorkers in community, state, and national governments. It also tells how New York's governments came to be and how they changed over time. As you read this book, you will learn about the leaders and laws in New York history. You will also read about leaders in New York today.

The study of government connects with civics. **Civics** is the study of citizenship. As you read this book, you will learn about the rights and responsibilities of citizens.

REVIEW How are government and civics different?

New York's state government is based in Albany.

Why Culture and Society Matter

VOCABULARY

culture   society   heritage

As you read this book, you will find out how people in the past helped make New York what it is today. You will learn where New York's early settlers came from, how they dressed, and what they believed. You will also learn about the languages they spoke and the foods they ate. All these things make up a **culture**, or way of life.

Each human group, or **society**, has a culture. Many groups of people have contributed to New York's culture. This book gives information about the different cultures that have come together in New York. It also describes New York's **heritage**, or the ways of life that have been passed down through history.

REVIEW How are culture and society related?

Traditional costumes and dances are often an important part of a culture's heritage.

The Land and Early People

The Big Idea

Geography

People in New York have always been influenced by their environment. They also have affected their environment.

What to Know

✓ What are the main physical features and resources of New York?

✓ How do New York's physical features and resources affect how people live?

✓ Who were the first inhabitants of New York State, and how did they

Niagara Falls

The Land and Early People

Reading Social Studies

Focus Skill Main Idea and Details

Why It Matters When you identify and understand the main idea and details, you can better understand what you read.

The **main idea** is the most important idea of a paragraph or passage. **Details** give more information about the main idea.

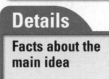

Main Idea

The most important idea of a paragraph or passage

Details

| Facts about the main idea | Facts about the main idea | Facts about the main idea |

- The main idea is often given at the beginning of a piece of writing.
- In a long article, each paragraph has a main idea and details. The article as a whole also has a main idea and details.

Unit 1

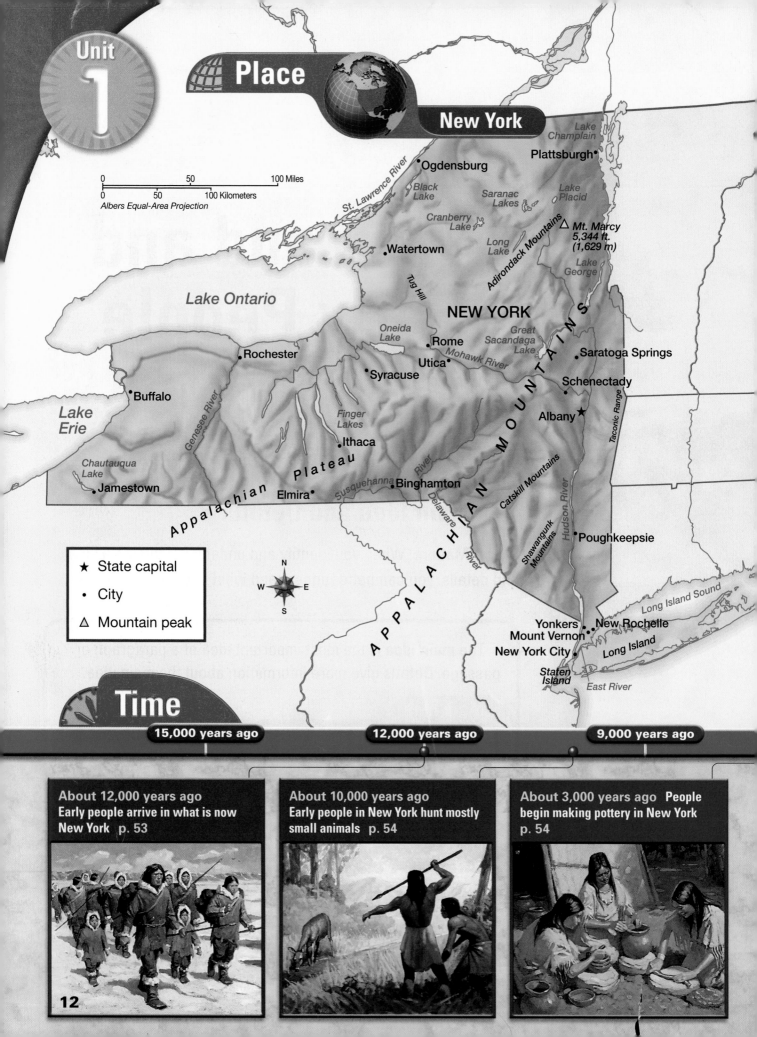

Lake Champlain

Plattsburgh

St. Lawrence River

Ogdensburg

Black Lake

Saranac Lakes

Lake Placid

Cranberry Lake

△ Mt. Marcy
5,344 ft.
(1,629 m)

Long Lake

Watertown

Adirondack Mountains

Lake George

Tug Hill

NEW YORK

Lake Ontario

Oneida Lake

Rome

Great Sacandaga Lake

Saratoga Springs

Rochester

Utica

Mohawk River

Schenectady

Syracuse

Albany ★

Taconic Range

Buffalo

Genesee River

Finger Lakes

Lake Erie

Ithaca

Catskill Mountains

Hudson River

Chautauqua Lake

Appalachian Plateau

Binghamton

Jamestown

Elmira

Susquehanna River

Delaware River

Shawangunk Mountains

Poughkeepsie

★ State capital

• City

△ Mountain peak

N
W E
S

APPALACHIAN MOUNTAINS

Long Island Sound

Yonkers
Mount Vernon

New Rochelle

New York City

Long Island

Staten Island

East River

0   50   100 Miles
0   50   100 Kilometers
Albers Equal-Area Projection

Time

15,000 years ago

12,000 years ago

9,000 years ago

About 12,000 years ago
Early people arrive in what is now New York p. 53

About 10,000 years ago
Early people in New York hunt mostly small animals p. 54

**About 3,000 years ago People begin making pottery in New York p. 54

People

Paleo-Indians

- About 12,000 years ago, were the first people to reach New York
- Probably came to North America from Asia by crossing a land bridge
- Hunted animals and gathered wild plants for food

Iroquois

- Lived in villages in northern, central, and western New York
- Called themselves Haudenosaunee, or "People of the Longhouse"

Algonquians

- Lived in the southeastern part of New York
- Built both longhouses and wigwams

ATLANTIC OCEAN

6,000 years ago	3,000 years ago	Present

About 1,000 years ago
People begin farming in New York
p. 54

About 1,000 years ago
Native Americans live in villages across New York   p. 54

About 600 years ago   Most Native Americans belong to the Iroquoian or Algonquian language groups   p. 55

Esther

by Sandra Weber and Peggy Eyres
illustrated by Lori Lohstoeter

In 1839, fur trappers were just about the only people who traveled up the Adirondack (a•duh•RAHN•dak) Mountains. Although several families had settled in the valleys there, no one went up the mountains just for the fun of it. No one did that until Esther McComb.

For as long as she could remember, 15-year-old Esther had longed to climb to the top of Whiteface Mountain. Every morning, from a window of her Wilmington Valley home, she would look at the mountain peak. Esther finally decided that she had to climb the mountain. She packed light, taking just a slice of bread and cheese. She was sure her journey would be a short one.

Esther struggled through thick bushes and trees, but she kept climbing. By late afternoon she had made her way to a clearing near the peak. Esther looked to see how much farther she had to go. To her horror she saw Whiteface Mountain in the distance! Somehow she had climbed the wrong mountain. But where was she? Read now the words to a song about Esther's adventure.

Esther grew up close to Whiteface Mountain,
Thought she heard it calling her name.
Her family told her, "Ladies don't go climbing."
Esther thought she'd try it just the same.

One morning just before the dawn was breaking,
Esther loaded up her brother's pack.
She left behind her petticoats and ribbons;
Esther wouldn't let them hold her back.

(Chorus)
Sometimes you have to climb a mountain.
Sometimes you have to wade a stream.
When the path you follow disappears among the trees,
Be brave and follow your dream.

By mid-morning she was tired and hungry.
Still she climbed beside a rocky creek.
By evening she fell down amid the hobble bush,
Not far from another mountains peak.

hobble bush a low plant with white flowers and red berries

Her family found her early the next morning,
Shivering cold but glad to be alive.
They named the peak she conquered, Esther Mountain,
For the young girl who was lost but still survived.

(Chorus)

If you dare to set out on a mountain,
And find you've somehow gone astray,
Though you miss your final destination,
Look at what you've learned along the way.

You took one step then followed with another,
Found the inner courage to go on.
You reached new heights and felt your heart's direction.
Now you finally see yourself as strong.

(Chorus)

No one knows for sure if Esther really climbed this mountain. However, her story made such an impression that the mountain was named for her.

Response Corner

1. **Focus Skill** **Main Idea and Details** How did Esther Mountain get its name?

2. What does the author feel about Esther's climb?

3. **Make It Relevant** Choose a place near where you live. Research how it got its name. Then write a poem or story that tells how the name came to be.

START THE UNIT PROJECT

Make a New York Atlas Working in a small group, make a New York atlas. Include at least four different kinds of maps, such as a political map, a physical map, a resource map, and a map of historic sites. As you read about New York, take notes on information that should go on each kind of map.

USE TECHNOLOGY

GO ONLINE

For more resources, go to www.harcourtschool.com/ss1

STUDY SKILLS

PREVIEW AND QUESTION

Previewing a lesson to identify main ideas, and asking yourself questions about those ideas, can help you read to find important information.

- **To preview a lesson, read the lesson title and the section titles. Look at the pictures, and read their captions. Try to get an idea of the main topic, and think of questions you have.**

- **Read to find the answers to your questions. Then recite, or say the answer aloud. Finally, review what you have read.**

New York's Geography

Preview	Questions	Read	Recite	Review
Lesson 1 You can describe New York's location in different ways.	In which region of the United States is New York?	✓	✓	✓
Lesson 2				

New York's Geography

Hudson River Valley

Where Is New York?

YOU ARE THERE

Your new pen pal in Brazil has asked you where you live. What do you say? You could give your street address. You might also tell him that you live north of Brazil. You tell your pen pal that you live in the state of New York. "Where in the world is New York?" he writes back.

WHAT TO KNOW
What are different ways to describe the location of New York?

VOCABULARY
continent p. 20
hemisphere p. 21
equator p. 21
relative location p. 22
region p. 23

MAIN IDEA AND DETAILS

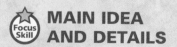

New York's Global Address

New York is one of the 50 states in the United States of America. Since the United States is part of North America, New York is also in North America. North America is one of Earth's seven **continents**, or largest land areas. The other continents are Africa, Antarctica, Asia, Australia, Europe, and South America.

FAST FACT Although New York is ranked twenty-seventh in land area among the 50 states, it has the third-largest population.

NORTH AMERICA

THE UNITED STATES

Earth is shaped like a sphere, or ball, so half of Earth is called a **hemisphere**. *Hemi* means "half." One way to divide Earth is into an Eastern Hemisphere and a Western Hemisphere. North America is in the Western Hemisphere.

Earth can also be divided into a Northern and a Southern Hemisphere. The **equator** is the imaginary line that divides Earth into these two hemispheres. On a map or globe, you can see the equator halfway between the North Pole and the South Pole. North America is located north of the equator, in the Northern Hemisphere.

REVIEW **Which of Earth's hemispheres are part of New York's global address?**

New York's Borders

On a map New York looks like a boot with a pointed heel. The boot's toe is the western tip of the state. It touches Lake Erie, one of the five Great Lakes. It also touches the northwestern corner of Pennsylvania. The tip of the heel touches the Atlantic Ocean. New York is the only state that borders both the Great Lakes and the Atlantic Ocean.

After people in Ogdensburg have crossed this bridge across the St. Lawrence River, they are in Canada.

The southern tip of the heel is part of New York City. Lying off the tip are several islands, including Staten Island and Manhattan. These islands are part of New York City. To the east is a larger island called Long Island. The western part of this island is part of New York City.

NEW YORK

THE NORTHEAST

Analyze Diagrams **New York is one of the 50 states in the United States.**

❓ Which usually covers a larger area, a country or a continent?

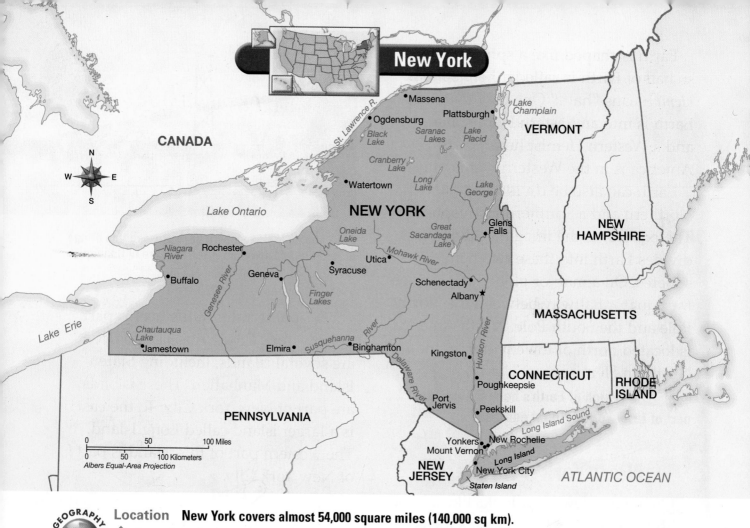

Location New York covers almost 54,000 square miles (140,000 sq km).

On a clear day people at the top of the Empire State Building in New York City can see four of New York's five bordering states. Which states do you think they are?

New York State shares its eastern border with the states of Connecticut, Massachusetts, and Vermont. Lake Champlain (sham•PLAYN) forms part of the New York–Vermont border.

To the south of New York are the states of New Jersey and Pennsylvania. New York's longest river, the Hudson River, forms part of the state's border with New Jersey. Another large river, the Delaware River, forms part of its border with Pennsylvania.

Two of the Great Lakes—Lake Erie and Lake Ontario—form part of New York's western and northern borders. New York also shares part of its border with another country—Canada. The St. Lawrence River and the Niagara River form parts of this border.

REVIEW Which states border New York?

A Northeastern State

Knowing New York's borders can help you describe its relative location. The **relative location** of a place is where it is, compared with one or more other places. When giving directions to a friend, you might say that the library is located next to your school. "Next to" describes the relative location of the library compared to your school.

You can describe New York's relative location in the same way. You might say that New York is south of Lake Ontario or that it borders New Jersey. These examples show New York's relationship to other places.

Another way to give New York's relative location is to describe where it is in the United States. New York is in a region called the Northeast. A **region** is an area on Earth with similar features. States in the same region may have the same kinds of landforms or be in the same part of the country.

New York is one of 14 states that border the Atlantic Ocean. This makes them Atlantic coast states. Because of their location along the coast, New York, Pennsylvania, New Jersey, and Delaware are sometimes called the Middle Atlantic states.

REVIEW In which region of the United States is New York located?

· SCIENCE AND TECHNOLOGY ·

Global Positioning System

Early mapmakers often made mistakes. One of the tools mapmakers use today to make better maps is the Global Positioning System, or GPS. Twenty-four GPS satellites orbit Earth. They send signals that are picked up by GPS receivers. A GPS receiver can display its position on Earth.

A satellite (below) and a handheld GPS unit (right)

REVIEW

1. **WHAT TO KNOW** What are three ways to describe New York's location on Earth?

2. **VOCABULARY** Define the word **equator**.

3. **GEOGRAPHY** With which country does New York share a boundary?

4. **CRITICAL THINKING** What is the location of your community relative to Lake Ontario?

5. **MAKE A GRAPHIC ORGANIZER** Write down these terms: *the Northeast, Earth, New York, Western Hemisphere, North America,* and *United States.* Put them in order from the largest region to the smallest. Then explain New York's global address.

6. **MAIN IDEA AND DETAILS** On a separate sheet of paper, copy and complete this graphic organizer.

Focus Skill

Main Idea

There are several ways to describe New York's location.

Details

·SKILLS·
MAP AND GLOBE

Use Latitude and Longitude

▶ WHY IT MATTERS

An exact way to tell where a place is is to describe its **absolute location**, or exact position on Earth. You can do this by using latitude and longitude.

▶ WHAT YOU NEED TO KNOW

Latitude and longitude are lines that mapmakers draw on maps and globes. One set of lines runs east and west. These are called **lines of latitude**. Lines of latitude are measured in degrees (°) north

and south from the equator. They go from 0° at the equator to 90° at each of the poles. Lines of latitude north of the equator are marked N for *north*. Lines south of the equator are marked S for *south*.

A second set of lines runs north and south between the poles. These lines are called **lines of longitude**. The starting point for lines of longitude is called the **prime meridian**. Lines of longitude go from 0° at the prime meridian to 180° halfway around the globe. Lines of longitude west of the prime meridian are

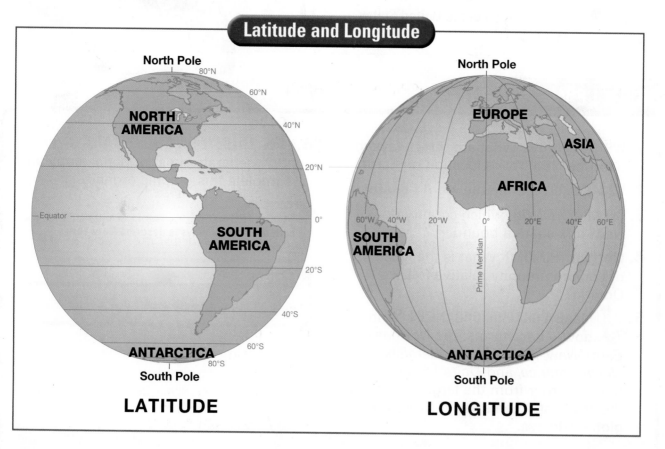

Latitude and Longitude

LATITUDE

North Pole
80°N
60°N
NORTH AMERICA
40°N
20°N
Equator — 0°
SOUTH AMERICA
20°S
40°S
ANTARCTICA
60°S
80°S
South Pole

LONGITUDE

North Pole
EUROPE
ASIA
AFRICA
60°W 40°W 20°W 0° 20°E 40°E 60°E
SOUTH AMERICA
Prime Meridian
ANTARCTICA
South Pole

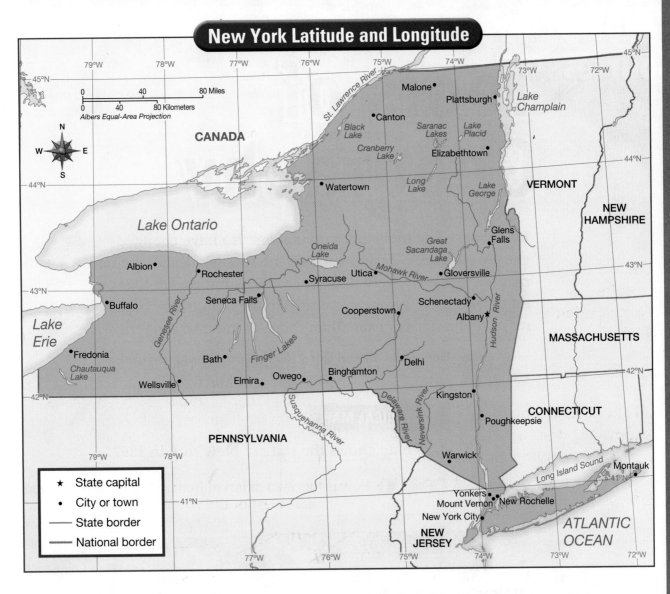

New York Latitude and Longitude

marked W for *west*. Lines east of it are marked E for *east*.

Together, lines of latitude and longitude on a map or globe form a grid. This grid can help you describe the absolute location of any place on Earth. You give the location by naming the closest lines of latitude and longitude.

Study the map of New York. At the left-hand side, find 43°N. At the bottom, find 79°W. The city of Buffalo is near where these lines cross. You can say that Buffalo is near 43°N, 79°W.

▶ **PRACTICE THE SKILL**

Use the map to answer the questions.

1️⃣ What line of longitude is closest to the city of Poughkeepsie?

2️⃣ What city is near 43°N, 76°W?

3️⃣ What lines of latitude and longitude best give the location of Watertown?

▶ **APPLY WHAT YOU LEARNED**

Write a paragraph telling a friend how he or she can find the absolute location of another place in New York.

Practice your map and globe skills with the **GeoSkills CD-ROM**.

MAP AND GLOBE SKILLS

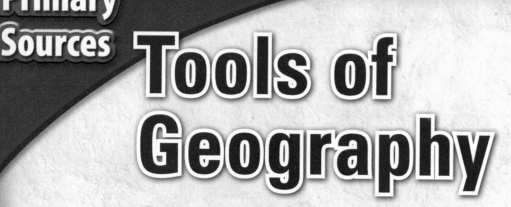

Primary Sources

Tools of Geography

Background The tools that mapmakers use have changed greatly over time. Early maps often had mistakes. As better mapmaking tools were developed, maps improved. Today mapmakers use computers and satellites to quickly make maps that are more exact than those of the past.

DBQ **Document-Based Questions** Study these primary sources, and answer the questions.

HISTORICAL MAP

This map shows the state of New York in 1867.

DBQ **1** How is this map different from a map of New York today?

COMPASS

Tools such as this compass from the 1700s helped both mapmakers and explorers.

 2 A compass tells a person whether he or she is going north, south, east, or west.

DBQ How did the compass help explorers?

FOLDING RULE

This folding rule from the 1580s had a hinge. It helped mapmakers draw curved lines.

DBQ **3** Why might mapmakers need a tool like the folding rule to draw a map?

SURVEYING LINE

In the 1700s a surveying line was used to measure short distances.

DBQ **4** How do you think the surveying line worked?

WRITE ABOUT IT

Mapmakers make different kinds of maps to show different information. Find three different kinds of maps of your community. Explain what they tell about your community.

GO ONLINE For more resources, go to www.harcourtschool.com/ss1

Lesson 2

Land and Water

WHAT TO KNOW
What are New York's major landforms?

VOCABULARY
glacier p. 28

plateau p. 29

sea level p. 29

mountain range p. 30

tributary p. 32

harbor p. 32

coastal plain p. 32

sound p. 33

estuary p. 33

drumlin p. 34

MAIN IDEA AND DETAILS

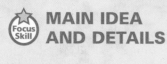

YOU ARE THERE You have just arrived in Massapequa after driving from Plattsburgh with your family. You were surprised to see how many different landscapes New York has. You saw rolling hills, tree-covered mountains, wide valleys, and windswept beaches. You also crossed many rivers and lakes.

A Landscape Formed by Glaciers

Much of New York's land and many of its lakes were shaped by **glaciers** (GLAY•sherz). Those huge, slow-moving masses of ice formed thousands of years ago. At that time Earth was much colder than it is today. The ice built up until some glaciers were hundreds of feet deep.

As the glaciers moved, they scraped their way across the land. As Earth warmed, the glaciers melted. Some areas were left with poor, rocky soil. In other areas a thick layer of fertile, or rich, soil remained. Fertile soil is good for farming.

Many kinds of animals, including bears, can be found in the Catskill Mountains.

In some places, glaciers carved deep holes. When the glaciers melted, their water filled the holes to form lakes. These lakes include Lake Champlain, the Saranac Lakes, the Finger Lakes, Lake Placid, and Oneida Lake.

Glaciers also wore down some mountains to form high, level land areas called **plateaus** (pla•TOHZ). In other places, glaciers carved valleys into the land, leaving mountains around them.

REVIEW How did glaciers shape New York's land?

Along the Van Hoevenberg Trail in the Adirondack Mountains, you can see the effect of glaciers.

Regions of Higher Land

The Adirondack (a•duh•RAHN•dak) Mountains cover most of northeastern New York. They have thick forests and hundreds of lakes and waterfalls.

Geographers call much of the northeastern part of our state the Adirondack Upland region. An upland is any area of high land. New York's tallest mountain, Mount Marcy, is in the eastern Adirondacks. It rises 5,344 feet (1,629 m) above sea level. **Sea level**, the level of the ocean's surface, is the starting point for measuring the height of land.

Much of the Adirondack Upland has been preserved as Adirondack Park. Verplanck Colvin, who explored the region in the late 1800s, urged the state to protect this land. Today, Adirondack Park has the largest wilderness area in the eastern United States. Other areas in the Adirondack Upland are used for lumbering and mining.

To the south of the Adirondacks are the Catskill Mountains. The Catskills attract visitors from New York City. Water from lakes in the Catskills provides most of New York City's fresh water.

At the southern end of the Catskills are the Shawangunk (SHAHNG•guhnk) Mountains. These mountains run from New York south into New Jersey and Pennsylvania.

The Catskill and Shawangunk Mountains and most of New York's other upland regions are part of the larger Appalachian mountain range. A **mountain range** is a group of connected mountains. The Appalachians cover much of the eastern United States, stretching from Alabama to Canada.

The Catskill and Shawangunk Mountains mark the eastern part of an area of high land called the Appalachian Plateau. Also called the Allegheny (a•luh•GAY•nee) Plateau, it is the state's largest land region. It covers most of southern New York. Several streams and large rivers, including the Delaware, the Susquehanna (suhs•kwuh•HA•nuh), and the Genesee (jeh•nuh•SEE), flow through the region.

There are few cities in this region. Instead, there are many vegetable and dairy farms. The region's most fertile land is near the Finger Lakes and along rivers. Much of this land is used to grow grapes.

People enjoy New York's mountains all year round.

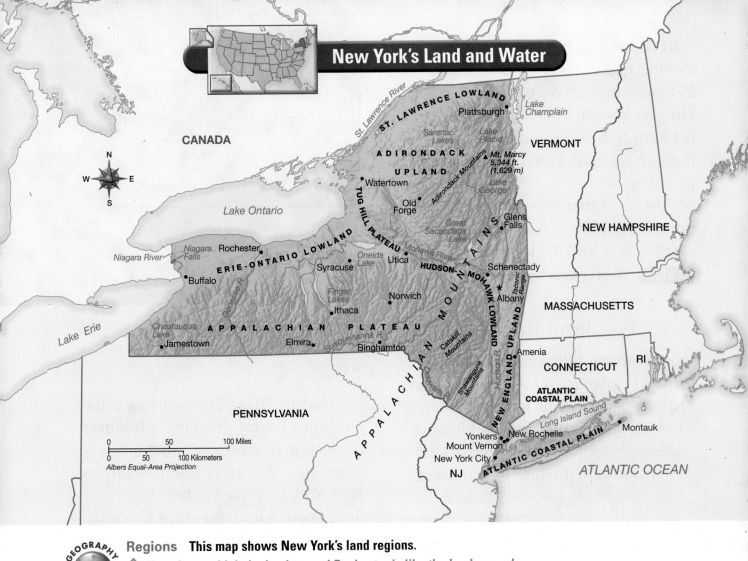

CANADA

VERMONT

NEW HAMPSHIRE

MASSACHUSETTS

CONNECTICUT

RI

PENNSYLVANIA

NJ

ATLANTIC OCEAN

ST. LAWRENCE LOWLAND

St. Lawrence River

Plattsburgh

Lake Champlain

Saranac Lakes

Lake Placid

ADIRONDACK

UPLAND

Mt. Marcy 5,344 ft. (1,629 m)

Watertown

Adirondack Mountains

Lake George

Old Forge

Great Sacandaga Lake

Glens Falls

TUG HILL PLATEAU

Lake Ontario

Niagara Falls

Rochester

ERIE-ONTARIO LOWLAND

Niagara River

Syracuse

Oneida Lake

Utica

Mohawk River

HUDSON-

MOHAWK LOWLAND

Schenectady

ADIRONDACK MOUNTAINS

Taconic Range

Buffalo

Genesee R.

Finger Lakes

Norwich

Ithaca

Albany

Amenia

Lake Erie

Chautauqua Lake

APPALACHIAN PLATEAU

Catskill Mountains

Hudson R.

NEW ENGLAND UPLAND

Jamestown

Elmira

Binghamton

Susquehanna R.

Shawangunk Mountains

ATLANTIC COASTAL PLAIN

APPALACHIAN

Delaware R.

Long Island Sound

Montauk

Yonkers

Mount Vernon

New Rochelle

New York City

ATLANTIC COASTAL PLAIN

0   50   100 Miles
0   50   100 Kilometers
Albers Equal-Area Projection

GEOGRAPHY THEME

Regions   This map shows New York's land regions.

How do you think the land around Rochester is like the land around Buffalo?

In many places, rivers have cut steep, narrow valleys called gorges into the land. Where the Genesee River flows through Letchworth State Park, south of Rochester, it has cut a gorge so large that it is sometimes called the Grand Canyon of the East. Along the walls of the gorge at Watkins Glen, near Seneca Lake, there are 19 separate waterfalls. At a height of 215 feet (about 66 m), Taughannock (tuh•GA•nuhk) Falls, near Cayuga Lake, is the highest waterfall in the northeastern United States.

The northern part of the Appalachian Plateau is called the Tug Hill Plateau.

Few people live in this high, flat, rocky area. The soil is poor, and winters are generally very harsh. In fact, this area receives more snow than any other part of the state.

Another upland region, called the New England Upland, covers much of southeastern New York. It is made up of part of New York City, including Manhattan. The Taconic (tuh•KAH•nik) Range, with some of the oldest mountains in the United States, is in this region. It runs along New York's eastern border with Connecticut, Massachusetts, and Vermont.

In one part of the New England Upland region, stone cliffs called the Palisades (pa•luh•SAYDZ) line the lower Hudson River for about 15 miles (24 km). Native American Indians thought the cliffs looked like trees. In fact, they called the cliffs *wee-awk-en*, or "the rocks that look like trees." Europeans thought they looked like a palisade, a wall made of log poles.

REVIEW **What is New York's highest point?**

Built where several bodies of water meet, New York City has many bridges.

Lowland Regions

Between the Adirondack and New England Uplands and the Tug Hill and Appalachian Plateaus is a low, mostly flat region called the Hudson-Mohawk Lowland. A lowland is an area of land that is lower and flatter than most of the land around it. The Hudson-Mohawk Lowland includes most of the Hudson and Mohawk River valleys. This small region has soil that is good for farming.

In this lowland region, near Albany, the Mohawk River joins the Hudson River. The Mohawk is the Hudson's largest tributary. A **tributary** is a stream or river that flows into a larger stream or river. From Albany to New York City, the Hudson River is deep enough for large ships to use.

At New York City the Hudson River flows into New York Bay, a part of the Atlantic Ocean. This bay is one of the country's largest natural harbors. A **harbor** is a part of a body of water where ships can dock safely.

New York Bay is shaped partly by Staten Island and Long Island. These islands are part of a larger lowland region called the Atlantic Coastal Plain. A **coastal plain** is an area of low, mostly flat land next to an ocean. The Atlantic Coastal Plain lies along most of the eastern coast of the United States, from Massachusetts to Florida.

LOCATE IT

NEW YORK

Montauk Point

Long Island is 118 miles (190 km) long and 12 to 20 miles (19 to 32 km) wide. Off the island's broad and sandy southern coast are smaller islands, including Long Beach and Fire Island.

Long Island's northern shore is jagged and rocky. Long Island Sound lies between the north shore of Long Island and Connecticut. A **sound** is a narrow body of water that lies between a mainland and an island.

The East River separates the western end of Long Island from Manhattan. The East River is not really a river. It is an **estuary** (ES•chuh•wair•ee), or a body of water where fresh water from a river or lake mixes with salt water from the ocean. The East River connects the Harlem River, Upper New York Bay, and Long Island Sound.

REVIEW How is a lowland region different from an upland region?

Other Lowland Regions

Another lowland region—the St. Lawrence Lowland—covers part of northern New York. It lies along the St. Lawrence River from Lake Ontario to the shores of Lake Champlain.

Where Lake Ontario meets the St. Lawrence River, there is a group of about 1,800 islands. This area is often called the Thousand Islands. Some of the islands are large enough to include small cities. Others are so tiny that they do not have even a single tree.

Montauk Point is New York's easternmost point.

GEOGRAPHY ESSENTIAL ELEMENTS

Howe Caverns
Understanding Physical Systems

Howe Caverns is a series of caves that lie 156 feet (48 m) underground west of Albany. The caves were named for Lester Howe, who found them in 1842.

The caves were formed by an underground stream, which carved them in the limestone. Visitors can reach the caves by elevator. They are advised to bring a jacket because the temperature is always a chilly 52°F (11°C). Visitors can see interesting rock formations and ride in boats on the Lake of Venus. This lake was formed by the River Styx, which flows along the floor of the caves.

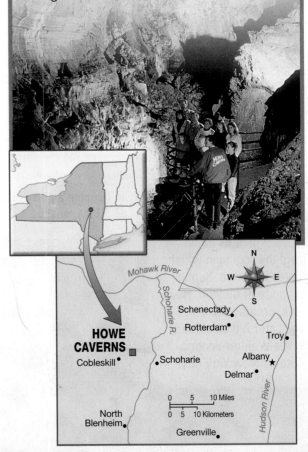

The drumlins shown in the center of the photograph rise above the surrounding farmland.

The Thousand Islands area is among New York's most popular places to visit. Visitors can reach Wellesley Island, Heart Island, and others from cities along the river, including Alexandria Bay and Fishers Landing. Many of the islands are linked to the mainland by a system of bridges.

Along the shores of Lake Ontario and Lake Erie is still another lowland region—the Erie-Ontario Lowland.

Three of New York's largest cities, Syracuse, Rochester, and Buffalo, are located in this region.

This region's soil is good for growing grapes and vegetables and for raising cows. In some lower places, however, there are swamps. In other places oval-shaped hills, called **drumlins**, rise as much as 200 feet (about 60 m) above the surrounding land. They were formed from pebbles and soil dropped by glaciers. About 10,000 drumlins can be found between Syracuse and Rochester.

One river in this region provides one of New York's most famous landmarks. The Niagara River flows only 34 miles (about 55 km), from Lake Erie to Lake Ontario. Along the way, however, it flows over a steep cliff to form two enormous waterfalls known as Niagara Falls. The American Falls are on the New York side of the Niagara River, and the Horseshoe Falls are on the Canadian side.

FAST FACT Thousand Island salad dressing gets its name from the region in which it was invented. Sophia LaLonde of Clayton, New York, created the dressing. Later it was served at the Waldorf-Astoria Hotel in New York City.

To become a part of the official count of the islands in the Thousand Islands area, an island must be above water 365 days a year and it must support two living trees.

Niagara Falls is considered one of North America's natural wonders.

The cliff over which the waters fall is made up of soft and hard stone. It was once only 35 feet (11 m) high, but over time, the rushing waters have washed away the softer rock below, making the drop greater. Today the American Falls are 190 feet (58 m) high and are 1,060 feet (323 m) across. The Horseshoe Falls are more than twice as wide but not as high as the American Falls. Millions of tourists visit both beautiful waterfalls each year.

REVIEW How has Niagara Falls changed over time?

REVIEW

1. WHAT TO KNOW What are New York's major landforms?

2. VOCABULARY What is an upland? Use the term **sea level** in your answer.

3. GEOGRAPHY How did glaciers change the land in New York?

4. CRITICAL THINKING How might the locations of rivers have affected where people chose to live in New York?

5. COMPARE REGIONS Make a Venn diagram to compare and contrast the landforms in your area and the landforms in another part of New York.

6. MAIN IDEA AND DETAILS On a separate sheet of paper, copy and complete this graphic organizer.

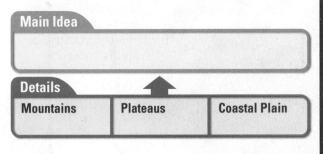

Main Idea

Details		
Mountains	Plateaus	Coastal Plain

Use an Elevation Map

VOCABULARY

elevation

relief

▶ WHY IT MATTERS

The height of land in New York is different around the state. Some regions are mostly low, while others have mountains. How can you tell how high or low the land is? How can you tell how much higher or lower one place is than another? To answer these questions, you need a map that shows elevation (eh•luh•VAY•shuhn). **Elevation** is the height of the land.

In this photo you can see Mount Marcy, covered in snow, in the distance.

▶ WHAT YOU NEED TO KNOW

The elevation of all land is measured from sea level. The elevation of land at sea level is zero. The top of Mount Marcy, New York's highest point, is 5,344 feet (1,629 m) above sea level.

The elevation map of New York on page 37 uses shading and color to show **relief** (rih•LEEF), or differences in elevation. The shading helps you see where hills and mountains are located, but it does not give you the elevations of those areas. To learn the elevation of a place, you must look up its color in the map key.

The map does not give exact elevations. Instead, each color stands for a range of elevations. That is, a color stands for an area's highest and lowest elevations and all the elevations in between. On this map, Rochester is in an area colored green. The key shows that the elevation there is between 0 and 655 feet (200 m) above sea level. Red is used to show land that is above 13,120 feet (4,000 m).

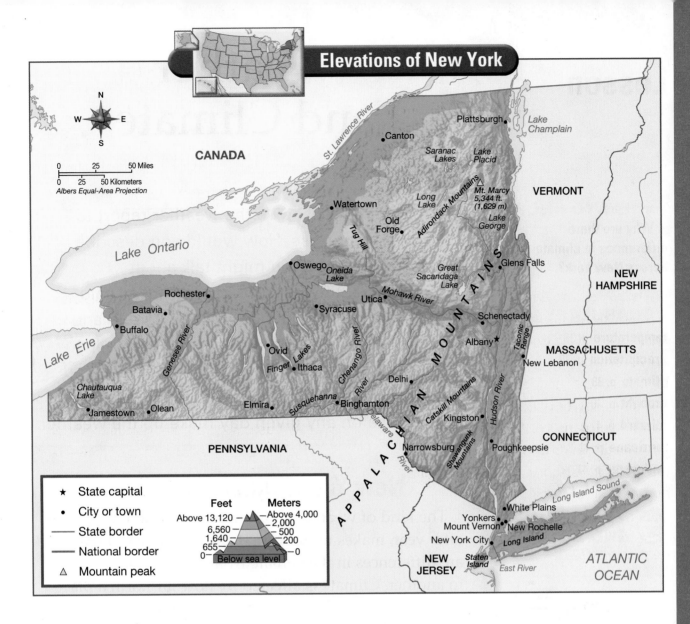

Elevations of New York

CANADA

VERMONT

NEW HAMPSHIRE

MASSACHUSETTS

CONNECTICUT

PENNSYLVANIA

NEW JERSEY

ATLANTIC OCEAN

Plattsburgh
Lake Champlain
Canton
Saranac Lakes
Lake Placid
Mt. Marcy 5,344 ft. (1,629 m)
Long Lake
Adirondack Mountains
Lake George
Watertown
Old Forge
St. Lawrence River
Tug Hill
Lake Ontario
Oswego
Oneida Lake
Great Sacandaga Lake
Glens Falls
Rochester
Batavia
Buffalo
Lake Erie
Syracuse
Utica
Mohawk River
Schenectady
Albany ★
Taconic Range
New Lebanon
Genesee River
Ovid
Finger Lakes
Ithaca
Chenango River
Delhi
Catskill Mountains
Kingston
Hudson River
Poughkeepsie
Chautauqua Lake
Jamestown
Olean
Elmira
Susquehanna River
Binghamton
Narrowsburg
Shawangunk Mountains
Delaware River
APPALACHIAN MOUNTAINS
White Plains
Yonkers
Mount Vernon
New Rochelle
New York City
Long Island
Long Island Sound
Staten Island
East River

Legend

- ★ State capital
- • City or town
- — State border
- — National border
- △ Mountain peak

Feet / Meters
Above 13,120 — Above 4,000
6,560 — 2,000
1,640 — 500
655 — 200
0 — 0
Below sea level

Scale: 0 25 50 Miles / 0 25 50 Kilometers
Albers Equal-Area Projection

PRACTICE THE SKILL

Use the elevation map of New York to answer these questions.

1. What range of elevation is shown by the color yellow?

2. Is the land near Rochester higher or lower than the land near Old Forge? Explain.

3. Which city has a higher elevation, Albany or Binghamton? How do you know?

4. Which mountains are higher, the Catskills or the Taconics?

APPLY WHAT YOU LEARNED

Imagine that you and your family are planning a trip between any two cities shown on the map. Place the edge of a ruler against the two cities on the map. Write down the elevation of the land near each city. Then write down the elevation of the highest and lowest land that you will cross on your trip.

Practice your map and globe skills with the **GeoSkills CD-ROM**.

MAP AND GLOBE SKILLS

Chapter 1 ▪ 37

Weather and Climate

temperature p. 38
precipitation p. 38
climate p. 38
drought p. 40
blizzard p. 41
hurricane p. 41
nor'easter p. 41

WHAT TO KNOW
Why are there differences in climate across New York?

VOCABULARY

temperature p. 38
precipitation p. 38
climate p. 38
drought p. 40
blizzard p. 41
hurricane p. 41
nor'easter p. 41

MAIN IDEA AND DETAILS

Main Idea

Details

YOU ARE THERE

You must give the weather report to your class. How would you describe today's weather? You might talk about **temperature**, the measure of how hot or cold the air is. You might also talk about wind and precipitation. **Precipitation** is water that falls to Earth's surface. It includes rain, sleet, hail, and snow. The temperature, precipitation, and wind in a place on any given day make up the weather.

New York's Different Climates

The kind of weather a place has most often, year after year, makes up its **climate**. In New York, there are differences in the climate from one part of the state to another. Climate is affected by how far north a place is, how high it is above sea level, and how close it is to a large body of water.

The temperature in any place depends partly on where it is. New York, like much of the rest of the United States, is located about halfway between the equator and the North Pole. This means that the temperatures in New York fall between the heat of places at the equator and the cold at the North Pole. Northern New York

Do you like to ride a bike when the weather is warm?

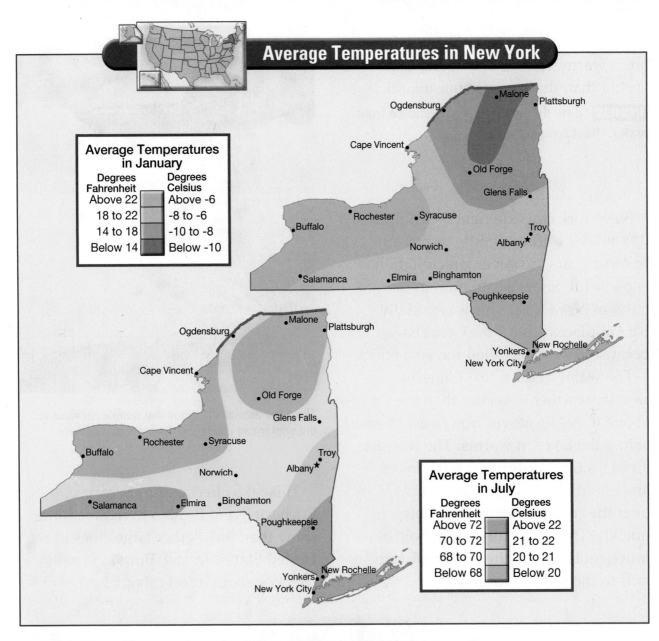

Average Temperatures in New York

Average Temperatures in January

Degrees Fahrenheit	Degrees Celsius
Above 22	Above -6
18 to 22	-8 to -6
14 to 18	-10 to -8
Below 14	Below -10

Average Temperatures in July

Degrees Fahrenheit	Degrees Celsius
Above 72	Above 22
70 to 72	21 to 22
68 to 70	20 to 21
Below 68	Below 20

GEOGRAPHY THEME

Place The maps above show the average temperatures in January and July in New York State.

❖ What is the average temperature for Syracuse in January? in July?

is usually the coldest part of the state. Southeastern New York is usually the warmest.

Elevation also affects temperatures. Generally, places at higher elevations are cooler. Because of this, winter temperatures are often coldest in upland regions. Even in summer, nights can be cool. In the Adirondacks the average temperature in July is just 66°F (19°C).

Distance from a large body of water, such as the Atlantic Ocean, affects temperatures, too. Water heats and cools more slowly than land. As a result, places near the ocean usually have warmer winters than places inland.

Like the Atlantic Ocean, the Great Lakes also affect temperatures in New York. The lakes' water takes longer to change temperature than the land does.

Because of this, the lakes keep nearby areas warmer in fall and cooler in spring than the areas farther inland.

REVIEW How do elevation and distance from water affect temperature?

Precipitation

New York can experience **droughts** (DROWTZ), or times of little or no rain. In most years, however, precipitation is plentiful. Snow is common in many parts of New York. This is especially true in places east of the Great Lakes because of what is called the lake effect.

The water in the Great Lakes is usually warmer in winter than the air above it. As air moves from west to east across the lakes, it warms. The warmer air picks up moisture from the lakes, and clouds form. When the clouds blow over the colder land, the air cools quickly. The cooler air cannot hold as much moisture, so the extra moisture falls to the ground as snow.

The large amounts of snow that Buffalo receives in the winter can cause problems for people there.

This lake effect causes Syracuse, Rochester, and Buffalo to receive more snow than most other large cities in the United States. In fact, Buffalo usually receives about 9 feet (about 3 m) of

Analyze Diagrams Because water cools more slowly than land, the water in the Great Lakes in the winter is usually warmer than the nearby land.

◆ What happens when cold air passes over the Great Lakes?

Lake Effect Snow

3 As the warmer air rises, it begins to cool. The moist air then forms clouds.

2 As the air passes over the lake, it is warmed from below. The warmer air picks up moisture from the lake.

1 Cold winds blowing from the west move over warm lake water.

snow each winter. In December 2001 a blizzard dumped about 7 feet (about 2 m) of snow on the city in just four days! A **blizzard** is a storm that combines heavy snow with high winds.

REVIEW Which areas of New York State receive the most snow? Why?

Severe Weather

Blizzards are just one kind of severe weather that can strike New York. Storms called hurricanes can form over the ocean. A **hurricane** is a powerful storm that has heavy rains and winds with speeds of 74 miles (119 km) or more per hour. Although hurricanes are rare in New York, they sometimes pass over Long Island.

Storms called **nor'easters** also affect New York. Nor'easters happen in cold weather, mostly in the eastern part of the state. They are named for the strong winds from the north and the east that blow before and during these storms. Nor'easters can bring flooding rains and heavy snowfalls.

REVIEW What are some kinds of storms that affect New York State?

4 When the clouds blow over the colder land, they cannot hold as much moisture. The moisture falls to the ground as heavy snowfall.

Lightning strikes during some severe storms.

REVIEW

1. **WHAT TO KNOW** Why are there differences in climate across New York?

2. **VOCABULARY** How are the terms **drought** and **precipitation** related?

3. **GEOGRAPHY** How are weather and climate different?

4. **CRITICAL THINKING** How do you think extreme weather might affect a farmer's earnings?

5. **CREATE A WEATHER CHART** Over a week, chart the temperature and precipitation in your community. Do the same for another. What conclusions can you draw about the climate in each place?

6. **MAIN IDEA AND DETAILS** On a separate sheet of paper, copy and complete this graphic organizer.

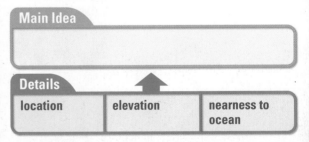

Main Idea

Details

| location | elevation | nearness to ocean |

Lesson 4

People and Resources

WHAT TO KNOW

How do the natural resources of New York affect the way people live?

VOCABULARY

natural resource p. 42
product p. 43
renewable p. 43
nonrenewable p. 43
quarry p. 43
reservoir p. 44
environment p. 44
urban p. 45
suburb p. 46
rural p. 46

 MAIN IDEA AND DETAILS

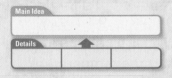

You ARE THERE

The buzzing alarm clock marks the start of another day. You head to the kitchen for breakfast. You eat a bowl of cereal and drink a glass of juice. Then you brush your teeth, wash, and dress. You toss an apple in your backpack as you rush to catch the bus to school.

Just an ordinary morning, right? Maybe, but none of it would be possible without New York's natural resources. A **natural resource** is something found in nature that people can use. Water, soil, rocks, and plants are all natural resources.

The Land

The land itself is one of New York's most important natural resources. About one-fourth of the land in New York is used for farming. Hay and corn are the state's leading crops. Farmers also grow fruits and vegetables, including beans, tomatoes, grapes, and apples.

More than half of the state's farms are dairy farms. They provide milk for drinking and for making products such as cream, butter, and cheese. A **product** is something that people make, grow, or raise, usually to sell. Other farmers raise animals for meat. These animals include beef cattle, sheep, hogs, chickens, and ducks.

Forests are another important natural resource in New York. They cover about half of the state. The trees are used to make lumber for houses and furniture. Wood is used to make other products, too, including the paper in this textbook. From the sap of maple trees, New Yorkers make syrup.

As trees are cut down, new trees are often planted in their place. Trees are a **renewable** resource, or one that can be made again by nature or by people.

New York is famous for its maple syrup.

Other natural resources in New York are found underground. All of these are called **nonrenewable** resources. They cannot quickly be made again by nature or by people.

Northern New York is a leading producer of garnets, which are used in watches and to make sandpaper. Salt and gypsum are mined mostly in central and western New York. Some oil and natural gas are also found in western New York.

In addition to granite, the most important stone found in the state's quarries (KWAWR•eez) is limestone. A **quarry** is a place where stone is cut or blasted out of the ground.

REVIEW Explain the difference between renewable and nonrenewable resources.

The milk you drink most likely comes from dairy farms like this one.

Water

Water is one of our state's most important natural resources. People need fresh water to use in their homes. Factories and farms also need water.

New York generally has a plentiful supply of fresh water. Much of that water is found in the state's many rivers and lakes. The largest amount of fresh water is in Lake Erie and Lake Ontario. Together, the five Great Lakes make up the largest group of freshwater lakes in the world. They hold one-fifth of the world's fresh water.

New Yorkers also meet their need for water in other ways. In some places they have dug wells. In others they have built dams across rivers to form reservoirs (REH•zuhr•vwarz). A **reservoir** is a human-made lake that stores water held back by a dam. Reservoirs provide many cities in New York with fresh water.

New York's waterways make fishing an important activity in New York. People catch many kinds of salt-water fish and shellfish in the waters off New York's Atlantic coast. Fresh-water fishing is also big business in Lake Ontario and Lake Erie. Water is an important resource for another reason.

Fishers catch lobsters in the waters off New York.

How Much Water?

USE	AMOUNT
Brushing teeth	1 to 2 gallons (4 to 8 L)
Flushing a toilet	5 to 7 gallons (19 to 26 L)
Running a dishwasher	9 to 12 gallons (34 to 45 L)
Taking a shower	15 to 30 gallons (57 to 114 L)
Washing dishes by hand	20 to 30 gallons (76 to 114 L)

Analyze Graphs Each American uses an average of about 140 gallons (530 L) of water a day.

◆ About how much water does a person use for brushing teeth?

Waterways serve as transportation routes in New York. Boats use the state's waterways to move people and goods from place to place.

REVIEW How do people use water resources?

Where New Yorkers Live

Once you understand New York's geography and the locations of its natural resources, you can understand why New Yorkers live where they do. Like people in most places, New Yorkers first settled along waterways or in areas with fertile soil. Fertile soil allowed them to grow their food. Waterways provided them with water and a way to travel. Later, cities grew up along those same waterways, and people moved to those cities to find jobs.

Most New Yorkers are still affected by their **environment** (in•VY•ruhn•muhnt), or surroundings. Often the kinds of work that people do depend on the natural resources around them. For example, in areas with fertile soil, many people are likely to earn their living by farming. In mountain regions, many people are likely to work in lumbering or mining. People along waterways may work in shipping or fishing.

Like people in the past, most New Yorkers today live near waterways or in areas with fertile soil. In fact, most live within one broad band of land. It runs from Long Island to New York City and up the Hudson River valley to Albany. From there it runs west along the Mohawk River valley and across the Erie-Ontario Lowland to Buffalo.

Most New Yorkers today live and work in cities. In fact, more than 8 out of every 10 people in New York State live in **urban**, or city, areas. Many of New York's largest urban areas are located near the coast, along rivers, or on the shores of the Great Lakes.

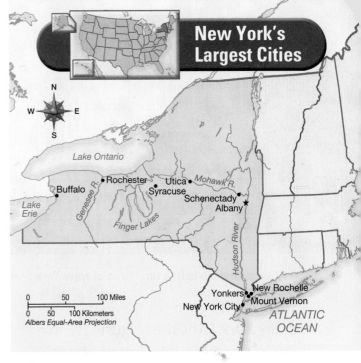

New York's Largest Cities

Human-Environment Interactions
New York's largest cities, such as New York City (below), are located on bodies of water.

❖ What two bodies of water do you think have helped Rochester grow?

The town of Hudson is in a rural area of New York State.

New York City, the largest city in New York and in the United States, grew up on New York Bay. New York City is now one of the busiest ports in the world. Even more people live in the suburbs of New York City, however. A **suburb** is a town or small city near a larger city.

While most New Yorkers live in urban areas, communities of many sizes are found in our state. Some are made up of just a few houses in **rural**, or country, areas.

In some areas, mountains and harsh climates have kept populations low. Fewer people live in northern New York and on the Appalachian Plateau than in other parts of the state. The land there is rugged, and the winters are harsh.

REVIEW **Where do most New Yorkers live? Why?**

REVIEW

1. **WHAT TO KNOW** How do the natural resources of New York affect the way people live?

2. **VOCABULARY** How are the terms **urban** and **suburban** related?

3. **ECONOMICS** What products are made from trees in New York's forests?

4. **CRITICAL THINKING** Why do you think many people live in cities?

5. **MAKE A CHART** Make a chart listing at least four of New York's natural resources. Then list as many jobs as you can that depend on that resource.

6. **MAIN IDEA AND DETAILS** On a separate sheet of paper, copy and complete this graphic organizer.

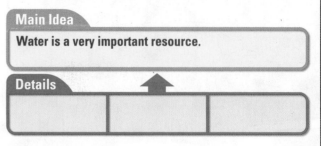

Main Idea

Water is a very important resource.

Details

Identify Fact and Opinion

▶ WHY IT MATTERS

A good reader or listener can tell facts from opinions. A **fact** is a statement that can be checked and proved to be true. An **opinion** is a statement that tells what the person who makes it thinks or believes. Knowing whether a statement is fact or opinion can help you better understand what you read or hear.

▶ WHAT YOU NEED TO KNOW

In the last lesson you read that more than 8 out of every 10 people in New York live in urban areas. You could check whether that statement is true by looking in an almanac or another kind of reference book.

It takes 42 gallons of sap to make one gallon of syrup.

Suppose someone said, "I think it is better to live in an urban area than in a rural area." There is no way to prove that living in a city or suburb is better than living in the country. This statement gives the speaker's opinion.

There are clues to help you know when a statement is an opinion. Words such as *think, believe, opinion,* and *doubt* tell you that you are reading an opinion. Words such as *beautiful, best, worst,* and *greatest* are often part of an opinion, too.

▶ PRACTICE THE SKILL

Identify each statement below as a fact or an opinion.

1. I think maple syrup made in New York is the best-tasting in the United States.
2. In forest regions of New York, many people earn their living by cutting down trees for wood.
3. Buffalo is a better place to live in than Albany.

▶ APPLY WHAT YOU LEARNED

Underline facts you read in a newspaper article. Then circle some opinions in the same article. Explain to classmates how you were able to tell the facts from the opinions.

READING SKILLS

Chapter Review

Summarize the Chapter

Focus Skill **Main Idea and Details** Complete this graphic organizer to show that you understand the important ideas and details about the geography of New York.

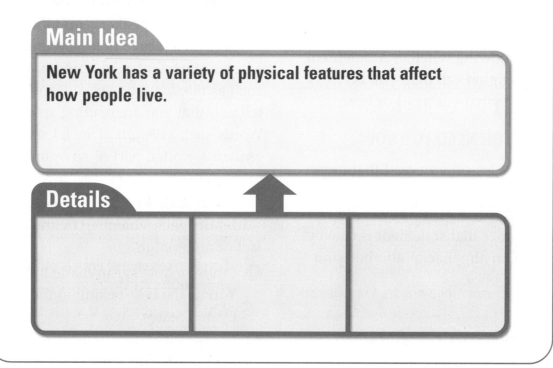

Main Idea

New York has a variety of physical features that affect how people live.

Details

THINK & WRITE

Write a Poem Think of a place in New York that is special to you. Write a poem about that place. In your poem, describe the geography of the place you chose, and explain why the place is special to you.

Write a Journal Entry Adventurers, such as Verplanck Colvin, often write journal entries about the landforms they explore. Write a journal entry about the landforms in your area.

USE VOCABULARY

Identify the term that correctly matches each definition.

region (p. 23)
sea level (p. 29)
harbor (p. 32)
climate (p. 38)
reservoir (p. 44)

1. the kind of weather a place has most often

2. the level of the ocean's surface

3. an area on Earth with similar features

4. a human-made lake that stores water held back by a dam

5. a part of a body of water where ships can dock safely

RECALL FACTS

Answer these questions.

6. Why are New York and its neighboring states called the Middle Atlantic states?

7. How did the movement of ancient glaciers form lakes in New York?

8. What mountain range are the Catskills and the Shawangunk Mountains a part of?

Write the letter of the best choice.

9. **TEST PREP** Which is NOT one of the cities in the Erie-Ontario Lowland?
   A Rochester
   B Syracuse
   C New York City
   D Buffalo

10. **TEST PREP** Because of the lake effect—
   F New York experiences droughts.
   G snow is common in the areas east of the Great Lakes.
   H hurricanes often hit New York.
   J it never snows near Lake Erie.

11. **TEST PREP** All resources found underground in New York are—
   A fuels.
   B renewable.
   C stone.
   D nonrenewable.

THINK CRITICALLY

12. Why is it important to protect wilderness areas such as Adirondack Park?

13. Choose a region of New York where you do not live. If you moved there, how would the weather and the environment there change the way you live?

APPLY SKILLS

Use Latitude and Longitude
Use the latitude and longitude map on page 25 to answer these questions.

14. Between which two lines of latitude is Rochester located?

15. What is the absolute location of Binghamton?

Use an Elevation Map
Use the elevation map on page 37 to answer these questions.

16. Which city has a higher elevation, Buffalo or Old Forge?

17. Would the elevation of the land increase or decrease if you traveled from the Tug Hill Plateau to the Atlantic Ocean?

Identify Fact and Opinion

18. Write a fact and an opinion about a place pictured in Chapter 1.

STUDY SKILLS

ANTICIPATION GUIDE

An anticipation guide can help you anticipate, or predict, what you will learn as you read.

- **Read the lesson titles and section titles for clues.**

- **Read the question at the end of each section.**

- **Predict what you will learn as you read.**

Native Americans in New York		
Iroquois		
Question	Prediction	Correct?
How did the Iroquois use the resources in their environment to meet their basic needs?	They made clothing out of animal skins, and they used trees to make shelters.	✓
Algonquian		
Question	Prediction	Correct?

New York's Early People

Ganondagan State Historic Site

Early People

YOU ARE THERE

"Shhh! I see one," the hunter next to you whispers. Standing in the distance is a woolly mammoth. You're excited—and a little scared. This mammoth will provide meat for many days. Its hide will provide warmth and shelter.

WHAT TO KNOW
How did people first come to live in New York, and how did their ways of life change over time?

VOCABULARY
nomad p. 53
ancestor p. 53
extinct p. 54
adapt p. 54
agriculture p. 54
culture p. 54
tribe p. 54
language group p. 55
artifact p. 55
archaeologist p. 55

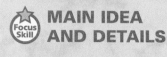

MAIN IDEA AND DETAILS

Main Idea

Details

The Land and People Long Ago

At different times in the past, Earth has had long periods of freezing cold. During these periods, known as Ice Ages, much of Earth's water was frozen in glaciers. So much water was trapped in glaciers that the water levels in the oceans dropped. This uncovered a "bridge" of dry land between Asia and North America each time.

Many scientists believe that people from Asia may have traveled across this land bridge and reached North America. Other scientists believe that people may have come to the Americas even earlier in boats.

These early people were most likely nomads. A **nomad** is a person who keeps moving from place to place. They followed herds of animals, which they hunted for food and for skins from which to make clothing.

Over thousands of years those early people's children and their children's children slowly spread out all over North America and South America. They were the **ancestors**, or early family members, of present-day Native Americans. Native Americans are also called American Indians.

About 12,000 years ago people reached the area that is now New York State. At that time, the climate was cooler than it is today. Huge animals such as mastodons and woolly mammoths roamed the land. Early people hunted these animals. They also gathered plants for food. Groups of people who get their food in these ways are called hunters and gatherers.

REVIEW How may glaciers have made it possible for early people to come to North America?

Early people worked together to hunt mastodons and mammoths. Some mammoths were 14 feet (4 m) tall.

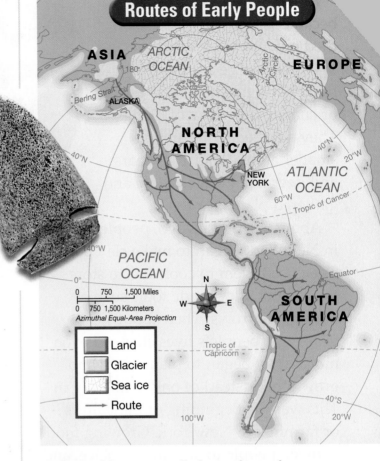

Routes of Early People

Movement Early people may have followed these routes to the Americas.

In what direction did people travel once they left what is now Alaska?

A Time of Change

Over time, New York's climate slowly became warmer and wetter. The glaciers melted, and the water levels in the oceans rose. Long Island, which had been part of the mainland, became surrounded by water. Forests covered the land, and many plants that the large animals ate could no longer grow.

result, those animals **extinct** (ik•STINGT), or ___t, about 10,000 years ago.

Without large animals to hunt, early people had to **adapt**, or change their way of living. They adapted by hunting smaller animals, such as bears and deer. They fished more and gathered plants for food.

About 3,000 years ago, people in New York began to make clay pots. They used them to cook and to store food. Later, they made tools such as bows and arrows. Then about 1,000 years ago, people's lives changed even more. They began to plant seeds and grow food instead of only gathering it. This was the beginning of **agriculture**, or farming, in New York. Growing food allowed people to stay in one place, and villages grew.

REVIEW How did agriculture affect early people?

Ancient pottery

New Ways of Life

Early people in New York were alike in many ways. They all made tools and pottery and settled in villages. They used natural resources to meet their needs. Over time, however, different groups came to have different ways of speaking and behaving. They developed different **cultures**, or ways of life.

Like other Native Americans, those in New York formed what are today called tribes. **Tribe** is a term often used to describe Native American groups that have the same leaders or share the same culture or land. Each tribe's culture is different from the cultures of other tribes.

The people of New York's many tribes spoke different languages. Many of those languages, however, belonged

Early people in what is now New York State used tools, such as digging sticks, to farm.

to the same language group. All the languages in a **language group** are alike in some way. In what is now New York State, most Native Americans spoke either Iroquoian (ir•uh•KWOY•uhn) languages or Algonquian (al•GAHNG•kwee•uhn) languages.

REVIEW What were the two major language groups in New York?

Clues from the Past

Early people in New York left no written records. What we know about them today comes from the artifacts they left behind. An **artifact** is any object made by people who lived in the past. Scientists called **archaeologists** (ar•kee•AH•luh•jists) study artifacts to learn how people lived long ago.

Native American artifacts have been found at sites across New York. From artifacts found at Grouse Bluff, on the Hudson River, archaeologists have

Archaeologists uncover artifacts at a site in the Schoharie Valley.

learned that early people gathered there to feast and exchange goods. At another site, early people heated stone to make it easier to chip into spear points and arrowheads.

REVIEW What do artifacts tell us about Native Americans in New York?

REVIEW

1. **WHAT TO KNOW** How did the early people in New York adapt to changes in the environment?

2. **VOCABULARY** Which is generally larger, a **tribe** or a **language group**? Explain.

3. **CULTURE** How did early people's lives change when they began farming?

4. **CRITICAL THINKING** Do you think it would be easier to survive as a hunter and gatherer or as a farmer? Explain.

5. **FIND YOUR OWN ARTIFACT** Imagine that you are an archaeologist of the future who finds an artifact from today. Describe the artifact and what it tells you about life in New York in the early 2000s.

6. **Focus Skill** **MAIN IDEAS AND DETAILS** On a separate sheet of paper, copy and complete this graphic organizer.

Main Idea

Native Americans' way of life changed when the resources around them changed.

Details

·SKILLS·

MAP AND GLOBE

Use a Cultural Map

VOCABULARY

cultural region

▶ WHY IT MATTERS

To know where people who belonged to different language groups lived, you can use a cultural map. A cultural map shows **cultural regions**, areas in which people share a similar language or some other cultural trait.

The culture of each Native American language group was often affected by where the group lived. Knowing where a Native American group lived can help you better understand how its environment and culture were related.

▶ WHAT YOU NEED TO KNOW

The cultural map on page 57 shows where the two major Native American language groups in New York lived. It also shows where the languages are unknown or where they were mixed.

Each color on the map represents a different cultural region. Most of the people who lived in a cultural region spoke similar languages and had similar ways of life. Labels show where each of the major tribes that made up a language group lived.

In which cultural region would these Native Americans most likely have lived? How can you tell?

Native American Language Groups of New York

0 40 80 Miles
0 40 80 Kilometers
Albers Equal-Area Projection

St. Lawrence River
Lake Champlain
Lake Ontario
MOHAWK
WENRO
Oneida Lake
ONEIDA
Mohawk River
MAHICAN
Lake Erie
CAYUGA
ONONDAGA
SENECA
Genesee River
ERIE
Finger Lakes
Chautauqua Lake
Hudson River
DELAWARE
WAPPINGER
Susquehanna River
Delaware River
MUNSEE
Long Island Sound
MONTAUK
ATLANTIC OCEAN

Algonquian group
Iroquoian group
Unknown or mixed
Present-day border

PRACTICE THE SKILL

Use the map above to answer these questions.

1 To which language group did more of the tribes in New York belong?

2 Which language group lived closer to Lake Erie?

3 Which language group lived closer to the Atlantic Ocean?

4 Which tribe lived in the area where the Mohawk River flows into the Hudson River?

APPLY WHAT YOU LEARNED

Compare the map on this page with a physical map of New York. On a sheet of paper, list five physical features shown on the physical map. Next to the name of each feature, write the name of the main language group that lived there. Share your list with classmates. Then talk about how the physical features may have affected the way of life of the different tribes.

Practice your map and globe skills with the **GeoSkills CD-ROM**.

2

The Iroquois

YOU ARE THERE

You are playing a ball game with other Iroquois children. You scoop up the ball in the small leather basket at the end of your stick and run toward the other team's goal. You fling the ball. Score! Your skillful play in this traditional Iroquois game will bring honor to you and your family.

WHAT TO KNOW
How did the Iroquois tribes in New York use natural resources, and how did they govern themselves?

VOCABULARY
palisade p. 59

longhouse p. 59

trade p. 60

wampum p. 60

clan p. 60

sachem p. 61

legend p. 61

confederacy p. 62

council p. 63

Focus Skill **MAIN IDEA AND DETAILS**

Iroquois Ways of Life

The Iroquois tribes lived in what is now northern and western New York. Thick forests covered their lands. They used wood from those forests to build shelters and to make tools, such as hoes and digging sticks. Iroquois men fished in waterways and hunted animals. Women prepared the fish and meat for eating. They used the animals' skins to make blankets, clothing, and moccasins. The men made tools out of antlers and bones.

The Iroquois gathered berries and nuts for food, and they used maple syrup to sweeten their foods. They were also skilled farmers.

The Iroquois grew three main crops—corn, beans, and squash. They called these crops the "Three Sisters" because they were all planted together in the same field. After a field was farmed for about ten years, the soil would become less fertile. The Iroquois would then move to another location.

Hundreds of people sometimes lived in a single Iroquois village. For protection against enemies, the Iroquois built **palisades**, or walls made of tall wooden poles, around their villages.

The Iroquois' own name for themselves was Haudenosaunee (hoh•dee•noh•SHOH•nee), or "People of the Longhouse." That is because they lived in **longhouses**, or long, narrow buildings with curved roofs.

A CLOSER LOOK
An Iroquois Village

Iroquois villages were usually built on high ground and were surrounded by a palisade.

1. The Iroquois may have played a game similar to lacrosse.

2. Before the crops were planted, workers cleared the land. To kill the trees, men cut the bark all around the trees. After the trees died, the men burned them. Then the women planted their crops in the cleared area. This is called the slash-and-burn method of farming.

3. The palisade could be as high as 20 feet (6 m).

4. Most villages had eight or ten longhouses. A longhouse might be home to as many as 20 families.

5. Each family in a longhouse slept on a platform. Under the platform, families stored weapons, tools, and baskets. On shelves above the platform, they stored pots, food, and animal skins.

❖ What are some ways the Iroquois used the natural resources near their villages?

Iroquois canoes were usually covered with the bark of elm or spruce trees.

The frame of a longhouse was made of poles cut from young trees. The poles were bent and tied and then covered with bark. Longhouses had no windows. Smoke from cooking fires escaped through holes in the roof.

Inside, a longhouse was divided into sections. Each section was home to two families, who built sleeping benches along the walls of their living space. A longhouse might be home to as many as 20 families.

Iroquois villages were usually located on hillsides near water and surrounded by forests. These waterways and forests provided food and many resources. However, no single place could provide people with everything they might need or want.

To get goods they could not make or find, the Iroquois had to leave their

What resource did the Iroquois make this spoon out of?

villages. They traveled in canoes to trade with people in other villages. **Trade** is the exchanging, or buying and selling, of goods. Over time, the Iroquois developed trade routes that stretched for hundreds of miles. They also built trails between their villages.

Beads cut from shells were sometimes traded and exchanged for goods such as food or cooking pots. These beads, called **wampum**, were also strung into belts with fancy designs. These belts had many uses. They were used to send messages and to mark agreements. Their designs usually told stories about the Iroquois and their past.

REVIEW How did the Iroquois use the resources in their environment to meet basic needs?

Family Life

While an Iroquois Indian belonged to one of several Iroquois tribes, he or she lived in a smaller group called a **clan**. Clans were made up mostly of relatives. A clan's men hunted together, and a clan's women helped one another with cooking and planting. The Iroquois had ten clans altogether. These were named for animals and birds. Clan names included turtle, bear, wolf, snipe, eel, hawk, heron, deer, beaver, and eagle.

Membership in a clan followed the mother's side of the family. If she was in the Turtle Clan, for example, her children were all in the Turtle Clan, even if their father was from another clan.

Women owned the crops and longhouses. They also chose a clan's **sachem** (SAY•chuhm), or chief. The oldest or most respected woman in an Iroquois village was called the Clan Mother. The Clan Mother and her advisers chose the sachem for a whole village.

REVIEW What were clans named for?

Working Together

The five largest Iroquois tribes were the Cayuga, Mohawk, Oneida, Onondaga (ah•nuhn•DAW•guh), and Seneca. These tribes were known as the Five Nations. The Iroquois were fierce warriors, and the Five Nations often battled each other over control of hunting areas. Even within a tribe, people sometimes fought to settle arguments between clans.

An Iroquois legend tells the story of an argument between tribes. A **legend** is a story handed down by a group of people over time. According to this legend, an Iroquois warrior named Hiawatha (hy•uh•WAW•thuh) saw his family killed by members of another tribe. Tradition said that Hiawatha had to kill those who had killed his family. Hiawatha, however, wanted the fighting to stop.

Hiawatha left his village and met another Iroquois named Deganawida (deh•gahn•uh•WEE•duh), who became known as the Peacemaker. They began

The Iroquois often displayed wampum belts at meetings. They were considered symbols of wealth.

talking to leaders about a plan for peace. In time, they persuaded the Five Nations to unite. The nations agreed to stop fighting one another and to work together as a group. The group they formed was called the Iroquois League. Deganawida said that the Iroquois League would have "only one body, one head, and one heart."

REVIEW How were Hiawatha and Deganawida important to the Iroquois?

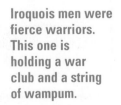

Iroquois men were fierce warriors. This one is holding a war club and a string of wampum.

Iroquois League council meetings were held "across the council fire." No one chief or one nation ruled over the others at these meetings.

The Iroquois League was a kind of representative government. In a representative government each group chooses a person to represent, or speak for, its members. That person listens to the people's ideas and shares those ideas with other leaders before decisions or laws are made. Each Iroquois tribe chose leaders to represent it on the Grand Council. There were about 50 chiefs representing their tribes on the Grand Council.

Analyze the Value

1. In a representative government, why is it important for many people to take part?
2. What are the benefits of a representative government?
3. **Make It Relevant** New York and the rest of the United States have a representative government. Find out who represents your community in the New York State government and in the United States government. Find out what kinds of issues in your community they deal with.

The Iroquois League

The Iroquois League was a large and powerful group. For a time it controlled much of what is today the northeastern United States and southeastern Canada. When the Five Nations formed the Iroquois League, they acted as a confederacy (kuhn•FEH•duh•ruh•see). A **confederacy** is a loose group of governments working together.

As members of a confederacy, each group continued to live as a separate nation. Each kept its own name, culture, and leaders. However, the Five Nations also worked together to make the league stronger.

A group called the Grand Council settled disputes among the tribes.

The Hiawatha Belt

Background The Iroquois used wampum to record important events. The Hiawatha Belt represents the joining of the five Iroquois nations.

1 Each symbol on the belt—a square or tree—represents one of the tribes.

2 The Great Tree of Peace in the center represents the Onondaga, where the confederacy's central council is kept.

DBQ **Document-Based Question** What do you think the lines linking the five shapes showed?

A **council** is a group that makes laws. The Grand Council made decisions about boundaries and about matters such as war and trade that were important to all the tribes. Each tribe sent leaders to serve on the Grand Council. They met once a year at a village near present-day Syracuse.

In the early 1700s a sixth group of Native Americans, the Tuscarora, joined the Five Nations. They had moved to New York from North Carolina. By 1722 the Iroquois people were known as the Six Nations.

REVIEW How did the Iroquois confederacy work?

REVIEW

1. **WHAT TO KNOW** How did the Iroquois use natural resources?

2. **VOCABULARY** What is the role of a **council** in a government?

3. **HISTORY** How did Hiawatha and Deganawida convince the Five Nations to stop fighting?

4. **CRITICAL THINKING** What role did Iroquois women play in tribal government?

5. **GIVE A SPEECH** Imagine that you are an Iroquois leader who wants to persuade other tribes to join a confederacy. Prepare a speech that tells why others should join the confederacy.

6. **MAIN IDEA AND DETAILS** On a separate sheet of paper, copy and complete this graphic organizer.

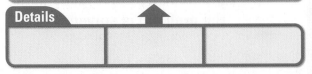

Main Idea

Five Iroquois tribes were united in a confederacy.

Details

· SKILLS · Solve a Problem

▶ WHY IT MATTERS

Think about a problem you have had recently. Perhaps you had trouble completing one of your assignments. How did you solve the problem? People everywhere have problems at some time. Being able to solve problems is an important skill that you can use now and in the future.

▶ WHAT YOU NEED TO KNOW

Here are steps you can follow to solve a problem.

Step 1 **Identify the problem. If it is big, divide it into smaller parts.**

Step 2 **Think of ideas for solving the problem or each part of it.**

Step 3 **Compare your ideas. Ask yourself what is good and bad about each. Choose the best idea.**

Step 4 **Plan how to carry out your idea. Can you do it yourself, or do you need help?**

Step 5 **Follow your plan, and then think about how well it worked.**

Step 6 **If your plan does not solve the problem, try other ideas until the problem is solved.**

▶ PRACTICE THE SKILL

You have read about how the Iroquois solved the problem of fighting among the tribes. Think about the steps for solving problems as you answer the following questions.

1 What might have been some of the possible solutions the Iroquois leaders thought of?

2 What did the leaders do to carry out the solution they chose?

3 How did the idea the leaders chose solve the Iroquois' problem?

▶ APPLY WHAT YOU LEARNED

What problems do you see in your school? Which is the most important to you? Using the steps listed on this page, write a plan to solve that problem.

This symbol of the Iroquois League shows four deer facing outward from a central circle.

The Algonquians

YOU ARE THERE

The Iroquois visitors from the north have just left your village. You are Algonquian and speak a different language from theirs. You noticed, however, that they wore clothes similar to yours and ate the same kind of food as you. You wonder, "Are they like us in other ways as well?"

Meeting Basic Needs

At one time, Native Americans who spoke Algonquian languages lived throughout much of New York. By about 1400, however, the Iroquois had pushed them into the southeastern part of the state. After that time, the Algonquians lived mostly along the southern Hudson River and on Manhattan Island, Staten Island, and Long Island. In all, there were fewer Algonquians than Iroquois in New York.

Algonquian tribes who lived in New York included the Delaware, Wappinger (WAH•pin•jer), Montauk, and Mahican (muh•HEE•kuhn). The Algonquian tribes were usually friendly and traded with each other. For the Mahicans, however, fighting was a regular part of life. They lived closest to the Iroquois Mohawks, who often attacked their villages.

WHAT TO KNOW
How did the Algonquian tribes in New York use the natural resources around them?

VOCABULARY
wigwam p. 66
division of labor p. 68
specialize p. 68
scarce p. 68
tradition p. 69
ceremony p. 69

MAIN IDEA AND DETAILS

Main Idea

Details

Delaware Indians often used wooden drumsticks like these in tribal ceremonies.

Making a Birchbark Canoe

1 A birchbark canoe began with a frame made of poles cut from young trees.

2 Sheets of bark from birch trees were stretched over the frame.

The Birchbark Canoe

The Algonquians found that birchbark canoes were good for traveling. They were light enough to carry over the land between rivers or around dangerous waters. They were sturdy, fast, and easy to paddle and steer even when heavily loaded. Materials used to build and repair birchbark canoes were also easy to find.

Like their Iroquois neighbors, the Algonquians hunted in nearby forests and fished in waterways. They also gathered maple syrup, wild berries, nuts, and plants for food. The Algonquians did not rely on their crops for food as much as the Iroquois did. However, they did plant corn, squash, and beans.

The Algonquians lived in villages near where they hunted, fished, and farmed. Most of their villages were smaller than those of the Iroquois.

Many Algonquians built longhouses similar to those of the Iroquois. Others lived in wigwams. A **wigwam** is a round, bark-covered shelter. To make wigwams, the Algonquians cut down small trees and tied the trunks together into a dome shape. Then they covered the frame with bark.

The Algonquians made their clothing mostly out of deerskins. Men wore shirts, leggings, and moccasins. They usually tied one or two eagle feathers to their hair. Women wore either dresses or skirts and blouses. Both men's and women's clothing was decorated with feathers, shells, and the sharp quills of

3 After cutting the sides of the canoe to the right height, workers painted tree sap or tar on the outside of the canoe to make it waterproof.

4 Finally, to make the canoe stronger, strips of wood were placed inside the canoe lengthwise and widthwise.

Analyze Diagrams The Algonquians were expert canoe builders. They often traveled long distances in their canoes to trade with other tribes.

◆ What made the birchbark canoe strong?

porcupines. For special events, they wore brightly colored capes made from feathers.

Like the Iroquois, the Algonquians used natural resources to make tools and weapons. From stones, branches, grasses, and animal bones, they made spears, clubs, nets, and traps. Using birch-bark, the Algonquians built light yet strong canoes. These canoes were highly valued by the Iroquois because they were faster than Iroquois elm bark canoes. In fact, Iroquois warriors stole Algonquian canoes whenever they could!

REVIEW What were two kinds of houses in which Algonquians lived?

Algonquian Ways of Life

The Algonquians, like the Iroquois, lived in clans. When Algonquian clans combined, they took a name from nature—usually the name of an animal or a plant. As with the Iroquois, Algonquian clan membership usually followed the mother's side of the family.

Unlike the Iroquois, the Algonquians were not united. Each tribe and village had its own leader. Although they were not united, Algonquian tribes often traded with each other.

Algonquian beeswax doll

For most of the year, the Algonquians lived in villages. In winter a group might leave its village and move into a forest to be closer to wood for fuel and animals to hunt. By moving with the seasons, the Algonquians made good use of the natural resources around them.

In Algonquian villages, as in Iroquois villages, the work was divided among the people. Dividing jobs among workers is called **division of labor**. Division of labor made it easier for villagers to meet their needs.

In a division of labor, people often specialize (SPEH•shuh•lyz). To **specialize**

An Algonquian bowl carved from elm

is to work at one kind of job that a person can do well. Some men made arrow points or bows. Others made traps, fishing nets, or other kinds of tools. When they were not hunting or fishing, men cleared fields for crops. They also cut bark for homes and canoes.

Algonquian women raised the children. They planted, cared for, and picked the crops. They cooked the food they grew and the animals the men brought from hunting and fishing. Women also stored food to eat in the winter, when it would be **scarce**, or hard to find. Often when a group

Making Pottery

Analyze Diagrams Algonquians in what is now New York State used clay to make bowls, jars, and other useful items.

◆ Why did the Indians mix plant fibers and crushed rocks or shells with the clay?

1 **Mix plant fibers and crushed rock or shells with clay to make the clay stronger.**

2 **Shape the clay into bowls, jugs, and cooking pots.**

3 **Place the pottery in a fire to make it hard and ready to use.**

moved, women took the shelters apart, carried them to the new camp, and put them together again.

Both Iroquois and Algonquian children learned about their tribe's traditions by listening to stories. A **tradition** is an idea, a belief, or a way of doing something that has been handed down from the past.

Both the Algonquians and the Iroquois held many ceremonies. A **ceremony** is a series of actions performed during a special event. For example, there were ceremonies to announce the names of new babies and to show thanks for a good harvest.

Marriage ceremonies were simple. If a man wanted to marry a woman, he would take her a gift of meat from an animal he had hunted himself. This was to show that he was a good hunter. If the woman wanted to marry him, she

Algonquians lived in wigwams. To keep time during dances, Algonquians shook rattles (left) made out of gourds.

would accept the gift of meat and cook it. This was to show that she was a good homemaker. When the couple shared the meal, they were considered married.

REVIEW How did Algonquian children learn their tribe's traditions?

REVIEW

1. **WHAT TO KNOW** How did the Algonquians use natural resources?

2. **VOCABULARY** Use the terms **tradition** and **ceremony** in a sentence about the Algonquians' ways of life.

3. **CIVICS AND GOVERNMENT** How did the Algonquians organize and govern themselves?

4. **CRITICAL THINKING** If you lived in an Algonquian village, would you rather harvest crops or go hunting? Explain.

5. **MAKE A CHART** In a chart, list ways the Algonquians and Iroquois were alike and ways they were different.

6. (Focus Skill) **MAIN IDEA AND DETAILS** On a separate sheet of paper, copy and complete this graphic organizer.

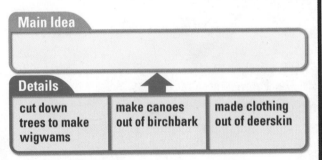

Main Idea		

Details		
cut down trees to make wigwams	make canoes out of birchbark	made clothing out of deerskin

Use Tables to Group Information

VOCABULARY

comparison   classify

▶ WHY IT MATTERS

How many ways can you think of to describe yourself? You might describe your height, your weight, and your age. You might also make comparisons between yourself and other people you know. To make a **comparison**, you say how two or more things are the same and how they are different.

When you make comparisons, you can use a table to show the information. A table lets you quickly compare numbers, facts, and other information. Before you can show the information, however, you must first decide how you want to **classify**, or group, it.

▶ WHAT YOU NEED TO KNOW

The tables on page 71 show information on the language groups in New York. Both tables show the same information, but they classify it in different ways.

In Table A, the first column lists the two major language groups in alphabetical order. The second column lists the tribes that belonged to each language group. Table B shows the same information about the language groups.

This drawing shows an artist's view of a Manhattan Indian village.

Table A	
LANGUAGE GROUP	TRIBES
Algonquian	Delaware
	Mahican
	Montauk
	Shinnecock
	Wappinger
Iroquois	Cayuga
	Mohawk
	Oneida
	Onondaga
	Seneca

Table B	
TRIBE	LANGUAGE GROUP
Cayuga	Iroquois
Delaware	Algonquian
Mahican	Algonquian
Mohawk	Iroquois
Montauk	Algonquian
Oneida	Iroquois
Onondaga	Iroquois
Seneca	Iroquois
Shinnecock	Algonquian
Wappinger	Algonquian

In this table, however, the Native American tribes of New York are listed in alphabetical order in the first column. The second column lists the language group to which each tribe belonged.

▶ PRACTICE THE SKILL

Examine the tables above. Then use the tables to answer the following questions.

1 Study Table A. Name two tribes listed in the table that spoke Algonquian languages. Name two tribes that spoke Iroquoian languages.

2 Now study Table B. To which language group did the Seneca belong? the Montauk?

3 Which table makes it easier to find out which tribes spoke a language belonging to a certain language group? Explain your answer.

4 Which table makes it easier to find out to which language group a certain tribe belonged? Explain your answer.

▶ APPLY WHAT YOU LEARNED

Tables can be used to compare many different types of information. Tables can compare peoples' likes and dislikes, the populations of cities and towns, students' grades, and the types of cars people drive. Think of some information that you would like to organize in a table. Maybe it is information that you learned from asking questions or doing a survey. For example, you could do a survey showing your friends' choices of colors or video games. Display the results in a table.

An Iroquois comb

Lesson 4

A Lasting Influence

 WHAT TO KNOW
How do Native American history and culture affect New York State today?

VOCABULARY
heritage p. 73
reservation p. 74
generation p. 75

 **MAIN IDEA AND DETAILS**

Main Idea

Details

YOU ARE THERE

"I'm sitting here as the seventh generation because seven generations ago these people were looking out for me. Seven generations from now someone will be here, I know. So each generation makes sure that seven generations is coming, all the time."

With these words Chief Oren Lyons, a member of the Onondaga Nation and a Faithkeeper of the Turtle Clan, explains the responsibility of each generation to keep Native American culture alive. Today Native American history and culture affect the lives of all New Yorkers.

Native Americans in New York today continue to keep their culture alive. This Iroquois man is performing a traditional dance outside a reconstructed longhouse.

Lacrosse

The sport of lacrosse is based on an old Native American game. The Iroquois may have played a game closest to the one played today. In the Iroquois game two teams played against each other, trying to score goals by using wooden sticks. The sticks had a net on one end so that team-mates could pass a wooden ball to each other and score a goal. A visitor once described how popular the game was among the Iroquois: "In summer they play a great deal at la crosse, twenty or more on each side."

A Lasting Tradition

New York's Native American heritage may be easiest to see in the names of many places in our state. **Heritage** is a way of life that has been passed down from one's ancestors. Many cities, towns, rivers, and lakes across New York have names that come from Native American words. Counties in New York that have Native American names include Saratoga, which means "the side hill"; Otsego, which means "place of the rock"; and Genesee, which means "good valley." Oswego, the name of a city, county, and river, comes from an Iroquois word for "the outpouring."

Many rivers and lakes in New York also have Native American names. These include the 11 Finger Lakes. *Chautauqua* (shuh•TAW•kwuh), is an Iroquois word that means "where the fish were taken out." *Canandaigua* (ka•nuhn•DAY•gwuh) means "the chosen place."

Places all over Long Island and the New York City area also have Native American names. The name Manhattan comes from *mannahatta*, a Native American word meaning "island." The names Montauk, Massapequa, Mamaroneck, Manhasset, and Tuckahoe also come from Native American words, to name just a few.

Native Americans have contributed far more to New York than names. When Europeans first arrived in New York in the 1600s, they learned important skills from the Native Americans already living there. By watching them, the Europeans learned to survive in their new land. They learned to plant Native American crops and to hunt the way Native Americans did. They learned to use natural resources as Native Americans had for thousands of years.

REVIEW What are some examples of New York's Native American heritage?

Native Americans Today

About 82,000 Native Americans from at least seven different groups live in New York today. About 27,000 of them live on reservations. A **reservation** is land set aside by a government for use by Native Americans. There are Algonquian reservations on Long Island, and there are Six Nations reservations in northern and western New York.

Native Americans in New York work at all kinds of jobs, and they live in all parts of the state. No matter where they live, however, many of them are working to keep their cultures alive. Some communities on reservations have traditional tribal governments, much like the ones their ancestors used. Clans on the Onondaga, Tuscarora, and Tonawanda Seneca Reservations still choose traditional chiefs. Today, council fires—signs of Iroquois cooperation—burn on Native American reservations in the United States and Canada. One of these fires burns at the Onondaga Reservation in New York.

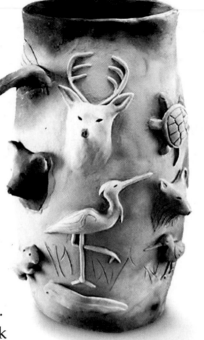

An Iroquois artist made this vase, which shows clan symbols.

Native American groups in New York often gather to celebrate their cultures and to take part in traditional ceremonies. At these gatherings, people wear traditional clothing, dance to traditional drum music, and share stories.

Museums also help keep Native American cultures alive. People can go to these museums to learn about the different Native American groups who have lived in New York. One of the best known of these museums is the

• BIOGRAPHY •

Joanne Shenandoah   1958 –
Character Trait: Individualism

Joanne Shenandoah is a Native American singer and composer. She is a Wolf Clan member of the Oneida Nation. As a child, Shenandoah was surrounded by the Oneida and Onondaga cultures. She often listened to tribal stories told by her parents. Today Shenandoah shares her Native American heritage with others. She writes music and sings songs that are inspired by her Oneida ancestors.

For more resources, go to
www.harcourtschool.com/ss1

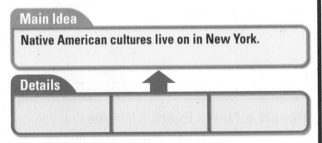

These Oneida children are learning the tradition of making cornhusk dolls.

National Museum of the American Indian's George Gustav Heye Center in New York City. Other museums in New York are run by Indian nations.

Native Americans keep their culture alive by teaching it to their children. Every Six Nations council meeting began with a member speaking these words, "In our every deliberation [discussion] we must consider the impact [effect] of our decisions on the next seven generations." A **generation** is the average time between the birth of parents and the birth of their children. The Iroquois believed that they should think of how their actions might affect not just their own lives, but the lives of children born seven generations in the future.

REVIEW How do Native Americans in New York work to keep their culture alive?

REVIEW

1. **WHAT TO KNOW** How have New York's Native American history and culture affected the state?

2. **VOCABULARY** Use **reservation** in a sentence.

3. **CULTURE** How do Native Americans make sure their culture lives on?

4. **CRITICAL THINKING** Why is it important to understand the contributions Native Americans have made to New York?

5. **DRAW A MAP** Does your county or town have a Native American name? What streets or geographic features have Native American names? Show these on a map.

6. **MAIN IDEA AND DETAILS** On a separate sheet of paper, copy and complete this graphic organizer.

Main Idea

Native American cultures live on in New York.

Details

Chapter Review

Summarize the Chapter

Main Idea and Details Complete this graphic organizer to show that you understand important ideas and details about how Native Americans in New York lived.

Main Idea

Native Americans in New York adapted to their environment and used the natural resources around them to meet their needs.

Details

THINK & WRITE

Report a News Event   Imagine that you are a reporter. Archaeologists have dug up some Native American pottery and tools near the Finger Lakes. Write a news report on the discoveries. Tell how the discoveries can help people understand how Native Americans in that part of New York lived long ago.

Write a Heritage Story   Native Americans often tell stories to share their heritage. Talk with older family members to learn about your family's heritage. Then write a story about it, and share it with the rest of the class.

USE VOCABULARY

Use a term from this list to complete each sentence.

archaeologist (p. 55)

longhouses (p. 59)

confederacy (p. 62)

traditions (p. 69)

reservations (p. 74)

1 Native Americans learn about their tribe's ____ by listening to stories.

2 About 27,000 Native Americans in New York live on the state's ____.

3 The people in Iroquois villages lived in ____.

4 An ____ studies artifacts to learn what life was like long ago.

5 A ____ is a loose group of governments working together.

RECALL FACTS

Answer these questions.

6 What caused the large animals that lived in what is now New York to become extinct?

7 How was a wigwam made?

Write the letter of the best choice.

8 **TEST PREP** Which of the following was NOT one of the "Three Sisters," the three main crops of the Iroquois?
 A corn
 B beans
 C tomatoes
 D squash

9 **TEST PREP** Which of the following place names does NOT come from a Native American word?
 F Manhattan
 G Oswego
 H Chautauqua Lake
 J Long Island

10 **TEST PREP** Iroquois warriors stole Algonquian birchbark canoes because
 A the Iroquois did not have canoes.
 B Algonquian canoes were faster than Iroquois canoes.
 C Algonquian canoes were bigger than Iroquois canoes.
 D the Iroquois did not have the natural resources to make canoes.

THINK CRITICALLY

11 Why do you think working together made the tribes of the Iroquois League stronger?

12 How might our knowledge of early people in New York be different if no archaeological discoveries had been made there?

APPLY SKILLS

Use a Cultural Map
Use the map on page 57 to answer these questions.

13 Which language group occupied most of central New York?

14 Which language group probably fished and traveled on most of the Hudson River?

Solve a Problem

15 Read a newspaper article about a problem in your community. Use the steps on page 64 to think of a solution to this problem.

Use Tables to Group Information

16 Make two tables that show the same information about Native American groups in New York today. Tell how you classified the information in each table. Explain the purpose of each table.

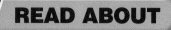

FIELD TRIP

READ ABOUT

Shako:wi Cultural Center is a place where members of the Oneida Indian Nation can share their heritage with others. In fact, *Shako:wi* is an Oneida name that means "He gives."

The center is locate near Oneida. Inside the center are many traditional arts and crafts. Also at Shako:wi, ceremonies are held honoring Oneida culture. If you visit, you might hear a story told by an Oneida storyteller, or you might learn how to make your own cornhusk doll.

FIND

NEW YORK

Oneida

SHAKO:WI
Cultural Center

This stained glass window shows a wolf, a turtle, and a bear. Each animal represents one of the three clans of the Oneida Indian Nation.

This student makes a cornhusk doll on his visit to Shako:wi.

Visitors can watch a ceremony or hear a story. This person is telling the story of how the Iroquois Nation was formed.

This Oneida woman and a visitor are using an Oneida tool.

A VIRTUAL TO

GO
ONLINE

For more re
www.ha

08

VISUAL SUMMARY

Write a Paragraph Study the pictures and captions below to help you review Unit 1. Then choose one picture. Write a paragraph that describes what the picture shows about Native American life.

USE VOCABULARY

For each pair of terms, explain how the terms are related.

1. **hemisphere** (p. 21), **equator** (p. 21)

2. **temperature** (p. 38), **climate** (p. 38)

3. **renewable** (p. 43), **nonrenewable** (p. 43)

4. **artifact** (p. 55), **archaeologist** (p. 55)

5. **longhouse** (p. 59), **wigwam** (p. 66)

RECALL FACTS

Answer these questions.

6. What are New York's lowland regions?

7. What are some of New York's most important farm products?

8. What was the Iroquois League?

Write the letter of the best choice.

9. **TEST PREP** Which of the following states does NOT share a border with New York?
   A Pennsylvania
   B Rhode Island
   C New Jersey
   D Connecticut

10. **TEST PREP** In what region is Mount Marcy located?
    F Tug Hill Plateau
    G New England Upland
    H Adirondack Upland
    J Appalachian Plateau

11. **TEST PREP** Which of the following tribes was NOT a part of the Iroquois League?
    A Delaware
    B Mohawk
    C Cayuga
    D Onondaga

Time

| 15,000 years ago | 12,000 years ago | 9,000 years ago |

About 12,000 years ago
Early people arrive in what is now New York p. 53

About 10,000 years ago
Early people in New York hunt mostly small animals p. 54

About 3,000 years ago People begin making pottery in New York p. 54

12 TEST PREP Which of the following was NOT a typical job for an Algonquian man?

F hunting

G fishing

H clearing fields

J raising children

THINK CRITICALLY

13 In what region of New York would you most want to spend the summer? In what region would you most want to spend the winter? Explain.

14 How do people change their environment when they use natural resources?

15 Why do you think Native American groups with similar languages had similar ways of life?

16 Why do you think New York's Native Americans work to keep their cultures alive?

APPLY SKILLS

Use a Cultural Map

Use the cultural map to answer the following questions.

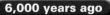

17 Which language group has the most reservations in New York?

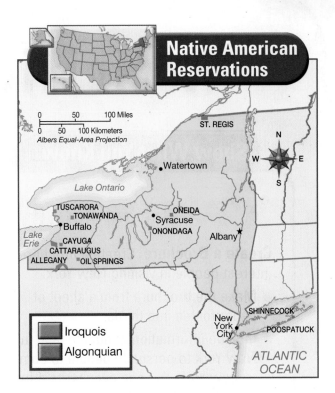

Native American Reservations

0   50   100 Miles
0   50   100 Kilometers
Albers Equal-Area Projection

ST. REGIS

Watertown

Lake Ontario

TUSCARORA
TONAWANDA
Buffalo

Lake Erie

CAYUGA
CATTARAUGUS
ALLEGANY   OIL SPRINGS

ONEIDA
Syracuse
ONONDAGA

Albany

New York City

SHINNECOCK

POOSPATUCK

ATLANTIC OCEAN

Iroquois
Algonquian

18 Which reservation is the farthest north? To which language group do the Native Americans who live there belong?

19 Which reservations are close to the Atlantic Ocean? To which language group do the Native Americans who live there belong?

20 To which language group do the Native Americans living on the reservations closest to the Great Lakes belong?

6,000 years ago   3,000 years ago   Present

About 1,000 years ago
People begin farming in New York
p. 54

About 1,000 years ago
Native Americans live in villages across New York p. 54

About 600 years ago **Most Native Americans belong to the Iroquoian or Algonquian language groups** p. 55

81

Activities

Show What You Know

✏️ Unit Writing Activity

Create a Brochure Create a brochure to interest people in visiting New York.

- Make the brochure from a sheet of paper folded into thirds.
- Include information about the land in New York to persuade people to come to New York. You can even write a fun slogan about New York.
- Include pictures of places to see in New York.

🖌️ Unit Project

Make a New York Atlas Make at least four outline maps to include in an atlas of New York.

- Use your textbook and other resources to make different kinds of maps, such as a physical map, a latitude and longitude map, and a cultural map.
- Include labels and give your maps titles. Also explain in map keys any symbols you use on your maps.

Read More

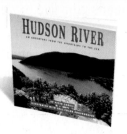

- *Hudson River: An Adventure from the Mountains to the Sea* by Peter Lourie. Boyds Mills Press.

- *The Rough-Face Girl* by Rafe Martin. Putnam Juvenile.

- *Anna, Grandpa, and the Big Storm* by Carla Stevens. Puffin.

 For more resources, go to
www.harcourtschool.com/ss1

Newcomers Arrive

The Big Idea

Encounters

The exploration and settlement of New York led to interaction between diverse peoples.

What to Know

- ✔ Why did Europeans explore and settle in New York?

- ✔ What was life like for the different groups that settled in colonial New York?

- ✔ What kinds of governments and economies developed in colonial New York?

- ✔ How did the French and Indian War affect New York?

A replica of Henry Hudson's ship, the *Half Moon*

Newcomers Arrive

Reading Social Studies

(Focus Skill) Generalize

Why It Matters Being able to generalize can help you better understand and remember what you read.

When you **generalize**, you make a statement that shows how different facts in a passage are related.

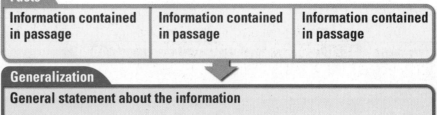

Facts

Information contained in passage	Information contained in passage	Information contained in passage

Generalization

General statement about the information

- A generalization is always based on facts.
- Words such as *most, many, some, generally,* and *usually* are clues to generalizations.

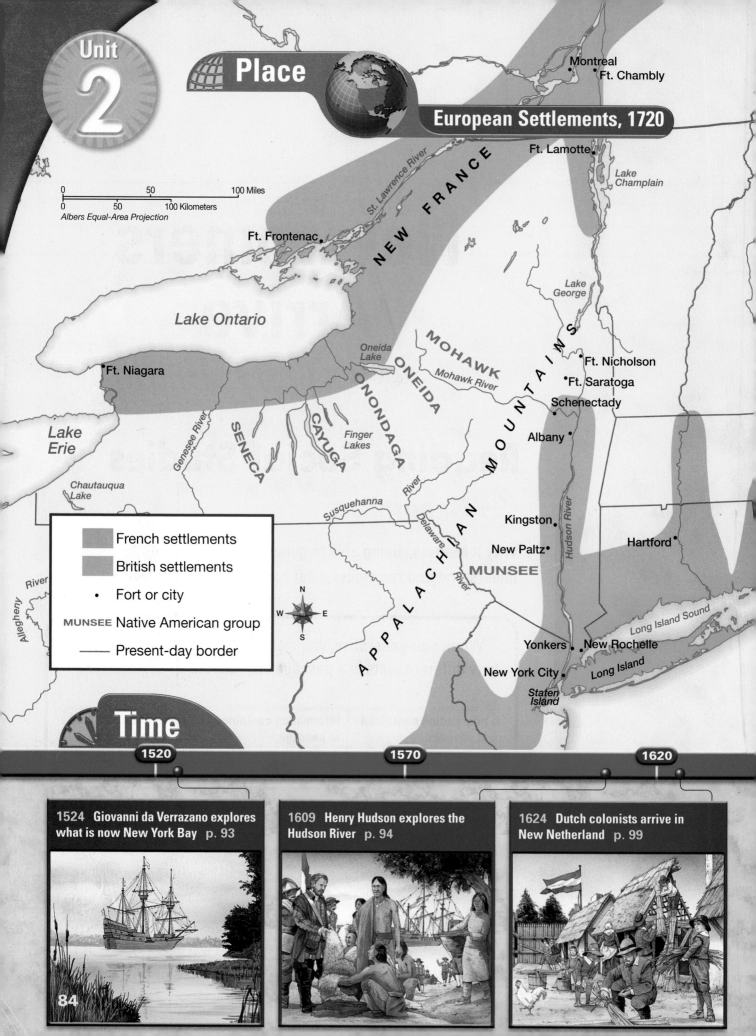

Place

European Settlements, 1720

100 Miles
100 Kilometers
Albers Equal-Area Projection

Montreal
Ft. Chambly

Ft. Lamotte

Lake Champlain

St. Lawrence River

NEW FRANCE

Ft. Frontenac

Lake Ontario

Lake George

MOHAWK

Ft. Nicholson

Oneida Lake

ONEIDA

Mohawk River

Ft. Saratoga

Schenectady

Ft. Niagara

ONONDAGA

Albany

Lake Erie

SENECA

CAYUGA

Finger Lakes

APPALACHIAN MOUNTAINS

Genesee River

Chautauqua Lake

Kingston

Hudson River

Hartford

New Paltz

Susquehanna River

Delaware River

MUNSEE

French settlements

British settlements

• Fort or city

MUNSEE Native American group

— Present-day border

Allegheny River

N
W E
S

Long Island Sound

Yonkers   New Rochelle

New York City   Long Island

Staten Island

Time

1520   1570   1620

1524 Giovanni da Verrazano explores what is now New York Bay p. 93

1609 Henry Hudson explores the Hudson River p. 94

1624 Dutch colonists arrive in New Netherland p. 99

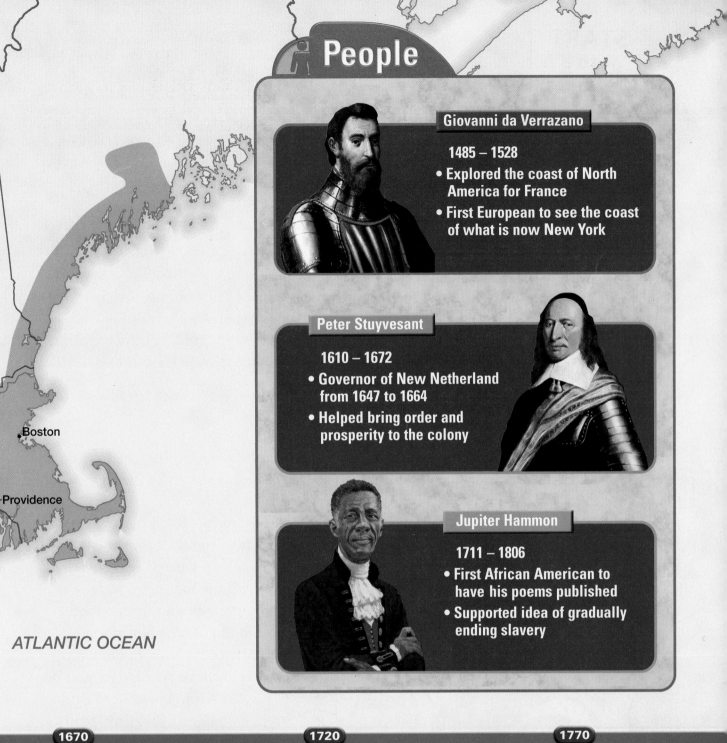

People

Giovanni da Verrazano

1485 – 1528
- Explored the coast of North America for France
- First European to see the coast of what is now New York

Peter Stuyvesant

1610 – 1672
- Governor of New Netherland from 1647 to 1664
- Helped bring order and prosperity to the colony

Jupiter Hammon

1711 – 1806
- First African American to have his poems published
- Supported idea of gradually ending slavery

Boston

Providence

ATLANTIC OCEAN

1670

1720

1770

1664   New Netherland becomes New York p. 119

1683   The first New York Assembly meets p. 122

1763   The French and Indian War ends p. 136

85

Marretje Haring
APRIL, 1687
FROM ADVENTURES FROM THE PAST

BY ALICE GERARD
ILLUSTRATED BY CYNTHIA VON BUHLER

In 1624, thirty Dutch families arrived in what is now New York. By the late 1600s many Dutch families had moved up the Hudson River from the present-day New York City area into what is now Rockland County. Among them were Marretje (ma•RET•yuh) Haring and her family. They moved to Tappan, which is now part of Orangetown. Marretje's stepfather, Daniel, and her older brothers, Peter, Cornelius, and Cozyn, were already in Tappan. Read now about the day Marretje arrived at her new home.

A cold wind blew from the river. Eight-year-old Marretje pulled her jacket close around her and squeezed closer to Brechje, her twelve-year-old sister.

"Are you warm enough?" asked Brechje. She put her arm around Marretje, which helped a little. The boat moved slowly up the Sparkill Creek, low in the water because it was so heavily laden. The two young men pulling on the long oars were strangers, but they seemed friendly enough and understood Dutch. Marretje looked around at the others: her mother Grietje, with six-year-old Abraham on her lap, her brother Jacobus beside her, and her sister Vroutje, twenty years old, an adult, really. Vroutje's shoulders were

laden	loaded

hunched together; she looked cold and unhappy. Their slave Helena sat with her baby in the front of the low, flat boat. Boxes and packages filled the rest of the space.

"I wonder if they are as excited as I am," Marretje thought. "How soon will we be there?" she asked.

"Soon," answered her mother. "Be patient, child. . . ."

Marretje tried to imagine what Tappan would be like. Peter had told her there were bears and wolves and panthers and birds everywhere. He said there were no roads and no houses nearby, but there was all the good land one could want, huge trees, and lots of water. She leaned against Brechje, making pictures in her mind of the new home. She was excited, looking forward to the adventure of a new house in a new place. But she was also a little unhappy at leaving the Bouwery village where she had been born and lived all her life. . . .

Helena called out and pointed. Ahead in the distance were people waving from the shore. Behind them was a small house. Marretje started to stand up, but Brechje pulled her down. "It's Father and the boys," her mother told her. "And that's our house."

The boatmen pulled strongly on the oars, steering the boat to the side of the creek. They reached the shore and Marretje could at last stand up and climb out. She was stiff and tired from sitting still for so long. She looked at the house. It was smaller than their old house and looked new and unfinished still. The roof was <u>thatched</u> and the outside walls were made of long <u>planks</u>. There were three windows and one door.

Stepfather Daniel called out, "Welcome to our new home!" They were all glad to see each other, and the boys <u>boasted</u> of all the work they had done to get ready. Peter picked Marretje up and hugged her. Cornelius started unloading the boat. Cozyn and Lewis, Helena's husband, came out of the house, where they had been working.

| thatched | covered with straw | planks | heavy, thick boards |

| boasted | bragged |

The boys helped carry in the baggage they had brought, and Marretje had a chance to look around the house. There were two rooms, the bigger one with a large fireplace at the end. This room had a long, narrow, wooden table with benches in the middle of the room, and beds by the wall. There was also a big chest, the kas, to hold linen sheets, napkins, and tablecloths. To get to the other room she went through a door beside the fireplace. This smaller room also had a fireplace. Mother called it the back kitchen and said that Helena and Lewis and their baby would sleep there. The boys put the feather beds they had brought onto the bedsteads and began to set other packages on the table in the big room.

Abraham called her. "Marretje, come up here! See what I found!" She looked up and saw his face leaning over the edge of a wide loft that ran the length of the room below. Marretje climbed the ladder and stood up beside him. Abraham, Jacobus, and the older boys would sleep up here on straw mattresses that were already laid out.

"Marretje," called her mother from down below, "Come here and help! There is still a lot of work to do!" Reluctantly she climbed down. Her mother gave her a broom and told her to sweep the wooden floor. All the tramping in and out with the baggage had brought in leaves and dirt. The boys had carried in more firewood, and Brechje and Vroutje were laying out the pewter spoons and wooden plates, called trenchers, so that they could eat supper soon. Mother was plumping up the feather beds where they would sleep. A pot of venison was warming in the fireplace, and Helena stirred it from time to time. . . .

After dinner, once the table was cleared and the beds all set up, Mother helped Brechje and Marretje get into the bed they would share. It was cozy and warm, with a feather bed under them and feather quilt on top.

She sat beside them and sang a nursery song, one they knew from when they were small. They were really too old for it now, but it made them feel more at home. . . . Before they knew it they were sound asleep.

Response Corner

1. (Focus Skill) **Generalize** How did Marretje feel about her move to Tappan?

2. Why do you think Marretje felt as she did?

3. **Make It Relevant** How would you feel if you had to move from your home to a new place that is very different?

START THE UNIT PROJECT

Stage a Play With your classmates, begin planning a play about the European exploration and settlement of New York. As you read this unit, choose at least three people or events you want to include in the play. Do research to find more information about each. This will help when you are ready to write scenes for your play.

USE TECHNOLOGY

GO ONLINE For more resources, go to www.harcourtschool.com/ss1

USE VISUALS

Looking at visuals, such as photographs, charts, and maps, can help you better understand and remember what you read.

- **Visuals often show the same information that is in the text but in a different way.**

- **Many visuals have titles, captions, or labels that help you understand what is shown.**

✓	What kind of visual is shown?
✓	What does the visual show?
✓	How does the visual help you better understand the subject that you are reading?

Exploration and Settlement

Old Hook Mill, East Hampton

Lesson Early European Explorers

1520 — 1645 — 1770

1520–1620

WHAT TO KNOW
Why did European explorers travel to the Americas?

VOCABULARY
claim p. 93
raw material p. 93
Northwest Passage p. 93
expedition p. 93
Columbian Exchange p. 95

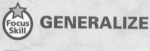 GENERALIZE

Facts

Generalization

YOU ARE THERE The year is 1524. You're a sailor exploring the east coast of North America. At each place along the way, you've learned about many new things and people. As you enter New York Bay, you imagine that this land has great riches. However, stormy weather tosses your ship. Your leader, Giovanni da Verrazano, decides to sail back to sea. You look back and wonder what you've missed.

Exploring New York

In 1492 a European explorer named Christopher Columbus sailed west across the Atlantic Ocean in three small ships. He was looking for a new trade route to Asia. Columbus reached a small island off the coast of North America. He believed he was in the part of Asia called the Indies, so he called the people he saw Indians.

Giovanni da Verrazano

Soon others sailed to North America. The Spanish, the Dutch, the French, and the English all began to **claim** or say they owned, lands there. They wanted gold and other raw materials, such as wood and fur. A **raw material** is a resource that can be used to make a product.

The Europeans began to search for a way to sail around or through North America. They hoped there might be such a route that started on the northern coast of North America. They called this route the **Northwest Passage**.

In 1524 the king of France hired Giovanni da Verrazano to lead an expedition to find the Northwest Passage. An **expedition** is a journey into an area to learn more about it. Verrazano sailed into Lower New York Bay. He became the first European to see the coast of what is now New York. Verrazano claimed this land for France, but he did not find the Northwest Passage.

In 1534 Jacques Cartier (ZHAHK kar•TYAY) of France tried to find the Northwest Passage. He and his crew sailed more than 994 miles (1,600 km) inland on a river he called the St. Lawrence. Cartier did not find the Northwest Passage, but he did become the first European to reach inland Canada.

In 1608 a French mapmaker named Samuel de Champlain

Samuel de Champlain

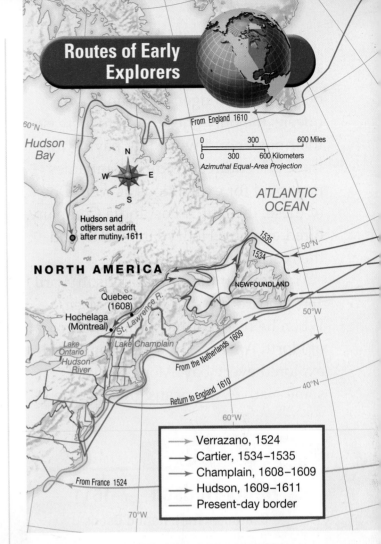

Routes of Early Explorers

Movement **Early explorers sailed along the northeastern coast of North America.**

❯ From what direction did Champlain travel into what is now New York State?

explored and mapped areas in what is now southeastern Canada. He set up a trading post there, which he named Quebec (kwih•BEK). Later, Algonquian Indian guides led Champlain into what is now northern New York State. There he saw the lake now named for him.

REVIEW Why did Europeans want to find the Northwest Passage?

Chapter 3 ■ **93**

Henry Hudson's Voyages

By the 1600s exploration was big business. No longer were kings and queens the only ones trying to increase their power and wealth by paying for these adventures. Trading companies now paid for expeditions as well. One of these, the Dutch East India Company, hired explorer Henry Hudson to find the Northwest Passage.

Hudson left the Netherlands in April 1609 aboard the ship the *Half Moon*. When he reached the northeastern coast of North America, he sailed south and explored every bay. Along the way, some Native Americans greeted Hudson and his crew. They shared meals and traded goods. Soon, however, misunderstandings between Hudson and some other Native Americans led to fights.

In September 1609 Hudson reached New York Bay. He sailed the *Half Moon* through the narrows and up a wide river. In time this waterway became known as the Hudson River. Hudson wrote that the land he saw was

66 **the finest . . . that I ever in my life set foot upon, and it also abounds in [has a lot of] trees of every description.** 99

mizzenmast

• BIOGRAPHY •

Henry Hudson   ?–1611
Character Trait: Heroic Deeds

Henry Hudson's final search for the Northwest Passage began in 1610. On this voyage for England, Hudson followed a broad waterway into a large bay. He spent three months exploring the bay. When winter came, the ship was icebound. By spring the crew had no food left. The crew forced Hudson, his son, and seven other sailors into a small boat. They left them there and sailed home. Hudson and his companions were never seen again. The waterways that he and his group had explored became known as Hudson Strait and Hudson Bay.

GO ONLINE For more resources, go to www.harcourtschool.com/ss1

officers' quarters

rudder

About 150 miles (241 km) upstream, the water became so shallow that the *Half Moon* could go no farther. Hudson had to quit his search for the Northwest Passage and turn back.

Leaders in the Netherlands read the descriptions of the rich land in New York. Instead of continuing to look for the Northwest Passage, they set up trading companies. One company, the New Netherland Company, claimed the right to trade in the land between the Delaware and Connecticut Rivers. The region included parts of New York, New Jersey, Pennsylvania, Connecticut, and Delaware. The company named it New Netherland.

REVIEW Why did leaders in the Netherlands stop looking for the Northwest Passage?

Two Worlds Come Together

Soon after Native Americans and Europeans met, they began to trade. This exchange of goods, plants, animals, and ideas between the Europeans and the Native Americans came to be known as the **Columbian Exchange**. It was named after Christopher Columbus.

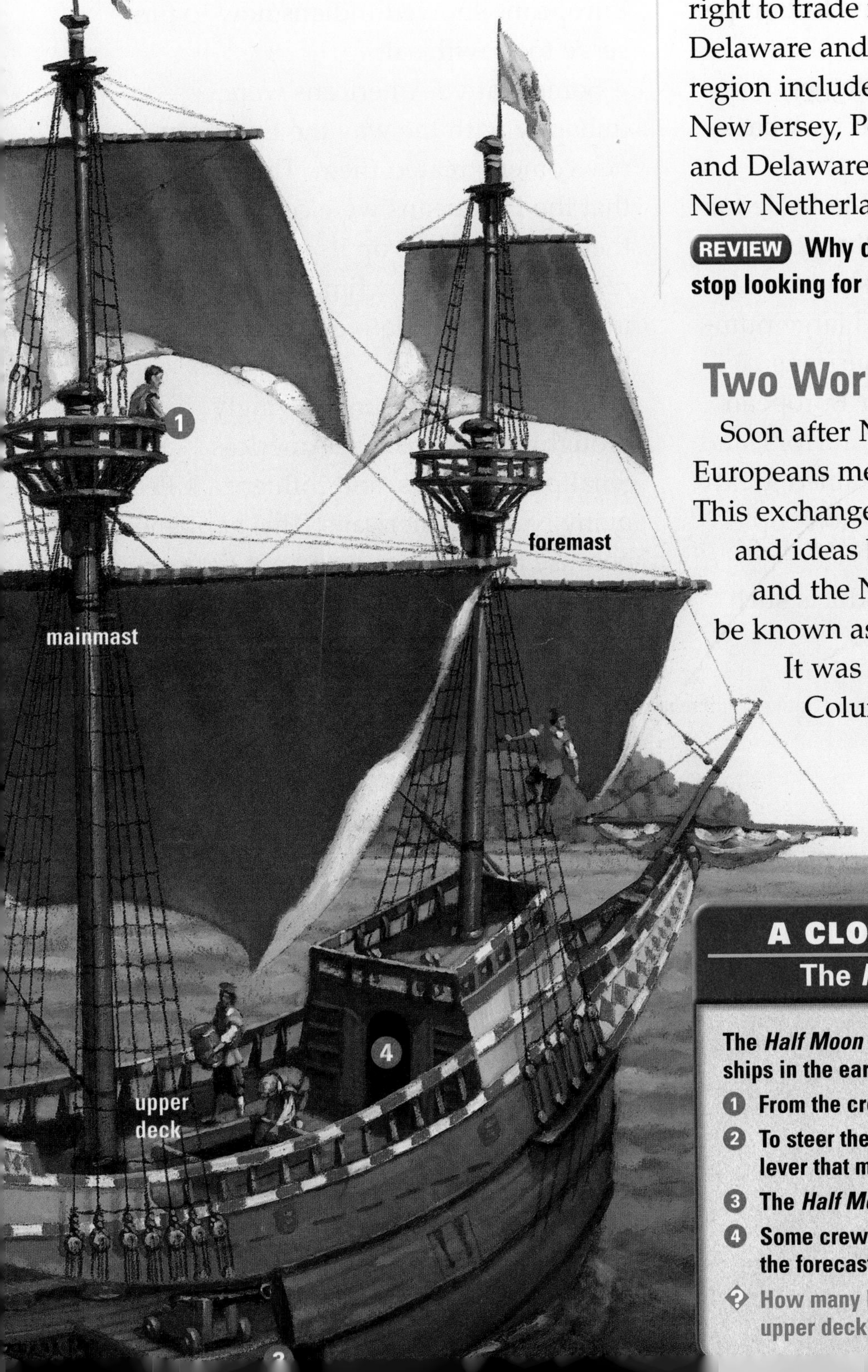

mainmast

foremast

upper deck

A CLOSER LOOK
The *Half Moon*

The *Half Moon* was typical of European sailing ships in the early 1600s.

❶ From the crow's nest, sailors looked for land.

❷ To steer the ship, sailors adjusted a long lever that moved the ship's rudder.

❸ The *Half Moon* could hold 80 tons of cargo.

❹ Some crew members had their quarters in the forecastle (FOHK•suhl).

❓ How many levels are shown below the ship's upper deck?

Because of the Columbian Exchange, many plants and animals that we know today were brought to the Americas. Before the Europeans came, Native Americans had never seen cattle, horses, pigs, chickens, or honeybees.

In turn, explorers returned to Europe from the Americas with new plants, including cotton, cocoa, potatoes, tomatoes, and corn. They also took back guinea pigs and turkeys.

Many Europeans wanted to trade for fur—especially beaver fur. In the 1600s beaver hats had become fashionable in Europe. North America had large numbers of beavers. Native Americans would trade beaver furs for European guns, metal pots and tools, mirrors, and beads. In turn, Europeans gained great wealth from selling the furs to people in Europe.

Over time, European products such as metal sewing needles, wool yarn, and iron knives became part of Native American life. Native Americans made copper kettles into necklaces and cutting tools. They turned iron knives and ax heads into other kinds of tools. Also, Europeans showed Indians how to preserve food with salt.

Some Native Americans were unhappy with the way the European newcomers treated them. They believed that the Europeans were coming to take their land and use up its natural resources. This sometimes led to fighting between the Native Americans and the Europeans.

Some Europeans unknowingly brought diseases to the Americas. Smallpox, measles, and influenza killed many Native Americans. This happened because their bodies could not fight off the European diseases. The new

Henry Hudson and his crew traded beads, knives, and other goods with Native Americans for food and furs.

East to West
- Pigs
- Sheep
- Horses
- Chickens
- Cows
- Goats
- Bees
- Iron

West to East
- Potatoes
- Cotton
- Corn
- Squash
- Turkeys
- Peas
- Cocoa
- Tomatoes

Can you imagine some of your favorite Italian foods without tomato sauce? Europeans did not bring tomatoes from the Americas to Italy until the 1500s.

diseases spread quickly and often killed whole villages.

The first Europeans to come to North America brought changes to the lives of the Native Americans. Soon many more Europeans would be arriving. Life for the Native Americans would change even more.

REVIEW Why did Europeans want to start a fur trade in North America?

REVIEW

1. **WHAT TO KNOW** Why did European explorers travel to the Americas?

2. **VOCABULARY** Use **claim** and **expedition** in a sentence about Europeans in North America.

3. **CULTURE** What happened when Native Americans and Europeans met?

4. **CRITICAL THINKING** Look at a globe. Why do you think Europeans tried sailing west instead of east to reach Asia?

5. **WRITE A DIARY ENTRY** Imagine that you are a sailor on the *Half Moon*. Write a diary entry describing your first view of New York Bay. Also explain how you feel about arriving in this unfamiliar place.

6. **GENERALIZE** On a separate sheet of paper, copy and complete this graphic organizer.

Facts

Generalization

Europeans had different reasons for exploring New York.

Lesson 2

The Dutch Settle New Netherland

1520 ———————— **1645** ———————— **1770**

1620–1645

WHAT TO KNOW
Why did the Dutch settle New Netherland?

VOCABULARY
colony p. 98
colonist p. 99
permanent p. 99
patroon p. 102

GENERALIZE

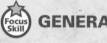

You ARE THERE

"Start packing," your father shouts, "we're sailing to New Netherland!" A few years ago, your family left France because they wanted to practice their religion freely. Now your father wants to move all the way across the Atlantic Ocean. "Don't worry," he explains. "The Dutch West India Company has offered to pay for the trip. They've also promised to give us land and help us buy farm animals."

The First Settlers Arrive

In 1621 the Dutch government gave a new company, the Dutch West India Company, control over all fur trade in areas of North America claimed by the Dutch. It also allowed the company to set up a colony in New Netherland. A **colony** is a settlement started by people who leave their own country to live in another land.

Dutch settlers in New Netherland

In 1624 a ship owned by the Dutch West India Company landed off the island of Manhattan. It carried 30 families from a French-speaking group called Walloons (wah•LOONZ). Earlier, the Walloons had moved to the Netherlands from France because they wanted to practice their religion freely. They left the Netherlands for New Netherland in search of wealth and land.

The Dutch West India Company paid for the Walloons' voyage. In return, these **colonists**, or people of the colony, would trade with the Native Americans for furs. The company would then sell the furs to merchants in Europe.

After arriving in New Netherland, the colonists set out to find good places to build settlements and to start farms. Eighteen families traveled up the Hudson River. They settled near the present location of Albany and built Fort Orange. It was the first **permanent**, or long-lasting, European settlement in New York.

In 1625 the Dutch West India Company hired Willem Verhulst (ver•HULST) to be New Netherland's leader. The company also chose a group of colonists to help Verhulst. The group was called the council.

REVIEW Who were the first European settlers in New Netherland?

This is how Fort Orange may have looked in 1635.

One story says that Manhattan Island was bought from Native Americans for goods that were worth 60 Dutch guilders, or about $24. Today that amount is equal to several thousand dollars.

The Founding of New Amsterdam

By 1626, New Netherland had a new leader—Peter Minuit (MIN•yuh•wuht). During Minuit's time as leader of the colony, the Dutch bought Manhattan Island from the Native Americans who were living there. However, the Native American ideas about owning land were different from those of the Europeans. The Native Americans believed that land was for all people to use. They thought the Dutch were paying them only for the use of the resources on the land, not for the land itself.

At the same time, a war between the Mohawks and the Mahicans began near Fort Orange. The fort's head officer supported the Mahicans. As a result, the Mohawks attacked Dutch soldiers and threatened the fort. They also tried to stop settlers from trading for furs.

To be safe from future attacks, Minuit ordered the colonists at Fort Orange to move to Manhattan Island. The settlers on the Delaware and Connecticut Rivers also moved to Manhattan. The colonists built a new settlement at the southern end of the island. They named their settlement New Amsterdam, after a city in the Netherlands.

New Amsterdam was built next to a harbor where the Hudson River flows into the Atlantic Ocean. This location proved to be good for trade, and the settlement started to grow. Traders traveled down the Hudson River in boats loaded with furs. They stopped at New Amsterdam to unload their furs and get supplies. Ships waited in the harbor to carry furs to Europe. The harbor rarely froze in the winter, so trade could take place all year round.

By the 1630s New Amsterdam had about 200 people and 30 houses. There was a countinghouse where workers kept track of furs and money. There were also warehouses in which to store food and furs. A mill, powered by a windmill, produced lumber for building houses. For protection the colonists also built a fort with high walls made of stone.

REVIEW Why did colonists build New Amsterdam at the southern tip of Manhattan Island?

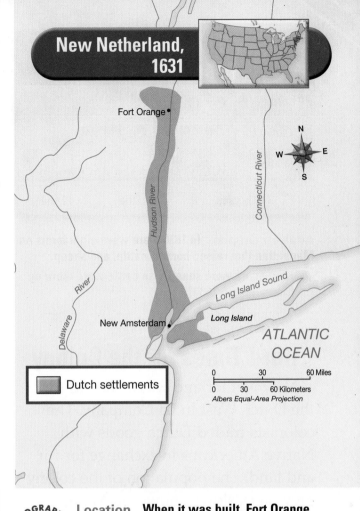

New Netherland, 1631

Fort Orange

Hudson River

Connecticut River

Delaware River

Long Island Sound

Long Island

New Amsterdam

ATLANTIC OCEAN

Dutch settlements

0   30   60 Miles
0   30   60 Kilometers
Albers Equal-Area Projection

GEOGRAPHY THEME

Location When it was built, Fort Orange was farther inland than any other European settlement in North America.

◆ About how far was Fort Orange from the ocean?

Dutch West India Company orchard

sheep pasture

A CLOSER LOOK
New Amsterdam, 1640s

New Amsterdam continued to grow. By 1643 more than 400 people lived there. French-speaking Walloons no longer made up most of the population. In fact, 18 different languages were spoken in the settlement.

❶ Ships arrived at the public dock on the East River.

❷ The center of New Amsterdam grew up around the fort. The marketplace, the church, and the windmill were there.

❸ Streets were developed from the paths that farmers used for travel to and from the town center.

◆ Why do you think the windmill was built near the town center?

Livestock on Manhattan, 1630

Horses	🐎🐎🐎🐎🐎
Cattle	🐄🐄🐄🐄🐄🐄🐄
Sheep	🐑🐑🐑🐑🐑🐑🐑🐑🐑

🐎 = 10 horses   🐄 = 10 cattle   🐑 = 10 sheep

Analyze Graphs **In 1630 there were eight farms on Manhattan that raised horses, cattle, and sheep.**

◈ How many more sheep than cattle were there on Manhattan in 1630?

Hard Times for the Colony

New Netherland was a success for the Dutch West India Company. The colonists traded Dutch goods with Native Americans in exchange for fur and land. The population of the colony grew very slowly, however. Many colonists thought that New Netherland needed more farms and workers in order to grow.

In June 1629 the company approved a plan to bring more settlers to New Netherland. Under this plan, members of the Dutch West India Company could receive large pieces of land. In return, the company asked the **patroons** (puh•TROONZ), or the new landowners, to each bring 50 new settlers to the colony. The settlers were to farm the patroon's land, pay rent to the patroon, and follow the rules of the Dutch West India Company.

The company hoped the patroon system would bring many new settlers to New Netherland. However, the system was largely a failure. Kiliaen Van Rensselaer (KEE•lee•uhn vahn ren•suh•LIR) founded the colony's only successful patroonship. Van Rensselaer was given lands near Fort Orange, where he started a settlement called Rensselaerswyck (ren•suh•LIRZ•wik).

Then, in 1638, the Dutch West India Company hired William Kieft (KEEFT) to lead New Netherland. Kieft faced many challenges. The colony was making less money from the fur trade. Also, conflicts with Native Americans had increased. This was because the settlers had cleared more land for farms.

Over the next several years, the colonists and Native Americans attacked each other's farms and villages. Kieft decided he could end the war by sending a large army against the Native Americans. The army destroyed Native American villages all over New Netherland.

Kiliaen Van Rensselaer and the seal of the Van Rensselaer family

Colonists and Native Americans sign a peace treaty.

In 1645 the two sides signed a peace treaty. Although the fighting ended, many colonists and Native Americans had already been killed. In fact, the Algonquian-speaking population of New York had nearly been wiped out.

The colonists blamed Kieft for the wars. It was not long before the Dutch West India Company ordered Kieft to return to the Netherlands.

REVIEW What problems did New Netherland face when Kieft took over as its leader?

REVIEW

1. **WHAT TO KNOW** Why did the Dutch settle New Netherland?

2. **VOCABULARY** Explain the difference between a **colonist** and a **patroon**.

3. **CIVICS AND GOVERNMENT** What were some of the jobs of the leaders of the New Netherland colony?

4. **CRITICAL THINKING** What kind of place would you choose to settle if you were starting a colony? Why?

5. **MAKE A LIST** Imagine that you are starting a colony in the 1600s in what is now New York. Make a list of the jobs that the colonists will need to do when they arrive in the new land.

6. **GENERALIZE** On a separate sheet of paper, copy and complete this graphic organizer.

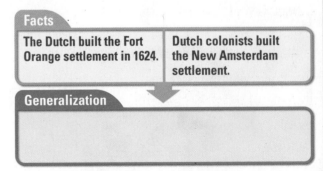

Facts	
The Dutch built the Fort Orange settlement in 1624.	Dutch colonists built the New Amsterdam settlement.

Generalization

Read a Time Line

VOCABULARY		
time line	decade	century

➡ WHY IT MATTERS

To understand the history of New York, you need to know when important events happened. A **time line** can help you with that. A time line is a diagram that shows the important events that took place during a certain period of time. It shows the order in which the events happened and the amount of time that passed between them. A time line can show how events are connected.

➡ WHAT YOU NEED TO KNOW

The time line below shows when some important events in the early history of New York took place. The earliest date is at the left, and the most recent date is at the right.

Like a map, a time line has a scale. The scale on a time line shows units of time, not distance. Time lines can show different units of time. Some time lines show events that took place during one day,

Early New York History

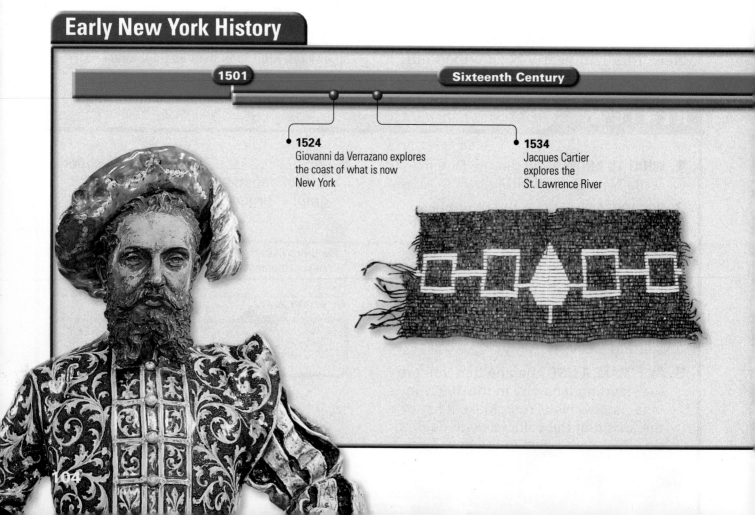

1501   Sixteenth Century

1524
Giovanni da Verrazano explores the coast of what is now New York

1534
Jacques Cartier explores the St. Lawrence River

one month, or one year. Others show events that took place over longer periods, such as a **decade**, or a period of ten years.

On the time line below, the space between two marks stands for one **century**, or a period of 100 years. The first part of the time line shows events that happened during the sixteenth century. The sixteenth century includes the years from 1501 to 1600. The next part of the time line shows the seventeenth century—from 1601 to 1700.

▶ **PRACTICE THE SKILL**

Use the time line to answer these questions about New York's history.

❶ In which century did the Dutch settle in New Amsterdam?

❷ In what year did Verrazano explore the coast of what is now New York?

❸ Which event took place first, Cartier's voyage or Hudson's voyage?

❹ How many years after Henry Hudson explored the Hudson River did the Dutch establish the patroon system in New Netherland?

▶ **APPLY WHAT YOU LEARNED**

Make a time line that shows the twentieth and twenty-first centuries. Label the first and last years of both centuries, the year you were born, and every five years since then. Show the year you began school and the year you will graduate from high school. Then mark the years of some other important events for you in the past and in the future. Add photographs or drawings, and display your time line on a bulletin board.

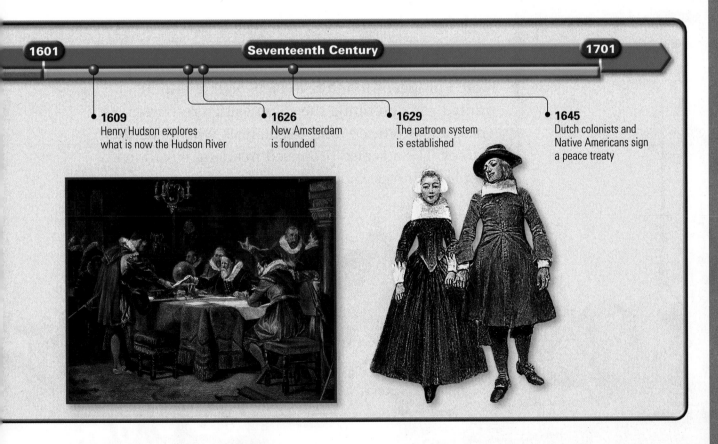

1601

Seventeenth Century

1701

1609
Henry Hudson explores what is now the Hudson River

1626
New Amsterdam is founded

1629
The patroon system is established

1645
Dutch colonists and Native Americans sign a peace treaty

Lesson 3

Life in New Netherland

1520   1645   1770

1645–1665

WHAT TO KNOW
Who came to New Netherland in the mid-1600s?

VOCABULARY
indentured servant p. 107

slave p. 108

slave trade p. 108

plantation p. 109

bouwery p. 109

apprentice p. 110

GENERALIZE

Facts		

Generalization

YOU ARE THERE

"Here he comes!" It's 1647, and you have joined a crowd waiting to greet the colony's new leader. The Dutch West India Company has chosen Peter Stuyvesant (STY·vuh·suhnt) to direct New Netherland. Stuyvesant tells the crowd he'll rule "as a father would his children." He promises to bring peace to your troubled colony. You hope he also brings prosperity.

A Time of Growth

The Dutch West India Company tried again to get more Europeans to move to New Netherland. It printed ads describing the colony's rich resources. These ads promised land to colonists who made the journey. The ads also promised freedom, which many people in Europe did not have.

Soon hundreds of families arrived in New Netherland. Children were born there, too. In 1660 about 5,000 colonists lived there. By 1664 the colony had about 9,000 people. Many of these settlers came from the Netherlands, but others came from Germany, France, England, Sweden, and Finland. Those who wanted to come to the colony but could not pay for the trip came as **indentured servants**. They agreed to work without pay for a set time for the person who paid for their trip.

New Amsterdam quickly became the colony's largest town. The fort built in the 1620s remained at the southern tip of Manhattan. A windmill sat to the west of the fort. Running north from the fort was Broadway, a dirt road that followed an old Indian trail. By 1661, Broadway and all the city's other streets had been paved with cobblestones.

At the north end of Broadway, a protective wall extended east and west across the island. Present-day Wall Street, in New York City, follows the path of this wall. A small canal east of Broadway ran north through the town.

· BIOGRAPHY ·

Peter Stuyvesant
1610–1672
Character Trait: Civic Virtue

In 1647 the Dutch West India Company made Peter Stuyvesant leader of New Netherland. Stuyvesant had already led the company's colony in Curaçao in the Caribbean Sea. Stuyvesant became known as a strict leader. Even though many colonists did not agree with his rules, he helped New Netherland grow and prosper. He set up the first paid police force in North America to help bring order to the colony.

 For more resources, go to www.harcourtschool.com/ss1

The town hall and the director's house stood near the banks of the East River. Behind the house was a beautiful garden. The place where the director's house stood is called Whitehall today.

REVIEW How did the Dutch West India Company attract more settlers to New Amsterdam?

The windmill in New Amsterdam, shown here in 1653, was located near the Hudson River. The windmill was similar to those that were common in the Netherlands.

The first slave auction in New Amsterdam was held in 1655.

The company said his demand was unfair and that Jews were free to live and worship in New Netherland.

Most of the people who came from Africa to New Netherland were slaves. **Slaves** are people held against their will and forced to work without pay. The first enslaved Africans in New Netherland were brought in 1626 by the Dutch West India Company. They lived in a house built by the company.

In 1655 a ship carrying 500 enslaved Africans arrived in New Netherland. In the years that followed, the **slave trade**, or the buying and selling of enslaved persons, increased. The slaves were sold to colonists, who used them to do the work on farms, in shops, and in homes. Other slaves had to help build ships and work on loading docks.

Not all Africans in New Netherland were slaves. The Dutch West India Company freed some slaves. Other slaves were able to buy their freedom. Former slaves were not completely free, however. Each year they had to pay their employers in money or goods in order to remain free. Also, children of former slaves remained enslaved until their parents could buy their freedom. In 1660 Stuyvesant gave some land on Manhattan to about 40 former slaves. This land, which stretched from today's Chinatown to Greenwich Village, became New Netherland's first community of free Africans.

REVIEW How did some slaves in New Netherland gain their freedom?

New Groups Arrive

Some people also came to New Netherland from Africa and from Dutch colonies in South America. In 1654 some Dutch colonists who were Jewish arrived from a Dutch colony in Brazil, in South America. At first Stuyvesant did not want people of other religions in New Netherland. He asked the Dutch West India Company to make them leave.

This wooden box from New Amsterdam has Dutch-style carvings.

New Amsterdam in 1660

Background This view of New Amsterdam in 1660 shows 342 homes and other buildings.

1 Breede Wegh, later known as Broadway, ran south to the Bowling Green.

2 A canal ran along the path of present-day Broad Street.

3 A wall 2,340 feet (713 m) long had been built along where Wall Street now is to protect the town.

DBQ **Document-Based Question** Compare this map with the illustration of New Amsterdam on pages 100 and 101. How did the town change from 1643 to 1660?

A Farming Colony

Unlike earlier colonists, who often returned to Europe, New Netherland's new settlers planned to stay. While many moved to towns such as New Amsterdam and Fort Orange, most newcomers came to New Netherland to farm the land. As a result, farming replaced fur trading as the main source of money for the colony. Settlers started farms mostly in the Hudson River valley and on parts of Manhattan Island. In fact, the part of New York City that is now Harlem was once a farming region.

On large farms called **plantations**, some settlers in New Netherland grew grains and vegetables.

Some planted orchards with peach, pear, and apple trees. Many colonists wanted to work on plantations because they could earn twice as much as they could farming in Europe. Farms that had both livestock and crops were called **bouweries** (BOW•uh•reez). *Bouwery* is Dutch for "farm." Stuyvesant owned a bouwery on Manhattan. Today that part of New York City is called the Bowery.

In New Netherland, farm animals such as cattle, pigs, and goats roamed freely. Often the animals destroyed people's fields and gardens.

Jugs from New Amsterdam

So Stuyvesant ordered that all farm animals be fenced in. On Manhattan this rule caused a problem. Wood needed for building was hard to find. So some people stole fences and used the wood to build houses. Stuyvesant then passed laws making fence stealing illegal. People who broke the law faced punishment or even death.

REVIEW How did the way people in New Netherland earn money change in the mid-1600s?

Dutch settlers in the 1600s had brightly colored pottery.

The Dutch Way of Life

Although many new groups of people lived in New Netherland, the colony seemed Dutch. Dutch was the official language. Colonists built their homes in the Dutch style, with sloped roofs, narrow first stories, and wide second stories. Many front doors were divided, in the Dutch style, into upper and lower sections. This allowed a person in the house to talk with others outside by opening only the top half of the door. In front of the door was a stoop, or uncovered porch, with benches.

Colonists filled their homes with Dutch-style furniture. Beds were usually hidden in the daytime by doors or curtains. Some were built into the wall and opened like cupboards. The Dutch used blue-and-white tiles to decorate their homes. They also cooked Dutch foods such as waffles and doughnuts.

Children went to school six days a week all year round. After finishing school, boys often became apprentices (uh•PREN•tuh•suhz). An **apprentice** worked for a skilled craftsperson for

Among the items that a Dutch family in New Netherland might have used in their home were large cupboards called *kasts* (left), iron firebacks (center), and cradles (right) made of mahogany.

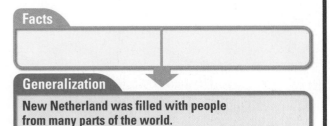

Dutch settlers brought the game of bowling to North America.

three years or more to learn a trade. Most girls learned how to cook, spin thread, weave cloth, and sew. They also made soap and candles. Dutch women made beautiful lace. They also wove a strong cloth called linsey-woolsey, a combination of linen and wool. From Native Americans they learned to dye their cloth bright colors by using plants and berries.

In their free time, families in New Netherland raced sailboats and horses and enjoyed sledding, sleigh riding, and ice-skating. The Dutch sport of *kolven* (KAWL•vuhn) also was popular in the colony. The game of hockey that some people today play is very similar to *kolven*.

REVIEW What were some traditions that the Dutch brought to New Netherland?

REVIEW

1. **WHAT TO KNOW** Who came to New Netherland in the mid-1600s?

2. **VOCABULARY** Explain the difference between an **indentured servant** and a **slave**.

3. **ECONOMICS** What was New Netherland's main source of income?

4. **CRITICAL THINKING** Do you think Peter Stuyvesant was a good leader or a poor leader? Explain your reasons.

5. **WRITE AN ADVERTISEMENT** Write an advertisement that will attract settlers to New Netherland. Include reasons why New Netherland is a good place to live.

6. **GENERALIZE** On a separate sheet of paper, copy and complete this graphic organizer.

Facts	

   ↓

   Generalization
   New Netherland was filled with people from many parts of the world.

Chapter Review

Time

1520

1524
Giovanni da Verrazano
explores the coast
of what is now
New York

Summarize the Chapter

Focus Skill **Generalize** Complete this graphic organizer to make a generalization about the exploration and settlement of New York.

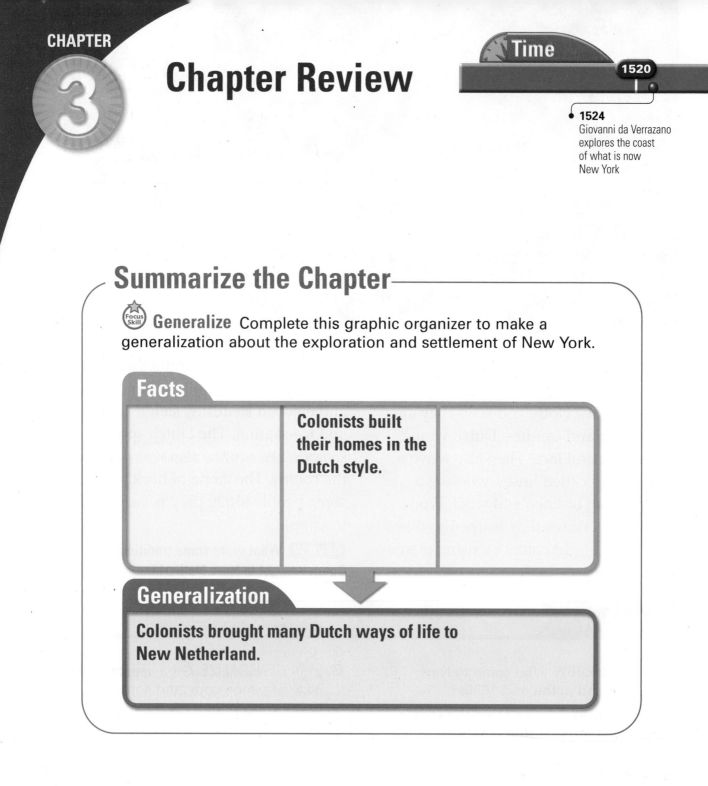

Facts

| | Colonists built their homes in the Dutch style. | |

Generalization

Colonists brought many Dutch ways of life to New Netherland.

THINK & WRITE

Write a Report Look on a map of New York for cities and landforms with Dutch names. Where are most of these places? Do you see any patterns? Write a one-paragraph report telling why you think the places with Dutch names appear where they do.

Write a Letter Imagine that you are one of the European colonists who arrived in New Netherland in 1624. Write a letter describing your new home to a family member who is still in Europe. Be sure to include details about your daily life.

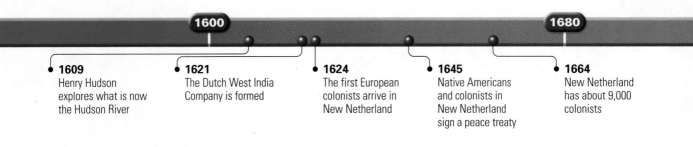

1609
Henry Hudson explores what is now the Hudson River

1621
The Dutch West India Company is formed

1624
The first European colonists arrive in New Netherland

1645
Native Americans and colonists in New Netherland sign a peace treaty

1664
New Netherland has about 9,000 colonists

USE THE TIME LINE

Use the chapter summary time line to answer these questions.

1 How many years after Verrazano explored the coast of what is now New York did the first European colonists arrive in New Netherland?

2 Did New Netherland have 9,000 colonists before or after the colonists signed a peace treaty with Native Americans?

USE VOCABULARY

Write a sentence that explains the meaning of each word.

3 claim (p. 93)

4 colony (p. 98)

5 permanent (p. 99)

6 indentured servant (p. 107)

7 apprentice (p. 110)

RECALL FACTS

Answer these questions.

8 Who were some of the European explorers of what is now New York State?

9 Why did the Walloons leave the Netherlands?

10 Settlers from what countries came to New Netherland?

Write the letter of the best choice.

11 **TEST PREP**   Peter Minuit ordered the colonists to move to Manhattan Island in order to—
   A start another trading center.
   B protect them from attacks by Native Americans.
   C start larger farms.
   D practice their religion freely.

12 **TEST PREP**   Who founded New Netherland's only successful patroonship?
   F Peter Minuit
   G Kiliaen Van Rensselaer
   H William Kieft
   J Willem Verhulst

THINK CRITICALLY

13 What Dutch traditions can you see in New York today?

14 Do you think William Kieft made the right decision to send an army against the Native Americans? Why or why not?

APPLY SKILLS

Read a Time Line

15 Look at the time line on pages 104–105. What events occurred in the 1600s?

STUDY SKILLS

POSE QUESTIONS

Learning to pose, or ask, questions as you read can help improve your understanding.

- **Think of questions that might be answered by reading. For example, you might ask how events are related.**

- **Use the questions to guide your reading. Look for answers as you read.**

Questions	Answers
What changes did English rule bring to colonial New York?	The English elected new leaders and passed new laws.
How did New York's economy grow in the early 1700s?	

An English Colony

Johnson Hall Historic Site, Johnstown

Lesson 1

New Netherland Becomes New York

WHAT TO KNOW

How did New Netherland become the English colony of New York?

VOCABULARY

tyrant p. 117

self-government p. 117

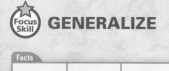

Focus Skill GENERALIZE

YOU ARE THERE The sun is setting over the steep roofs of the homes in Fort Orange. As you walk home for dinner, you wonder, "What's going to happen to my village?" Like many of your Dutch neighbors, you're afraid that the English are going to take over your colony. The English have started colonies to the south and northeast of New Netherland. Most of them are growing faster than your Dutch colony. Peter Stuyvesant has asked the English government to stop setting up towns on Dutch lands, but they have refused.

In 1664 the village near Fort Orange was renamed Albany. Years later, Dutch-style buildings still lined Pearl Street.

New Challenges

In New Netherland, people in Dutch towns and English towns had to be loyal to the Dutch West India Company and follow its laws. However, each town had its own kind of government. The biggest difference between these town governments was that in English towns, landowners voted to elect their leaders. In Dutch towns the colony leaders appointed other leaders.

New Amsterdam was a Dutch city. However, its government was different from those of other Dutch towns. One reason for this was the power of the merchants. Since trade was the main business in New Amsterdam, wealthy merchants had a strong voice in city life. Many of them did not like the way Stuyvesant ran the city. They felt that his orders were too strict.

Stuyvesant made laws that controlled the prices of goods, such as bread and meat. Another law forced everyone to go to church on Sundays. Many people believed that Stuyvesant had become a **tyrant** (TY•ruhnt), or a leader who rules harshly.

In 1649, city leaders asked the Dutch West India Company to let them set up **self-government** for the city. This would allow the colonists to make their own laws and decisions.

Dutch and German coins called thalers were used in New Amsterdam.

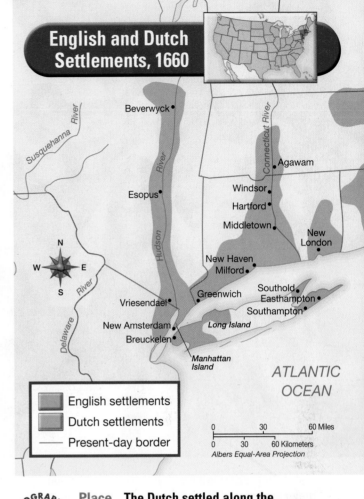

English and Dutch Settlements, 1660

Beverwyck

Susquehanna River

Connecticut River

Agawam

Esopus

Windsor

Hartford

Middletown

New London

New Haven

Milford

Vriesendael

Greenwich

Southold

Easthampton

Southampton

New Amsterdam

Long Island

Breuckelen

Delaware River

Hudson River

Manhattan Island

ATLANTIC OCEAN

English settlements

Dutch settlements

Present-day border

0   30   60 Miles

0   30   60 Kilometers

Albers Equal-Area Projection

GEOGRAPHY THEME

Place The Dutch settled along the Hudson River, while the English had many settlements along the Connecticut River.

◆ Was Esopus a Dutch settlement or an English settlement?

The company granted New Amsterdam self-government. Under this system of government, a group of city leaders and merchants would help Stuyvesant govern. However, instead of holding elections, Stuyvesant chose the leaders himself. Stuyvesant believed that he was doing what was best for the people, but many of the colonists disagreed.

REVIEW What was the biggest difference between English and Dutch town governments?

Peter Stuyvesant left New Netherland for Amsterdam on August 29, 1664. He had been governor of New Netherland for 17 years.

The English Take Control

In 1664 King Charles II of England decided to give his brother James, the Duke of York and Albany, all the land between the Connecticut and Delaware

The English flag in 1664

Rivers. The Duke of York's new lands included almost all of New Netherland!

The Duke of York sent four warships to take New Netherland away from the Dutch. The English ships arrived off the coast of New Amsterdam in August 1664. English Colonel Richard Nicolls ordered Stuyvesant to give up New Amsterdam. He said that if Stuyvesant did not surrender the city, the English would attack. Panic spread through New Amsterdam.

Stuyvesant tried to get the colonists to fight the English, but the colonists refused. They knew they were outnumbered. New Amsterdam had fewer than 150 soldiers, while the English had more than 300.

Colonel Nicolls offered Stuyvesant a peace agreement. Under this agreement Dutch colonists could keep their homes, businesses, and farms. City leaders and merchants told Stuyvesant to surrender.

On August 27 Stuyvesant and the city leaders agreed to turn over New Netherland to the English. Soon after, the Dutch colonists near Fort Orange also surrendered to the English. Stuyvesant left the colony after its surrender, but he later returned to live in the area.

The English renamed many of the colony's settlements in honor of the Duke of York. New Netherland became the English colony of New York, and New Amsterdam became New York City. The village near Fort Orange became the city of Albany.

REVIEW Why did the colonists of New Netherland surrender to the English?

A Lasting Dutch Influence

Some Dutch colonists returned to the Netherlands. However, many others stayed in the new English colony. The Dutch people living in New York worked to keep their culture alive. They continued to speak the Dutch language for many years. More than 80 years after New York became an English colony, a visitor to Albany wrote about the people whose families had been Dutch settlers,

66 **They speak Dutch, have Dutch preachers and . . . [their] manners are likewise quite Dutch.** 99

The Dutch heritage can still be seen in New York State today. Words such as *cookie, coleslaw, sleigh*, and *waffle* come from Dutch. Dutch building styles can still be seen in communities along the Hudson River and in New York City.

The Tulip Festival in Albany begins with a ceremonial street sweeping. Street sweeping is a Dutch tradition that dates back to the 1600s.

• HERITAGE •

Dutch Festivals in New York

The Dutch brought many of their traditions to North America. One of those traditions was a springtime religious celebration they called Pinkster. The first Pinkster festivals included Dutch traditions such as sharing dyed eggs and scrubbing the streets. During Pinkster enslaved Africans were allowed to stop working and take part in African celebrations. Over time, other celebrations, such as Albany's Tulip Festival, grew out of Pinkster. The Wyckoff House in Brooklyn has both a Tulip Festival and a Pinkster celebration.

Tulips remain a symbol of Dutch culture in New York today. Some parts of Harlem, in New York City, are known for their historic Dutch-style buildings.

Parts of New York City are still called by their Dutch names—the Bowery, Brooklyn, Harlem, and Coney Island. Outside of the city are other places with Dutch names, such as Rensselaer, Rotterdam, and Peekskill.

The Dutch heritage includes some special celebrations. For example, the Dutch observe a holiday in December called Saint Nicholas Day. The Dutch call Saint Nicholas *Sinter Klaas*, which sounds like *Santa Claus* to an English speaker. Santa Claus later became a part of the American Christmas tradition.

REVIEW **What are some examples of Dutch heritage seen in New York today?**

REVIEW

1. WHAT TO KNOW How did New Netherland become the English colony of New York?

2. VOCABULARY Use the word **tyrant** in a sentence about why colonists wanted **self-government**.

3. CULTURE What are some Dutch words that are still used today?

4. CRITICAL THINKING Why do you think Dutch colonists did not want to fight the English?

5. ✎ **WRITE A JOURNAL ENTRY** Imagine that you are a Dutch colonist. Write a journal entry telling how you feel about the English takeover.

6. (Focus Skill) **GENERALIZE** On a separate sheet of paper, copy and complete this graphic organizer.

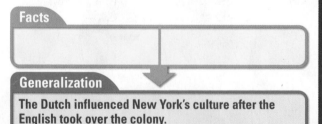

Facts

Generalization

The Dutch influenced New York's culture after the English took over the colony.

Identify Multiple Causes and Effects

▶ WHY IT MATTERS

Sometimes events in history have more than one cause and more than one effect. A **cause** is an event or an action that makes something happen. An **effect** is what happens as a result of that event or action. Sometimes an effect has more than one cause. One cause can also lead to several effects. Understanding how events are related as causes and effects can help you figure out why things happen.

▶ WHAT YOU NEED TO KNOW

The following steps can help you see how causes and effects are related.

Step 1 Look for the effects.

Step 2 Look for all the causes of each effect.

Step 3 Think about how the causes and effects relate to one another.

▶ PRACTICE THE SKILL

Copy the chart below. Then decide whether each of the following statements describes a cause or an effect. Write each statement in the proper place on your chart.

1 Dutch colonists did not want to fight a large English army.

2 England took control of New Netherland.

3 The king of England gave his brother James land that included New Netherland.

4 Dutch colonists near Fort Orange surrendered to the English.

▶ APPLY WHAT YOU LEARNED

Interview one of your school's teachers. Ask how your school has changed over time. Then use the steps you learned to identify the causes and effects of the changes. Share your findings with your classmates.

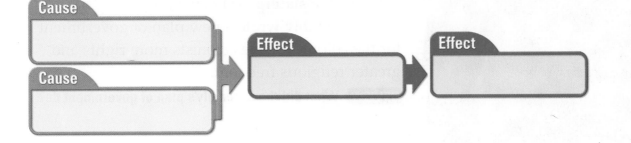

Cause

Cause

Effect

Effect

Lesson 2

The New York Colony

1520   1645   1770

1660–1750

WHAT TO KNOW
How did English rule change life in New York?

VOCABULARY
governor p. 122
representative p. 122
legislature p. 122
jury p. 125

Focus Skill GENERALIZE

Facts		

Generalization

YOU ARE THERE The year is 1664. King Charles II of England has given his brother, the Duke of York, control over the lands that used to be part of New Netherland. The Duke sends Colonel Richard Nicolls to claim New York. He gives Nicolls four warships. "We don't want to fight the Dutch, but we can't let them stand in our way."

English Rule Brings Changes

The Duke of York appointed Richard Nicolls to be New York's first governor. A **governor** is the leader of a colony or state. Governor Nicolls said that all Dutch colonists who stayed in New York had to promise to be loyal to the king of England.

In 1683 New York's new governor, Thomas Dongan, met with representatives elected by the colony's leaders. A **representative** is a person chosen by a group and given power to make decisions for the group's members. These representatives made up the first New York Assembly. This was the colony's **legislature**, or lawmaking group.

The assembly wrote a new plan of government for the colony. It gave colonists more rights and greater religious freedom.

REVIEW What did the assembly's plan of government do?

The Duke of York

A Mix of Cultures

Under the English, the population of the colony increased. In New York City the population grew so fast that by the early 1700s the city had more families than houses. One leader wrote, "I have eight in a family and know not yet where to fix [settle] them, houses are so scarce [few] and dear [expensive] . . . in this place."

In 1685 thousands of Huguenots (HYOO•guh•nahts), who were French Protestants, left France to find religious freedom. About 1,000 of them settled in New York. They founded the towns of New Rochelle and New Paltz.

In the early 1700s many families left Germany because of war and a lack of jobs there. Some of these families came to New York hoping to find land to farm. Many Germans moved to the Hudson River valley and started settlements such as Germantown and

Rhinebeck. Germans also helped build towns in the Mohawk River valley. These towns included German Flats and Schoharie.

The African population also grew. By 1723 more than 6,000 Africans—both free and enslaved—lived in New York.

Population of New York, 1700–1760

Number of People (y-axis): 0, 20,000, 40,000, 60,000, 80,000, 100,000, 120,000
Year (x-axis): 1700, 1720, 1740, 1760

Analyze Graphs   The population of New York in 1760 was nearly six times what it was in 1700.

❖ What was the population of New York in 1740?

Analyze Diagrams   **Huguenot Street in New Paltz has been preserved as a historic district.**

❖ What family had two homes on Huguenot Street?

Huguenot Street

Freer 1694-1735

Abraham Hasbrouck 1694-1717

DuBois Fort 1705

Huguenot St

Jean Hasbrouck 1694-1912

Bevier-Elting 1698-1735

Cemetery

French Church 1717

Deyo 1692

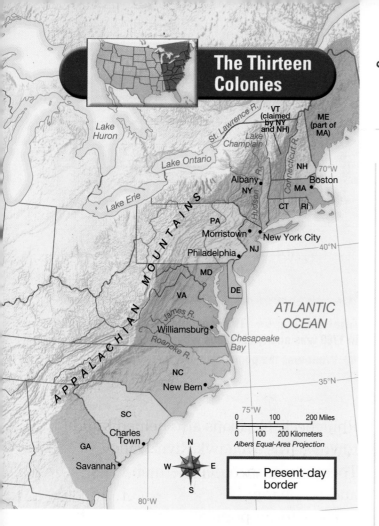

The Thirteen Colonies

GEOGRAPHY THEME

Regions This map shows the English colonies in North America.

❓ What physical feature lay between the colonies and the Great Lakes?

there to settle the rich lands. Slaves rarely lived with their own families because slave owners often sold away children, mothers, fathers, and other relatives.

Jupiter Hammon was a slave on a Long Island farm. Unlike most slaves, Hammon was given the chance to learn to read and write. He became the first African American poet to have his work published.

REVIEW What groups of people came to New York in the late 1600s and early 1700s?

The Zenger Case

New York's mix of cultures meant that its people did not always hold the same opinions about their leaders. In 1733, New Yorkers who did not like Governor William Cosby started a newspaper to voice their opinions.

The printer and editor of the *New York Weekly Journal* was a New Yorker named

However, free and enslaved Africans had fewer rights under English rule than under the Dutch. English laws made it hard for slaves to earn their freedom.

Slavery slowly moved up the Hudson River valley as more people moved

The trial of John Peter Zenger was an important step toward freedom of the press. What do you think newspapers in the United States would be like today if Zenger had been found guilty?

DEMOCRATIC VALUES
Freedom of the Press

The trial of John Peter Zenger introduced the idea of freedom of the press. Freedom of the press means citizens can publish facts, ideas, and opinions without the government's approval. A free press lets people know what is going on in their community and around the world. This helps people stay informed about the actions of their local, state, and national governments. Today freedom of the press is protected in the United States Constitution.

Analyze the Value

1. What is freedom of the press?
2. Why did the jury decide that Zenger had the right to print the articles in his newspaper?
3. **Make It Relevant** Work with classmates to create a newspaper for your class. The newspaper should include an article about why freedom of the press is an important right.

John Peter Zenger. He published articles against Cosby written by New Yorkers. This angered Cosby. He had Zenger arrested, saying that he printed lies.

In 1735 Zenger's case went to court. At the trial Zenger's lawyer said that the articles Zenger had printed were not lies. He said that Cosby had arrested Zenger because he did not like the articles written about him. The jury found Zenger not guilty. A **jury** is a group of citizens that decides a case in court.

REVIEW Why is the trial of John Peter Zenger important?

REVIEW

1. **WHAT TO KNOW** How did English rule change life in New York?

2. **VOCABULARY** Explain how the words **representative** and **legislature** are related.

3. **CULTURE** Who were the Huguenots?

4. **CRITICAL THINKING** How do you think the breaking up of slave families affected Africans in New York?

5. **WRITE A SCENE** Write a scene for a play about a debate that might have taken place between two of the jurors at the trial of John Peter Zenger. One juror believes Zenger was arrested unfairly. The other juror believes that Zenger printed lies about Cosby.

6. **GENERALIZE** On a separate sheet of paper, copy and complete this graphic organizer.

Facts	
About 1,000 Huguenots settled in New York in the 1680s.	By 1723 more than 6,000 Africans lived in New York.

Generalization

Colonial Artifacts

Background In the late 1600s and early 1700s, many colonists settled in New York. Some of these colonists came from France, while others came from Germany. Many families brought their household items and tools with them on their long journey across the Atlantic Ocean. Others bought new items once they were settled.

 Document-Based Question Study these primary sources and answer the questions.

ROCKING HORSE

This wooden rocking horse was made in Switzerland and later brought to New York.

DBQ ❶ Why did colonists own so many things from other places?

FUNNEL

This funnel was hand-carved from a single piece of wood.

DBQ ❷ How do you think this funnel was used?

SPOON AND PEPPER SHAKER

Silver goods like this spoon and pepper shaker were usually found in the homes of wealthy colonists.

DBQ ❸ Why do you think silver goods were usually found only in wealthy homes?

PITCHER

Wooden pitchers would have been found in many colonists' homes.

DBQ ❹ Why do you think colonists made many objects out of wood?

WRITE ABOUT IT

Make a list of five everyday items that you think will give future archaeologists useful information about life in the early twenty-first century. Write a paragraph explaining why you made the choices you did.

For more resources, go to
www.harcourtschool.com/ss1

Living in Colonial New York

1520 **1645** **1770**

1700–1760

YOU ARE THERE

"Watch out!" someone yells. Before you can turn around, a whale crashes into the side of your small boat. You lose your breath as you are thrown into the cold water. Working on a whaling ship is dangerous. This time, you are lucky that another boat is there to save you.

WHAT TO KNOW
What was life like for those living in colonial New York?

VOCABULARY
economy p. 128
industry p. 129
manufacturing p. 129
manor p. 131
tenant farmer p. 132

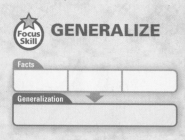
Focus Skill GENERALIZE

Facts

Generalization

Growing Industries

During the early and middle 1700s, New York had a growing economy that attracted many people. An **economy** is the way a region's people use resources to meet their needs. To meet these needs, the people of the

Whaling was a major industry in the mid-1700s. Merchants sold whale oil to Britain, where it was used as lamp fuel.

colony had to think about three things: what goods and services to produce, how to produce them, and for whom to produce them.

Many of the goods and services produced in colonial New York were used by the people of New York and the other English colonies. Other products were sent to England, or Britain, as it became known. Trade and shipping became important parts of New York's economy. Ships sailing out of New York Harbor carried fruits and vegetables, grains, and meats to other colonies and to Britain.

Many of New York's colonists worked in industries related to shipping. An **industry** includes all the businesses that make one kind of product or provide one kind of service. New York's forests provided much of the lumber needed to build ships.

In the 1740s Philip Livingston and his son, Robert, began a new industry in New York when they founded an ironworks in Ancram. Workers mined iron ore there and melted it to remove the iron. Robert Livingston sold the iron to merchants in New York City and Albany. It was used in **manufacturing** (man•yuh•FAK•chuh•ring), or the making of products. Workers in New York City used iron to make nails that were used in the building of ships and houses. Blacksmiths in Albany made

iron into metal tools such as axes and plows.

Most colonists worked in smaller businesses that they ran from their homes. Craftspeople produced baked goods, clothing, jewelry, wooden barrels, and rope. Many of these goods supported larger industries such as shipbuilding and trade. For example, shipbuilders climbed walkways made of rope. Merchants often packed their goods in wooden barrels.

REVIEW What new industry did Philip and Robert Livingston start in New York?

A Smith.

_WR.fc._

The ironworks at Ancram, New York, was successful because the raw materials needed to make iron were nearby. The area also had skilled workers to make the iron.

Farmers and craftspeople took their products to the market in Albany. There they traded with one another for farming tools and food. Merchants bought goods from both farmers and craftspeople and shipped them to New York City.

Many people moved to New York City to work as lawyers, teachers, doctors, and merchants. Other people there provided services, such as driving carriages, running inns, and policing city streets.

By 1749 more than 13,000 people lived in New York City. Culture groups included Jews, Dutch, French, British, Germans, and free and enslaved Africans. At that time each culture group lived in its own neighborhood with its own places of worship and schools.

Most children went to school for three years. After they had finished school, they went to work in their family's business. The entire family helped run the business.

REVIEW What kinds of jobs did people in cities have?

During colonial times, children of all ages learned together in one room. Instead of having textbooks, students studied from "hornbooks" like this one.

Town Life

By 1756 Albany had more than 2,000 people and about 330 buildings. The largest of these were the English church, the Dutch church, and the city hall. Albany also had warehouses, mills, shops, and brick and wooden houses.

A typical scene of the east side of Market Street in Albany in the early 1800s.

This photograph of the dining room in the mansion at Van Cortlandt Park shows how it would have looked in the 1700s. What Dutch influences can you see?

· GEOGRAPHY ·

GEOGRAPHY ESSENTIAL ELEMENTS

Van Cortlandt Park
Understanding Places and Regions

In 1888 New York City gained a large part of the Van Cortlandt manor and preserved it as a public park and historical museum. Today Van Cortlandt Park covers 1,146 acres in the Bronx. The park has trails, ball fields, and playgrounds. The Van Cortlandt mansion still stands in the park's southwest corner. Visitors to the Van Cortlandt mansion can learn what life was like in New York in the 1700s and 1800s.

0   5   10 Miles
0 5 10 Kilometers

Ossining
Spring Valley
CONNECTICUT
NEW JERSEY
Hudson R.
White Plains
Long Island Sound
VAN CORTLANDT PARK
Yonkers
New Rochelle
N W E S
Long Island
Levittown
New York City
Hempstead
ATLANTIC OCEAN

Farm Life

While many people worked in industries in cities, most made their living as farmers. Small farms lined the western bank of the Hudson River between Albany and New York City. Other farms were on Long Island and in the Bronx. Most farms covered fewer than 250 acres.

Farm life remained much the same as in Dutch times. Families generally lived in small homes. Large fireplaces provided heat and a place to cook. Around the farmhouse were fields of grain and hay and herds of livestock. Farm families lived on what they raised, and sold what they did not need in local markets.

While most farms in New York were small, there were some large farms called **manors**. These farms covered thousands of acres. They produced food to sell in the colonies and overseas. In the 1700s manor owners controlled much of New York's best farmland. This gave them a powerful voice in how the colony was run. Many of them served in the colony's assembly.

The Van Cortlandt family owned a manor in the Bronx. It stretched for 16 miles (26 km) along the Hudson River. The Van Cortlandts farmed and also milled wheat on the manor.

Colonists might have cooked food in an iron Dutch oven and drunk from silver tankards.

In 1748 they built a three-story stone house known as the Van Cortlandt mansion.

The Philipsburg manor lay north of the Van Cortlandt manor near what is now Sleepy Hollow. A wealthy merchant named Frederick Philipse (FIL•uhps) owned it. Large manors like Philipsburg used slaves to work in the fields, to run the mill, and to take care of the manor house.

Manors like Philipsburg also had tenant farmers. A **tenant farmer** was a person who farmed land belonging to a manor owner. Tenant farmers paid rent to the manor owner for the use of the land. They also did work, such as putting up barns and fences, for the owner.

Tenant farmers often had to work long days to grow enough food to feed their families and to pay their rent. In contrast, manor owners and their families had more free time. Many of the men went on hunting trips. The women enjoyed quilting parties. Families often gathered at each other's homes for dances and dinner parties.

REVIEW What were some differences between a manor owner and a tenant farmer?

REVIEW

1. **WHAT TO KNOW** What was life like for those living in colonial New York?

2. **VOCABULARY** Use **tenant farmer** and **manor** in a sentence about colonial farms.

3. **ECONOMICS** How did smaller businesses support larger industries such as shipbuilding?

4. **CRITICAL THINKING** How did New York's economy change between the years 1650 and 1750?

5. **MAKE A CHART** Make a chart showing some of the jobs people had in Albany, in New York City, and in the countryside in the mid-1700s.

6. **GENERALIZE** On a separate sheet of paper, copy and complete this graphic organizer.

Facts

Generalization

The whaling and iron industries were important to colonial New York's economy.

Growing Conflict with the French

4 Lesson

1520	1645	1770

1750–1765

WHAT TO KNOW
Why did Britain and France fight each other in the French and Indian War?

VOCABULARY
ally p. 135
congress p. 135
delegate p. 135
alliance p. 135
proclamation p. 137

GENERALIZE
Focus Skill

Facts		

Generalization

YOU ARE THERE The year is 1757. You've been standing guard for hours at Fort William Henry, on the Hudson River. All of a sudden, you see a large group of soldiers marching toward you. "It's the French!" you shout. "They're attacking!" You're tired and scared, but you must fight to keep France from gaining control of this land.

Troubles Grow

By the early 1700s, Britain had set up 13 colonies along the Atlantic coast of North America. France had colonies in Canada, in an area known as New France. Both countries claimed lands in the Ohio River valley and around the Great Lakes. These lands included northern and western New York.

A reenactor at Fort William Henry, on the Hudson River

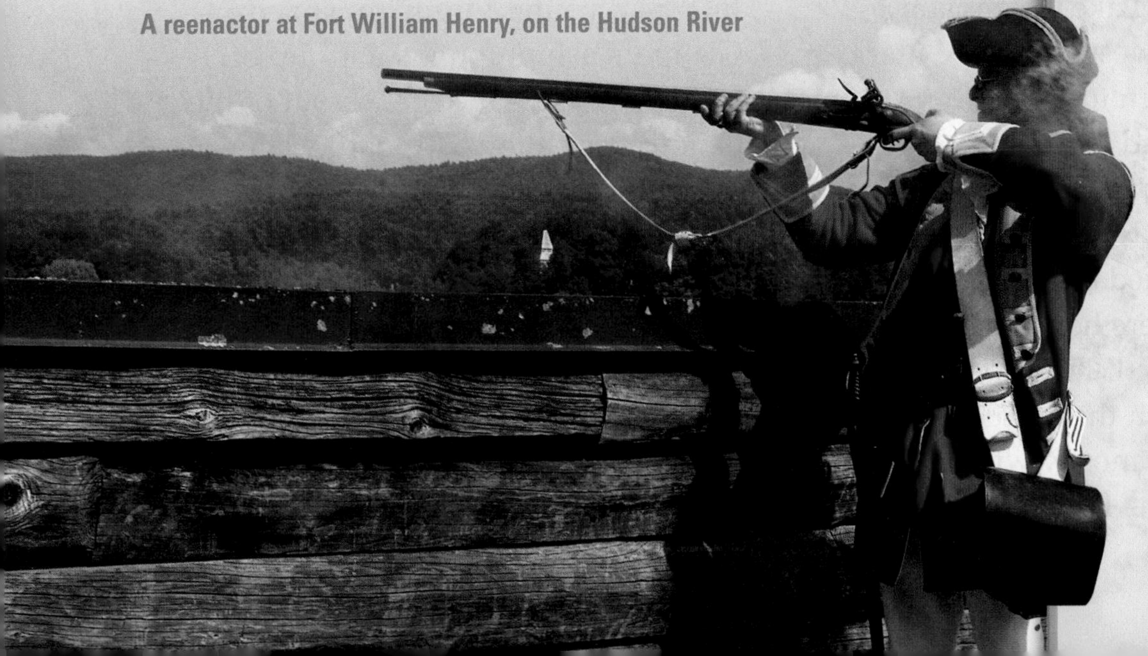

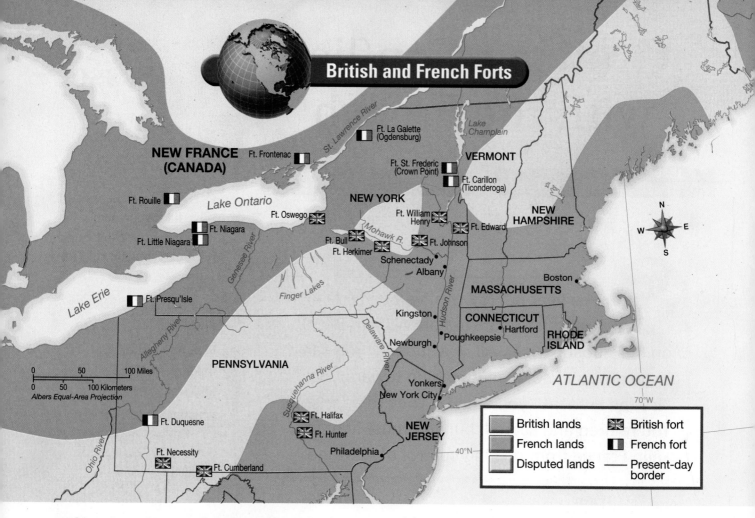

British and French Forts

NEW FRANCE (CANADA)

Ft. La Galette (Ogdensburg)

Ft. Frontenac

St. Lawrence River

Lake Champlain

VERMONT

Ft. St. Frederic (Crown Point)

Ft. Carillon (Ticonderoga)

Ft. Rouille

Lake Ontario

NEW YORK

NEW HAMPSHIRE

Ft. Oswego

Ft. William Henry

Ft. Edward

Ft. Niagara

Mohawk R.

Ft. Little Niagara

Ft. Bull

Ft. Johnson

Ft. Herkimer

Genesee River

Schenectady

Albany

Finger Lakes

Boston

Lake Erie

MASSACHUSETTS

Ft. Presqu'Isle

Allegheny River

Kingston

CONNECTICUT

Hartford

RHODE ISLAND

Newburgh

Poughkeepsie

Delaware River

PENNSYLVANIA

Susquehanna River

Yonkers

New York City

ATLANTIC OCEAN

70°W

Ft. Duquesne

Ft. Halifax

NEW JERSEY

Ohio River

Ft. Hunter

Philadelphia

Ft. Necessity

40°N

Ft. Cumberland

British lands	British fort
French lands	French fort
Disputed lands	Present-day border

GEOGRAPHY THEME

Location Lands controlled by Native American tribes lay between the lands claimed by France and Britain.

❖ Which two French forts were closest to Fort William Henry?

The French and the British built forts in North America to protect the lands they had claimed. The French forts in New York included Fort Carillon (KAR•uh•lahn) on Lake Champlain. Fort Niagara, on western Lake Ontario, was another French fort. British forts in the region included Fort Oswego, on eastern Lake Ontario, and Fort William Henry, on the Hudson River.

The lands claimed by both the French and the British were home to many Native Americans. While the British traded mostly with the Iroquois, the French traded mostly with the Algonquians. Some French traders lived in Algonquian villages and learned Algonquian ways of life.

By the early 1750s, Britain and France seemed to be heading toward war. In 1754 a young Virginian named George Washington led a group of soldiers to force the French out of the Ohio River valley. This battle, later called the Battle of Fort Necessity, turned out to be the start of a long war between the French and the British. This war became known in North America as the French and Indian War.

REVIEW Why did the French and the British build forts in North America?

The Albany Congress

After the Battle of Fort Necessity, the British government asked colonial leaders to meet with the Iroquois. The British hoped to make the Iroquois their **allies**, or partners in war. In the summer of 1754, the colonial leaders met with the Iroquois leaders in Albany, New York. This meeting became known as the Albany Congress. A **congress** is a formal meeting of representatives.

Seven colonies sent **delegates**, or representatives, to the congress. These delegates included James Delancey from New York and Benjamin Franklin from Pennsylvania. Franklin and the others knew that the colonists needed more than Indian allies to defeat the French. They felt that the colonies needed to be united in the war against the French.

The plan that Franklin introduced was called the Albany Plan of Union. It was one of the first plans to call for the uniting of all the colonies under one government. The colonial leaders could not agree on how to do this. However, they did form an **alliance**, or agreement, with the Iroquois. The British gave the Iroquois guns and supplies. In return, the Iroquois agreed to help them fight the French. The Iroquois had become one of Britain's most important Native American allies.

REVIEW What was the result of the Albany Congress?

POINTS OF VIEW
The Albany Plan of Union

BENJAMIN FRANKLIN, writer of the Albany Plan of Union

❝ I should hope that the people of Great Britain and the people of the colonies would learn to consider themselves as . . . belonging to . . . one community with one interest. ❞

WILLIAM CLARKE, a delegate from Boston, Massachusetts

❝ The Commissioners [delegates] at Albany . . . have set up a Scheme [plan] for the destroying of the liberties and privileges of every British Subject upon the Continent. ❞

Analyze the Viewpoints

❶ What views about the Albany Plan of Union did each person hold?

❷ **Make It Relevant** Look at the Letters to the Editor section of your local newspaper. Find two letters that express different viewpoints on the same issue. Then write a paragraph that summarizes the viewpoint of each letter.

JOIN, or DIE.

Benjamin Franklin drew this cartoon to convince the colonies to approve his Albany Plan of Union. What do you think the parts of the snake stand for?

Chapter 4 ■ **135**

New York and the War

The British lost many of the war's early battles. In 1756 the French captured Fort Oswego. Fort William Henry fell a year later. About 2,000 British soldiers died at the Battle of Fort William Henry.

The French and their Indian allies attacked farms in the Mohawk and Hudson Valleys. As a result, many colonists decided to move nearer to cities in more settled areas. Their families could be safe there. Some settlers who did not leave lost their lives.

Merchants in New York City turned the war to their advantage. They made agreements with the British government to provide soldiers with supplies. Some merchants even hired pirates to attack and rob the French ships sailing to New York. Many merchants grew rich by selling stolen goods.

A Native American tomahawk used in the French and Indian War

British leaders knew that they needed a new plan to win the war. The British government began paying colonists to become soldiers. Britain also sent thousands more of its own soldiers to North America.

Working together, British and colonial soldiers began to win more battles. In 1759 British forces captured the city of Quebec, the capital of New France. One year later France surrendered. The agreement that ended the war in 1763 took away most of France's land in North America. The British gained Canada and most of the lands east of the Mississippi River.

With the end of the war, New Yorkers looked forward to settling in the western part of the colony.

This powderhorn is engraved with a map showing some of the major battles of the war, including the battles of Fort Ticonderoga. In July 1758, the British lost Fort Ticonderoga to the French. In June 1759, the British recaptured it.

Regions When the French and Indian War ended in 1763, the French had lost to the British most of the land they claimed in North America.

❖ What European country claimed most of the land in eastern North America?

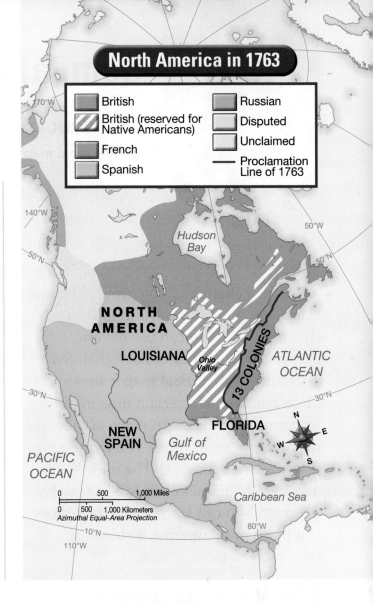

North America in 1763

British		Russian	
British (reserved for Native Americans)		Disputed	
French		Unclaimed	
Spanish		Proclamation Line of 1763	

170°W · 140°W · 50°W · 50°N · 50°N · Hudson Bay · NORTH AMERICA · LOUISIANA · Ohio Valley · 13 COLONIES · ATLANTIC OCEAN · 30°N · 30°N · NEW SPAIN · FLORIDA · Gulf of Mexico · PACIFIC OCEAN · Caribbean Sea · 80°W · 10°N · 110°W

0 500 1,000 Miles
0 500 1,000 Kilometers
Azimuthal Equal-Area Projection

However, Britain soon issued a **proclamation**, or order, known as the Proclamation of 1763. It said that all the lands to the west of the Appalachian Mountains belonged to the Native Americans. This angered many New Yorkers. They felt the proclamation took away their rights as British citizens to travel and settle where they wanted.

The end of the war also brought money troubles. Without an army to sell to, some merchants went out of business. This caused their workers to lose their jobs. The war had also cost the British government a lot of money. It began to look to the colonists to help pay war debts.

REVIEW What was the Proclamation of 1763?

REVIEW

1. **WHAT TO KNOW** Why did Britain and France fight each other in the French and Indian War?

2. **VOCABULARY** Use the words **congress** and **delegate** in a sentence about the Albany Congress.

3. **GEOGRAPHY** What areas of North America did the French control in the early 1700s?

4. **CRITICAL THINKING** Why do you think the Iroquois became British allies?

5. **MAKE A MODEL** Research what a fort in the Great Lakes region looked like in the 1700s. Make a model of one.

6. **GENERALIZE** On a separate sheet of paper, copy and complete this graphic organizer.

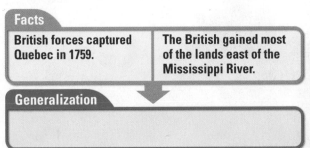

Facts	
British forces captured Quebec in 1759.	The British gained most of the lands east of the Mississippi River.

Generalization

·SKILLS· Compare Historical Maps

MAP AND GLOBE

VOCABULARY

historical map

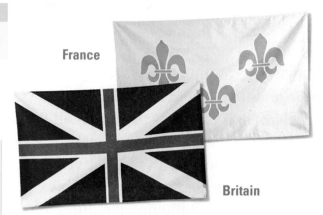

France

Britain

▶ WHY IT MATTERS

You will change as you grow older and learn new things. The world is always changing, too. You can use historical maps to see how places have changed over time. A **historical map** shows a place as it was at a certain time in history. By comparing historical maps of the same region at different times, you can see how that place has changed. The region's borders and the names of its towns may be different. You can learn about the history of a place by comparing the details shown on historical maps.

▶ WHAT YOU NEED TO KNOW

You have read about the French and Indian War which the British and the colonists fought against the French. In the years that followed the war, the boundaries of European colonies in North America changed.

The two historical maps on page 139 show New York as it appeared in two different years. You will see that different countries claimed the region in 1750 and in 1763.

▶ PRACTICE THE SKILL

Study the map keys to learn what the lines and colors on the maps stand for. Then answer these questions.

The British and the French fought for control of land in the western part of New York.

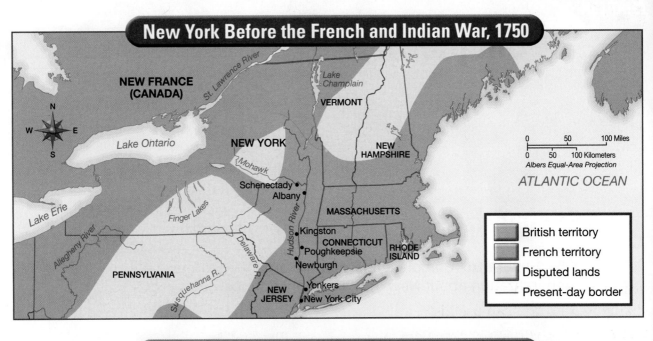

New York Before the French and Indian War, 1750

NEW FRANCE (CANADA)
St. Lawrence River
Lake Champlain
VERMONT
NEW YORK
Lake Ontario
Mohawk
NEW HAMPSHIRE
Schenectady
Albany
MASSACHUSETTS
Lake Erie
Finger Lakes
Kingston
CONNECTICUT
Poughkeepsie
RHODE ISLAND
Allegheny River
Delaware R.
Newburgh
ATLANTIC OCEAN
PENNSYLVANIA
Susquehanna R.
Yonkers
NEW JERSEY
New York City
Hudson River

0 50 100 Miles
0 50 100 Kilometers
Albers Equal-Area Projection

British territory
French territory
Disputed lands
Present-day border

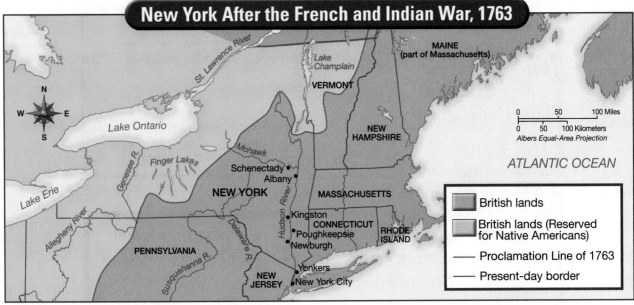

New York After the French and Indian War, 1763

St. Lawrence River
Lake Champlain
MAINE (part of Massachusetts)
VERMONT
Lake Ontario
Mohawk
NEW HAMPSHIRE
Genesee R.
Finger Lakes
Schenectady
Albany
NEW YORK
MASSACHUSETTS
Lake Erie
Allegheny River
Kingston
CONNECTICUT
Poughkeepsie
RHODE ISLAND
Newburgh
Delaware R.
ATLANTIC OCEAN
PENNSYLVANIA
Susquehanna R.
Yonkers
NEW JERSEY
New York City
Hudson River

0 50 100 Miles
0 50 100 Kilometers
Albers Equal-Area Projection

British lands
British lands (Reserved for Native Americans)
Proclamation Line of 1763
Present-day border

1 What color is used on the maps to show the land claimed by the British? by the French?

2 In 1750, which country claimed most of the land around the St. Lawrence River?

3 Find the part of New York in which you live. Which country claimed that land in 1750? Which country claimed that land in 1763?

▶ **APPLY WHAT YOU LEARNED**

Write two or three sentences about the two maps. Include the dates of the maps in your sentences, but leave blanks where the dates belong. Then trade papers with a partner. Have your partner fill in the correct date to complete each sentence.

Practice your map and globe skills with the **GeoSkills CD-ROM**.

MAP AND GLOBE SKILLS

Time

1640

1649
New Amsterdam
asks for
self-government

Summarize the Chapter

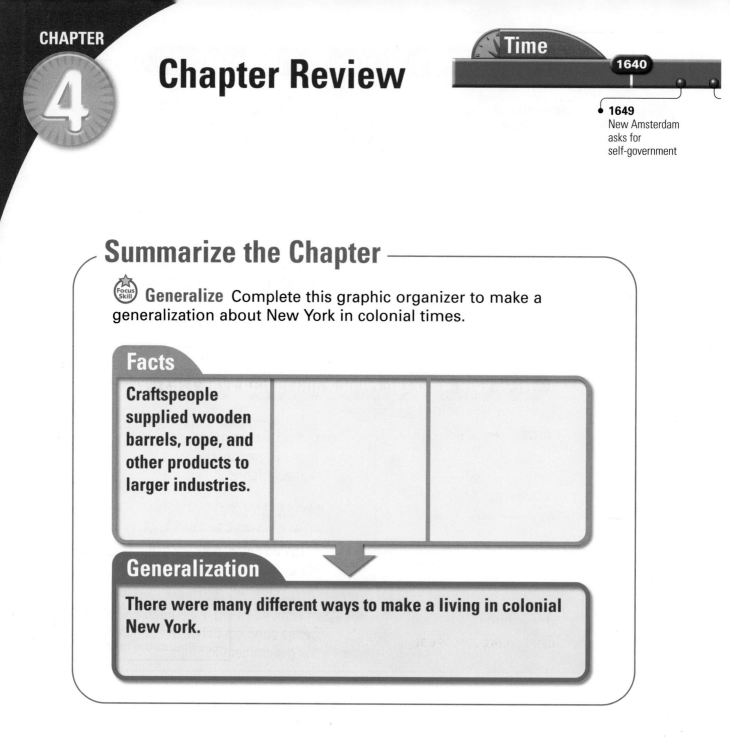

Focus Skill **Generalize** Complete this graphic organizer to make a generalization about New York in colonial times.

Facts

Craftspeople supplied wooden barrels, rope, and other products to larger industries.

Generalization

There were many different ways to make a living in colonial New York.

THINK & WRITE

Write a Dialogue Imagine that you are listening to a conversation that took place between a Dutch colonist and an English colonist. Write what they might have said to each other after the English took over New Netherland.

Write a Newspaper Story Think about one of the events of the French and Indian War. Write a newspaper headline and story describing the event. Be sure to include the *who, what, where, why,* and *how* of the event in your story.

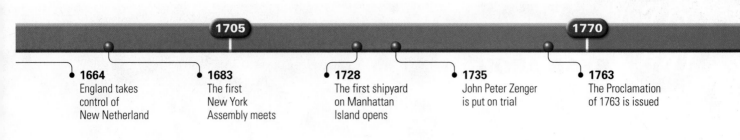
1664
England takes control of New Netherland

1683
The first New York Assembly meets

1728
The first shipyard on Manhattan Island opens

1735
John Peter Zenger is put on trial

1763
The Proclamation of 1763 is issued

USE THE TIME LINE

1 How many years after New Amsterdam asked for self-government did the English take over New Netherland?

2 Did the John Peter Zenger trial take place before or after the Proclamation of 1763 was issued?

USE VOCABULARY

Identify the term that correctly matches each definition.

tyrant (p. 117)

jury (p. 125)

economy (p. 128)

manor (p. 131)

allies (p. 135)

3 a group of citizens that decides a case in court

4 partners in war

5 a large farm

6 a leader who rules harshly

7 the way people use resources to meet their needs

RECALL FACTS

Answer these questions.

8 Why did a group of city leaders ask the Dutch West India Company for self-government in New Amsterdam?

9 What right did the John Peter Zenger trial introduce?

10 What are some of the ways people made a living in colonial New York?

Write the letter of the best choice.

11 **TEST PREP** The English renamed the village near Fort Orange. They called it—
A New York.
B New Amsterdam.
C Albany.
D Brooklyn.

12 **TEST PREP** What group of immigrants founded the towns of New Rochelle and New Paltz?
F the Swedish
G the Huguenots
H the Germans
J the Africans

THINK CRITICALLY

13 In the colonies, how were the Dutch ways of life and the English ways of life different? How were they the same?

14 In what ways did the French and Indian War cause conflicts between the colonists and the government in England?

APPLY SKILLS

Identify Multiple Causes and Effects

15 Identify an event that is described in this chapter. Make a chart like the one on page 121 to show the causes and the effects of the event.

Compare Historical Maps

16 Look at the historical maps on page 139. How did New York change from 1750 to 1763?

FIELD TRIP

READ ABOUT

Old Fort Niagara overlooks Lake Ontario at the mouth of the Niagara River in Youngstown, New York. The fort, once an important military base, was used from 1678 until 1946. It is now part of the 504-acre Fort Niagara State Park.

Today visitors can see what life was like for soldiers in colonial New York. They can see the castle, moat, drawbridge, and parade grounds that French, British, and United States soldiers once used.

FIND

Youngstown

NEW YORK

Old Fort Niagara

This entrance is called the Gate of the Five Nations. Its name honors the original Five Nations of the Iroquois League.

The British built the Bakehouse to replace a French bakery that was destroyed by fire.

The French Castle is the oldest building at Old Fort Niagara. The three flags that fly outside the Castle represent the three nations that have held the fort—France, Britain, and the United States.

Reenactors show visitors what battle was like long ago. These reenactors look like British troops of about 1770.

A VIRTUAL TOUR

GO ONLINE For more resources, go to www.harcourtschool.com/ss1

VISUAL SUMMARY

Write a Journal Entry Examine the events in the Visual Summary below. Write a journal entry from the point of view of a person present at one of the events shown.

USE VOCABULARY

Use the words from the list to complete the sentences below.

expedition (p. 93)   **colony** (p. 98)

self-government (p. 117)   **manufacturing** (p. 129)

1. The people of New Amsterdam wanted _____ so that they could make their own laws and decisions.

2. People living in the Dutch _____ traded for furs.

3. Workers in New York used iron in _____.

4. Giovanni da Verrazano led an _____ to North America.

RECALL FACTS

Answer these questions.

5. Why did many countries send explorers to North America?

6. What were the Native Americans' beliefs about land ownership?

7. Why did the population of New York grow so fast in the 1700s?

Write the letter of the best choice.

8. **TEST PREP** Jacques Cartier was the first European to—
   A find the Northwest Passage.
   B sail into New York Bay.
   C reach inland Canada.
   D see the coast of New York.

9. **TEST PREP** Why did colonial leaders hold the Albany Congress?
   F to meet with Iroquois leaders
   G to write a new plan of government
   H to establish new trade routes
   J to change the name of Albany

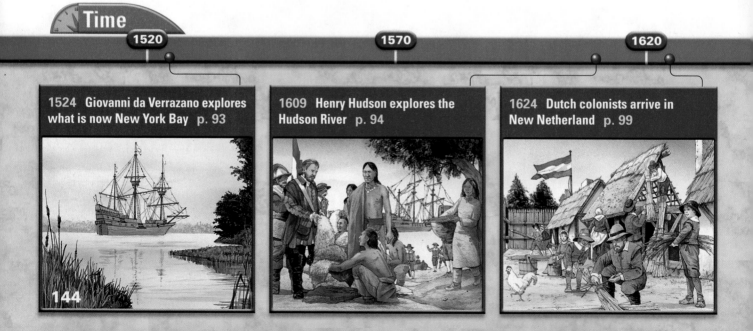

Time

1520   1570   1620

1524 Giovanni da Verrazano explores what is now New York Bay p. 93

1609 Henry Hudson explores the Hudson River p. 94

1624 Dutch colonists arrive in New Netherland p. 99

144

10 TEST PREP New Yorkers were angry about the Proclamation of 1763 because—

A they felt it took away their protection from the Native Americans.

B they felt it took away their rights as British citizens.

C they wanted to be ruled by France.

D they did not want to move to the western part of the state.

THINK CRITICALLY

11 How are the effects of the Columbian Exchange still felt today?

12 How do you think New Amsterdam might have developed if the Dutch had kept control of the colony?

13 Why do you think many colonial manufacturing businesses were located near cities?

APPLY SKILLS

Compare Historical Maps
Use the two historical maps on this page to answer the following questions.

MAP AND GLOBE SKILLS

14 What color is used to show the land claimed by the British?

15 Which European country claimed Louisiana in 1756? in 1763?

Map A: North America in 1756

0 250 500 Miles
0 250 500 Kilometers
Azimuthal Equal-Area Projection

NORTH AMERICA

NEW FRANCE

LOUISIANA

Ohio Valley

ATLANTIC OCEAN

BRITISH COLONIES

NEW SPAIN

FLORIDA

Gulf of Mexico

- British
- French
- Spanish
- Unclaimed
- Disputed lands

Map B: North America in 1763

0 250 500 Miles
0 250 500 Kilometers
Azimuthal Equal-Area Projection

NORTH AMERICA

LOUISIANA

Ohio Valley

ATLANTIC OCEAN

13 COLONIES

FLORIDA

Gulf of Mexico

- British
- British (reserved for Native Americans)
- Spanish
- Disputed lands

1670

1720

1770

1664 New Netherland becomes New York p. 119

1683 The first New York Assembly meets p. 122

1763 The French and Indian War ends p. 136

Activities

Show What You Know

Unit Writing Activity

Write a Narrative Imagine that you are a new settler in New Netherland. Write a story about life in your colony.

- Explain the role of government in your society.
- Explain how colonists earn a living.
- Make sure your narrative has a story.

Unit Project

Stage a Play Stage a play about the early history of New York. As a class, decide on the people and events you want to show. Then form small groups.

- Write one scene about a person, a group of people, or an important event.
- Make props and costumes.
- Perform it for invited guests.

Read More

- ***Peter Stuyvesant: Dutch Military Leader*** by Joan Banks. Chelsea House.

- ***Beyond the Sea of Ice: The Voyages of Henry Hudson*** by Joan Elizabeth Goodman. Mikaya Press.

- ***The Colony of New York*** by Susan Whitehurst. Rosen.

GO ONLINE For more resources, go to www.harcourtschool.com/ss1

A New Nation and State

The Big Idea

American Government

The United States Constitution established a form of government that reflects the democratic values fought for in the American Revolution.

What to Know

- How did the Revolutionary War impact New York State?

- How was the government of the United States formed?

- How did Americans begin to create a national identity?

- What is the structure and function of government at the national, state, and local levels?

Federal Hall, New York City

A New Nation and State

Reading Social Studies

⭐ (Focus Skill) Cause and Effect

Why It Matters Understanding cause and effect can help you see why events happen.

> A **cause** is an action or event that makes something else happen. An **effect** is what happpens as the result of that action or event.

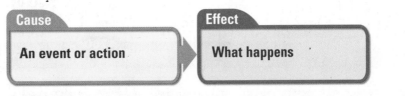

Cause	Effect
An event or action	What happens

- Words and phrases such as *because, since, so,* and *as a result* are clues of cause and effect.
- Sometimes the effect may be stated before the cause.

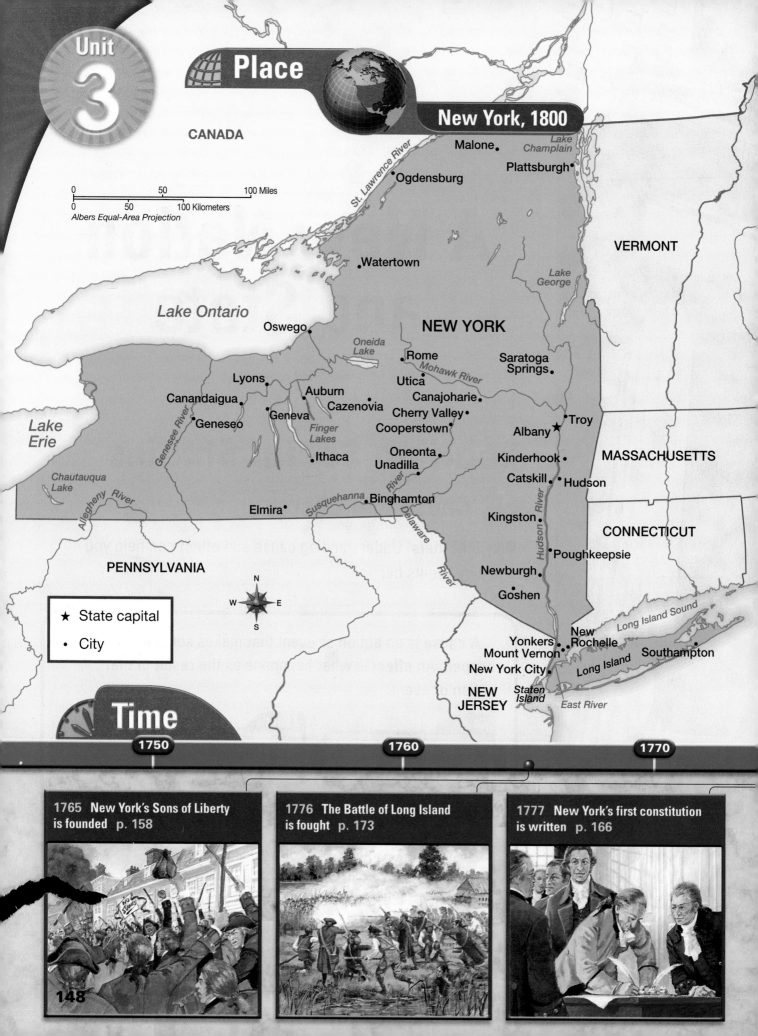

Place

New York, 1800

CANADA

0   50   100 Miles
0   50   100 Kilometers
Albers Equal-Area Projection

Lake Ontario

Lake Erie

Chautauqua Lake

PENNSYLVANIA

NEW YORK

Malone
Plattsburgh
Ogdensburg
St. Lawrence River
Lake Champlain
Lake George
VERMONT

Watertown

Oswego
Oneida Lake
Rome
Mohawk River
Utica
Saratoga Springs
Lyons
Auburn
Canajoharie
Canandaigua
Cazenovia
Cherry Valley
Troy
Geneva
Cooperstown
Albany
Geneseo
Finger Lakes
Oneonta
Kinderhook
MASSACHUSETTS
Ithaca
Unadilla
Catskill
Hudson
Genesee River
River
Elmira
Susquehanna
Binghamton
Kingston
CONNECTICUT
Allegheny River
Delaware River
Hudson River
Poughkeepsie
Newburgh
Goshen
Long Island Sound
New Rochelle
Yonkers
Mount Vernon
Southampton
New York City
Long Island
NEW JERSEY
Staten Island
East River

★ State capital
• City

N
W   E
S

Time

1765 New York's Sons of Liberty is founded p. 158

1776 The Battle of Long Island is fought p. 173

1777 New York's first constitution is written p. 166

1750   1760   1770

Still holding the plate, she whirled around. Pompey was waiting behind her. "Run!" she screamed. "Run! Get my father!"

Everyone stopped talking. Pompey looked at her in amazement. "Y-your father?" he stammered. . . .

Everyone in the dining room sat frozen. All eyes were on Phoebe. "General Washington!" she cried. "Mr. Hickey has put poison in your dinner! I saw him!" There was a gasp from the table.

"What jest is this?" roared General Gates, getting up from his place and reaching for the plate. But before he could take it from her, Phoebe ran to the open window and threw the whole plate out into the yard.

---

jest a joke

Samuel and Phoebe Fraunces were free African Americans. Samuel owned the Queen's Head Tavern in New York City. The tavern, which still exists today, is located on Broad and Pearl Streets. It looks very much the way it did when Phoebe and her father lived there.

Response Corner

1 **Cause and Effect** What do you think would have been the effect on the American Revolution had General Washington been poisoned?

2 Whom did Phoebe think was trying to harm General Washington?

3 **Make It Relevant** Would you have helped protect a leader like George Washington? Why or why not?

START THE UNIT PROJECT

Honor a Hero Help your classmates honor a New Yorker from the American Revolution. As you study this unit, take notes about the important people and events. Then decide which person to honor in a presentation to the class.

USE TECHNOLOGY

GO ONLINE For more resources, go to www.harcourtschool.com/ss1

STUDY SKILLS

CONNECT IDEAS

Graphic organizers can help you connect ideas.

- **On a bubble map, the main idea is written in the center bubble.**

- **Ideas that are related to the main idea are written in surounding bubbles.**

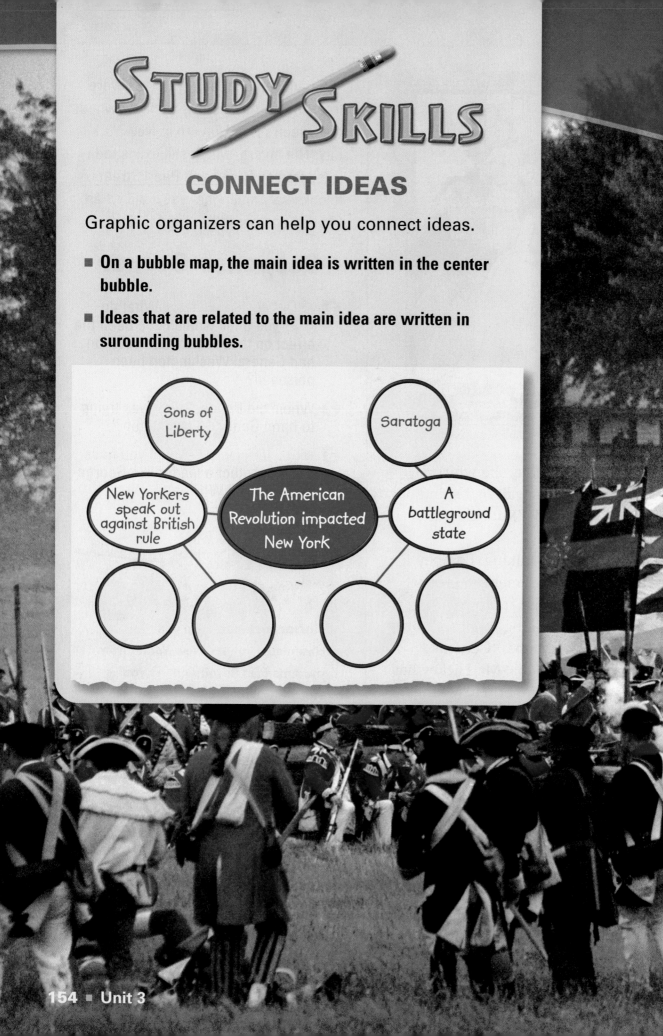

New York and the American Revolution

Saratoga National Historical Park

Unrest in the British Colonies

1750   1775   1800

1764–1770

WHAT TO KNOW
Why were colonists in New York angered by Britain's new colonial tax laws?

VOCABULARY

Parliament p. 156
export p. 157
import p. 157
representation p. 157
boycott p. 158
Patriot p. 158
liberty p. 158
repeal p. 158
Loyalist p. 159
neutral p. 159

CAUSE AND EFFECT

Cause		Effect
Cause		Effect

YOU ARE THERE

It is 1764. The French and Indian War is over at last. To help pay for the war, **Parliament**, Britain's legislature, is making the colonists pay more taxes. You are angry. You feel that you have helped enough by giving supplies. You also believe that the colonial leaders, not Parliament, should set taxes.

Taxes in the Colonies

New York, like the other colonies, was ruled by two levels of government. The king and Parliament ruled all of the 13 colonies from Britain. Each colony also had its own governor and assembly. The king usually chose the colony's governor. Landowners and other wealthy colonists elected the members of the assembly to make laws for the colony. All laws passed by the

King George III (left) and Parliament did not think the colonies had the right to print their own money (below).

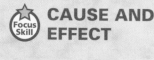

BY A LAW OF THE New-York, TH
pafs current
POUNDS.
the SECOND DAY of
Thoufand Seven Hun
Nine.

TWO POUNDS. No. 6195

BY a Law of the Colony of New-York, this BILL fhall be received in all Payments in the Treafury, for TWO POUNDS.
NEW-YORK,
February 16, 1771.

II.L.

'Tis Death to counterfeit.

assembly had to be approved by the governor.

In New York, members of the assembly felt it was their right to pass laws and set taxes for the people of New York. The governor believed that only Parliament and the king had those powers.

After the French and Indian War, Parliament passed even more laws for the colonies. The Currency Act kept the colonies from printing their own money. The Quartering Act said that colonists had to provide British troops with food and housing.

Parliament also passed laws to control **exports**, or goods sent from one country to another. It also passed new laws to control **imports**, or goods brought into one country from another. Many New Yorkers were merchants, so these laws directly affected them.

One of the most hated laws was the Stamp Act. It taxed many kinds of documents, as well as pamphlets, calendars, newspapers, and advertisements. A stamp placed on each item showed that the tax on it had been paid.

The new laws angered many New Yorkers. After all, they could not help make the laws they were supposed to obey. They had no **representation** in Parliament. They had no one to speak or act for them there. The colonists saw the new taxes as taxation without representation.

In 1765, delegates from the colonies met in New York City. This meeting was called the Stamp Act Congress. The delegates decided to ask people in all the colonies to refuse to buy any stamped item.

REVIEW Why did many colonists think the Stamp Act and other new laws were unfair?

New Yorkers were quick to protest the Quartering Act because there were more British soldiers in New York than in any other colony.

New Yorkers Speak Out

Soon after the Stamp Act Congress ended, about 200 New York City merchants began a boycott of British goods. A **boycott** is a refusal to buy goods in order to force the seller to change a rule. Most of New York's businesses stopped selling British goods. Merchants in other colonies soon joined the boycott.

The colonists who acted against Britain's new laws called themselves **Patriots**. They believed that the colonists had to take a stand against Parliament.

Many Patriots supported the boycott by making their own goods instead of buying them. Some spun wool to make thread. Others wove the thread into

Since Patriots destroyed most Stamp Act stamps, few New Yorkers ever saw stamps like these.

cloth. Still others made the cloth into shirts, pants, and dresses. Many wealthy New Yorkers stopped wearing British clothes and bought the homemade clothing.

As another way to protest the Stamp Act, some Patriots burned the stamps before they could be put on items. In New York City a group of Patriots formed a club called the Sons of Liberty. **Liberty** is another word for "freedom." The Sons of Liberty protested against the Stamp Act by making speeches and by marching with signs in the city streets. They organized attacks against stamp tax collectors.

The British government needed to end the protests against the Stamp Act. The boycott was hurting businesses in Britain. In March 1766 Parliament voted to **repeal**, or cancel, the Stamp Act. New York's colonists celebrated by setting off fireworks and ringing church bells.

New York's Sons of Liberty held protests like this one (left). The leather box below was used to hold stamps.

THE FOLLY OF ENGLAND
THE RUIN OF AMERICA

Alexander McDougall 1731–1786

Character Trait: Perseverance

Alexander McDougall was one of the founders of New York's Sons of Liberty. McDougall came to New York City from Scotland when he was a boy. McDougall published posters that stirred up people against the British. He was arrested for his actions. Even though he could have paid a fine to get out of jail, McDougall remained a prisoner to protest British rule. Today a street in Greenwich Village is named in his memory.

For more resources, go to
www.harcourtschool.com/ss1

Not all colonists supported the Patriots' actions. Many colonists, known as **Loyalists**, remained loyal to the king. Families were often torn apart as people chose to take either the Patriot side or the Loyalist side. Still other colonists did not support either side. They remained **neutral**.

REVIEW Who were the Sons of Liberty?

More Protests

On the same day that the Stamp Act was repealed, Parliament passed the Declaratory (dih•KLAIR•uh•tawr•ee) Act. It said that Parliament still had the right to make laws for the colonies. To further show its power over New Yorkers, the British government sent nearly 4,000 British soldiers to the colony.

New York's Daughters of Liberty helped support the Patriot cause by making homemade clothing and other goods.

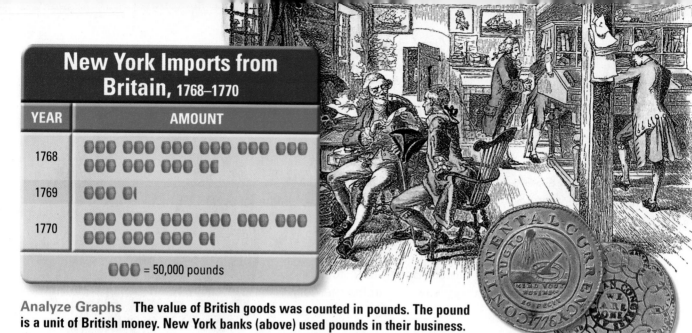

New York Imports from Britain, 1768–1770

YEAR	AMOUNT
1768	●●● ●●● ●●● ●●● ●●● ●●● ●●● ●●● ●●● ●●
1769	●●● ●(
1770	●●● ●●● ●●● ●●● ●●● ●●● ●●● ●●● ●●● ●(

●●● = 50,000 pounds

Analyze Graphs The value of British goods was counted in pounds. The pound is a unit of British money. New York banks (above) used pounds in their business.

◆ What was the value of New York imports from Britain in 1769?

In 1767 Parliament also passed the Townshend Acts, which taxed many goods that New York imported from Britain. New York merchants protested by once again boycotting British goods.

In 1770 Parliament repealed the Townshend Acts. This time New Yorkers did not have much to celebrate. The boycott had hurt New York's economy.

It had forced businesses to close, and many colonists had lost their jobs.

After the Townshend Acts were repealed, New Yorkers ended their boycott. The Sons of Liberty, however, continued to protest British laws that they thought were unfair.

REVIEW How did New Yorkers protest the Townshend Acts?

REVIEW

1. **WHAT TO KNOW** What caused disagreements between Britain and the colonies after the French and Indian War?

2. **VOCABULARY** Describe a **boycott**.

3. **CIVICS AND GOVERNMENT** How did New York's governor and assembly disagree about how the colony should be run?

4. **CRITICAL THINKING** Do you think New York's boycotts of British goods were a useful idea? Why or why not?

5. **DRAW A POSTER** Imagine that you are a Patriot protesting the Stamp Act. Draw a poster asking people not to buy any stamped goods.

6. **CAUSE AND EFFECT** On a separate sheet of paper, copy and complete this graphic organizer.

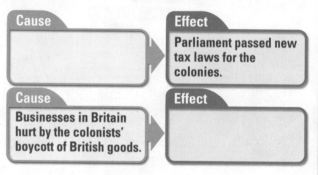

Cause	Effect
	Parliament passed new tax laws for the colonies.

Cause	Effect
Businesses in Britain hurt by the colonists' boycott of British goods.	

Determine Point of View

VOCABULARY

revolution

▶ WHY IT MATTERS

Looking for a writer's feelings and beliefs—or point of view—about his or her subject can help you better understand what you are reading. If you can identify the point of view, you will have a better idea of why the person wrote what he or she did.

▶ WHAT YOU NEED TO KNOW

In the 1770s people in New York could not agree on whether the colonies should separate from Britain. Some New Yorkers wanted to keep working with Britain. Others believed the time had come for a revolution. A **revolution** is a sudden and complete change, such as the overthrow of a government. The words of two New Yorkers on this page show different points of view about whether or not the colonies should break away from Britain.

> "I will not raise my hand against my Sovereign [king]—nor will I draw my sword against my Country . . ."
> —Isaac Wilkins, letter published in the *Gazetteer*, May 11, 1775

> "Every thing that is right or natural pleads for separation . . . the weeping voice of nature cries, 'TIS TIME TO PART."
> —Thomas Paine, *Common Sense*, 1776

▶ PRACTICE THE SKILL

1. What point of view about breaking away from Britain did Thomas Paine hold? How do you know?

2. What point of view did Isaac Wilkins have? How do you know?

3. Why might a merchant have wanted the colonies to remain part of Britain?

▶ APPLY WHAT YOU LEARNED

The next time you read a book, consider the writer's point of view. How might this viewpoint change your understanding of the work?

Thomas Paine

Lesson 2

New York Chooses Liberty

1750 — 1775 — 1800

1770–1780

WHAT TO KNOW
How did the colony of New York become a state with its own government?

VOCABULARY
independence p. 164
constitution p. 166
legislative branch p. 166
executive branch p. 166
judicial branch p. 166

CAUSE AND EFFECT

Cause		Effect
	▶	

Cause		Effect
	▶	

YOU ARE THERE

The year is 1774. For years now you have been unhappy living under British rule. You think it is unfair that you and your fellow colonists cannot help make the laws you are supposed to obey. You think that the colonists should have representation in the British Parliament. Lately, there has been talk of the colonies breaking away from Britain. Some people want the colonies to be a new nation. Some of your neighbors say they are willing to fight, and even die, to win liberty.

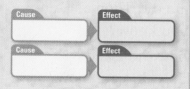

Liberty poles were raised in many New York communities.

Disagreements Grow

In 1766 the Sons of Liberty put up New York's first liberty pole, in what is now City Hall Park in New York City. A liberty pole was a tall wooden pole with a flag that supported the Patriot cause.

When British soldiers in New York City took down a liberty pole in 1770, Patriots protested. A fight broke out. One person was killed in the fight, which became known as the Battle of Golden Hill.

Most New Yorkers did not like such violence. New York remained calm until 1773. That year Britain passed the Tea Act to control the sale of tea.

The colonists again saw this as taxation without representation. In Boston, Massachusetts, some colonists protested by dumping 342 chests of tea into the harbor. Early the next year, New Yorkers had their own tea protest. Patriots threw 18 chests of tea into New York Harbor.

As punishment, British leaders passed laws that limited the freedom of the Massachusetts colonists. Many New Yorkers feared that Britain planned to limit the freedom of all colonists.

Colonial leaders met in Philadelphia, Pennsylvania, in 1774. This meeting became known as the First Continental Congress. New Yorkers hoped that the Congress could reach an agreement with Britain. Arguments between the two sides continued.

REVIEW How did most New Yorkers feel about violent protests?

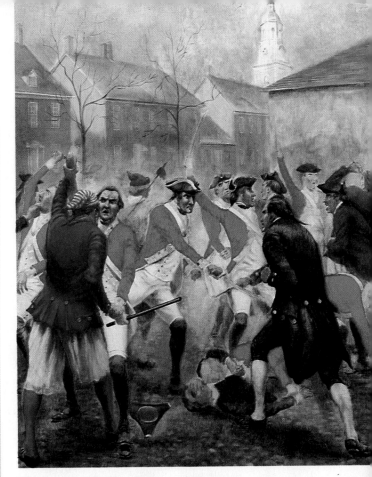

The Battle of Golden Hill

TEA THROWN INTO BOSTON HARBOR DEC 16 1773.

The War Begins

In April 1775, British soldiers and Patriots fought each other at the villages of Lexington and Concord, in Massachusetts. News of these battles spread quickly, and the colonies began preparing for war. In New York City, the Sons of Liberty boarded British ships. They took or destroyed supplies waiting to be sent to soldiers in Massachusetts.

One month after the fighting at Lexington and Concord, a battle took place at Fort Ticonderoga (ty•kahn•duh•ROH•guh), near Lake Champlain. Early one morning a small group of Patriot fighters set out to attack the fort.

They arrived while most of the British soldiers were still sleeping.

The Patriots, led by Ethan Allen and Benedict Arnold, captured the fort without firing a shot. This marked the first American victory of the Revolutionary War. The Patriots removed 59 British cannons from the fort. Later that year the cannons were moved down the Hudson River valley and pulled across the frozen river. They were then taken to Patriot forces in Massachusetts—a total distance of more than 200 miles (322 km). The cannons helped stop the British from capturing Boston.

Even after the fighting had started, many New Yorkers still hoped war could be avoided. In May 1775 the Second Continental Congress met in Philadelphia. Again the members tried to reach an agreement with Britain. New Yorkers were divided about what should be done. Many wanted **independence**, or the freedom to govern themselves. They did not want to separate from Britain, however.

Congress believed that it needed to form an army to protect the colonies. George Washington was asked to lead the new army, which was called the Continental Army.

GEOGRAPHY THEME

Movement Rivers were an important means of transportation in the colonies.

❓ In which direction did the Patriots travel along the Hudson River?

Patriots' Cannon Route

St. Lawrence R.

Lake Champlain

VERMONT (claimed by NY and NH)

MAINE (part of Massachusetts)

Fort Ticonderoga

Lake George

Connecticut River

NEW HAMPSHIRE

NEW YORK

Albany

MASSACHUSETTS

Cambridge
Boston

Springfield

Worcester

N
W E
S

Hudson River

Hartford

Providence

Delaware R.

CONNECTICUT

RHODE ISLAND

New Haven

NEW JERSEY

New York City

0   50   100 Miles
0 50 100 Kilometers
Albers Equal-Area Projection

→ Patriots' route
— Present-day border

Fort Ticonderoga

Historical paintings give an artist's view of an event. The women, small children, and the Native American family shown here would not really have been present at this event.

Even though Congress was preparing for war, it hoped for peace. New York's delegates even wrote to King George III to ask for an end to the fighting. By the time their letter reached Britain, however, the king had decided to go to war.

This decision to go to war would affect every colony, but New York was affected from the start. By July 1776 a group of British warships had arrived in New York Harbor. These ships carried more than 30,000 British soldiers, who soon marched ashore on Staten Island.

In Philadelphia, Congress was preparing to vote on independence. Thomas Jefferson, a Virginia delegate, was asked to write a statement explaining why the colonies wanted to break away from Britain. This statement became known as the Declaration of Independence. On July 4, 1776, Congress approved the Declaration.

One of its most famous sentences states that people have the right to

> **❝Life, Liberty, and the pursuit of Happiness.❞**

Word of the Declaration reached New York City a few days later. When Patriots there heard the news, they tore down a statue of King George III in the Bowling Green area of the city.

The Continental Army, which had gathered in New York, was made up of nearly 17,000 soldiers. However, only 10,000 of them had any military training. When George Washington arrived, he and his officers began to prepare the Continental Army for war. At the same time, New York's leaders prepared to create a new government for their new state.

REVIEW Why was the Declaration of Independence written?

New York's First Constitution

When the 13 colonies broke away from Britain, every colony had to form a new state government. A group led by John Jay began working on a **constitution**, or plan of government, for New York in late 1776. On April 20, 1777, the constitution was signed into law in the town of Kingston. New York became the first of the former 13 colonies to have its own constitution.

New York's first constitution set up three branches of government. The **legislative branch** would write laws for the state. It was to be made up of a senate and an assembly. The **executive branch** would carry out the laws. It was to be led by a governor. The **judicial branch** would decide if laws were fair. It was to be headed by a supreme court.

The writers of New York's first constitution knew that times would change, so they created a special rule. It said that every 20 years the voters could decide whether to rewrite the constitution. This gave future voters the chance to make changes if they felt they were needed.

When New York's constitution was written, not everyone in the state could vote. Only free white men who owned property or had a certain amount of money had that right.

The first state election was held in 1777. That year New York voters chose George Clinton of Ulster County as their governor. At the time of the election, Clinton

Primary Sources

British Troops Enter New York City

Der Einzug der Königlichen Völker in Neu Yorck

L'Entrée triumphale de Troupes royales a Nouvelle Yorck

Background In 1776, British troops entered New York City. They remained in the city until 1783.

1. Drummers marched in front of the soldiers. The drumbeat helped the soldiers march.
2. British soldiers marched in straight lines.
3. The drawing is labeled in German and French.

DBQ Document-Based Question Who do you think the people on horseback are? Why do you think this?

John Jay 1745–1829

Character Trait: Civic Virtue

A lifelong New Yorker, John Jay served his state in many different ways. After college he became a lawyer. During the Revolutionary War, Jay represented New York in the Second Continental Congress. He also served as the first chief justice of the New York Supreme Court. After the war he became the first chief justice of the United States Supreme Court. Jay later served as governor of New York.

For more resources, go to
www.harcourtschool.com/ss1

was serving as a general in the Continental Army. He was respected by his soldiers, and many of them voted for him. John Jay, another respected leader, became the first chief justice of the New York Supreme Court. These leaders and others helped shape New York's first state government.

REVIEW How could New York's constitution be changed?

REVIEW

1. **WHAT TO KNOW** How did New York become a state with its own government?

2. **VOCABULARY** Use **constitution** in a sentence about John Jay.

3. **CIVICS AND GOVERNMENT** What were the three branches of government set up by New York's first constitution?

4. **CRITICAL THINKING** Why do you think some New Yorkers wanted to be a part of Britain and be independent at the same time?

5. **WRITE A LETTER** Imagine you are at the Second Continental Congress. Write a letter to King George III persuading him to end the fighting between the Patriots and the British.

6. **CAUSE AND EFFECT** On a separate sheet of paper, copy and complete this graphic organizer.

Cause	Effect
	Colonial leaders formed the First Continental Congress.

Cause	Effect
British soldiers and Patriots fought each other at Lexington and Concord.	

SKILLS

Compare Bar and Line Graphs

VOCABULARY	
bar graph	line graph

▶ WHY IT MATTERS

In the mid-1700s New York was a busy trade center. Many ships carrying raw materials and finished goods passed through the colony's deepwater ports. You can report on trade in New York during this time by using graphs. Knowing how to read and make graphs can help you show information.

▶ WHAT YOU NEED TO KNOW

Bar graphs and line graphs show information in different ways. A **bar graph** uses bars of different lengths to stand for different amounts. The bar graph on page 169 shows the value of New York's exports to Britain from 1768 to 1774.

Bar graphs mainly compare amounts, but they can also show change over time. So can line graphs. A **line graph** is a graph that uses lines to show change over time.

The line graph on page 169 shows that the value of New York's imports changed from 1768 to 1774. The numbers along the left side of the graph show the value of imports. The years are listed across the bottom of the graph. As the red line moves from left to right, it shows how the value of imports changed.

Find the year 1773 on the line graph. Move your finger up from that date until you reach the red dot. Then move your finger to the left to the value numbers. Your finger will be a little below 300,000,

Trade with Britain brought wealth to New York.

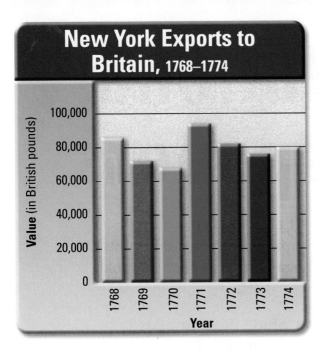

New York Exports to Britain, 1768–1774

Value (in British pounds)

100,000
80,000
60,000
40,000
20,000
0

1768 1769 1770 1771 1772 1773 1774

Year

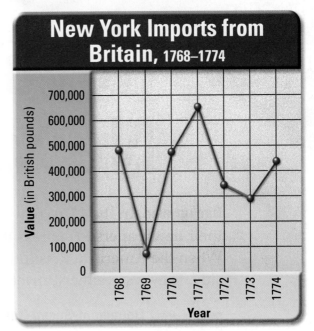

New York Imports from Britain, 1768–1774

Value (in British pounds)

700,000
600,000
500,000
400,000
300,000
200,000
100,000
0

1768 1769 1770 1771 1772 1773 1774

Year

so you will need to estimate the value. To estimate is to make a close guess. The value of imports in 1773 was about 290,000 British pounds. The pound is a unit of British money.

▶ PRACTICE THE SKILL

Use the information in the graphs to answer the following questions.

❶ Look at the bar graph. In which year did New York export the most goods?

❷ What happened to exports from 1771 to 1773?

❸ What happened to imports from 1771 to 1773?

❹ What happened to imports between 1769 and 1771?

❺ Compare the value of imports and the value of exports in 1774.

▶ APPLY WHAT YOU LEARNED

Think about the information shown on the graphs. Was the value of New York's imports or exports greater between 1768 and 1774?

Revolutionary Newspapers

Background In the 1770s newspaper publishers often used their newspapers to express their opinions on current events. When the American Revolution began, most publishers took a side. They were either Patriots or Loyalists.

 Document-Based Question Study these primary sources and answer the questions.

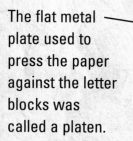

The flat metal plate used to press the paper against the letter blocks was called a platen.

PRINTING PRESS

The first printing press in the American colonies was set up in Cambridge, Massachusetts, in 1638.

DBQ ❶ It took at least two workers to run a printing press. Why do you think this was so?

The legs of a printing press had to be very strong because workers used great force to press the paper against the blocks.

A LOYALIST NEWSPAPER

James Rivington published this newspaper.

DBQ ❷ When was this newspaper published?

The masthead is the part of the newspaper where its name is printed.

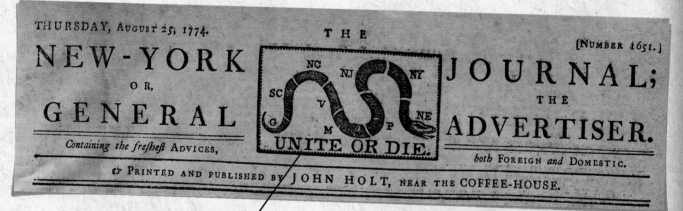

[N.º 136]

THURSDAY Nov. 23, 1775.

RIVINGTON'S

NEW-YORK GAZETTEER;
OR,
Connecticut, Hudson's River, THE New-Jersey, and Quebec
WEEKLY ADVERTISER.

PRINTED af his OPEN and UNINFLUENCED PRESS fronting HANOVER-SQUARE.

The British royal seal

THURSDAY, AUGUST 25, 1774.

[NUMBER 1651.]

NEW-YORK JOURNAL;
OR,
GENERAL THE ADVERTISER.
Containing the freshest ADVICES, both FOREIGN and DOMESTIC.

UNITE OR DIE.

PRINTED AND PUBLISHED BY JOHN HOLT, NEAR THE COFFEE-HOUSE.

A cartoon expressing a need for the colonies to unite

A PATRIOT NEWSPAPER

The New-York Journal was the first Patriot newspaper published in New York City.

DBQ ❸ Who was the publisher of *The New-York Journal?*

DBQ ❹ How did the publisher of this newspaper let readers know which side of the revolution the newspaper supported?

WRITE ABOUT IT

Imagine you are a New York newspaper publisher in the 1770s. Create a masthead for your newspaper. Your masthead should include your newspaper's name, the date, and a picture that shows whether you support the Patriots or the Loyalists.

 GO ONLINE For more resources, go to www.harcourtschool.com/ss1

Independence Is Achieved

WHAT TO KNOW
How did the American colonies win the Revolutionary War?

VOCABULARY
commander in chief p. 172
militia p. 174
turning point p. 176
traitor p. 177
treaty p. 178

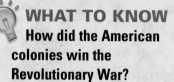

CAUSE AND EFFECT

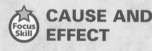

Cause		Effect
Cause		Effect

George Washington

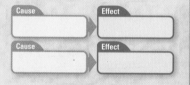

1750		1775		1800

1776–1784

YOU ARE THERE You overhear George Washington tell his officers how important New York is to winning the war. The general reminds them of what John Adams wrote: "New York is a kind of key to the continent." You wonder what he means.

New York's Importance

As **commander in chief**, or leader of all the military forces, George Washington understood how important New York was. Because of New York's location, Washington knew that if the British captured the colony, they could separate the 13 colonies and cut off communications and supplies. They would also use New York City's harbor to land more soldiers and supplies. The first goal of British General William Howe was to control New York. From there he could plan attacks against the other colonies.

REVIEW Why was New York's location important in the Revolutionary War?

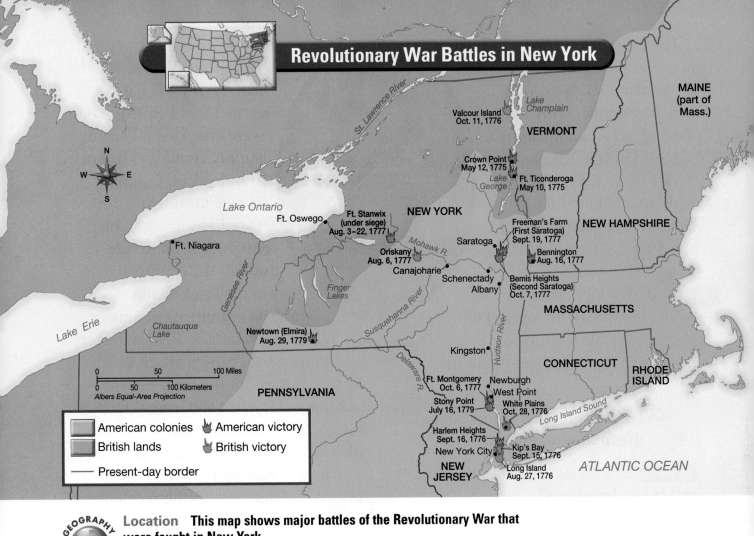

Revolutionary War Battles in New York

Valcour Island
Oct. 11, 1776

Lake Champlain

MAINE
(part of
Mass.)

VERMONT

Crown Point
May 12, 1775

Lake George

Ft. Ticonderoga
May 10, 1775

Lake Ontario

Ft. Oswego

Ft. Stanwix
(under siege)
Aug. 3–22, 1777

NEW YORK

Freeman's Farm
(First Saratoga)
Sept. 19, 1777

NEW HAMPSHIRE

Ft. Niagara

Oriskany
Aug. 6, 1777

Mohawk R.

Saratoga

Bennington
Aug. 16, 1777

Canajoharie

Schenectady

Bemis Heights
(Second Saratoga)
Oct. 7, 1777

Finger Lakes

Albany

Genesee River

Lake Erie

Chautauqua Lake

Susquehanna River

MASSACHUSETTS

Newtown (Elmira)
Aug. 29, 1779

Kingston

Hudson River

Delaware R.

CONNECTICUT

RHODE ISLAND

| 0 | 50 | 100 Miles |
| 0 | 50 | 100 Kilometers |

Albers Equal-Area Projection

PENNSYLVANIA

Ft. Montgomery
Oct. 6, 1777

Newburgh

West Point

Stony Point
July 16, 1779

White Plains
Oct. 28, 1776

Long Island Sound

Harlem Heights
Sept. 16, 1776

Kip's Bay
Sept. 15, 1776

New York City

NEW JERSEY

Long Island
Aug. 27, 1776

ATLANTIC OCEAN

American colonies
British lands
— Present-day border

American victory
British victory

Location **This map shows major battles of the Revolutionary War that were fought in New York.**

❖ **What major battles took place near Lake Champlain?**

The Battle for New York City

In the summer of 1776, General Washington prepared to defend New York City against the British. Patriots, including women and slaves, helped soldiers place cannons on the tops of buildings. They also built two forts on Manhattan. Fort Washington guarded the city on the eastern side of the Hudson River. Fort Lee protected it on the western side of the river.

The British soldiers who had arrived on Staten Island also began building forts. The British warships in New York Harbor kept guns aimed at the city.

General Washington ordered his army to set up camp at Brooklyn Heights on Long Island. On the morning of August 27, 1776, about 10,000 British soldiers attacked the Continental Army. By day's end 1,400 Americans had been killed or wounded.

The fighting continued, but General Washington knew he had to get his army off Long Island. On a foggy night three days later, Washington marched his troops from Brooklyn toward the East River. He warned them to be very quiet. Any noise could alert the British. More than 9,000 soldiers left Long Island for Manhattan on fishing boats.

The Continental Army then fled north to White Plains, and the British took New York City. The British army used the city as its headquarters.

Most Patriots left New York City when the British took over. A few, such as Nathan Hale, stayed and spied for the Continental Army. Hale gathered and passed on a lot of information before the British discovered he was a spy. Hale's last words before the British hanged him are said to have been,

> 66 I only regret that I have but one life to lose for my country. 99

REVIEW How did the Continental Army escape from Long Island?

Nathan Hale

A Battleground State

In April 1777, Patriots learned that British soldiers were attacking a Patriot supply center in Danbury, Connecticut. Colonel Henry Ludington, a New York Patriot, asked his daughter Sybil to ride through the countryside to warn the local **militia** (muh•LIH•shuh), or volunteer army, of the attack. Sybil's bravery helped the Patriots attack the British as they left the area.

Later in 1777 British General John Burgoyne (ber•GOYN) came up with a plan to win the war. He believed that a victory at Albany would allow the British to defeat the northern colonies.

• BIOGRAPHY •

Sybil Ludington   1761–1839

Character Trait: Heroic Deeds

On the night of April 26, 1777, 16-year-old Sybil Ludington rode 40 miles (64 km) across Dutchess and Putnam Counties. She told Patriot soldiers of a British attack on Danbury, Connecticut. Historical markers trace her route, and her hometown is named Ludington in her honor.

Contributors To The Cause.
U.S. 8¢
Sybil Ludington 🌼 Youthful Heroit

This statue of Sybil Ludington is in Carmel, New York.

GO ONLINE For more resources, go to www.harcourtschool.com/ss1

During the Battle of Oriskany, Nicholas Herkimer (sitting) was very badly wounded. Soon after the battle he died of his injuries. Today, a county in New York is named in his honor.

He ordered more British troops to move toward Albany to join those moving south from Canada. Together they would attack the city from the north, south, and west.

Burgoyne's plan might have worked, but the British troops never reached Albany. The troops coming from New York City were delayed by a battle in Philadelphia. The troops moving east met Patriots at Fort Stanwix, at the western end of the Mohawk River valley. Instead of going to Albany, the British surrounded the fort and waited there for the Americans to surrender.

A force of about 900 Americans, led by Nicholas Herkimer (HER•kuh•mer), set out to help the Patriots at Fort Stanwix. About 7 miles (11 km) from the fort, at Oriskany (aw•RIS•kuh•nee), they met the British.

During the battle that followed, many Native Americans fought alongside the British. One of their leaders was the Mohawk chief Joseph Brant. Brant had asked Native Americans to help the British because the British government had promised to protect Indian lands.

The fighting at Oriskany was fierce, and many American soldiers died. Of the nearly 900 American soldiers, only about 150 were unhurt. Because of their heavy losses, the Americans were forced to turn back.

Soon another American army, led by Benedict Arnold, arrived at Fort Stanwix. This time the British had to retreat. They were driven back to Fort Oswego. As a result, they were unable to join Burgoyne at Albany.

Joseph Brant

Meanwhile, Burgoyne and about 5,000 soldiers continued their march south from Canada. American general Horatio Gates was ready for them. He had ordered about 17,000 soldiers to position themselves along the road to Albany. Just south of Saratoga, the Americans attacked the British army.

The Battle of Saratoga was really two battles that took place over three weeks.

When the British troops that were to have joined Burgoyne's did not arrive, Burgoyne realized he was outnumbered. He decided to surrender.

The American victory at Saratoga was a turning point in the Revolutionary War. A **turning point** is an event that causes important changes. The victory led France to join the war on the side of the Americans. The French believed that with their help, the Americans could defeat Britain, France's longtime enemy.

With Albany lost to them, the British needed a big win. They wanted to gain control of the lower Hudson River valley. American soldiers at West Point, about 50 miles (80 km) north of New York City, protected the valley.

A CLOSER LOOK
Fighting at Saratoga

The weapons used in the Revolutionary War were not very accurate, so soldiers had to fight many hand-to-hand battles.

1. In most battles officers usually rode on horseback.
2. Both sides displayed their flags on the front lines.
3. Both sides fought in straight-line formation.

❖ Why do you think most officers rode on horseback?

John Burgoyne

August 6, 1777
The Battle of Oriskany is fought

September 19, 1777
The Battle of Freeman's Farm (first Saratoga) is fought

Benedict Arnold, the American commander at West Point, felt that his service to the Patriots' cause had been overlooked. Arnold's disappointment led him to decide to give the plans of West Point to the British.

Luckily, the Americans found out about Arnold's plan before he could carry it out. Arnold became known as a **traitor**, or a person who works to harm his or her own country. Before he could be arrested, however, Arnold left and joined the British army.

Horatio Gates

REVIEW Why did the British want to capture Albany?

New Yorkers and the War

New York City became a safe place for Loyalists. They moved to the city from other parts of New York and from other colonies. Many escaped slaves also went to New York City. The British promised them freedom in exchange for military service.

Some African Americans fought in the British army, and some fought in the Continental Army. They formed their own groups of soldiers. Native Americans also joined the war, mainly in support of the British.

October 7, 1777
The Battle of Bemis Heights (second Saratoga) is fought

October 17, 1777
Burgoyne surrenders to Gates at Saratoga (right)

Women in New York also played an important role in the war. Elizabeth Burgin helped more than 200 American soldiers escape from a prison ship in New York Harbor. Women also ran many farms and businesses while men fought in the army. Some women even disguised themselves so they could fight as soldiers.

Other New Yorkers also made contributions. The bravery of Alexander Hamilton at the Battle of Long Island was noticed by George Washington. Washington later asked Hamilton to be his personal assistant. New Yorker Robert Livingston took part in the Continental Congress and helped write the Declaration of Independence.

REVIEW How did New Yorkers take part in the Revolutionary War?

The Effects of the War

The last major battle of the American Revolution took place at Yorktown, Virginia. The Continental Army's victory there forced the British to surrender in October 1781.

The war officially ended on September 3, 1783, when Britain signed the Treaty of Paris. A **treaty** is an official agreement between groups or countries.

Britain agreed that the United States was a free and independent country. Britain also agreed to give up its lands east of the Mississippi River and south of Canada. Soon after, New York's modern boundaries were set. On November 25, 1783, the last British soldiers left New York City. Soon the American flag was once again flying above the city.

After the last British soldiers left New York City, George Washington led a tired troop of soldiers to reclaim the city. The water jug (above) celebrates that day, which is often called Evacuation Day.

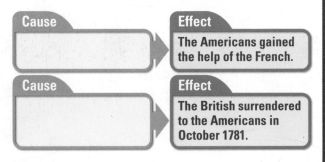

West Point
Understanding Human Systems

After the American Revolution, West Point remained an important location for the military. In 1802 the United States government opened a school there to train officers for the United States Army. The United States Military Academy at West Point now trains both young men and young women to be wise and honest army leaders. The academy's motto is "Duty, Honor, Country."

Many Native Americans who had fought on the side of the British moved to Canada. Those who did not were ordered to live on reservations in the northern, central, and western parts of New York. The war changed the Indians' ways of life forever.

REVIEW What happened as a result of the Battle of Yorktown?

REVIEW

1. **WHAT TO KNOW** How did the American colonies win the Revolutionary War?

2. **VOCABULARY** Write a sentence explaining the job of a **commander in chief**.

3. **GEOGRAPHY** Why was control of New York important to both the Americans and the British?

4. **CRITICAL THINKING** What do you think might have happened if the Americans had not won the Battle of Saratoga?

5. **DRAW A SCENE** Imagine that it is your job to draw a picture for an article about the British leaving New York City. Draw a picture that shows the event.

6. **CAUSE AND EFFECT** On a separate sheet of paper, copy and complete this graphic organizer.

Cause		Effect
	→	The Americans gained the help of the French.

Cause		Effect
	→	The British surrendered to the Americans in October 1781.

Compare Maps with Different Scales

➡ WHY IT MATTERS

Some maps have larger scales than other maps. Maps with large scales show more detail than maps with smaller scales. Maps with smaller scales show more area.

When you want to see all the states of the United States at one time, you look at a map with a small scale. When you want to see all the cities in New York, you look at a map with a larger scale. A map with an even larger scale could show you New York City's streets and well-known landmarks.

➡ WHAT YOU NEED TO KNOW

The maps on pages 180 and 181 both show the Battle of Long Island, but they have different scales. Map B shows a larger area than Map A, but Map A has more detail. You can use Map A to find where the troops were. Map B has a smaller scale than Map A. By studying Map B, you can learn where the Atlantic Ocean is located. Although they have different scales, Maps A and B can both be used to measure the distance between any two places that are shown on both of the maps.

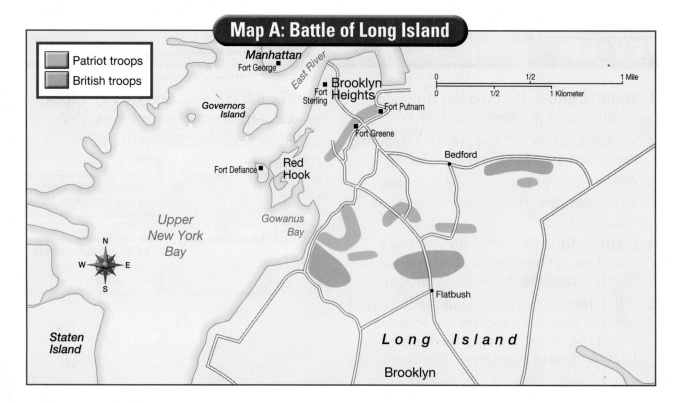

Map A: Battle of Long Island

Patriot troops
British troops

Manhattan
Fort George

East River

Brooklyn Heights
Fort Sterling

Fort Putnam

Governors Island

Fort Greene

Fort Defiance

Red Hook

Bedford

Upper New York Bay

Gowanus Bay

N
W · E
S

Flatbush

Staten Island

Long Island

Brooklyn

0   1/2   1 Mile
0   1/2   1 Kilometer

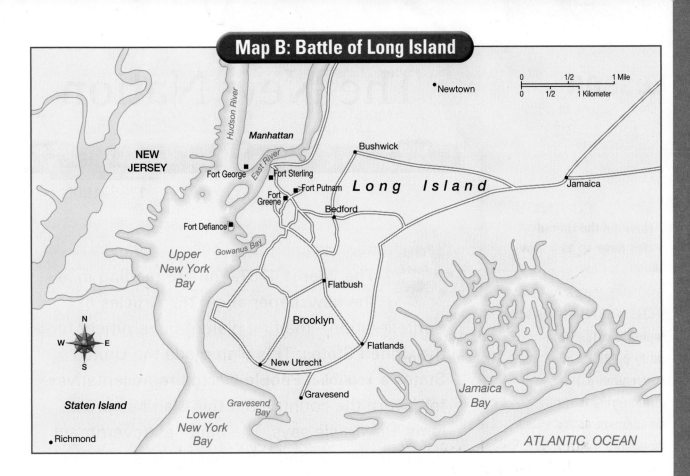

Map B: Battle of Long Island

▶ PRACTICE THE SKILL

Use Maps A and B to answer these questions.

1 Which map shows the distance of Patriot troops near Fort Greene from British troops near Flatbush?

2 Which map could you use to find the distance from Fort Defiance, in Upper New York Bay, to Jamaica Bay?

3 What is the distance in miles from Gravesend to Bedford? Which map shows both places?

▶ APPLY WHAT YOU LEARNED

When you take trips with your family, you probably use a map to help you find your way. You could use a small-scale map to find interstates and other highways. A large-scale map would help you find the home of a friend or relative in a particular town. Imagine that you are taking a trip to the city of Rochester. Use a large-scale map to find the sites you would like to visit in Rochester.

Practice your map and globe skills with the **GeoSkills CD-ROM.**

The New Nation

1750   1775   1800

1785–1800

WHAT TO KNOW
How did the United States develop as a new nation?

VOCABULARY

republic p. 182
ratify p. 183
convention p. 183
bill of rights p. 183
amendment p. 183
inauguration p. 184
stock p. 184
stock exchange p. 185

CAUSE AND EFFECT

Focus Skill

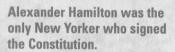

Alexander Hamilton was the only New Yorker who signed the Constitution.

YOU ARE THERE

The year is 1787. You are reading in the newspaper about the Articles of Confederation—the first plan of government for the United States. This plan made the United States a **republic**. People elected representatives to govern the country. But this plan has problems, the article says. The national government has little power. You read that leaders will meet to make the national government stronger.

A New Plan of Government

In May 1787, delegates from 12 of the 13 states met in Philadelphia. New York was represented by Alexander Hamilton, John Lansing, Jr., and Robert Yates. The delegates began working on a new plan of government. The

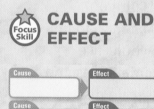

delegates studied both the Declaration of Independence and the Mayflower Compact. The Mayflower Compact was written by the Pilgrims, who settled in Massachusetts in 1620. It gave the settlers the right to govern themselves.

The delegates finally agreed on a new plan of government called the Constitution of the United States of America. Its Preamble, or opening statement, begins with the words,

"We the people of the United States . . ."

With these words the delegates were saying that the government should get its power from the people.

The Constitution had to be **ratified**, or approved, by 9 of the 13 states. Some New Yorkers, like Governor George Clinton, disliked the Constitution because it made the states less powerful. Others, such as Alexander Hamilton, supported it. They believed it would make the whole country stronger.

In June 1788 New York held a **convention**, or meeting, to vote on the Constitution. Most of the delegates at the convention decided to vote against the Constitution. Then they learned that nine states had ratified it. It was already law. Those who had voted against the Constitution agreed to change their votes if a **bill of rights**—a list of rights and freedoms—was added to it.

In 1791 ten **amendments**, or changes, were added to the Constitution. These first ten amendments, known as the Bill of Rights, describe freedoms that the national government cannot take away. These include freedom of religion, speech, and the press and the right to a trial by jury.

REVIEW What is the Bill of Rights?

The Empire State

New York is often called the Empire State. An empire is a collection of lands and peoples under one government. This nickname refers to the state's size and its many groups of people. Many believe it was George Washington who first called New York the Empire State. In 1785 Washington wrote a letter to New York City's mayor, James Duane, describing New York as the "Seat of the Empire." Some historians have written that people began calling New York the Empire State about the time the Erie Canal was completed. We may never be sure who gave New York its nickname, but it certainly fits.

A Growing American Identity

New York City was the capital of the United States from 1785 to 1790. The people of the new nation elected George Washington as their first President. The first presidential inauguration (ih•naw•gyuh•RAY•shuhn) took place in New York City on April 30, 1789. An **inauguration** is a ceremony in which a leader takes office.

President Washington called on the nation's wisest leaders to help him govern. He appointed Alexander Hamilton as secretary of the treasury. Hamilton helped New York open its first bank.

New York City was the country's economic center. Businesspeople called brokers began buying and selling stock for other people. A **stock** is a share of ownership in a company. The brokers earned money by charging their customers fees.

The brokers usually met near a buttonwood tree on Wall Street. In 1792

Alexander Hamilton (right) was an expert on money matters. The Tontine Coffee House (far left) was on the corner of Wall and Water Streets. It was a meeting place for brokers in the 1790s.

they decided to form a group in which all members would charge the same fees. Their Buttonwood Agreement was the start of the New York Stock Exchange, which is still located on Wall Street. A **stock exchange** is a place where people can buy and sell stocks.

After the Revolution, most Americans wanted to move away from British culture and British ways of thinking. They saw themselves as independent, hard-working people. They were ready to form their own traditions.

Americans began to develop their own styles of writing. New Yorker Washington Irving wrote short stories. Some of his characters, such as Rip Van Winkle, remain

Washington Irving

a part of American culture today. Another American, Noah Webster, began collecting American words. He put the words into the first dictionary of American English. Webster also wrote books to help American students learn how to read and write.

Perhaps Americans were most proud of their ability to govern themselves. The Constitution and the Bill of Rights helped set up a government that put power the hands of the people.

REVIEW How did Americans to develop their own culture

REVIEW

1. **WHAT TO KNOW** How did the United States develop as a new nation?

2. **VOCABULARY** Use the terms **ratify** and **amendment** to write about the Constitution.

3. **ECONOMICS** What was the Buttonwood Agreement?

4. **CRITICAL THINKING** Why did Americans want to form their own traditions?

5. **WRITE A LETTER** Imagine that it is 1787. Write a letter to the editor of a newspaper saying why you are for or against the new Constitution.

6. **CAUSE A**
   sheet of
   this graphic

   Cause
   The national g
   ment is weak
   Articles of
   Confederat

   Cause

Write a Lett
a Continental A
American Revo
to your family, e
is like.

Chapter Review

Summarize the Chapter

Focus Skill **Cause and Effect** Complete this graphic organizer to show that you understand the causes and effects leading to the American Revolution and the formation of a new nation.

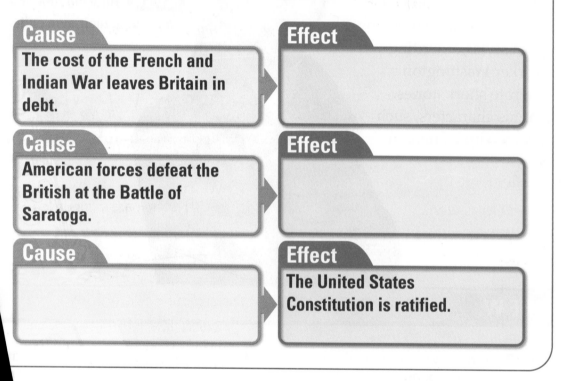

Cause	Effect
The cost of the French and Indian War leaves Britain in debt.	
American forces defeat the British at the Battle of Saratoga.	
	The United States Constitution is ratified.

THINK & WRITE

...er Imagine that you are ...rmy soldier fighting in the ...lution. Write a letter home ...xplaining what your life

Write a Newspaper Article Imagine that you are a newspaper reporter who has traveled to see George Washington's inauguration. Write a newspaper article telling why people think Washington will be a good President.

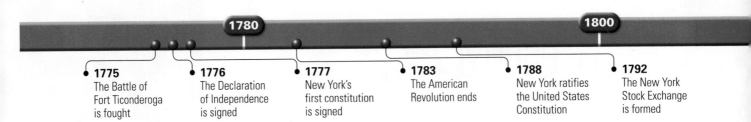

1780   1800

1775
The Battle of
Fort Ticonderoga
is fought

1776
The Declaration
of Independence
is signed

1777
New York's
first constitution
is signed

1783
The American
Revolution ends

1788
New York ratifies
the United States
Constitution

1792
The New York
Stock Exchange
is formed

USE THE TIME LINE

Use the chapter summary time line to answer these questions.

1 When was the Declaration of Independence signed?

2 Did New Yorkers approve the New York Constitution before or after the United States Constitution was ratified?

USE VOCABULARY

Write the term that correctly matches each definition.

liberty (p. 158)

repeal (p. 158)

constitution (p. 166)

militia (p. 174)

amendment (p. 183)

ratified (p. 183)

3 a plan of government

4 approved

5 to cancel

6 a change

7 a volunteer army

8 freedom

RECALL FACTS

Answer these questions.

9 What were the two levels of government in New York in the late 1760s?

10 What was the Stamp Act Congress?

11 According to New York's Constitution, what two groups make up the legislative branch?

12 What did Britain agree to in the Treaty of Paris

Write the letter of the best choice.

13 **TEST PREP** Why was the Battle of Saratoga considered a turning point in the American Revolution?

A The Patriot victory led France to join the war.

B The Patriots were encouraged by their victory over the British.

C General Washington had arranged a meeting with British leaders.

D The Patriots now controlled the entire East Coast.

THINK CRITICALLY

14 Do you think the British could have avoided war with the colonists? Explain.

15 Why do you think the Bill of Rights is an important part of the United States Constitution?

APPLY SKILLS

Determine Point of View

16 Explain how a Patriot's view on taxation may have been different from a Loyalist's view.

Compare Bar and Line Graphs

17 Study the graphs on page 169. Which graph would you use to see how the number of New York imports changed over time?

Compare Maps with Different Scales

18 Study the maps on pages 180–181. To find the distance from Fort Putnam to Fort Greene, is it easier to use Map A or Map B?

STUDY SKILLS

TAKE NOTES

Taking notes can help you remember important ideas.

- Write down only important facts and ideas. Use your own words. You do not have to write in complete sentences.

- One way to organize notes is in a chart. Write down the main ideas in one column and facts in another.

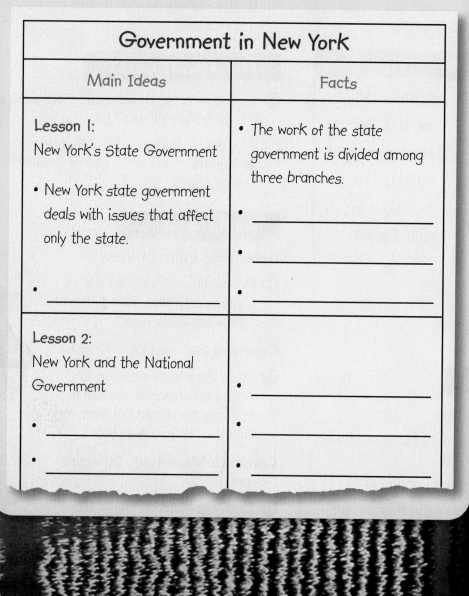

Government in New York

Main Ideas	Facts
Lesson 1: New York's State Government • New York state government deals with issues that affect only the state. • _____	• The work of the state government is divided among three branches. • _____ • _____ • _____
Lesson 2: New York and the National Government • _____ • _____	• _____ • _____ • _____

Government in New York

Empire State Plaza, Albany

1

New York's State Government

WHAT TO KNOW

What is the structure of the New York state government?

VOCABULARY

democracy p. 190
budget p. 192
bill p. 192
veto p. 193
appeal p. 194
justice p. 195

CAUSE AND EFFECT

Cause		Effect
	▶	

Cause		Effect
	▶	

YOU ARE THERE Imagine a place without any form of government. In this place, there would be no laws to protect people and their property. There would be no elected leaders to make decisions. There would be no military, police officers, or firefighters to help keep people safe.

Our American Democracy

The purpose of government is to protect the rights of citizens and to promote the common good. Governments do this by setting up laws. Laws, and the leaders who see that they are carried out, help protect people. A **democracy** (dih•MAH•kruh•see) is a form of government in which the people rule. In a democracy, people make decisions themselves or elect leaders to make decisions for them.

Americans' firm belief in democracy also helps unite them. Americans are united when they rise together to sing the national anthem. Americans promise to be loyal to the United States when they say the Pledge of Allegiance:

> **❝I pledge allegiance to the Flag of the United States of America, and to the Republic for which it stands, one Nation under God, indivisible, with liberty and justice for all.❞**

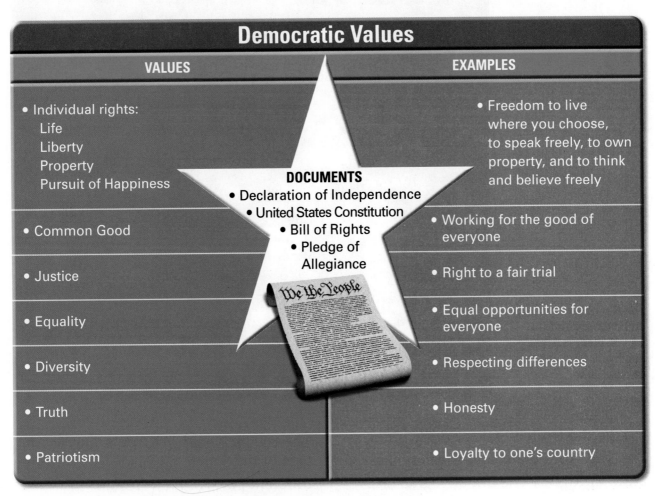

Democratic Values

VALUES	EXAMPLES
• Individual rights: 　Life 　Liberty 　Property 　Pursuit of Happiness	• Freedom to live where you choose, to speak freely, to own property, and to think and believe freely
• Common Good	• Working for the good of everyone
• Justice	• Right to a fair trial
• Equality	• Equal opportunities for everyone
• Diversity	• Respecting differences
• Truth	• Honesty
• Patriotism	• Loyalty to one's country

DOCUMENTS
- Declaration of Independence
- United States Constitution
- Bill of Rights
- Pledge of Allegiance

Analyze Diagrams Documents such as the Declaration of Independence and the United States Constitution protect democratic values and principles.

◈ How is the democratic value of justice protected in the United States?

Americans also share many common democratic values and principles. Among these are the right of people to life, liberty, and the pursuit of happiness. Americans also value justice and equal opportunity and their right to vote, to own property, and to worship as they wish. These values and principles, as well as others, are expressed in the Declaration of Independence, the Preamble to the United States Constitution, the Bill of Rights, and the Pledge of Allegiance.

REVIEW What are some of the documents in which democratic values and principles are expressed?

The New York Constitution

In the United States, the power to govern is shared by the national government and the 50 states. State governments—including New York's—deal with issues that affect only their state. These issues include state taxes, state elections, and state education.

In 1777, while still a colony, New York adopted its first state constitution. The writers of that constitution made sure that it could be amended or rewritten. Since 1777, New Yorkers have adopted three new constitutions. The present one was first used in 1894.

The New York Assembly and the New York Senate meet in Albany each year from January through June.

Like the United States Constitution, the New York State Constitution has a Bill of Rights. The Bill of Rights lists the basic rights and liberties of New Yorkers. The New York State Constitution is also like the United States Constitution in the way it divides the government into three branches.

REVIEW In what ways is the New York State Constitution like the United States Constitution?

The Legislative Branch

The legislative branch makes or changes state laws. The New York legislature is divided into two parts—the Assembly and the Senate. The two parts, or houses, meet at the Capitol building in Albany.

The Assembly has 150 members. Each one represents people in a different part of the state. Voters in each part elect a representative to the Assembly.

The Senate has 61 members. The members of the Senate are also elected from different parts of New York.

The legislature passes laws to protect the lives, freedoms, and property of New Yorkers. It also passes tax laws and votes on plans for spending tax money. A written plan for spending money is called a **budget**.

The money from state taxes is used to pay the costs of running the state government and providing state services. It pays for building and repairing state highways and ports and for keeping state parks clean and safe. State tax money is also spent on education.

A **bill**, or a plan for a new law, can be introduced in either house. More than half of the members in both houses must vote for a bill for it to pass.

REVIEW What are the two parts of the New York legislature?

The Executive Branch

The executive branch of the state government makes sure that laws are carried out. Voters in New York elect a governor to lead this branch. The governor serves a four-year term.

The governor suggests a budget and other bills to the legislature but cannot vote on them. However, all bills passed by the legislature must be presented to the governor. If the governor signs a bill, it becomes a law. If the governor does not agree to a bill, the governor has ten days to **veto**, or reject, it. If the governor does not veto the bill in ten days, it becomes law.

David Paterson became governor of New York in 2008.

If a bill is given to the governor after the legislative session is over, the governor has 30 days to sign the bill or to veto it. If the governor does not sign the bill within 30 days, it is vetoed.

People elected to work with the governor include the lieutenant (loo•TEH•nuhnt) governor, the attorney general, and the comptroller. Other employees in the executive branch work in departments that deal with agriculture, labor, and transportation.

REVIEW What are the duties of the governor?

Since 1875 the New York Executive Mansion in Albany has been home to New York's governors.

The Court of Appeals has one chief judge and six associate judges.

The Judicial Branch

The judicial branch of the New York state government makes sure that state laws agree with the state constitution. This branch is made up of courts that hear and decide legal cases. The judges decide how to punish a person who breaks the law.

New York has several levels of courts. In the low courts, juries decide cases. The highest court in New York is the Court of Appeals. In law, to **appeal** is to ask for another trial. Cases go to the Court of Appeals after they have gone through the lower courts. The Court of Appeals can change decisions made by the lower courts.

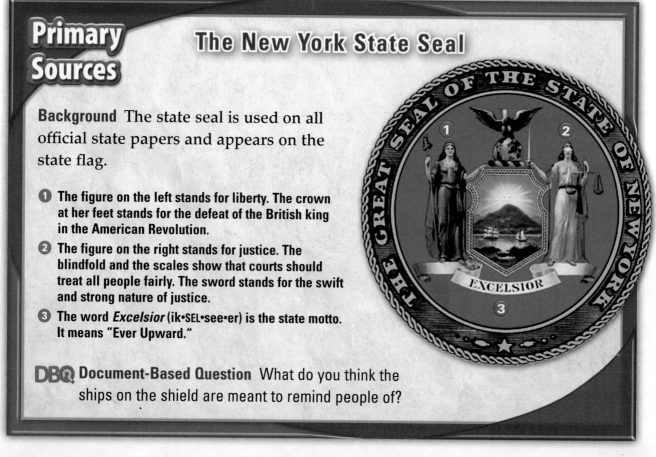

Primary Sources

The New York State Seal

Background The state seal is used on all official state papers and appears on the state flag.

1. The figure on the left stands for liberty. The crown at her feet stands for the defeat of the British king in the American Revolution.

2. The figure on the right stands for justice. The blindfold and the scales show that courts should treat all people fairly. The sword stands for the swift and strong nature of justice.

3. The word *Excelsior* (ik•SEL•see•er) is the state motto. It means "Ever Upward."

DBQ Document-Based Question What do you think the ships on the shield are meant to remind people of?

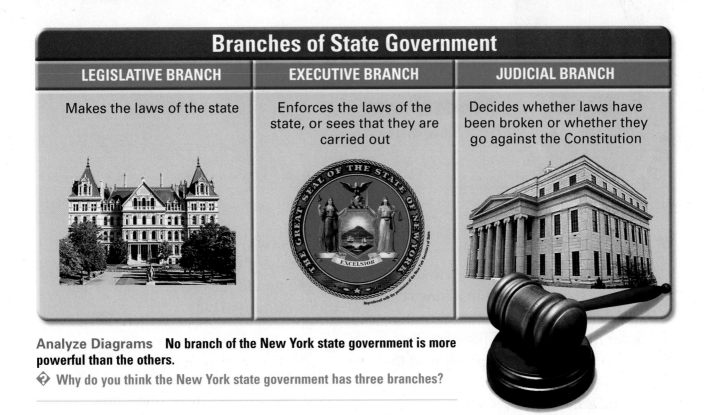

Branches of State Government

LEGISLATIVE BRANCH	EXECUTIVE BRANCH	JUDICIAL BRANCH
Makes the laws of the state	Enforces the laws of the state, or sees that they are carried out	Decides whether laws have been broken or whether they go against the Constitution

Analyze Diagrams **No branch of the New York state government is more powerful than the others.**

◆ Why do you think the New York state government has three branches?

The next-highest court in New York is the Supreme Court. The Supreme Court has 314 **justices**, or judges. They are located in different areas of the state. The voters in each area elect their Supreme Court justices.

Other courts in New York include county courts, family courts, and city courts. New York City has its own courts, including a civil court and a criminal court.

REVIEW Which is New York's highest court?

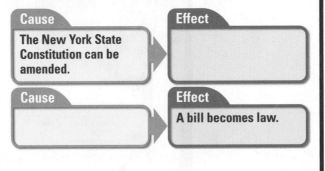

REVIEW

1. WHAT TO KNOW What is the structure of the New York state government?

2. VOCABULARY Use **veto** and **bill** to explain how state laws are made.

3. CIVICS AND GOVERNMENT What kinds of cases are heard in New York's courts?

4. CRITICAL THINKING What might happen if one branch of the state government had more power than the others?

5. CRITICAL THINKING What do you think would happen if there were no government in New York?

6. ROLE-PLAY Imagine that you are a leader in one branch of the state government. Describe the work you do and why your work is important.

7. CAUSE AND EFFECT On a separate sheet of paper, copy and complete this graphic organizer.

Cause		Effect
The New York State Constitution can be amended.	→	
Cause		Effect
	→	A bill becomes law.

Read a Flow Chart

VOCABULARY

flow chart

▶ WHY IT MATTERS

Sometimes a process is easier to understand when it is explained in a flow chart. A **flow chart** is a drawing that shows the order in which things happen. The arrows on a flow chart help you read the steps in the correct order.

▶ WHAT YOU NEED TO KNOW

The flow chart on page 197 shows how the New York state government passes new bills. A bill may begin in either house of the state legislature.

In the first step, a member of the Assembly or the Senate writes a bill.

In the second step, members of the Assembly or the Senate debate whether the bill would make a good law. Then they vote on the bill.

▶ PRACTICE THE SKILL

Read the remaining steps on the flow chart, and answer these questions.

❶ What happens if the members of both the Assembly and the Senate approve a bill?

❷ What happens if the governor signs a bill?

❸ How can a bill become a law if the governor vetoes it?

Members of the New York Assembly discuss important issues and new bills.

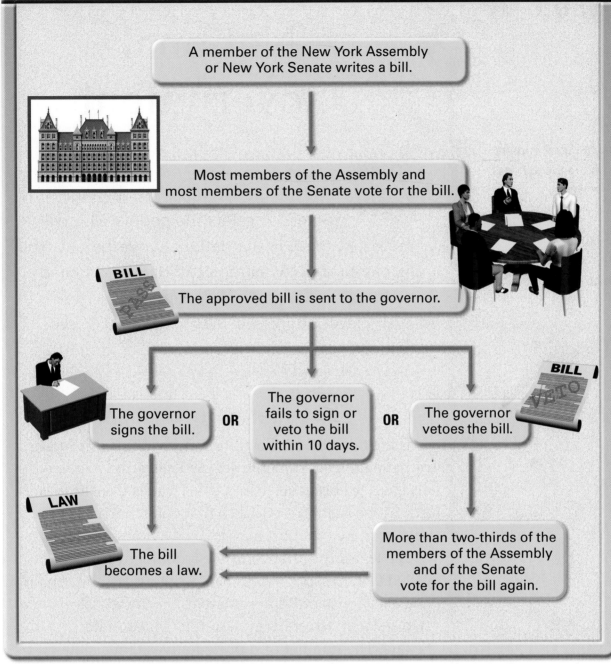

How a Bill Becomes a Law

A member of the New York Assembly or New York Senate writes a bill.

Most members of the Assembly and most members of the Senate vote for the bill.

BILL PASS

The approved bill is sent to the governor.

The governor signs the bill.

OR

The governor fails to sign or veto the bill within 10 days.

OR

BILL VETO

The governor vetoes the bill.

LAW

The bill becomes a law.

More than two-thirds of the members of the Assembly and of the Senate vote for the bill again.

► APPLY WHAT YOU LEARNED

Work with a partner to make a flow chart that explains to younger students how something works. Write each step on a strip of paper. Then paste the strips in order onto a sheet of posterboard, and connect the steps with arrows. Give your flow chart a title. You may also wish to illustrate each of its steps. Then use the flow chart to teach the process to a group of younger students.

New York and the National Government

WHAT TO KNOW

How do New Yorkers take part in the national government?

VOCABULARY
federal p. 198
Cabinet p. 199

CAUSE AND EFFECT

YOU ARE THERE Today is Election Day. It's time for New Yorkers to select the people who will represent them in the national government. You listened carefully as the candidates explained how they will help New Yorkers if they are elected to Congress in Washington, D.C. Who will voters pick?

The Federal Government

The United States Constitution divides the **federal**, or national, government into the legislative, executive, and judicial branches. The United States Constitution makes the branches equal so that one branch cannot rule over the other branches.

The legislative branch of the federal government is called Congress. Congress has two houses—the Senate and the House of Representatives. Each state elects two senators to represent it in the United States Senate. The number of representatives that a state

elects to the House of Representatives depends on how many people live in the state. States with large populations, such as New York, have the most representatives. New York has 29. Congress makes laws for the whole nation.

The main job of the executive branch is to make sure that the laws passed by Congress are carried out. The President is the head of the executive branch. Other members include the Vice President and the President's Cabinet. The **Cabinet** is a group of the President's most important advisers.

The judicial branch is made up of the United States Supreme Court and all the other federal courts. Justices on the Supreme Court are appointed by the President and approved by the Senate.

The Supreme Court decides whether laws passed by Congress or actions taken by the President agree with the Constitution. The Supreme Court also decides whether the laws and courts of New York and the other states follow the Constitution.

REVIEW What is the main job of the executive branch?

President Barack Obama lives and works in the White House.

New York and the Federal Government

New Yorkers have served in all three branches of the federal government. Seven New Yorkers have served as President of the United States.

The first New Yorker to serve as President was Martin Van Buren. He became President in 1837. In 1850, Millard Fillmore was the next New Yorker to become President.

Both the Senate and the House of Representatives meet in the United States Capitol in Washington, D.C.

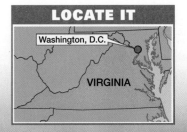

LOCATE IT
Washington, D.C.
VIRGINIA

LOCATE IT

The home of Franklin D. Roosevelt in Hyde Park, New York

NEW YORK

Hyde Park

Roosevelt served as Vice President before becoming President in 1901. In 1933 his cousin Franklin Delano Roosevelt became President. Franklin Delano Roosevelt served from 1933 to 1945, longer than any other President.

Hillary Rodham Clinton, the wife of former President Bill Clinton, was the first woman to serve as senator from New York. She is the only former First Lady to serve in an elected office. Kirsten Gillibrand became the second woman senator from New York in 2009.

A number of New Yorkers have also served on the United States Supreme Court. John Jay, from New York City, was the first chief justice of the Supreme Court. Other Supreme Court justices from New York City include Benjamin Cardozo (kar•DOH•zoh), Harlan Stone, and Thurgood Marshall. New Yorker Ruth Bader Ginsburg became a Supreme Court justice in 1993. She is only the second woman to serve on the Supreme Court.

Another New Yorker, Chester A. Arthur, served as Vice President before he became President in 1881. The next President from New York was Grover Cleveland. He served from 1885 to 1889 and again from 1893 to 1897. Theodore

Presidents Elected from New York

1825	1850	1875	1900
1837	1850	1881	1885

Martin Van Buren
Birthplace: Kinderhook, NY

Millard Fillmore
Birthplace: Locke, NY

Chester A. Arthur
Birthplace: Fairfield, VT

Grover Cleveland
Birthplace: Caldwell, NJ

Citizens of New York take part in the federal government when they elect a President and leaders to represent them in Congress. In 2008 the citizens of New York helped elect President Barack Obama. They also take part when they pay taxes to the federal government. These taxes provide the money to pay for the federal government and the services it provides. For example, the money pays for the nation's military. It pays to print and coin the money we use. It supports the postal system. It also helps support national parks, forests, and seashores.

Money from federal taxes is also used to help elderly people, people who have lost their jobs, and people who are too sick to work. When there is a natural disaster or other emergency, the federal government makes low-cost loans available to help people repair damage. It also helps New York and other states pay what is needed to protect and clean up the environment.

REVIEW Which New Yorker served longer than any other President?

Senators Charles Schumer and Kirsten Gillibrand represent New Yorkers in the national government. They are shown here with New York City Mayor Michael Bloomberg and Governor David Paterson.

REVIEW

1. **WHAT TO KNOW** How do New Yorkers take part in the national government?

2. **VOCABULARY** What do members of the President's **Cabinet** do in the **federal government**?

3. **ECONOMICS** For what does the federal government use tax money?

4. **CRITICAL THINKING** Why is it important for each of the 50 states to have representatives in Congress?

5. **DELIVER A SPEECH** Write a speech telling why people should elect you to the House of Representatives. Tell what you plan to do for your community, the state, and the nation.

6. **CAUSE AND EFFECT** On a (Focus Skill) separate sheet of paper, copy and complete this graphic organizer.

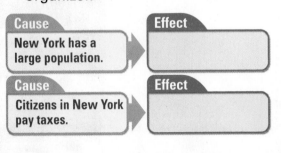

Cause	Effect
New York has a large population.	
Citizens in New York pay taxes.	

1925   1950
1901   1933

Theodore Roosevelt
Birthplace: New York, NY

Franklin D. Roosevelt
Birthplace: Hyde Park, NY

Lesson 3

Local Governments

WHAT TO KNOW
What do local governments in New York do?

VOCABULARY
county seat p. 202
board of supervisors p. 203
trustee p. 204
borough p. 205
special district p. 205

CAUSE AND EFFECT

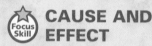

Local governments are responsible for providing services such as fire protection.

YOU ARE THERE
The mayor is visiting your class. As the leader of the city government, he explains how local governments see that life runs smoothly in villages, towns, cities, and counties. The mayor says he makes decisions about police and fire protection, garbage collection, and public transportation in your city. The county government, however, may be in charge of repairing streets and running schools, hospitals, and libraries.

County Government

New York is divided into 62 counties. In each county, one town serves as the county seat. The **county seat** is the center of government for a county. The leaders of a county government often meet at the county courthouse in the county seat.

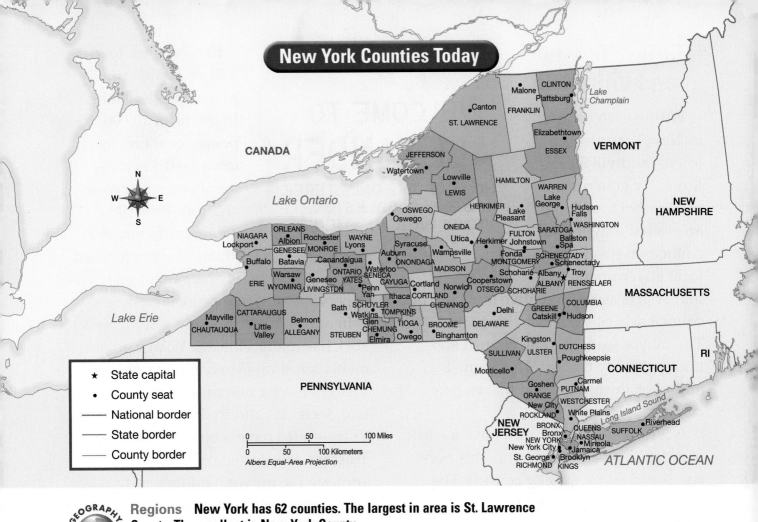

New York Counties Today

CANADA

Lake Ontario

Lake Erie

CLINTON
Malone
Plattsburg
Lake Champlain
FRANKLIN
Canton
ST. LAWRENCE
Elizabethtown
VERMONT
ESSEX
JEFFERSON
Watertown
Lowville
HAMILTON
WARREN
Lake George
Hudson Falls
Lake Pleasant
WASHINGTON
LEWIS
OSWEGO
Oswego
HERKIMER
FULTON
SARATOGA
Ballston Spa
ORLEANS
NIAGARA
Albion
Rochester
WAYNE
Lyons
ONEIDA
Utica
Herkimer Johnstown
Fonda
MONTGOMERY
SCHENECTADY
Schenectady
Troy
Lockport
GENESEE
MONROE
Syracuse
Wampsville
Buffalo
Batavia
Canandaigua
Auburn
ONONDAGA
MADISON
Cooperstown
Schoharie
Albany
ALBANY
RENSSELAER
Warsaw
Geneseo
ONTARIO
YATES
Waterloo
SENECA
CAYUGA
Cortland
Norwich
OTSEGO
SCHOHARIE
MASSACHUSETTS
ERIE
WYOMING
LIVINGSTON
Penn Yan
Ithaca
CORTLAND
CHENANGO
COLUMBIA
Bath
SCHUYLER
TOMPKINS
Delhi
GREENE
Catskill
Hudson
CATTARAUGUS
Watkins
Glen
Mayville
Belmont
CHEMUNG
TIOGA
BROOME
DELAWARE
CHAUTAUQUA
Little Valley
ALLEGANY
STEUBEN
Elmira
Owego
Binghamton
Kingston
DUTCHESS
RI
SULLIVAN
ULSTER
Poughkeepsie
CONNECTICUT
PENNSYLVANIA
Monticello
Goshen
Carmel
PUTNAM
ORANGE
WESTCHESTER
New City
ROCKLAND
White Plains
Long Island Sound
Riverhead
NEW JERSEY
BRONX
Bronx
QUEENS
SUFFOLK
NEW YORK
NASSAU
Mineola
New York City
Jamaica
St. George
Brooklyn
ATLANTIC OCEAN
RICHMOND
KINGS

Legend
- ★ State capital
- • County seat
- —— National border
- —— State border
- —— County border

0   50   100 Miles
0   50   100 Kilometers
Albers Equal-Area Projection

GEOGRAPHY THEME

Regions New York has 62 counties. The largest in area is St. Lawrence County. The smallest is New York County.

❖ Which counties border the state of Massachusetts?

Many counties are governed by a group of officials called a **board of supervisors**. Voters in the county elect representatives to serve on the board. The board holds meetings every month to talk about county issues. Other counties, such as Albany County, have a legislature. The legislature makes policies, or plans, for the county.

New York counties have other elected officials, too. Most counties have a sheriff, a supervisor of elections, and a clerk. The county sheriff's job is to see that laws are obeyed and to protect people in the county against crime. The supervisor of elections makes sure that elections are fair. The county clerk keeps important records of births, deaths, and marriages. Like the other levels of government, counties and other local governments collect taxes from citizens to pay for services and the cost of government.

REVIEW What are two kinds of county governments in New York?

In most counties, a sheriff runs the county jail.

Cities, Towns, and Villages

Within each county in New York are cities, towns, and villages. Most city governments in New York are led by an elected mayor and council. In this form of local government, the mayor acts as the executive branch. The council acts as the legislative branch. The mayor leads the city council and makes the city budget. The council approves the budget and makes new city laws.

A few cities in New York have a city manager instead of a mayor. This person is picked by the city council. The city manager supervises the work of each city department. The manager reports to the council.

WELCOME TO··
ALEXANDER
HOME OF THE ONLY THREE
STORY COBBLESTONE
TOWN HALL IN AMERICA

In New York towns, a town board usually makes the decisions. In towns of 10,000 people or more, the town board is made up of one supervisor and four council members. In smaller towns, the town board is made up of one supervisor and two council members.

In addition to cities and towns, New York has many villages. Village governments are similar to city governments. Villages elect a mayor to make important decisions and to draw up a budget. Villages also have a board of trustees. **Trustees** are elected officials who approve the mayor's budget and make laws for the village.

REVIEW What is the difference between a mayor and a city manager?

These elected officials (seated at table) listen to a citizen speak at a local government meeting in New York.

New York City and Special Districts

The government in New York City is different from that of other cities in the state. New York City spreads over five counties. These counties do not have county governments. Instead, New York City is divided into five districts called **boroughs** (BER•ohz).

The mayor leads all the boroughs of New York City. As in other cities, the mayor makes a budget. A city council approves the budget and passes laws.

New York and other states also have forms of local government called **special districts**. Each special district handles one problem, such as flooding, or one service, such as health care. Special districts in New York include school districts, library districts, the Port Authority of New York, and the New York Power Authority.

REVIEW How is the government of New York City different from that of other cities?

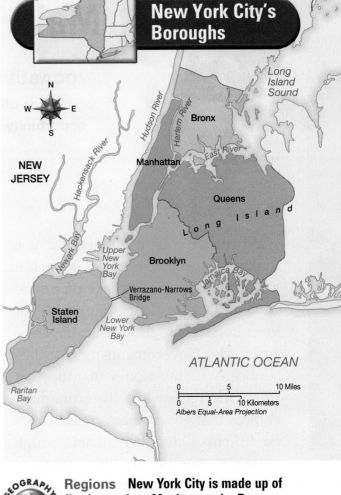

New York City's Boroughs

Regions New York City is made up of five boroughs—Manhattan, the Bronx, Queens, Brooklyn, and Staten Island.

❓ Which borough covers more area, Manhattan or Queens?

REVIEW

1. **WHAT TO KNOW** What do local governments in New York do?

2. **VOCABULARY** What is the difference between a **county seat** and a **borough**?

3. **CIVICS AND GOVERNMENT** What are some special districts in New York? What issue does each handle?

4. **CRITICAL THINKING** Why do you think New York City does not have five separate county governments?

5. **DRAW A CHART** Draw a chart that shows the form of city government in your community. Name each official, and describe their job.

6. **CAUSE AND EFFECT** On a separate sheet of paper, copy and complete this graphic organizer.

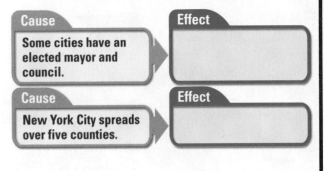

Cause		Effect
Some cities have an elected mayor and council.	→	
New York City spreads over five counties.	→	

Make Economic Choices

VOCABULARY

trade-off
opportunity cost

▶ WHY IT MATTERS

Whenever you buy something, you make an economic choice. Like people, governments have to make economic choices. It costs money to provide services such as fire protection, libraries, and parks. Governments pay for these services with tax money that they get from citizens. Some of the economic choices that governments make can be difficult. Often there is not enough money to pay for everything that people would like done.

▶ WHAT YOU NEED TO KNOW

To buy one thing, you often give up the chance to buy something else. Giving up one thing to get another is called a **trade-off**. What you give up is called the **opportunity cost** of what you get. People and governments can

use the following steps to make better economic choices:

Step 1 **Identify what you want to buy.**

Step 2 **Figure out how much you can spend.**

Step 3 **Think about trade-offs and opportunity costs. Decide whether you want the product enough to give up buying something else.**

▶ PRACTICE THE SKILL

Imagine that you are the mayor of a small town. The town council wants to build a new park and expand the community center. Your town does not have enough money to pay for both projects. List the benefits, trade-offs, and opportunity costs of each choice.

▶ APPLY WHAT YOU LEARNED

Imagine that you have $10 to spend. You want to buy a book and rent a movie, but you do not have enough money for both. Explain the trade-offs and opportunity costs of your choices.

Is building a new park the best economic choice?

New York Citizenship

YOU ARE THERE
"All persons born...in the United States...are citizens of the United States and of the State wherein they reside [live]." These words in the United States Constitution explain how you are a citizen of both New York and the United States. As citizens of each, you have certain rights and responsibilities. A **responsibility** is a duty—something that a person should do because it is right and important.

Becoming a Citizen

Throughout its history, the United States has attracted millions of immigrants. An **immigrant** is a person who comes from some other place to live in a country. Immigrants can in time become naturalized citizens of the United States. A **naturalized citizen** is an immigrant who has become a citizen by taking certain steps described in the law.

WHAT TO KNOW 💡
What does it mean to be a United States citizen?

VOCABULARY
responsibility p. 207
immigrant p. 207
naturalized citizen p. 207
register p. 209
patriotism p. 211

Focus Skill ☆ **CAUSE AND EFFECT**

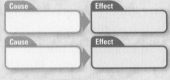

These immigrants are about to become citizens of the United States.

When an immigrant has lived in the United States for at least five years—or three years, if married to a United States citizen—that person may follow these steps to become a naturalized citizen. First, he or she must ask a judge, in writing, to become a citizen. The person must also pass a test to show that he or she can read, write, and understand English. Next, the person must pass a test on United States history and government. Finally, the person must promise to be loyal to the United States. When adults become naturalized citizens of the United States, their children under 18 years of age become citizens as well.

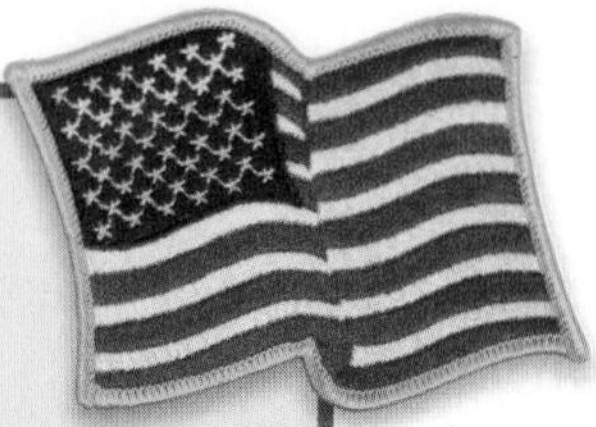

REVIEW **How can a person become a citizen of the United States?**

• HERITAGE •

Honoring the United States Flag

One way that citizens of the United States can show their loyalty to their country is by saying the Pledge of Allegiance. Francis Bellamy, a minister from Rome, New York, wrote the first Pledge of Allegiance in 1892.

In 1942 the United States Congress wrote guidelines for people to follow when they display the United States flag. It asked that people hang the flag so that the blue field of stars is on the upper left side. They also said that public buildings such as schools and post offices should have a flag flying daily. The flag should fly from sunup to sundown. Congress also said that in a parade, the United States flag should always be higher than and in front of any other flags.

Citizens Have Rights

Citizens of New York have the rights that are listed in the constitutions of both the United States and New York. They have the right to be treated fairly by their government, to own property, and to travel from state to state. They also have the right to a fair trial if they are accused of wrongdoing. Citizens have the right to free speech, and they enjoy freedom of

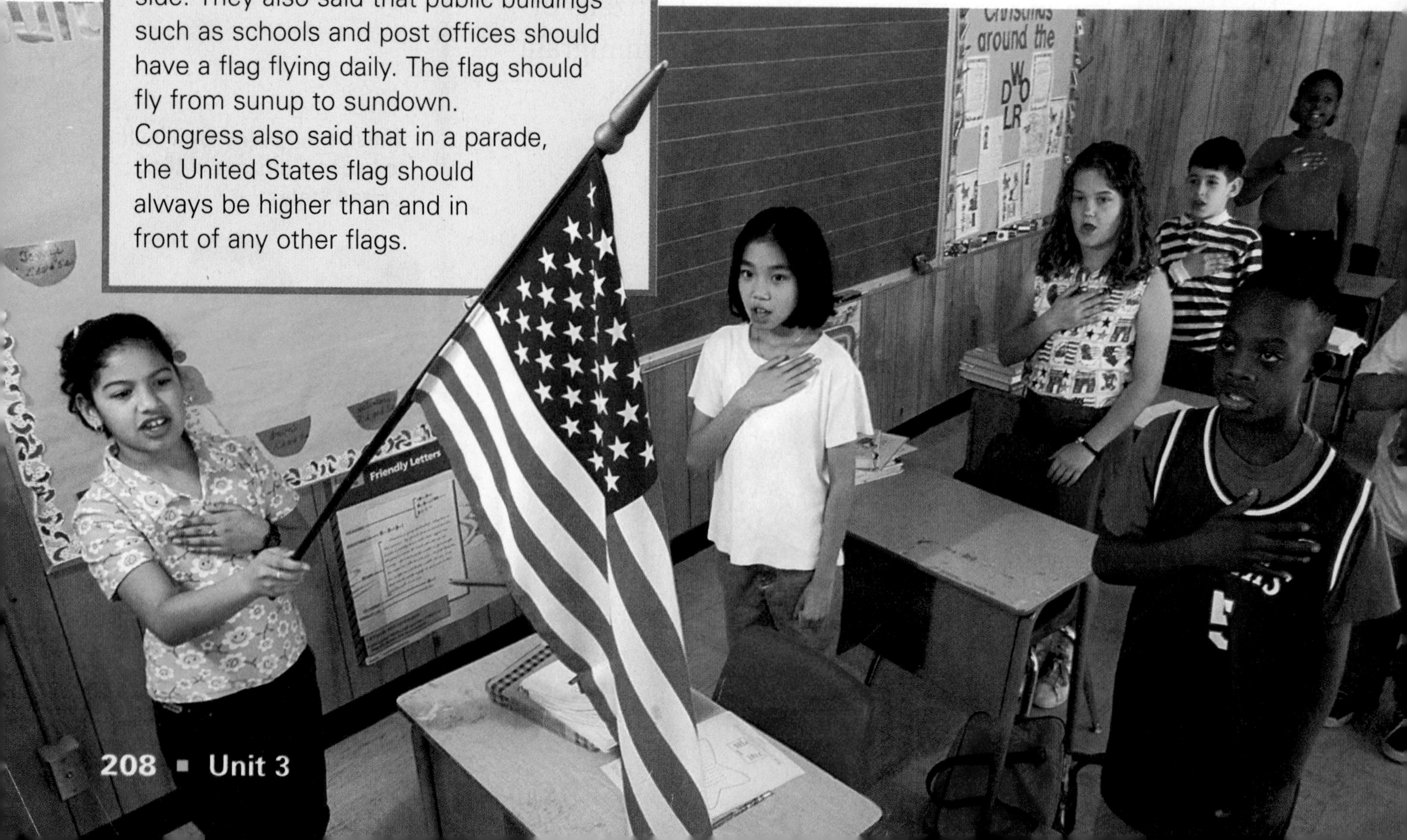

VOTE AQUÍ

I Voted

This citizen is receiving a ballot by which he will cast his vote. Why is voting important in a democracy?

the press. Citizens also have freedom of religion and freedom to gather in groups.

Among the most important rights of citizenship are the right to vote and the right to hold public office. By voting, citizens of New York can choose the leaders who will represent them in their local, state, and national governments.

Governments cannot take away a citizen's constitutional rights unless that person has been found guilty of a serious crime. However, some rights have certain limits. For example, the right to vote is limited to citizens who are at least 18 years old. State governments can also say that each citizen

REGISTER HERE ★★★★ VOTER REGISTRAR

must **register**, or sign up, before he or she can vote. People who move to New York from another state must live in New York for 30 days before they can vote in state elections.

People in the United States who are not citizens have many of the same rights and freedoms as citizens. However, they cannot vote, hold office, or serve on a jury.

REVIEW How are voting rights limited?

Citizens Have Responsibilities

With rights come responsibilities. With the right to vote, for example, comes the responsibility of voting.

Signs like this one tell people where they can register to vote.

In a democracy every citizen's vote is important. Taking part in political activities and voting are important responsibilities of citizenship. Being an informed citizen—someone who understands the problems that New York and the United States face—is also a very important responsibility. The information that citizens gather will help them make good decisions when they vote.

Some responsibilities of citizens are stated in laws. United States laws and New York laws say that it is a citizen's responsibility to be loyal to the United States. It is also a citizen's duty to pay taxes, to obey traffic rules, and to serve on a jury when called to do so. Some of these responsibilities, such as paying taxes and obeying laws, also apply to people who are not citizens. They apply to anyone who lives or works in New York or elsewhere in the United States.

Many citizens of New York and the United States take on additional responsibilities that make their communities better places in which to live. These citizens often offer their services as volunteers. New Yorkers have many opportunities to volunteer. They can help in elections. They can give out food at food banks to people in need. They can help by tutoring students or coaching youth sports teams.

There are many ways you, too, can be a good citizen. You can volunteer to help your family and neighbors. You can also be a good citizen by following rules at home and at school.

REVIEW What responsibilities come with having rights?

CITIZENSHIP

DEMOCRATIC VALUES
The Common Good

In the 1960s New Yorkers became worried about pollution in the Hudson River. Chemicals and wastes were being dumped into the river. Concerned people started an organization called Riverkeeper to clean up the Hudson and to stop it from becoming polluted again. To do its work, Riverkeeper depends on volunteers to report on problems. As boaters, fishers, and hikers travel up and down the Hudson, they report on any polluting they may see. Many of the polluters that Riverkeeper has stopped were discovered by volunteers. Because of the efforts of Riverkeeper, the Hudson River is much cleaner today.

Analyze the Value

❶ Why is protecting the Hudson River important for the common good?

❷ **Make It Relevant** What volunteer programs help people in your community?

Volunteers from Riverkeeper patrol the Hudson River, looking for possible sources of pollution.

How do national holidays, such as Independence Day, unite New Yorkers and other Americans?

Symbols of Pride

Good citizens also show patriotism for their country. **Patriotism** is love of one's country. Patriotic citizens of the United States honor important symbols of our nation, such as the United States flag. They participate in national holidays and celebrations, such as Independence Day, Memorial Day, and Flag Day.

Many citizens of New York show pride in their state by displaying the state flag. Some New Yorkers also like to sing the state song, "I Love New York." Words in the song tell how New Yorkers feel about their state:

> 66 . . . there's no place else on earth quite like New York . . . 99

REVIEW What are some ways New Yorkers show pride in their state?

REVIEW

1. **WHAT TO KNOW** What does it mean to be a United States citizen?

2. **VOCABULARY** Explain how an **immigrant** can become a **naturalized citizen**.

3. **CIVICS AND GOVERNMENT** What responsibilities are required of citizens by law?

4. **CRITICAL THINKING** Why is voting both a right and a responsibility?

5. **CRITICAL THINKING** How can citizens help make decisions and solve problems at the national, state, and local level?

6. **VOLUNTEER** Think of tasks with which your teachers could use help.

Volunteer to help them complete these tasks.

7. **(Focus Skill) CAUSE AND EFFECT** On a separate sheet of paper, copy and complete this graphic organizer.

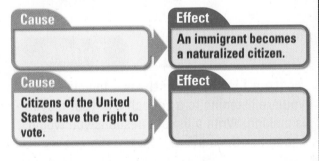

Cause	Effect
	An immigrant becomes a naturalized citizen.

Cause	Effect
Citizens of the United States have the right to vote.	

Chapter Review

Summarize the Chapter

Focus Skill **Cause and Effect** Complete this graphic organizer to show that you understand the causes and effects of government and citizenship in New York.

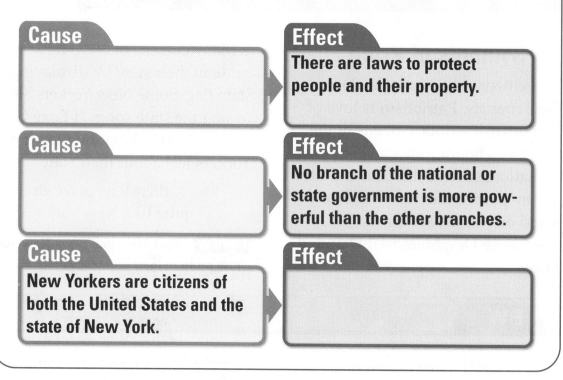

Cause

Effect
There are laws to protect people and their property.

Cause

Effect
No branch of the national or state government is more powerful than the other branches.

Cause
New Yorkers are citizens of both the United States and the state of New York.

Effect

THINK & WRITE

Write a List of Questions   Imagine that you are listening to a speech that your mayor is making. Write a list of questions you would like to ask the mayor.

Write a Song   Many patriotic songs have been written about the United States. Think of some things that make the United States special, and then write a song to honor the nation.

USE VOCABULARY

Use a term from this list to complete each of the sentences that follow.

democracy (p. 190)
federal government (p. 198)
trustees (p. 204)
naturalized citizen (p. 207)

1 In order to become a ____, an immigrant must take an oath to be loyal to the United States.

2 One way that New Yorkers take part in the ____ is by electing United States senators.

3 In a ____, the people rule.

4 In villages, the ____ help make laws.

RECALL FACTS

Answer these questions.

5 What is the job of New York's legislative branch?

6 What are the three branches of the federal government?

7 Who are some of the elected officials in a county government?

8 What rights do citizens of New York have?

Write the letter of the best choice.

9 **TEST PREP** The federal government makes decisions that affect—
  A only New Yorkers.
  B all the people in the United States.
  C all the people in the Northern Hemisphere.
  D only New York mayors.

10 **TEST PREP** When adults become naturalized citizens of the United States, their children under 18 years of age—
  F must take an oath to be loyal to the United States.
  G can vote in elections.
  H are asked to volunteer in schools and hospitals.
  J become citizens also.

THINK CRITICALLY

11 Why are there different levels of government in New York?

12 What role in the federal government do you think you would like to have? Explain why.

13 Why is it important for citizens to act responsibly?

14 What are some ways in which people can volunteer in New York?

APPLY SKILLS

Read a Flow Chart

15 Make a flow chart that shows what you do to get ready for school each morning. First, on a separate strip of paper, write each step you follow. Next, put the strips in order. Last, connect the strips with arrows.

Make Economic Choices

16 Suppose you must choose between buying a CD and going to a movie. How would you make this economic choice? Use the steps you read about on page 206 to help you make your choice.

FIELD TRIP

READ ABOUT

The New York State Capitol

When you see the roof of the New York state capitol, you might be reminded of the state motto, *Excelsior*, which means "Ever Upward." When the capitol opened in 1899, it was one of the largest government buildings of its time. Its three main staircases are decorated with stone carvings. There are more than 500 rooms in the capitol, including the Assembly Chamber, the Senate Chamber, and the Executive Chamber.

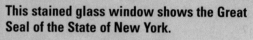

This stained glass window shows the Great Seal of the State of New York.

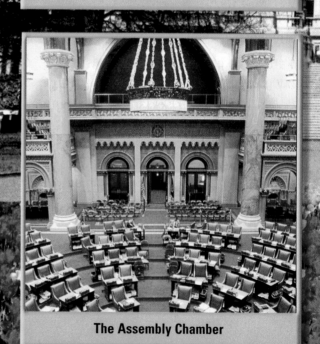

The Assembly Chamber

FIND

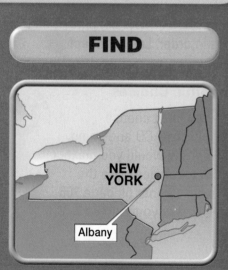

NEW YORK

Albany

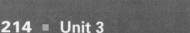

The Great Western Staircase took 14 years to build.

This stone sculpture of Frederick Douglass is one of 77 such faces inside the capitol.

The Executive Chamber was once the office of the governor. Today it is used mostly for special events.

A VIRTUAL TOUR

 **GO** **ONLINE** For more resources, go to www.harcourtschool.com/ss1

VISUAL SUMMARY

Write a List Study the pictures below to help you review Unit 3. Then write a list of people, places, and events that relate to each picture. Include at least three items in each list.

USE VOCABULARY

Use each of the following words in a sentence about the Revolutionary War or the new United States government.

1 **Parliament** (p. 156)

2 **Patriot** (p. 158)

3 **Loyalist** (p. 159)

4 **independence** (p. 164)

5 **democracy** (p. 190)

6 **budget** (p. 192)

7 **justice** (p. 195)

8 **Cabinet** (p. 199)

RECALL FACTS

Answer these questions.

9 Why did some escaped slaves help the British during the Revolutionary War?

10 What was the Buttonwood Agreement?

11 How is the government of New York City organized?

Write the letter of the best choice.

12 **TEST PREP** During the Revolutionary War, the first fighting in New York took place at —
A Fort Ticonderoga.
B Albany.
C Manhattan.
D Saratoga.

13 **TEST PREP** Why was New York so important during the war?
F George Washington always met colonial leaders there.
G All of the Patriots' supplies were there.
H Its location was useful.
J Many Loyalists lived in Albany.

Time

1750   1760   1770

1765 New York's Sons of Liberty is founded p. 158

1776 The Battle of Long Island is fought p. 173

1777 New York's first constitution is written p. 166

14 TEST PREP The United States Constitution makes the three branches of government equal so that—

A each branch has the same number of members.

B one branch cannot rule over the other branches.

C the branches can take turns ruling the nation.

D the President can rule over all three branches.

THINK CRITICALLY

15 Why do you think the British government believed it had the right to tax the colonists?

16 Why might some colonists have remained loyal to Britain during the Revolutionary War?

17 How would your community be different if none of its citizens volunteered?

APPLY SKILLS

Compare Maps with Different Scales

Use the two maps on this page to answer the following questions.

18 Which map would you use to find the movement of troops?

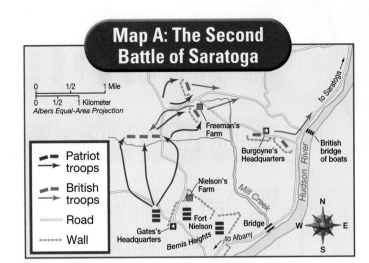

Map A: The Second Battle of Saratoga

Map B: The Second Battle of Saratoga

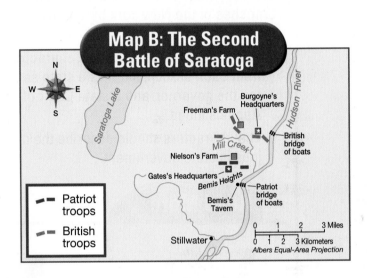

19 Which map shows the distance from Stillwater to Nielson's Farm?

20 Which map could you use to find the wall around Fort Nielson?

1780   1790   1800

1783 The American Revolution ends and the British leave New York p. 178

1789 George Washington becomes President of the United States p. 184

1792 The New York Stock Exchange is formed p. 185

Activities

Show What You Know

Unit Writing Activity

Write a Scene Write a scene in which the main characters are from different branches of the New York State government.

- There should be at least one character from each branch, such as a state senator, the governor, and a state Court of Appeals judge.
- The characters should describe their jobs in state government.

Unit Project

Honor a Hero Complete your presentation about a New York hero from the American Revolution.

- Write a speech about the hero, telling about the person's heroic deeds.
- You may also reenact an event from the war that involves your hero.
- Videotape your presentation and invite others to watch it, or perform the presentation live for them.

Read More

- *A More Perfect Union* by Betsy and Giulio Maestro. Harper Trophy.

- *The Big Tree* by Bruce Hiscock. Boyds Mills Press.

- *Charlotte* by Janet Lunn. Tundra Books.

GO ONLINE For more resources, go to www.harcourtschool.com/ss1

Becoming the Empire State

The Big Idea

Progress

Human activities and historical events caused New York to grow and change over time.

What to Know

- ✓ How did changes in transportation, communication, and technology help New York grow and change?

- ✓ What role did New York play in the Civil War?

- ✓ How did industrialization change New York?

- ✓ How did immigration and urbanization change New York?

Grand Central Terminal, New York City

Becoming the Empire State

Reading Social Studies

(Focus Skill) Compare and Contrast

Why It Matters Being able to compare and contrast people, places, objects, and events can help you understand how they are alike and how they are different.

When you **compare**, you tell how two or more things are alike, or similar. When you **contrast**, you tell how they are different.

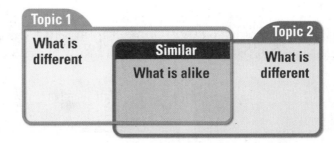

Topic 1 — What is different
Similar — What is alike
Topic 2 — What is different

- *Like, both, all, also, too, similar,* and *same* are words that compare.
- *But, instead, unlike, however, different,* and *differ* are words that contrast.

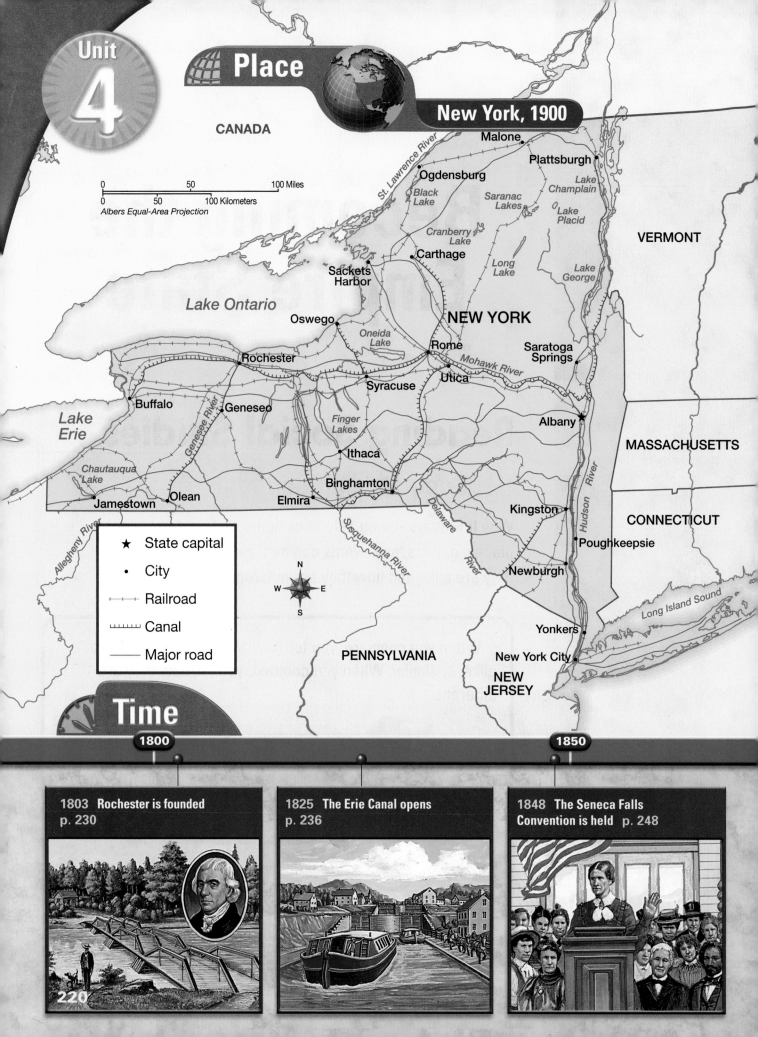

CANADA

0   50   100 Miles

0   50   100 Kilometers

Albers Equal-Area Projection

St. Lawrence River

Malone

Plattsburgh

Ogdensburg

Black Lake

Saranac Lakes

Lake Champlain

Cranberry Lake

Lake Placid

VERMONT

Carthage

Long Lake

Lake George

Sackets Harbor

Lake Ontario

Oswego

Oneida Lake

NEW YORK

Rome

Saratoga Springs

Rochester

Mohawk River

Utica

Syracuse

Buffalo

Genesee River

Geneseo

Finger Lakes

Albany

MASSACHUSETTS

Lake Erie

Ithaca

Chautauqua Lake

Binghamton

Elmira

Olean

Delaware River

Kingston

Hudson River

CONNECTICUT

Jamestown

Susquehanna River

Poughkeepsie

Newburgh

Long Island Sound

N
W   E
S

Legend

★ State capital

• City

⊢⊢⊢ Railroad

⊥⊥⊥ Canal

— Major road

Allegheny River

Yonkers

PENNSYLVANIA

New York City

NEW JERSEY

Time

1800

1850

1803   Rochester is founded
p. 230

1825   The Erie Canal opens
p. 236

1848   The Seneca Falls
Convention is held   p. 248

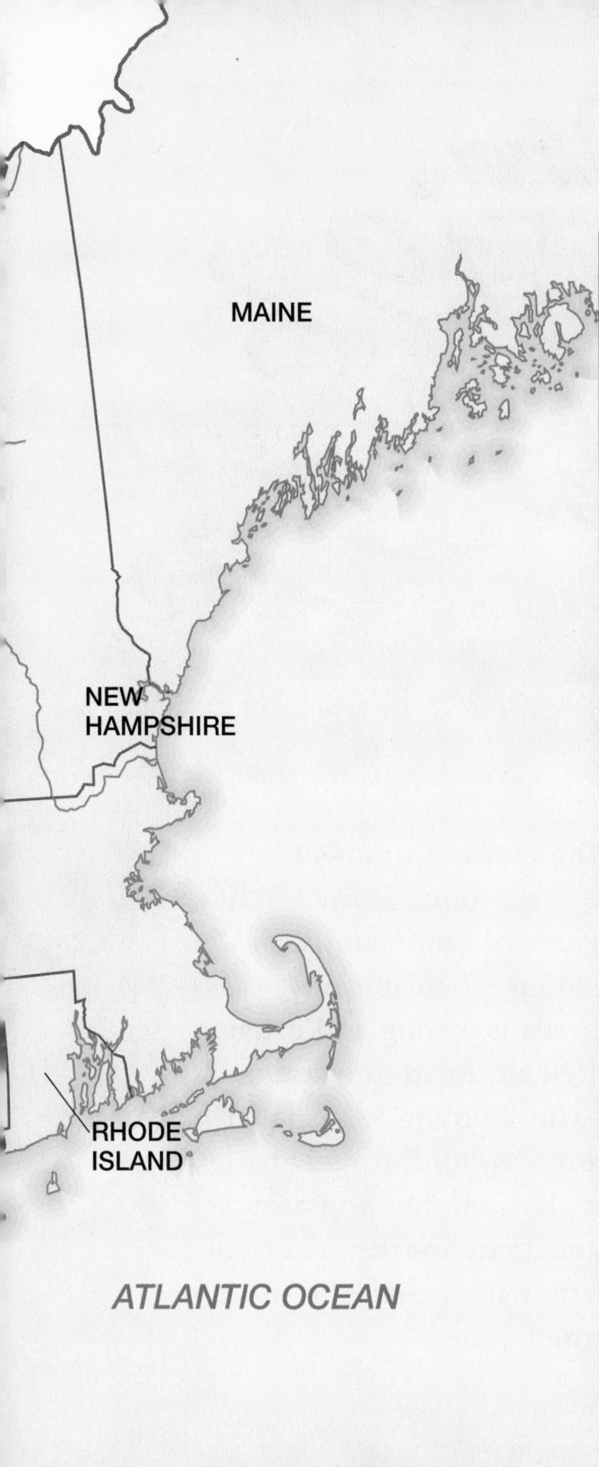

MAINE

NEW
HAMPSHIRE

RHODE
ISLAND

ATLANTIC OCEAN

People

DeWitt Clinton

1769–1828

- Governor of New York who helped plan the Erie Canal
- Federalist party candidate for President of the United States in 1812

Frederick Douglass

1818–1895

- Escaped from slavery when he was 20 years old
- Became world-famous for writing and speaking against slavery

Elizabeth Cady Stanton

1815–1902

- Women's rights leader who organized the Seneca Falls Convention
- Helped start the National Woman's Suffrage Association

1900

1950

1904 New York City's first subway opens p. 279

1905 Buffalo's first steel mill is built p. 262

1931 The Empire State Building opens p. 280

When Jessie Came Across the Sea

by Amy Hest
illustrated by P.J. Lynch

In the 1800s millions of people came to the United States in search of opportunity and freedom. Their journey across the sea was long and often difficult. Read now about Jessie, a young Jewish girl from Central Europe. She left her grandmother and a small village home for the chance to have a new life across the sea in the United States.

A week passed quickly, then two more, as Grandmother prepared Jessie for her journey. The morning the ship was to sail, it rained so hard there was no telling where the sky met the sea. "America! Good things await you there," Grandmother had promised.

Jessie stood at the rail, holding her hat against the wind and the rain. At her feet was a small trunk, packed with a few simple clothes and layers of lace. In Jessie's pocket was the tiny silver box with a tiny lace lining, but her mother's wedding band was not inside.

"Keep it safe for me, Grandmother," she had whispered as they kissed good-bye.

"Grandmother!" she called. But the boat slipped away from the dock, then into the channel and on toward the sea. Umbrellas faded in the mist. Rain pelted Jessie's face. It slid down the back of her collar.

> **channel**   a deep part of a river or harbor

Later, she sat on her trunk and cried. Passengers pitied the girl with the auburn hair and ginger-colored freckles. But what could they do? Crammed together and fearful, speaking strange languages, huddling close to keep warm, what could they do for Jessie?

The ship sailed west for many days.

At first it was stormy. Jessie lay curled on a mat, too ill to eat, too ill to sleep. She thought about Grandmother in the hut with the slanting roof, eating her soup alone.

On the fourth morning the sun came up and the passengers dried out.

They played cards and sang, and sometimes they argued. But mostly they talked, swapping stories and dreams. Dreams of America, where the streets were paved with gold. America, land of plenty.

Jessie began sewing to pass the time. Just to touch the soft lace was like touching Grandma again.

A little girl with almond eyes climbed on Jessie's lap. They sang and played finger games. Then Jessie sewed lace, a tiny heart pocket for the girl's plain dress. Miss Almond Eyes danced.

An old woman came along in a tattered coat. Jessie sewed lace, a collar and cuffs, and soon that coat was grand.

almond narrow, slanted-shaped eyes
tattered ragged, falling apart

A boy named Lou—he was a shoemaker's son—watched as Jessie sewed lace.

"How do you do?" he asked, tipping his hat.

Jessie smiled.

Lou took patches of leather from his splintered crate. He stitched shoes for a baby, who cried when his mother put them on his fat baby feet.

This time Jessie laughed.

Later, Lou and Jessie walked on the deck and talked. They shared black bread as the ship rolled and pitched in the wide, wide sea.

On a fine fall day they sailed past the Statue of Liberty. America! No one swapped stories or argued. Babies hushed. Even the oldest passengers, and the most seasick, stood against the rail. America!

And there it was, New York City with those tall, tall buildings that touched the sky.

Grandmother! Jessie thought.

If only you could see what I see now!

Response Corner

1. **Compare and Contrast** What did passengers do on the ship to pass the time?

2. How do you think travelers felt when they saw the Statue of Liberty?

3. **Make It Relevant** How would you feel if you moved to another country?

STUDY SKILLS

ORGANIZE INFORMATION

Graphic organizers can help you organize information.

- **Graphic organizers help you categorize, or group, information.**

- **Putting people, places, and events into categories makes it easier to find facts and understand what you read.**

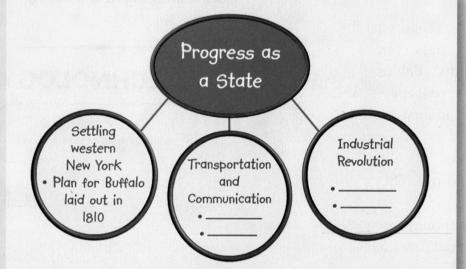

Progress as a State

Settling western New York
• Plan for Buffalo laid out in 1810

Transportation and Communication
• _____
• _____

Industrial Revolution
• _____
• _____

Erie Canal Village, Rome

Progress as a State

The Changing Frontier

1800   1850   1900   1950

1800–1825

WHAT TO KNOW
What parts of New York changed quickly after the American Revolution?

VOCABULARY

frontier p. 228

migration p. 228

land speculator p. 229

profit p. 229

turnpike p. 231

impress p. 232

COMPARE AND CONTRAST

YOU ARE THERE
"Wake up," your mother calls. "The sun is rising." You usually go to the barn early in the morning to get fresh eggs and milk. Then you spend the rest of the day helping with the farming. Tonight you have to complete some unfinished chores. Life in western New York requires hard work and a strong spirit.

Settling the Western Lands

After the American Revolution, thousands of people began moving to New York's western frontier. A **frontier** is land that lies beyond settled areas. This **migration**, or large movement of people, quickly changed life in the state.

The Genesee County Village and Museum

Under British rule, New York's western frontier had been set aside for Native Americans. The American Revolution, however, had weakened most tribes. New York's new state government forced tribes to agree to treaties that took away their remaining land. In return, the state set aside new places for Native Americans to live and work.

Reservations were started near Cayuga, Oneida, and Onondaga Lakes. Farther west, there were reservations at Allegany, Buffalo Creek, Cattaraugus (ka•tuh•RAW•guhs), and Tonawanda (tah•nuh•WAHN•duh).

The state sold most of the frontier lands to settlers—often in small sections at a very low price. Wealthy businesspeople, called land speculators (SPEK•yuh•lay•terz), also bought land from the state. A **land speculator** is a person who buys land at a low price with the hope of selling it later for a higher price. Unlike most settlers, land speculators often bought thousands of acres of land. Their goal was to sell it for a profit. In business, **profit** is the money left over after all costs have been paid.

A few land companies owned by speculators bought land directly from Native American tribes. The Holland Land Company, for example, wanted to buy much of the land west

Many Senecas, including Red Jacket, were unhappy with the Big Tree Treaty.

of the Genesee River from the Seneca Indians. A leader named Red Jacket warned his tribe not to sell its land. However, the other leaders signed the Big Tree Treaty, which let the company buy almost all of the Senecas' land.

At the Big Tree meeting, some of the land was set aside for Native Americans. Some land along the Genesee River was given to Mary Jemison. Jemison was a settler who years earlier had been captured by Native Americans and raised as a Seneca. Jemison's land was named the Gardeau Reservation.

FAST FACT
The Senecas gave Mary Jemison the name Dehgewanus. It means "Two Falling Voices."

REVIEW Why do you think New York sold frontier lands at low prices?

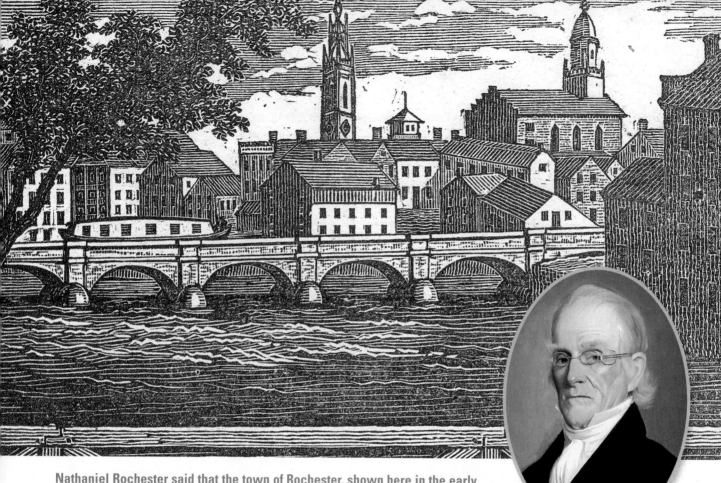

Nathaniel Rochester said that the town of Rochester, shown here in the early 1800s, "[had] sprung up like a mushroom." This was in part because the Genesee River "contributed so bountifully to [its] canals and mill-dams."

Western Movement Continues

As people continued to move west, new towns sprang up in central and western New York. In 1784, Hugh White founded Whitestown in Oneida County. In the 1780s, other pioneers set up a trading post and saltworks at the former capital of the Iroquois Confederacy. This settlement later became the city of Syracuse. Judge William Cooper helped found Cooperstown at the southern tip of Otsego Lake. Utica, along the Mohawk River, became a village in 1798. Utica became the starting point for the Genesee Road. Thousands of settlers used that road to reach their new land on the frontier.

Joseph Ellicott, who worked for the Holland Land Company, laid out a plan for Buffalo in 1801. Two years later Colonel Nathaniel Rochester and two partners settled near the falls of the Genesee River. They drew up plans for Rochester.

Over time, as more people moved west, towns such as Rochester grew larger. People built sawmills to cut trees into lumber and gristmills to grind wheat into flour. They built more homes and started new businesses and farms. They also built markets and schools.

REVIEW How did central and western New York change as more people moved there?

Building Early Roads

As New York grew, people in the state needed better ways to travel. They also needed faster, cheaper ways to take their crops, lumber, and other goods to market. In the early 1800s private companies built roads called **turnpikes** and charged people to use them. A long pole, or pike, blocked the entrance to each section of road. When a traveler paid the toll, a company worker turned the pike to let the traveler pass.

By 1809 two separate turnpikes crossed New York State. However, these turnpikes were narrow and bumpy. In wet weather, the unpaved roads became so muddy that wagons could not use them at all. Some people traveled the roads by sleigh, but that was possible only in the winter. The roads were so bad that few people moved into the towns along them.

Other roads linked communities such as Oswego, Bath, Ithaca, and Auburn to the main routes or to each other.

By 1822, about 4,000 miles (6,437 km) of highway crossed central and western New York. However, like earlier roads, these roads were often muddy and rough. Travel on them was difficult.

REVIEW Why was travel on New York's early roads often difficult?

Another War with Britain

In the early 1800s, longtime enemies Britain and France were at war with each other again. Neither country wanted the United States to trade with the other. Both the British and French captured American trading ships.

• GEOGRAPHY •

The Great Western Turnpike

Understanding Environment and Society

The Great Western Turnpike, which is today known as U.S. Route 20, is one of New York's oldest roads. Recently, the state celebrated the road's 200th anniversary. The road began as an Iroquois trading path. It was later used by settlers moving upstate and to lands in western New York. The first part of the road connected Albany to Cherry Valley—a distance of 52 miles (84 km).

The Battle of Lake Champlain was the last battle of the War of 1812 to be fought in New York.

British sailors **impressed**, or forced, American sailors to work on British ships. In June 1812, Congress declared war on Britain. The War of 1812 began.

Because Britain still controlled Canada, many battles took place along the New York–Canada border. British troops attacked New York cities, including Ogdensburg, Sackets Harbor, Buffalo, and Black Rock. The Americans and British fought battles on Lake Erie and Lake Champlain. The War of 1812 ended three years later.

REVIEW What caused the War of 1812?

REVIEW

1. **WHAT TO KNOW** What parts of New York changed quickly after the American Revolution?

2. **VOCABULARY** Why were New York's early roads called **turnpikes**?

3. **GEOGRAPHY** Why did so many battles of the War of 1812 take place in New York?

4. **CRITICAL THINKING** Why do you think the War of 1812 is often called the "Second War for Independence"?

5. **DRAW A MAP** Draw a map of a town in New York's western frontier. Show what you will build to help settlers live a good life in your town.

6. **COMPARE AND CONTRAST** On a separate sheet of paper, copy and complete this graphic organizer.

Topic 1
Frontier settlers

Similar

Topic 2
Wealthy land speculators

The Erie Canal

1800   1850   1900   1950

1800–1835

WHAT TO KNOW 💡
What problems did New York leaders believe the Erie Canal would solve?

VOCABULARY
canal p. 233
lock p. 233
aqueduct p. 235

COMPARE AND CONTRAST
Focus Skill

YOU ARE THERE

It's November 4, 1825. You're celebrating the opening of the new waterway built across the state. "Governor Clinton deserves a lot of credit for sticking with the project," you tell a friend. "I didn't think he could get it built." President Thomas Jefferson once called the plan "a little short of madness."

Planning and Building the Canal

In the early 1800s, the best way to move people and goods was on the state's waterways. A group of people led by DeWitt Clinton of New York City suggested building a canal across the state. A **canal** is a waterway dug across land.

Building the Erie Canal was a daring and expensive idea. Workers would have to cut it through more than 350 miles of forests and hills. The canal would link Buffalo, on Lake Erie, with Troy, on the Hudson River. From Troy, boats could sail down the Hudson River to New York City and the Atlantic Ocean.

Clinton knew that linking Lake Erie and the Hudson River would increase trade. He helped plan the canal's route and the system of locks that would make the canal work. A **lock** is a section of canal between two watertight gates. It works like an elevator.

DeWitt Clinton

When one gate is opened, water flows in and raises a boat to the level of the water ahead. Then the other gate opens, and the boat sails on. The process is reversed when a boat is to be lowered.

DeWitt Clinton convinced people that a canal could be built. In 1817 he became New York's governor. A short time later, on July 4, 1817, work on the canal began. It started in the middle, between Utica and Rome. This was one of the easiest parts of the canal to build, but it still took two years to complete. From that part, construction moved both east and west.

The Erie Canal was one of the greatest building projects in history. Nothing like it had ever been done before. There were no bulldozers, trucks, or power tools at the time. Many workers were local people. Other workers were immigrants from European countries such as Ireland and Germany. Workers dug with shovels and moved soil and rock in wheelbarrows. Horses and mules pulled wagons to haul supplies in and carry dirt out.

Workers often had to figure out what to do—and how to do it—as they went along. As problems came up, they had to invent new ways to solve them. Their inventions included a better system

A CLOSER LOOK
The Erie Canal

Lake Erie's elevation is nearly 600 feet (183 m) higher than the Hudson River's. To move between the lake and the river, boats must be raised or lowered in locks. After a boat enters the lock, the gates close behind the boat. The water level inside the lock is then raised or lowered. When the water level matches the water level ahead of the lock, the gate at the far end opens and the boat goes on its way.

❶ gates controlled by balance beam
❷ watertight gates
❸ towing rope
❹ canal towpath

◈ How were boats moved through the lock?

of locks, a way to pull up tree stumps, and a special kind of concrete that could harden under water.

The eastern part of the Erie Canal was finished first. It reached the Hudson River in 1823. The western part of the canal reached Lake Erie at Buffalo in 1825.

When the whole Erie Canal was completed, it was 363 miles (584 km) long and 40 feet (12 m) wide. There were 83 locks that moved boats through a change in elevation of 565 feet (172 m). Eighteen **aqueducts** (A•kwuh•duhkts) acted as water bridges to carry the canal over rivers, streams, and swamps.

REVIEW Why was the Erie Canal built?

The Erie Canal Song

Thomas S. Allen wrote the Erie Canal Song in 1905. The song was written to protest the fact that machines were going to replace mules in pulling the boats. Today many New Yorkers learn the Erie Canal Song, also called "Low Bridge."

I've got a mule, her name is Sal,
Fifteen miles on the Erie Canal.
She's a good ol' worker and a good ol'
  pal,
Fifteen miles on the Erie Canal.
We've hauled some barges in our day,
Filled with lumber, coal, and hay,
And we know ev'ry inch of the way,
From Albany to Buffalo.

Chorus:
Low bridge, ev'rybody down!
Low bridge, for we're comin' to a town!
And you'll always know your neighbor,
You'll always know your pal,
If you've ever navigated on the Erie
  Canal!

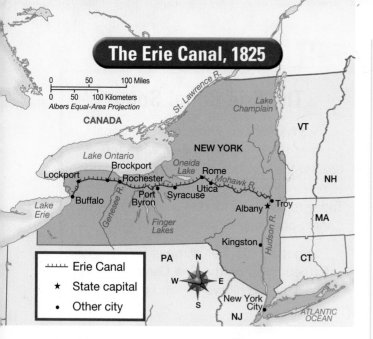

The Erie Canal, 1825

0 50 100 Miles
0 50 100 Kilometers
Albers Equal-Area Projection

Erie Canal
★ State capital
• Other city

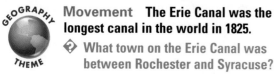

Movement **The Erie Canal was the longest canal in the world in 1825.**

❓ **What town on the Erie Canal was between Rochester and Syracuse?**

The Canal Causes Growth

The Erie Canal officially opened on October 26, 1825. Suddenly, shipping goods across the state was twice as fast and ten times as cheap. Before the canal, it had cost about $100 to ship a ton of goods from Buffalo to New York City. Now the same trip cost $10 or less.

People in western and central New York used the canal to ship their goods to the East. Factories in eastern New York used the canal to ship their products west.

Using the Erie Canal, businesses could make more money. More people started businesses and farms in New York. New York quickly became a major wheat-growing region. The state's lumber industry also grew.

New towns, such as Port Byron, Lockport, and Brockport, grew up along the canal. The populations of Albany, Utica, Syracuse, Buffalo, and Rochester increased. Rochester, which became known as "The Flour City," became a center for grinding wheat into flour. The flour was shipped on the Erie Canal to New York City. This kind of trade helped make New York City the busiest port in the country.

The populations of counties along the canal's route more than tripled. Today, nearly four out of every five people in central and western New York live within 25 miles (40 km) of the canal.

On November 4, 1825, Governor DeWitt Clinton celebrated the opening of the Erie Canal by pouring water from Lake Erie into the Atlantic Ocean. This ceremony was called "The Marriage of the Waters." Clinton poured the water from this barrel.

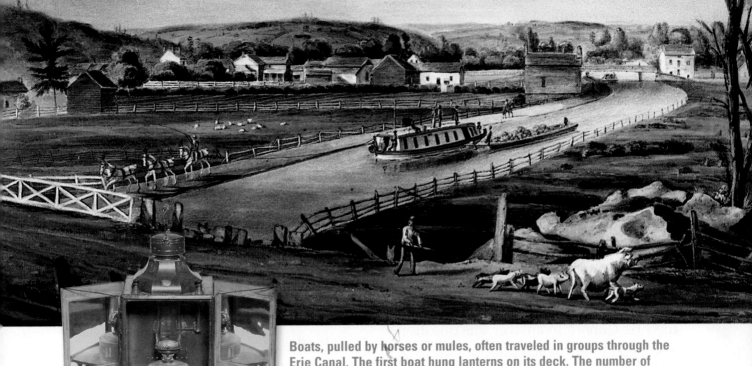

Boats, pulled by horses or mules, often traveled in groups through the Erie Canal. The first boat hung lanterns on its deck. The number of lanterns showed how many boats were traveling together.

The state of New York soon built more canals. These smaller canals connected more New York cities and waterways with the Erie Canal. By 1835 the Erie Canal was so busy that leaders decided to make it wider and deeper.

This allowed more boats to use it. Later the Erie Canal and the smaller canals were renamed the New York State Barge Canal System.

REVIEW How did the Erie Canal help businesses in New York grow?

REVIEW

1. **WHAT TO KNOW** What problems did New York leaders believe the Erie Canal would solve?

2. **VOCABULARY** Explain the difference between a **canal** and an **aqueduct**.

3. **GEOGRAPHY** Why were locks needed on the Erie Canal?

4. **CRITICAL THINKING** How might New York be different today if the Erie Canal had never been built?

5. **WRITE A NEWS STORY** Imagine that you are reporting on the grand opening of the Erie Canal. Write a news story describing the events you see. Use quotes from people who are there.

6. **COMPARE AND CONTRAST** On a separate sheet of paper, copy and complete this graphic organizer.

Topic 1
Albany

Similar

Topic 2
Rochester

Read a Double-Bar Graph

VOCABULARY

double-bar graph

> **WHY IT MATTERS**

What cities in New York grew the most as a result of the building of the Erie Canal? To answer this question you need to know the populations of some cities before and after the canal was built. A good way to compare two sets of information is to study them on a double-bar graph. **Double-bar graphs** are graphs that compare two sets of numbers. By studying the double-bar graph, you can learn how the populations of the cities changed.

> **WHAT YOU NEED TO KNOW**

The graph on this page compares the populations of some cities along the Erie Canal in 1820, before the canal was built, and in 1850, after the canal was built. Two different colors are used to show information for the two years. The key on the graph tells you that green bars stand for populations in 1820 and purple bars stand for populations in 1850.

The cities are listed across the bottom of the graph, and the populations are listed along the left-hand side. Find Syracuse at the bottom, and place your finger on the purple bar. Run your finger to the top of the bar and then to the left. Look at the closest number

to estimate the population of Syracuse in 1850.

> **PRACTICE THE SKILL**

Use the double-bar graph on this page to answer these questions.

① What was the population of Albany in 1820? in 1850?

② By about how much did the population of Buffalo increase?

③ Which city had the greatest population growth between 1820 and 1850?

> **APPLY WHAT YOU LEARNED**

Make a double-bar graph showing your test scores in social studies and in another subject. Make a key showing what each bar in your graph stands for.

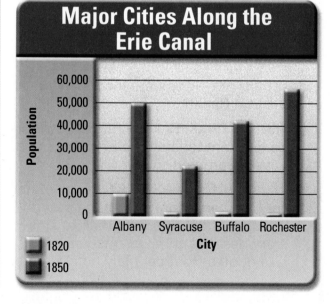

Major Cities Along the Erie Canal

Travel and Communication

1800 — 1850 — 1900 — 1950

1800–1870

WHAT TO KNOW
How did travel and communication in New York change in the early 1800s?

VOCABULARY
technology p. 239
locomotive p. 240
telegraph p. 242

COMPARE AND CONTRAST

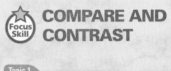

YOU ARE THERE

"Here it comes!" A big boat chugs around a bend in the Hudson River. Black smoke pours from its chimney. You and your sister wave your hats in the air. People wave back at you from the boat's deck. For the rest of the day, you dream about someday becoming a boat captain.

Traveling by Steamboat

As New York grew, people used new technologies to improve travel and communication. **Technology** is the use of new ideas and knowledge to do things.

Robert Fulton and others developed boats powered by steam engines. Fulton's first steamboat left New York City on August 17, 1807. Its engine turned two huge paddlewheels.

Robert Fulton's steamboat was useful for businesses because it was fast and could carry heavy loads.

Chapter 7 239

They pushed the boat through the water at about 5 miles (8 km) per hour. The trip from New York City to Albany took just 32 hours! This sounds slow today, but it was much faster than the four days it took sailboats to make the same trip.

Fulton renamed his ship the *Clermont*, after Livingston's home on the Hudson River in Columbia County. Soon the *Clermont* carried paying passengers along the Hudson River. Before long, larger and faster steamboats traveled on New York's rivers.

REVIEW How did steamboats change how people traveled in New York?

• SCIENCE AND TECHNOLOGY •

The *DeWitt Clinton*

The *DeWitt Clinton* was New York's first steam-powered locomotive. In a steam engine, water is heated to make steam. The steam, which is under great pressure, turns parts of the engine. The steam is then released through an opening. When the pressurized steam is released, it makes a "choo!" sound. This is where the "choo-choo" sound of a train comes from.

Traveling on Rails

Early steam engines were also used to power locomotives. A **locomotive** is a train engine used to move railroad cars.

The first railroad in New York was called the Mohawk and Hudson Railroad. Its 16-mile (26-km) track connected Albany and Schenectady.

On August 9, 1831, thousands of people gathered for the railroad's opening. Everyone waited with great excitement. When the *DeWitt Clinton* locomotive began moving down the tracks, the crowd cheered.

On its first trip the *DeWitt Clinton* pulled three passenger cars. It had to travel over steep hills. More than once, passengers were asked to leave the train and walk beside it while it went up a hill. Even with these delays, the train made the trip in about an hour. At times it reached speeds of as much as 30 miles (about 48 km) per hour!

Many people were curious to see the *DeWitt Clinton*, New York's first steam-powered locomotive.

At first, people saw railroads only as a way to help the canals, not replace them. The locks between Albany and Schenectady made that part of a canal trip very slow. To save time, a passenger might sail to Albany and then take a train from Albany to Schenectady. The passenger could then travel west on the Erie Canal from Schenectady.

The success of the Mohawk and Hudson Railroad led to a boom in the building of railroads. In 1833 a railroad opened between Schenectady and Saratoga Springs. By 1842, a person could travel all the way from Albany to Buffalo by train. To do that, a person had to use six different railroads. In 1853 Erastus Corning combined the rail lines into one company. It was called the New York Central Railroad.

People were slower to want railroads in the Hudson Valley because steamboats worked so well there. Still, by 1850 rail lines stretched along the Hudson River to Albany. By then, the state had 1,649 miles (2,654 km) of track, and another 1,000 miles (1,609 km) were

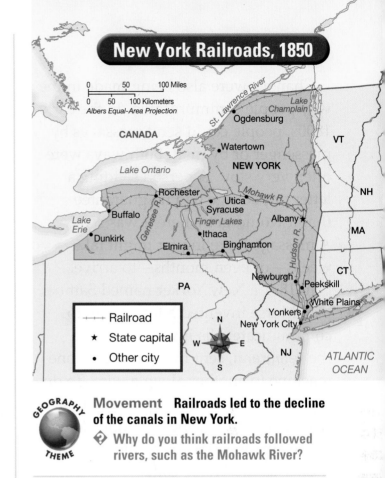

New York Railroads, 1850

Movement **Railroads led to the decline of the canals in New York.**

❖ Why do you think railroads followed rivers, such as the Mohawk River?

being built. Railroads gave people a fast, low-cost form of transportation. This helped businesses and trade in New York grow rapidly.

REVIEW **What effect did railroads have on life in New York?**

The Telegraph

Changes were also being made in the way people communicated. In the early 1800s, people could send messages by messenger or by mail. Both ways were often very slow. A person sending a letter or package had no guarantee that it would get where it was sent. A message traveling far might take weeks—or even months—to arrive.

In 1837 a New Yorker named Samuel F. B. Morse invented a faster way to communicate. His invention, called the **telegraph**, sent messages from one machine to another along a wire. To do this, Morse invented a code system in which dots and dashes stand for letters of the alphabet. We know the dots and dashes as the Morse code.

The telegraph sent those electronic dots and dashes across a wire. At the other end an operator translated them back into letters and words. On May 24, 1844, Morse sent the first long-distance telegraph message. It traveled 35 miles (56 km) between Washington, D.C., and Baltimore, Maryland.

Suddenly, messages that once took days or weeks to send took only seconds! Before long, telegraph lines connected places all over New York and the nation. By 1861 a telegraph wire connected California to states on the East Coast of the United States.

Soon people and businesses wanted a way to communicate across the ocean. New York business owner Cyrus Field led the project of laying a telegraph cable across the Atlantic Ocean.

The telegraph allowed news to travel faster than people could. Here, Samuel F. B. Morse (seated) shows how the telegraph works.

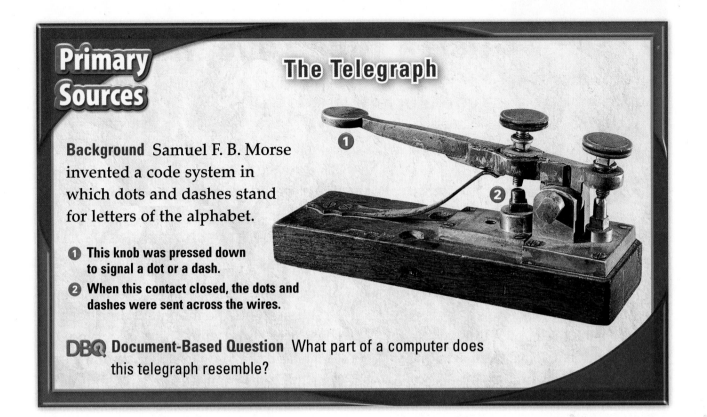

Primary Sources

The Telegraph

Background Samuel F. B. Morse invented a code system in which dots and dashes stand for letters of the alphabet.

① This knob was pressed down to signal a dot or a dash.

② When this contact closed, the dots and dashes were sent across the wires.

DBQ Document-Based Question What part of a computer does this telegraph resemble?

The cable broke twice, and another attempt worked for just one month.

By 1866, a working cable connected Europe and North America. The queen of England and the United States President exchanged the first messages, and people around the world celebrated the new technology. A poet expressed the excitement of the moment:

> ❝'We are one!' said the nations, and hand met hand, in a thrill electric from land to land. ❞

REVIEW How did the telegraph change the way people communicated?

REVIEW

1. WHAT TO KNOW How did travel and communication in New York change in the early 1800s?

2. VOCABULARY Use the term **locomotive** in a sentence about the *DeWitt Clinton*.

3. HISTORY Why was boat travel difficult before Robert Fulton's steamboat?

4. CRITICAL THINKING In 1850, how would you have divided state spending between canals and railroads?

5. ✎ **WRITE A MESSAGE** Write a short message in Morse code. Swap messages with a partner.

6. (Focus Skill) **COMPARE AND CONTRAST** On a separate sheet of paper, copy and complete this graphic organizer.

Topic 1
Robert Fulton

Similar

Topic 2
Samuel F. B. Morse

Use a Time Zone Map

▶ WHY IT MATTERS

The coming of the railroad made it necessary to create a single way of keeping time. Before then, each town across the United States set its own time, using the sun as a guide. Clocks were set at noon, when the sun was highest in the sky. As Earth turns, however, it is noon in different places at different times. Because of this, the towns along train routes all had their own times. It was impossible for the railroads to make and keep schedules.

A group of people was asked to study the problem. The group decided to divide Earth into 24 time zones—one for each hour of the day. A **time zone** is a region in which people use the same time. To figure out the time anywhere in the United States, you can use a time zone map like the one on page 245.

All the people in a time zone use the same time.

▶ WHAT YOU NEED TO KNOW

The United States has six time zones. They are the eastern time zone, the central time zone, the mountain time zone, the Pacific time zone, the Alaska time zone, and the Hawaii-Aleutian time zone. Earth rotates from west to east, so time zones to the west of you always have an earlier time than your time zone. Houston, Texas, is in a time zone west of Rochester, so the time in Houston is earlier than the time in Rochester.

▶ PRACTICE THE SKILL

1 Find New York City on the time zone map. In which time zone is New York City?

2 Find the eastern time zone clock. What time does the clock show?

3 Find Omaha. It is in the central time zone. What time does the clock above this time zone show? When it is 10:00 A.M. in the eastern time zone, it is 9:00 A.M. in the central time zone. Moving west, you must subtract one hour as you enter each new time zone.

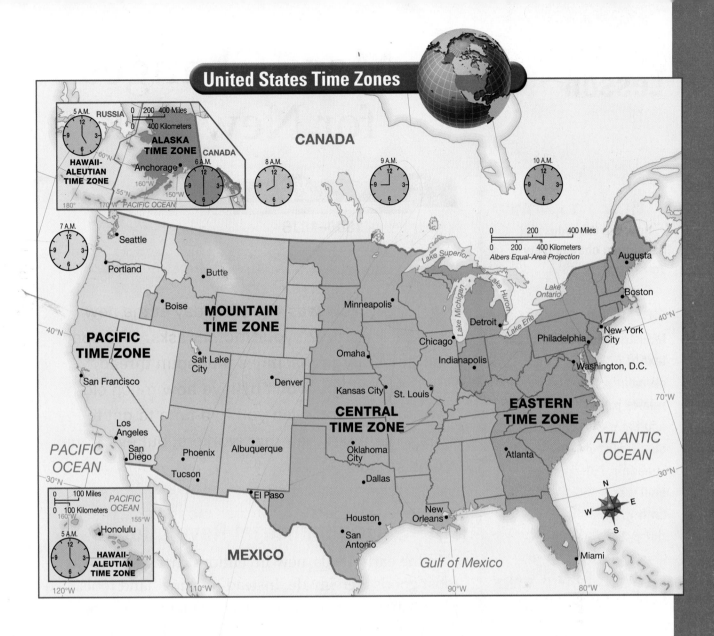

United States Time Zones

4. Now find Denver. In which time zone is it? When it is 8:00 A.M. in the mountain time zone, it is 9:00 A.M. in the central time zone. Moving east, you must add one hour as you enter each new time zone.

5. Imagine you are in San Francisco. Is the time earlier than, later than, or the same as the time in Chicago?

6. If it is 4:00 P.M. in Phoenix, what time is it in Washington, D.C.? in Seattle?

▶ APPLY WHAT YOU LEARNED

Look at a watch or a classroom clock. What time is it in your time zone? Now figure out what time it is in each of these cities:

Anchorage	Boston	Miami
Honolulu	Boise	Minneapolis

Practice your map and globe skills with the **GeoSkills CD-ROM**.

More Changes for New York

| 1800 | 1850 | 1900 | 1950 |

1800–1875

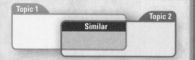

YOU ARE THERE

"How was your first day at the new factory?" your mother asks. "We spent all day at large machines that spun thread," you reply. "You won't believe how much cloth we made!" You wish you had time to get to know some of the other workers, but everyone was so busy.

The Industrial Revolution

In the early 1800s, new inventions changed the way most goods were made. Instead of using hand tools, people began to use machines to make many goods. So many machines were invented and put to use during this time that it became known as the **Industrial Revolution**.

Factory workers began to use machines to spin thread and to weave **textiles**, or cloth. The use of better sewing machines helped the **garment**, or clothing, industry grow. New York City became a center of that industry. It remains so today.

Other cities in New York became known for their industries, too. Syracuse developed a major salt

Workers in factories in New York made carpets, gloves, and woolen and cotton cloth.

Central Park
Understanding Environment and Society

By the mid-1800s New York City had become crowded. Some New Yorkers, such as writer William Cullen Bryant, wanted the center of Manhattan to be free of buildings. City leaders agreed and purchased 843 acres of land to build Central Park. Today, the park has a zoo, a museum, an ice-skating rink, tennis courts, and ball fields.

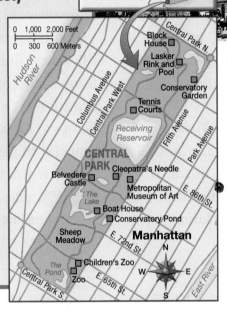

industry. Machine parts were made in Rochester, and iron products were made in Troy.

REVIEW **What was the Industrial Revolution?**

Changes in Society

Factories needed workers to run their machines, and many people moved to cities to find jobs. People from other countries were also moving to New York in great numbers. By 1850, New York had more people than any other state, and it led the nation in manufac-turing. Ten years later, New York City became the first city in the nation with more than a million people.

Leaders in New York City wanted to have an outdoor area where people could go to relax. In 1856, the city set aside land in Manhattan for a public park. Central Park, as it became known, opened in 1876.

Central Park was just one example of how New Yorkers worked to **reform**, or change for the better, the state. In 1812, the state legislature passed the Common School Act. It set up a system of free public schools in New York.

Another effort at reform had to do with women's rights. In the early 1800s the law usually gave a woman's husband control of her money and property. Women were not allowed to vote. They could not hold most jobs.

Lucretia Mott

Elizabeth Cady Stanton

Elizabeth Blackwell

Sojourner Truth

In 1848, Lucretia Mott and New Yorker Elizabeth Cady Stanton organized a women's rights convention at Seneca Falls. The delegates approved the Declaration of Sentiments, which said "All men *and women* are created equal." It was modeled after the Declaration of Independence.

Another woman from New York, Amelia Bloomer, soon became a famous women's rights reformer, too. Susan B. Anthony, who lived much of her life in Rochester, joined the cause later.

By the mid-1800s women were able to control their own property and money. They still could not vote. It would be many years before they won that right.

Some women found new careers. Elizabeth Blackwell became the first female doctor in the United States. She graduated from a medical college in Geneva, New York, in 1849. Blackwell worked to get all medical schools to admit women.

REVIEW Why was the Seneca Falls Convention important?

• BIOGRAPHY •

Susan B. Anthony   1820–1906

Character Trait: Perseverance

In 1826 Susan B. Anthony and her family moved from Massachusetts to New York. As an adult, Anthony looked for a way to help women gain the same rights that men had. One of these rights was the right to vote.

Anthony traveled across the country speaking in favor of women's rights. Some people made fun of Anthony or insulted her, but she kept working for what she believed in. The work of Anthony and women like her finally paid off. In 1920 all women in the United States were given the right to vote in all elections.

GO ONLINE For more resources, go to www.harcourtschool.com/ss1

Working to End Slavery

Many people who worked for women's rights also worked to **abolish**, or end, slavery. By 1827 New York had freed all enslaved people living there. However, slavery still existed in the Southern states.

People who wanted to abolish slavery in the United States were called **abolitionists** (a•buh•LIH•shuhn•ists). One way they spoke out against slavery was in newspapers. In 1827 Samuel Cornish started *Freedom's Journal* in New York City. It was the country's first African American newspaper. Another well-known abolitionist, Frederick Douglass, lived in Rochester. He published *The North Star*, an abolitionist newspaper, there.

New York-born Isabella Baumfree was one of the first African American women to speak out against slavery. In the 1840s she changed her name to Sojourner Truth. She traveled the country speaking against slavery.

Many abolitionists worked with the Underground Railroad. The Underground Railroad was not a railroad, and it was not underground. It was made up of secret routes along which runaway slaves could find safe stops on the way to the North and freedom.

Helping a slave escape was against the law. To keep from being caught, people used code words. "Stations" were places where

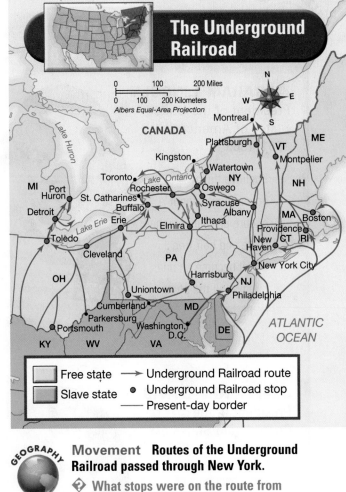

The Underground Railroad

0   100   200 Miles
0   100   200 Kilometers
Albers Equal-Area Projection

Free state
Slave state
→ Underground Railroad route
● Underground Railroad stop
— Present-day border

Movement Routes of the Underground Railroad passed through New York.

❓ What stops were on the route from Albany to Watertown?

slaves could hide, eat, rest, and get supplies. There were stations in homes and in churches all over New York.

People who led runaway slaves from station to station were called "conductors."

One of them was Harriet Tubman, a former slave. She lived in Auburn and led more than 300 slaves to freedom.

REVIEW How did some New Yorkers work to end slavery?

Frederick Douglass

CITIZENSHIP

POINTS OF VIEW
Slavery and States' Rights

ABRAHAM LINCOLN, President of the United States of America, 1861–1865

❝I believe this government cannot endure permanently half slave and half free . . . It will become all one thing or all the other . . . in all the States . . . North as well as South.❞

JEFFERSON DAVIS, President of the Confederate States of America, 1861–1865

❝The inhabitants of an organized Territory of the United States, like the people of a State . . . [must] decide for themselves whether slavery . . . shall be maintained or prohibited.❞

Analyze the Viewpoints

1 What did Abraham Lincoln believe would happen if some states remained free states, while others continued to allow slavery?

2 What did Jefferson Davis believe about the right of the states to decide for themselves whether they wanted to permit slavery?

3 **Make It Relevant** Abraham Lincoln was hoping to be a United States senator when he expressed this viewpoint on slavery in 1858. Do you think it is still important for leaders to hold debates on important issues before elections? Explain your answer.

New York and the Civil War

In March 1861 Abraham Lincoln became President of the United States. Many people in the South believed that Lincoln might outlaw slavery. Seven Southern states decided to **secede** (sih•SEED), or separate from, the United States. They formed a new nation called the Confederate States of America, or the Confederacy. Four other Southern states later joined the Confederacy.

In April 1861 Confederate soldiers fired on Fort Sumter in South Carolina. The fort was held by soldiers of the United States, or the Union. This battle was the beginning of the Civil War. A **civil war** is a war between two groups in the same country.

New York factories produced guns, ships, and uniforms. New York provided more money, supplies, and soldiers than any other state. Many of those soldiers were immigrants. In fact, one group of soldiers, the 39th Infantry, was made up of soldiers who had immigrated from Spain and Portugal.

Most New Yorkers supported the war, but many were upset when a military draft began. A **draft** is a way to force people into the military. Many New Yorkers believed the draft was unfair, because the men who were drafted but could pay a $300 fee did not have to serve.

In July 1863 **riots**, or violent protests, broke out in New York City. Rioters destroyed property and burned buildings. They attacked draft officials, police, and African Americans. They blamed African Americans for the war

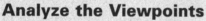

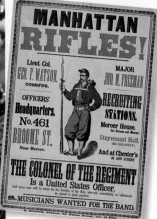

Members of the 8th New York State Militia posed for a photograph in 1861. Some people joined the military because of posters like the one above.

and the draft. After all, they were being asked to fight a war to help end slavery. After a week of riots, more than 100 people were dead and more than 300 others were injured. More than a million dollars' worth of property had been destroyed.

After more than four years of fighting, the Civil War finally came to an end in April 1865. The Union was saved, and slavery was ended everywhere in the United States.

REVIEW Why did many New Yorkers feel that the draft was unfair?

REVIEW

1. **WHAT TO KNOW** How did the Industrial Revolution change New York?

2. **VOCABULARY** Write a sentence explaining how the terms **reform** and **abolitionist** are related.

3. **HISTORY** Why did the Southern states secede from the Union?

4. **CRITICAL THINKING** Why do you think people were willing to risk their own safety or freedom to help slaves on the Underground Railroad?

5. **MAKE A MAP** Do research to find the locations of stops and other important parts of the Underground Railroad in New York. Make a map to record the information you find.

6. **COMPARE AND CONTRAST** On a separate sheet of paper, copy and complete this graphic organizer.

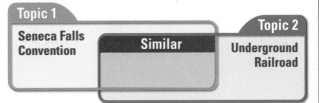

Topic 1
Seneca Falls Convention

Similar

Topic 2
Underground Railroad

Chapter Review

Summarize the Chapter

Focus Skill **Compare and Contrast** Complete this graphic organizer to compare and contrast inventions that changed New York during the 1800s.

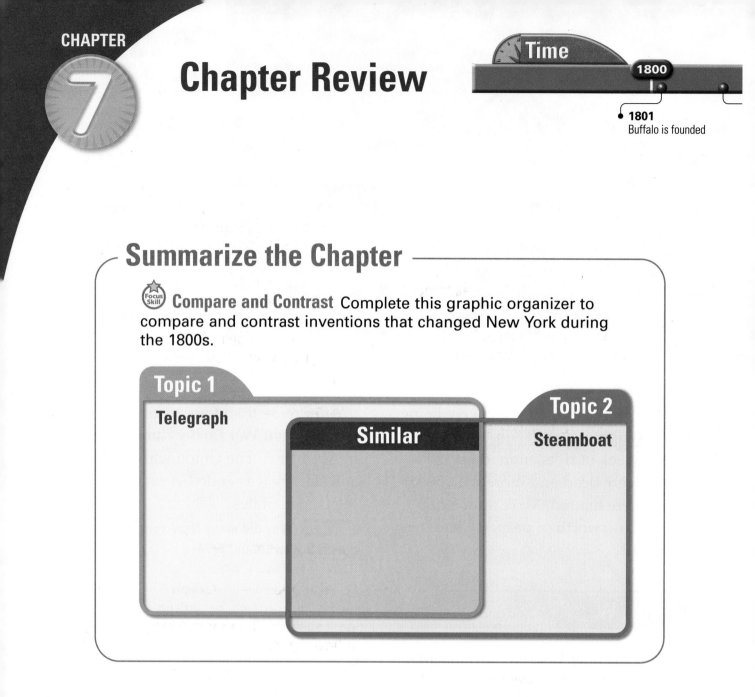

Topic 1

Telegraph

Similar

Topic 2

Steamboat

THINK & WRITE

Write a Travelogue Imagine that it is 1825 and you are on a boat traveling on the Erie Canal. Write a travelogue describing some of the people, places, and things you see on your journey. Be sure to include the names of cities that you visit.

Write a List of Questions Imagine that you are a newspaper reporter who has been sent to cover the Seneca Falls Convention. Write a list of questions that you would like to ask the convention's organizers.

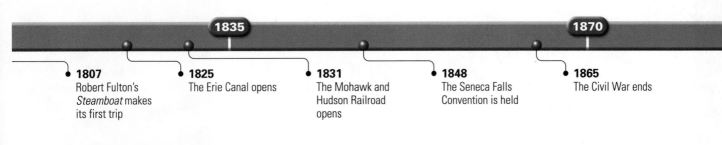

1807
Robert Fulton's
Steamboat makes
its first trip

1825
The Erie Canal opens

1831
The Mohawk and
Hudson Railroad
opens

1848
The Seneca Falls
Convention is held

1865
The Civil War ends

USE THE TIME LINE

Use the chapter summary time line to answer these questions.

1 How many years after Buffalo was founded did the Erie Canal open?

2 Was the Mohawk and Hudson Railroad built before or after the Civil War ended?

USE VOCABULARY

For each pair of terms, write a sentence that explains how the terms are related.

3 **land speculator** (p. 229), **profit** (p. 229)

4 **canal** (p. 233), **lock** (p. 233)

5 **technology** (p. 239), **telegraph** (p. 242)

6 **textiles** (p. 246), **garment** (p. 246)

7 **abolish** (p. 249), **abolitionist** (p. 249)

RECALL FACTS

Answer these questions.

8 What happened to Native Americans who were living in New York in the late 1700s?

9 How did the Civil War affect New Yorkers?

Write the letter of the best choice.

10 **TEST PREP** One of the advantages of railroad travel was that—
 A it was invented before steamboat travel.
 B the New York Central Railroad opened before the Erie Canal.
 C trains never broke down.
 D it gave people a fast, low-cost form of transportation.

11 **TEST PREP** One way New Yorkers tried to reform their state in the 1800s was by—
 F making British sailors work on American ships.
 G joining the Confederate States of America.
 H setting up a system of free public elementary schools.
 J giving women the right to vote.

THINK CRITICALLY

12 Why do you think the New York State government forced Native American tribes to give up most of their land?

13 How did the building of canals and railroads change where people lived in New York?

APPLY SKILLS

Read a Double Bar Graph
Study the double bar graph on page 238. Then answer the following questions.

14 What was the population of Rochester in 1820? in 1850?

15 By how much did the population of Albany increase?

Use a Time Zone Map
Use the time zone map on page 245 to answer the following questions.

16 If it is 9:00 A.M. in New York City, what time is it in San Francisco?

17 Imagine that you are in Miami. Is the time earlier than, later than, or the same as the time in New York City?

STUDY SKILLS

VOCABULARY

Using a dictionary can help you learn new words.

- A dictionary shows the meanings of a word and tells its origin, or where it came from.

- You can use a chart to organize unfamiliar words.

investor (in•ves′tər) *n.* [from the Latin *investire*, to cover with clothing] 1. Someone who spends money on a project with the hope of earning back more money in return.

Word	Syllables	Origin	Definition
investor	in•ves•tor	Latin	Someone who spends money on a project

Statue of Liberty, Liberty Island

Growth and Change

CHAPTER

8

Immigration and Migration

| 1800 | 1850 | 1900 | 1950 |

1840–1910

 WHAT TO KNOW
Why did many immigrants come to New York during the 1800s and early 1900s?

VOCABULARY
immigration p. 256
famine p. 257
discrimination p. 257

COMPARE AND CONTRAST
Focus Skill

| Topic 1 | | Topic 2 |
| | Similar | |

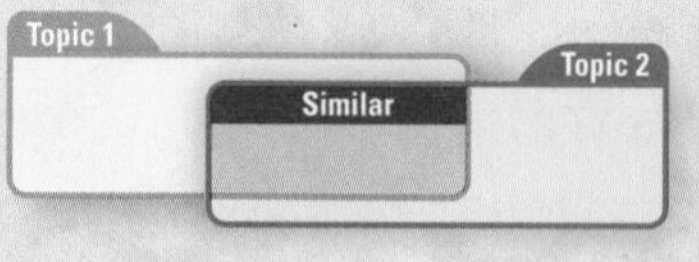

YOU ARE THERE

"Wait for us!" As you rush off the ship, your father tells you to head for the round building near the dock. Everyone must check in there before they can enter the United States. Your aunt and uncle will meet you outside of the building. It's a day you'll never forget.

The Great Irish Migration

From its very beginning, New York has attracted people from many different places. This **immigration**, or moving to one country from another, continued throughout the 1800s. Most immigrants came through the port of New York. Many of them made New York City their home.

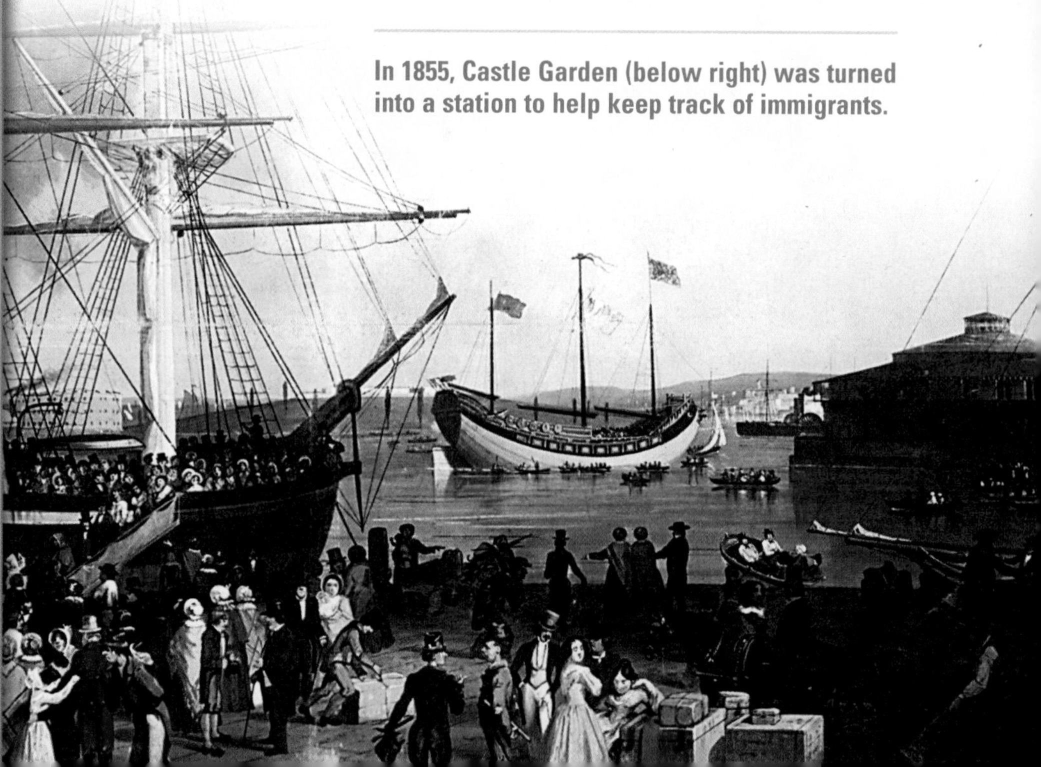

In 1855, Castle Garden (below right) was turned into a station to help keep track of immigrants.

In the early and middle 1800s, most immigrants came from western Europe. Many came from Ireland. Between 1845 and 1849 a disease killed most potato crops in Ireland. People called this time the Potato Famine. A **famine** (FA•min) is a time when food is limited and people starve. More than a million others left Ireland. Many of them moved to New York. In some parts of New York City, by 1855 one out of every four people had been born in Ireland.

REVIEW What was the Irish Potato Famine?

Challenges and Opportunities

Many immigrants in New York faced discrimination. **Discrimination** is the unfair treatment of people because of their background, religion, or race. Sometimes immigrants were not hired for certain jobs. Often they were made to live in separate neighborhoods.

Despite these hardships, many immigrants found better jobs and more freedom than they had in their homelands. Between 1840 and 1856 more than 3 million immigrants passed through the Port of New York. Nearly 17 million immigrants passed through the port between 1880 and 1919.

In the second half of the 1800s, most immigrants came from southern and eastern Europe, including Italy and Russia. Many of them were Catholics and Jews. Many came because of problems in their home countries.

As many as 500,000 African Americans left the South during the Great Migration.

Immigration to the United States, 1850–1890

Number of People / Year

Analyze Graphs Immigration to the United States increased greatly after the Civil War.

❖ About how many people immigrated to the United States in 1870?

Starting in the 1890s, large numbers of African Americans from the South moved to northern cities to find jobs in the factories there. This movement was called the Great Migration. By 1930 the African American population of New York State had doubled. The Harlem area of New York City became the largest African American community in the United States.

REVIEW What was the Great Migration?

The Statue of Liberty

Beginning in 1886 a new sight greeted immigrants who arrived in New York Harbor. It was the Statue of Liberty. The statue was a gift to the people of the United States from the people of France. Frédéric-Auguste Bartholdi (fray•day•REEK oh•GOOST bar•TAHL•dee) built the Statue of Liberty out of sheets of copper hammered over a steel frame. Alexandre-Gustave Eiffel (a•lek•SAHN•druh gus•TAHV EYE•fuhl), the same man who built the famous Eiffel Tower in Paris, France, built that frame.

It was up to the United States to raise the money needed to build a pedestal, or base, for the Statue of Liberty. New York newspaper publisher Joseph

New York quarter

Pulitzer (PU•luht•ser), an immigrant from Hungary, called on people to donate money. Many children helped by giving what was in their piggybanks. New Yorker Emma Lazarus (LAZ•uh•ruhs) wrote the famous poem that appears on the statue's base. Part of it reads:

> 66 **Give me your tired, your poor, Your huddled masses yearning to breathe free . . .** 99

The statue was too big to ship to New York in one piece, so it was taken apart and shipped in 214 crates. The Statue of Liberty arrived in New York on June 15, 1885. It took more than a year to put it back together and attach it to the pedestal. The statue was first shown to the public on October 28, 1886.

1876

1878

To build the Statue of Liberty, Frédéric-Auguste Bartholdi (left) made full-sized models of the parts of the statue. These models were made of wooden frames covered with plaster.

The head of the Statue of Liberty was put on display in Paris in 1878. People could pay to climb onto it. The money helped pay for the statue.

The statue became a symbol of hope for immigrants. Most had made the trip to the United States crammed into a ship's crowded steerage, or lowest level. There was little food and no privacy. Seeing the statue meant that the difficult voyage was almost over. A Polish man said,

> 66 The bigness of Mrs. Liberty overcame us. No one spoke a word for she was like a goddess and we knew she represented the . . . country which was to be our future home. 99

REVIEW Why was the Statue of Liberty important to immigrants?

A CLOSER LOOK
The Statue of Liberty

The Statue of Liberty was once the tallest monument in the world. The statue itself is 151 feet (46 m) high and stands on an 89-foot (27-m) pedestal.

1 The torch that Liberty holds stands for knowledge and truth.

2 The model for Liberty's face was Bartholdi's mother. Many people say the seven points on Liberty's crown represent the seven continents and the seven seas.

3 The statue's inner framework is made up of wrought-iron bars that cross each other diagonally to give the greatest support to the frame.

4 A staircase winds through the central tower. There are 171 steps to the viewing room in the crown.

❓ Why do you think it took eight years to build the Statue of Liberty?

1884

Construction of the Statue of Liberty was finished in Paris in 1884.

1886

On October 28, 1886, the Statue of Liberty was dedicated to the people of the United States.

Ellis Island

Another immigrant described what happened once a ship passed the Statue of Liberty. "They [took us] to Ellis Island. We got off the boat. . . . You got your bag in your hand and went right into the building. Ah, that day [there] must have been about five to six thousand people."

Ellis Island was built to keep track of the large numbers of people entering the country. At Ellis Island, officials gave each new arrival a medical exam. They asked everyone a long list of questions: "Where did you come from? Can you read and write? Do you have a job waiting for you?"

People who were sick might be held on the island until they were well again. People who were too sick to work or

Ellis Island was an immigration center from 1892 to 1954. In 1907, its busiest year, Ellis Island welcomed more than one million newcomers.

who had broken the law might be sent back home. Those who passed inspection, however, were free to begin their new lives and seek new opportunities in the United States.

REVIEW What happened to immigrants when they arrived at Ellis Island?

REVIEW

1. **WHAT TO KNOW** Why did many immigrants come to New York during the 1800s and early 1900s?

2. **VOCABULARY** Explain how **immigration** to the United States was affected by a **famine**.

3. **HISTORY** What was the Great Migration?

4. **CRITICAL THINKING** Why do you think so many immigrants were willing to leave their homes to come to the United States?

5. **WRITE A SCRIPT** Imagine that you are a tour guide at the Statue of Liberty. Write a script of the information you want guests to know about the statue. Include a list of questions you

think people might ask you, and provide the answers to those questions.

6. **(Focus Skill) COMPARE AND CONTRAST** On a separate sheet of paper, copy and complete this graphic organizer.

Topic 1
The Great Irish Migration — Similar — Topic 2 The Great Migration from the South

Make a Thoughtful Decision

VOCABULARY

consequence

▶ WHY IT MATTERS

Each decision you make has consequences (KAHN•suh•kwen•sihz). A **consequence** is the result of a decision or an action. Thinking about the consequences before you decide will help you make a good decision.

▶ WHAT YOU NEED TO KNOW

Here are some steps you can use to make a thoughtful decision.

Step 1 Know you have to make a decision, and identify a goal.

Step 2 Make a list of choices that might help you reach that goal.

Step 3 Think about the good and bad consequences of each choice.

Step 4 Decide which choice you think will have the best consequences.

Step 5 Think about your choice. Could it have bad consequences you have not yet thought of? If so, make a different decision.

Step 6 Make a choice and take action.

▶ PRACTICE THE SKILL

Imagine that it is 1900. You need to decide whether to start a new life and leave for the United States or remain in your homeland with your family. Think about your decision to leave your country and your family and the possible consequences of that decision.

1 If you went to the United States, what might the consequences be?

2 What might the consequences be if you stayed in your homeland?

▶ APPLY WHAT YOU LEARNED

What were the consequences of a decision you made recently? Do you think your decision was a thoughtful one? Explain.

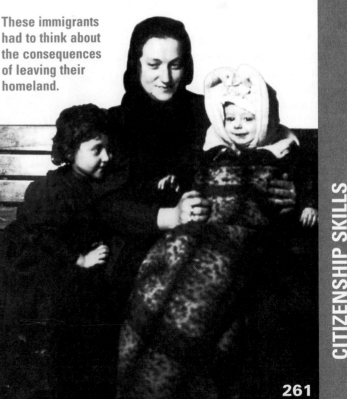

These immigrants had to think about the consequences of leaving their homeland.

Building New Lives

WHAT TO KNOW
What were some of the problems that immigrants faced?

VOCABULARY
tenement p. 263
entrepreneur p. 265

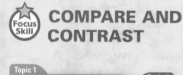
COMPARE AND CONTRAST

 You Are There

The year is 1900. Your cousin has been trying to convince you to move to the United States. You keep telling him that you don't have much money and can't speak English. "It doesn't matter," he says. "We can stay at our uncle's place. Most of the people in his neighborhood come from our country. They'll make us feel right at home."

Working, Living, and Learning

Immigrants settled in many areas of New York State. In Buffalo's Italian community many young men had come to work on the railroads or canals. A large Polish community also grew in Buffalo. Many found jobs in Buffalo's steel mills.

This photograph from 1900 shows a busy day on Mulberry Street, on the Lower East Side of New York City.

Street peddlers, like this bread seller, sold everything from pots and pans to old coats and hats. A successful peddler could earn up to 15 or 20 dollars per week.

Large groups of Poles, Italians, and Syrians (SIR•ee•uhnz) settled in New York Mills, near Utica. There they worked in factories that produced clothing, shoes, and other goods. In time, a growing community of Chinese joined the Irish and others in Albany. Immigrants provided much of the workforce for copper and locomotive businesses in Schenectady and Rome. Jamestown became home to a successful community of Swedish furniture makers.

Many immigrants who settled in New York City lived in one of the city's immigrant neighborhoods, such as Little Italy and Chinatown. Many Jewish immigrants from Russia, Poland, and other European countries lived in an area called the Lower East Side.

These neighborhoods were lively places. Thousands of people lived close together. Neighbors would often gather on their front stoops and chat with each other in their native languages. With few parks and playgrounds in their neighborhoods, children often played games in the street. The shouts of pushcart vendors selling fruit, bread, or newspapers could be heard all day long.

With little money, many immigrants had to live in run-down apartment buildings called **tenements** (TEH•nuh•muhnts). As many as 20 people lived together in a two-room apartment. Often four or five children had to share a single bed.

Immigrant children, like this newspaper seller, often had to work to help their families earn money.

Tenement apartments were almost always overcrowded. On New York City's Lower East Side, sometimes more than 3,000 people lived on a single city block.

Usually one room served as a kitchen and living space. The other room was a bedroom. Tenements had few windows and were dark and stuffy.

Immigrants had to work long hours to afford these tiny apartments and buy food for their families. Adults and children often worked 14-hour shifts in factories.

Life was difficult for immigrants in other ways, too. Many of them faced prejudice—both from other recent immigrant groups and from people whose families had lived in New York for a long time. In time, some people began to see the need for reform in New York City's immigrant neighborhoods. By 1900, people such as Jacob Riis (REES), a reporter, and Lillian Wald, a nurse, were working to improve conditions in tenements. Catholic nun Mother Frances Cabrini (kuh•BREE•nee)

founded schools, hospitals, and children's homes.

In communities around New York, immigrants adapted to their new way of life. They also kept the customs, languages, and cultures of their homeland. Many of these cultural influences still exist in New York neighborhoods today.

REVIEW Who were some New Yorkers who worked to improve immigrant neighborhoods?

The Contributions of Immigrants

Immigrants helped build the Erie Canal. They now provided workers for New York's factories, railroad lines, and other industries. Many worked on the state's docks, loading and unloading ships. Some found jobs on construction sites, helping to build many of New York's landmarks.

Henry Steinway   **John Jacob Bausch**   **Henry Lomb**   **Irving Berlin**

Some of the immigrants who settled in New York became **entrepreneurs** (ahn•truh•pruh•NERZ), or people who start new businesses. Among them was German-born Henry Steinway, who built and sold pianos. Steinway pianos are still made in a factory in Queens. John Jacob Bausch (BOWSH) and Henry Lomb (LAHM), also from Germany, started a business making eyeglass lenses. Other immigrants ran grocery stores, restaurants, and laundries.

Immigrants also made important contributions in the arts. Book publishers Alfred A. Knopf (kuh•NAWPF) and Albert Boni (BOH•ny) came from immigrant families. Walter Damrosch (DAM•rahsh), a former conductor of the New York Symphony and a music educator, was born in what is now Poland. Songwriter Irving Berlin was born in Russia. Berlin wrote some of the world's most popular songs, including "White Christmas" and "God Bless America."

• BIOGRAPHY •

Saint Frances Xavier Cabrini   1850–1917

Character Trait: Compassion

Mother Frances Cabrini was born Maria Francesca Cabrini in Italy. She became a nun, and in 1889 the Catholic Church sent her to the United States to help care for poor immigrants in New York. Soon after arriving in New York, she started an orphanage, or home for children without families. For the next 28 years, Mother Cabrini traveled throughout the United States founding schools, hospitals, and orphanages. In 1909 Mother Cabrini became a United States citizen.

Mother Cabrini was declared a saint by the Catholic Church in 1946. She was the first United States citizen to receive this honor. For her work with immigrants, she was named the patron saint of immigrants by Pope Pius XII in 1950.

GO ONLINE
For more resources, go to
www.harcourtschool.com/ss1

265

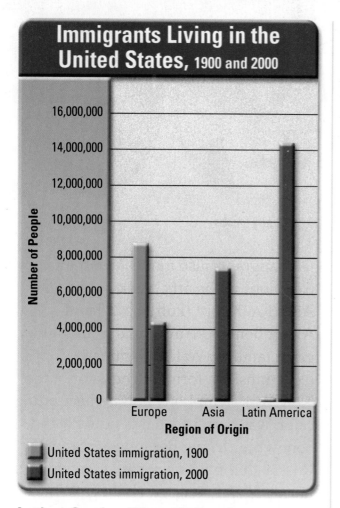

Immigrants Living in the United States, 1900 and 2000

Number of People

16,000,000
14,000,000
12,000,000
10,000,000
8,000,000
6,000,000
4,000,000
2,000,000
0

Europe   Asia   Latin America
Region of Origin

■ United States immigration, 1900
■ United States immigration, 2000

Analyze Graphs This graph shows how many immigrants living in the United States came from different parts of the world in 1900 and 2000.

◆ How did the number of Latin American immigrants change between 1900 and 2000?

Another famous musician, George Gershwin, was born in Brooklyn of Russian Jewish parents. Songs that Gershwin wrote for Broadway shows in the 1920s and 1930s were hits of their day.

REVIEW What kinds of contributions have immigrants made to American culture?

Immigration Continues

New York State continues to attract people from around the world. Since 1960 more than 4 million immigrants have come to the state. In fact, in 2000, one out of every three children in New York was an immigrant or the child of immigrants.

Most of the immigrants who came to New York in the 1800s and early 1900s were from countries in Europe. Today immigrants come from more than 200 different countries. Most come to New York from countries in Latin America, Asia, or Africa. The highest number come from the Dominican Republic. The next-highest number come from China, followed by Jamaica.

The way immigrants travel to the United States is also different from the way they did in the past. Today a newcomer to this country is likely to pass through an airport, not a ship port.

The places where immigrants settle in New York have also changed over time. A recent study

Foreign language newspapers and ethnic businesses are common in some neighborhoods in New York.

showed that immigrants have added to the population of almost every county in the state.

Many of the reasons immigrants come to the United States remain the same, however. Many of them still come to seek freedom or to escape poverty, war, or prejudice in their homelands. They think carefully about whether to leave their homelands for life in an unfamiliar land.

Carrie Hung, who as a child came to New York from China with her parents, feels her family made the right decision in coming to the United States. "There are many things I really like about the free society [in the United States]. You can experience more things, and there are more ways for you to grow. [For] my parents, there were no such opportunities . . . [in China]."

As in the past, immigrants today make many contributions to New York. Today, immigrants work in nearly every

Carrie Hung and her family moved to the land many people in China call *mei guo,* or "beautful country," so that she could get a good education.

industry. Among other things, they are doctors, scientists, teachers, taxicab drivers, and business owners.

REVIEW From where do most immigrants to New York today come?

REVIEW

1. **WHAT TO KNOW** What were some of the problems that immigrants faced?

2. **VOCABULARY** Use the word **tenement** in a sentence about the need for reform in immigrant neighborhoods.

3. **GEOGRAPHY** Why did many immigrants want to live among people from their home country?

4. **CRITICAL THINKING** What hopes do you think immigrants today share with immigrants of the past?

5. **MAKE A GUIDE BOOK** Make a guidebook that explains how immigrants have contributed to your

community. Think about businesses that are run by immigrants or landmarks that are named for immigrants.

6. **COMPARE AND CONTRAST** On a separate sheet of paper, copy and complete this graphic organizer.

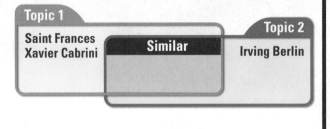

Topic 1
Saint Frances Xavier Cabrini

Similar

Topic 2
Irving Berlin

Jacob Riis's Photographs

Background Jacob Riis is considered the nation's first photo-journalist. The Danish-born photographer traveled throughout New York City during the 1880s and 1890s, taking thousands of photographs. Riis documented the lives of men, women, and children of all nationalities at home, at work, and at leisure. His photographs appeared in newspapers and in his books, such as *How the Other Half Lives*.

DBQ **Document-Based Question** Study these primary sources and answer the questions.

BAXTER STREET ALLEY IN MULBERRY ROW

"At 59 Baxter Street … is an alley leading in from the sidewalk with tenements on either side crowding so close as to almost shut out the light of day."

—from the *New York Sun,* February 12, 1888

DBQ ❶ What does this photograph show about city life during the 1890s?

CAMERA This camera is similar to the kind Jacob Riis used.

DBQ ❷ Why do you think there is a handle on top of this camera?

AN OLD REAR TENEMENT IN ROOSEVELT STREET

"It is Thursday, but patched linen is hung upon the pulley-line from the window ... It is wash-day all the week round, for a change of clothing is scarce among the poor."

—from *How the Other Half Lives*, 1890

DBQ ❸ How might a photograph taken today differ from this photograph?

A "SLIDE" IN HAMILTON STREET

"A dozen years ago [1890], I gave a stockbroker a good blowing up [yelling at] for hammering his cellar door full of envious nails to prevent the children using it as a slide. It was all the playground they had."

—from *The Battle with the Slum*, 1902

WRITE ABOUT IT

Write a paragraph describing the people, the activities, and the scenes of life in most cities today. If Jacob Riis were taking pictures today, how would they differ from his older pictures? How might they be similar?

GO ONLINE · For more resources, go to www.harcourtschool.com/ss1

DBQ ❹ What does Jacob Riis's explanation say about the lives of the children shown in the photograph?

Industries Grow and Expand

| 1800 | 1850 | 1900 | 1950 |

1865–1915

WHAT TO KNOW
What led to the growth of new industries in New York?

VOCABULARY
industrialization p. 270

human resource p. 270

capital resource p. 271

demand p. 272

supply p. 272

hydroelectric power p. 272

investor p. 273

sweatshop p. 274

labor union p. 275

strike p. 275

COMPARE AND CONTRAST

Topic 1 — Similar — Topic 2

 YOU ARE THERE
"Next stop Grand Central Depot!" As your train approaches the station, you can't believe what you see. "At least two dozen trains are in there." Later in the day, you learn that Grand Central Depot can hold nearly 100 trains at once. They can carry about 15,000 passengers every day.

A Center of New Industries

The late 1800s was a time of rapid **industrialization**, or growth of industries. New York's industries had three kinds of resources to use in manufacturing products. The state's natural resources included deep harbors and good waterways, as well as wood and minerals. Because of its large population, New York had many workers, or **human resources**. It also had many large banks to

Grand Central Depot opened in 1871.

By 1910 more than half of the factory workers in the United States were immigrants. Many of them worked in steel mills.

provide the third kind of resource—capital resources. **Capital resources** are the money, buildings, machines, and tools needed to run a business.

Railroads were a key part of New York's industrial growth, and Cornelius Vanderbilt was key to the growth of the state's railroads. Vanderbilt bought several small railroad companies and combined them with the New York Central Railroad. Vanderbilt also built new railroads. By the early 1900s nearly every community in the state was on a railroad line.

Vanderbilt also built New York City's original Grand Central Terminal. At the time, it was the largest train station ever built. Its construction provided thousands of New Yorkers with jobs.

REVIEW How did Cornelius Vanderbilt change New York's railroad service?

Thomas Edison

Inventions and Industries

In the late 1800s new inventions changed the way people lived and worked. One of these inventions was the telephone. Invented in 1871, the telephone was more than just a new way to communicate. It created new kinds of jobs. Some workers made telephones, while others served as operators. Other workers strung and repaired wires.

The electric lightbulb also changed New York. In 1879 Thomas A. Edison built the first working lightbulb. With the support of banker J.P. Morgan and the Vanderbilt family, Edison started the Edison Electric Light Company in New York. His company built the world's first power station, in lower Manhattan. It provided electricity to a large area of the city.

Lewis H. Latimer 1848–1928

Character Trait: Inventiveness

In 1880, people still used candles and fuel-burning lamps for light. Thomas Edison had already invented a lightbulb, but his design had problems. Its filament (FIH•luh•muhnt), the glowing wires inside the bulb that make light, burned out quickly. In 1881 Lewis H. Latimer invented a carbon filament that lasted much longer than filaments made from other materials. In time, Latimer went to work for Edison at the Edison Electric Light Company. He became the first African American member of the "Edison Pioneers," a group of Edison's best engineers.

GO ONLINE For more resources, go to
www.harcourtschool.com/ss1

Lewis Latimer was an African American who worked for Edison's company. He improved the lightbulb so that it would burn brighter and last longer. As a result, the demand for electricity increased. A **demand** is a desire for a good or a service by people who are willing to pay for it. Within a few years, communities all over New York had power stations.

Other New Yorkers invented ways to increase the state's supply of electricity.

A **supply** is an amount of a good or service that is offered for sale. The supply of a good or service usually rises or falls to meet the demand. This means that businesses will produce more of something if people want to buy more of it.

In the 1880s German immigrant Jacob Schoellkopf (SHOH•uhl•kawpf) built a power plant on the Niagara River. It made **hydroelectric power**—electricity made by machines that are turned by running water. Croatian-born Nikola

George Eastman (left) of Rochester invented an easy-to-use camera. In 1874 Philo Remington (right) started the country's first typewriter factory in Ilion.

Tesla invented a way to send power from the plant on the Niagara River to Buffalo. Another New Yorker, George Westinghouse, also developed a way to improve the transmission of electricity.

All across the state, New Yorkers were inventing new products and starting factories to manufacture them. In 1868, Amory Houghton (HOHT•uhn) brought a new type of glassmaking to Corning. His company invented a kind of glass that would not break when heated. In the 1890s George Eastman opened a camera factory in Rochester. Soon his cameras were being sold across the country. In 1902 Willis Carrier invented a machine that could cool the air. He then started a company in Syracuse to make air conditioners.

REVIEW How was the Niagara River used to help meet New York's demand for electricity?

Hetty Green

New Wealth

Many inventors in New York became very wealthy. So did the investors who helped them start their businesses. An **investor** is someone who spends money on a project with the hope of earning back more money in return. Among these investors were Cornelius Vanderbilt, John D. Rockefeller, and Edward H. Harriman. Banker J.P. Morgan made millions of dollars by lending money to companies and by buying and selling stock in them. Other people, such as Hetty Green, made their fortune by buying and selling stock and land. Green was one of only a few women who invested in businesses at this time.

REVIEW Why do investors spend money on other people's ideas?

New York's first Metropolitan Opera House opened in 1883. Wealthy business owners donated the money to build it.

The Labor Movement and Child Labor

By 1900 New York led the nation in manufacturing. New York businesses provided thousands of jobs. Often, the jobs were in factories with dangerous working conditions. In these crowded **sweatshops**, as they were called, people had to work long hours for little pay.

Pauline Newman, a Jewish immigrant, said, "We started work at 7:30 in the morning, and during the busy season we worked until 9:00 in the evening. . . . The employers had a sign that said *If you don't come in on Sunday, don't come in on Monday.* You were expected to work every day if they needed you."

In some families children as young as six years old had to work. These shoe shiners carried their tools with them.

In 1911, a fire in New York City's Triangle Shirtwaist Factory brought attention to the problems in factories. That factory's owners kept the doors locked so that workers could not leave for breaks. When fire broke out in the factory, workers were trapped. More than 146 workers died.

In poor families, even children worked. Like their parents, they often worked in unsafe factories. Others sold newspapers or shined shoes. In 1900 in the United States, more than 2 million children worked.

• HERITAGE •

Labor Day

Labor Day honors American workers. Many people believe that Matthew Maguire, a machine worker, and Peter McGuire, a carpenter, came up with the idea. They thought a day should be set aside to recognize the importance of workers. The first Labor Day parade was held on September 5, 1882, in New York City. In 1894 Congress made Labor Day a national holiday. Americans continue to celebrate it on the first Monday in September.

In the early 1900s, New York passed new laws to help protect workers and children. In time, a law was passed that said children had to be at least 14 years old to work and could work only after school. To work during school hours, a child had to be at least 16.

To improve their working conditions and pay, some workers formed labor unions. A **labor union** is a group of workers who act together to improve their working conditions. Workers knew that if they asked for changes as a large group, employers would have to listen. If an employer said no to their demands, the workers could **strike**, or refuse to work, until the changes were made.

REVIEW What laws were passed to protect child workers?

**Labor Union Membership,
1898–1920**

Analyze Graphs One of the first successful unions was the American Federation of Labor (AFL). It was formed in 1886 and was led by New Yorker Samuel Gompers.

✦ By how much did membership in labor unions increase between 1904 and 1920?

REVIEW

1. **WHAT TO KNOW** What led to the growth of new industries in New York?

2. **VOCABULARY** Use **labor union** and **strike** to explain how employees worked for their rights.

3. **ECONOMICS** Explain what happens when a business produces more of a product than there is a demand for.

4. **CRITICAL THINKING** For years, industries tried to make labor unions illegal. Why do you think this was true?

5. **CREATE AN ADVERTISEMENT** Create a poster or brochure that would have convinced businesspeople in 1900 that New York was the best place for them to do business.

6. **COMPARE AND CONTRAST** On a separate sheet of paper, copy and complete this graphic organizer.

Topic 1
Telephone

Similar

Topic 2
Electric lightbulb

Resolve Conflict

▶ WHY IT MATTERS

People sometimes have different ideas about how to do things. That can lead to conflict. There are many ways to resolve, or settle, a conflict. Working out a compromise is a peaceful and positive way.

▶ WHAT YOU NEED TO KNOW

To reach a compromise, or agreement, you can follow these steps.

Step 1 **Identify what is causing the conflict.**

Step 2 **Tell the people on the other side what you want. Also listen to what they want.**

Step 3 **Decide which things are most important to you. Make a plan for a compromise. Explain your plan, and listen to the other side's plan.**

Step 4 **If you still do not agree, make a second plan. Give up one of the things that are most important to you. Ask the other side to do the same.**

Step 5 **Keep talking until you agree on a compromise. Plan your compromise so it will work for a long time.**

▶ PRACTICE THE SKILL

As you have read, labor unions worked with business owners to improve working conditions in some factories. To resolve their conflicts, the labor unions and the business owners had to make some compromises.

❶ Use the steps to think of a way labor unions and business owners compromised to resolve their conflicts.

❷ What do you think would have happened if the workers and the business owners had not reached a compromise?

▶ APPLY WHAT YOU LEARNED

With your classmates, choose an issue that you do not all agree on, such as which game to play. Work out a compromise to resolve the conflict.

Many immigrants joined labor unions in the early 1900s.

CITIZENSHIP SKILLS

The Spread of City Life

1800 1850 1900 1950

1860–1950

WHAT TO KNOW
How did the ways New Yorkers lived and worked change in the late 1800s and early 1900s?

VOCABULARY
urbanization p. 277
commute p. 280
metropolitan area p. 280
interdependence p. 281

COMPARE AND CONTRAST

Topic 1   Topic 2
         Similar

> **YOU ARE THERE**
> It's May 24, 1883. Everyone has the day off to go to the opening of the Brooklyn Bridge. You arrive just in time to see President Chester Arthur in the afternoon parade. Once you cross over to Manhattan, you wait to see the closing fireworks. The fireworks display lights up the bridge for more than an hour. What a great finish to this special day!

The Brooklyn Bridge

As industries grew, more and more people moved to cities to find jobs. This **urbanization** (er•buh•nuh•ZAY•shuhn), or spread of city life, changed New York's landscape forever. In 1867 an immigrant named John Roebling (ROHB•ling) designed a bridge to cross New York City's East River. His plans called for a suspension bridge, one supported by steel cables that hung from high towers.

In 1869, John Roebling was killed in an accident at the bridge site. The job of building the bridge then passed to his son, Washington. The younger Roebling soon became ill. His wife, Emily, took over the job.

Emily Roebling taught herself engineering and math in order to oversee the construction of the Brooklyn Bridge.

Building the bridge was difficult. Part of the time, workers had to dig beneath the bed of the river. The work was hot and dirty, and many workers got sick.

The Brooklyn Bridge was finally completed in 1883. By using it, people could quickly cross the East River. In 1898, Brooklyn—along with the Bronx, Queens, and Staten Island—united with Manhattan to form Greater New York.

REVIEW Why was the Brooklyn Bridge important to New York City?

A CLOSER LOOK
The Brooklyn Bridge

Like all suspension bridges, the Brooklyn Bridge suspends, or hangs, a roadway from huge cables. These cables rest on top of high towers and are anchored on land at each end.

1. The Brooklyn Bridge's four main suspension cables each weigh nearly 2 million pounds (907,200 kg). A total of 380 suspender ropes hang from each cable.

2. The 277-foot-high (84-meter-high) towers support most of the weight of the roadway.

3. The main span of the bridge stretches 1,595 feet (486 m) across the East River.

4. To build the underwater foundations for the towers, workers had to dig underneath the riverbed in watertight air chambers called caissons (KAY•sahnz).

◇ The roadway is 135 feet (41 m) above the East River. Why do you think the roadway had to be so high?

Subways and Skyscrapers

In the early 1900s New York City's streets were becoming more crowded. Leaders began thinking of a way to move people under the ground. On March 24, 1900, workers began building a subway system.

Subways were hard to build. Workers had to dig deep ditches down streets. Then they had to line the ditches with steel, lay tracks inside, and cover the ditches up again. In some places the trains had to come above ground. In other places they had to travel under bodies of water.

The first line on New York City's subway system opened on October 27, 1904. It ran from City Hall in lower Manhattan to Harlem. Today, with 722 miles (about 1,162 km) of track, New York City has the longest subway system in the world. About four million people use the subways each day.

While working in Yonkers in the late 1800s, Elisha Otis designed the first elevator that could safely carry people. A New York department store was the first business to move people from floor to floor by elevator.

At the time, few buildings had more than four or five stories. Most people did not want to walk up the many flights of stairs that taller buildings would require. However, elevators could now take people to the top floors of tall buildings quickly and easily. They made skyscrapers practical.

In 1904, it cost five cents to ride the subway in New York City.

Buffalo's 13-story Guaranty Building was one of the first skyscrapers to be built in New York. It opened in 1896. However, most of the early skyscrapers in New York were built in New York City. Manhattan's geography makes it a good place to build tall buildings.

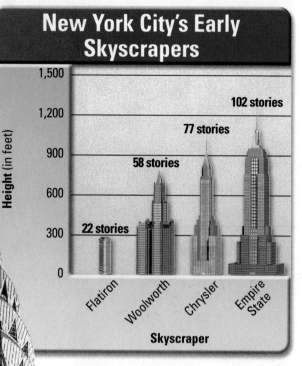

New York City's Early Skyscrapers

Height (in feet)

- 1,500
- 1,200
- 900
- 600
- 300
- 0

102 stories
77 stories
58 stories
22 stories

Flatiron — Woolworth — Chrysler — Empire State

Skyscraper

Analyze Graphs For a few months in 1930, the Chrysler Building (left) was the tallest building in the world, until the Empire State Building was finished.

◆ About how much taller is the Empire State Building than the Chrysler Building?

Beneath the ground is a layer of rock to which building supports can be attached. New York City has many famous skyscrapers. The Flatiron Building is the city's oldest. Some people say that it looks like an old-fashioned flat iron. Other skyscrapers include the Woolworth Building, the Chrysler Building, and the Empire State Building.

REVIEW What invention made skyscrapers practical?

Suburbs Grow

As transportation improved, people no longer had to live near where they worked. Across New York, many people began to move out of cities and into suburbs. From there, they could **commute**, or travel back and forth, to work each day.

People who worked in New York City spread out into suburbs on Long Island and up the Hudson River valley. Others moved to suburbs in New Jersey and Connecticut. In time, the New York City area became the largest metropolitan (meh•truh•PAH•luh•tuhn) area in the nation. A **metropolitan area** is a large city together with its suburbs.

Some of New York City's suburbs were specially planned with brand-new homes, schools, and shopping centers. Levittown, a suburb built on Long Island, was one of them. By 1960, Levittown was home to 82,000 people, and communities like it were popular across the United States.

REVIEW How did improvements in transportation change where people lived?

Levittown and many other suburban communities were built after World War II. Houses that looked very much alike filled block after block.

Linking Regions

As more people moved to urban areas, they no longer grew their own food. Instead, they depended on farmers. Farmers used land in rural areas to raise livestock and grow crops. They sold their products to markets or businesses in the cities.

With the money they earned, farmers could buy goods made by workers in the cities. Many farmers bought tractors and other machines that allowed them to grow more crops. These crops fed New York's people. In this way people in cities and on farms depended on one another. Depending on one another for resources is called **interdependence**.

New roads also connected people. The roads were built to link cities with their suburbs and to link large cities with other large cities. In the 1950s the

People compared the New York Thruway to the Erie Canal. How were the two alike?

United States government began building a system of interstate highways that today crisscrosses the nation. The New York Thruway from New York City to Buffalo opened to drivers in 1955.

REVIEW How did farmers and people in cities grow to depend on one another?

REVIEW

1. **WHAT TO KNOW** How did the ways New Yorkers lived and worked change in the late 1800s and early 1900s?

2. **VOCABULARY** Write a sentence about the different ways people **commute**.

3. **GEOGRAPHY** How did the Brooklyn Bridge make it easy for people to travel between Brooklyn and Manhattan?

4. **CRITICAL THINKING** As people began moving out of cities and into suburbs, what new problems do you think the cities may have had?

5. **BUILD A MODEL** Build a model of a New York City skyscraper or another New York City landmark.

6. **COMPARE AND CONTRAST** On a separate sheet of paper, copy and complete this graphic organizer.

Topic 1
Brooklyn Bridge

Similar

Topic 2
Empire State Building

Use a Road Map and Mileage Table

VOCABULARY

mileage table

WHY IT MATTERS

Imagine that this is the first day of your family's vacation. You and your family pack the car, buckle your seat belts, and are on your way. About an hour later your little brother asks, "How much farther do we have to go?"

To answer his question, you can use a road map. A road map shows the routes between places. It provides information about the kinds of roads that connect places. Different kinds of lines on a road map stand for different kinds of roads. Knowing the kinds of roads helps you choose good routes.

Road Map of New York

- Interstate highway
- United States highway
- State highway

New York Mileage Table

CITY	ALBANY	BUFFALO	JAMESTOWN	POUGHKEEPSIE	ROCHESTER	SYRACUSE
Albany		294	343	75	219	137
Buffalo	294		66	338	75	157
Jamestown	343	66		346	141	206
Poughkeepsie	75	338	346		287	205
Rochester	219	75	141	287		82
Syracuse	137	157	206	205	82	

▶ WHAT YOU NEED TO KNOW

Suppose your family will travel by car from Binghamton to Schenectady. You can use the road map to find out which highways connect the two cities.

To find the distance between cities, you can use a mileage table. A **mileage table** gives the number of miles between listed cities. Suppose you want to find the distance from Poughkeepsie to Syracuse. On the mileage table on this page, find the point where the row and column for these two cities cross. You will see that the driving distance is 205 miles.

▶ PRACTICE THE SKILL

Use the road map on page 282 and the mileage table above to answer these questions.

1. If you wanted to travel quickly west across all of New York, which highway should you use? What cities would you pass through?

2. What three interstate highways meet at Albany?

3. Which interstate highways would you use to drive from Utica to Watertown? What state highway connects those cities?

4. How many miles is it from Buffalo to Albany? How did you determine this?

5. What is the best route between New York City and Saranac Lake?

▶ APPLY WHAT YOU LEARNED

Plan a trip by car to three large cities shown on the New York mileage table. Begin your trip in the city of Albany. Use the road map to decide on the route you will take. Then use the mileage table to find the number of miles you will travel.

Practice your map and globe skills with the **GeoSkills CD-ROM**.

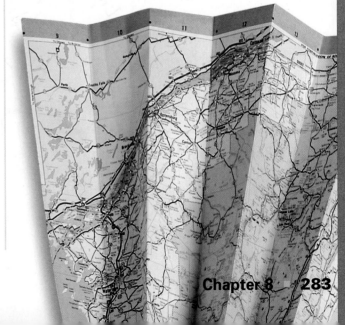

Chapter Review

Summarize the Chapter

Focus Skill

Compare and Contrast Complete this graphic organizer to compare and contrast information about past and present New Yorkers.

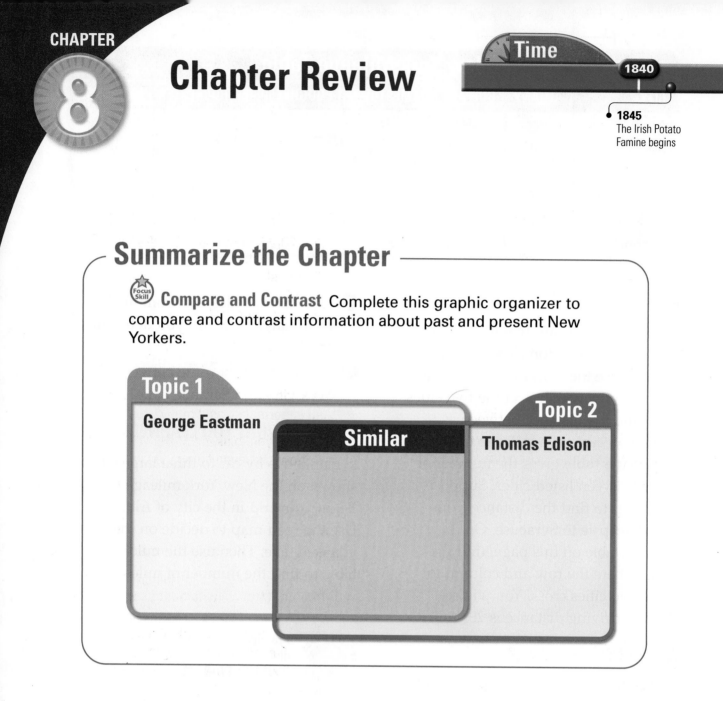

Topic 1

George Eastman

Similar

Topic 2

Thomas Edison

THINK & WRITE

Write a Packing List for a Journey
Think about the kinds of things you would need to pack if you were an immigrant coming to the United States in the early 1900s. Make a list of these items.

Write a Conversation Imagine that you are an immigrant on a ship that has just sailed into New York Harbor. Write a conversation that might take place between you and another immigrant who is seeing the United States for the first time.

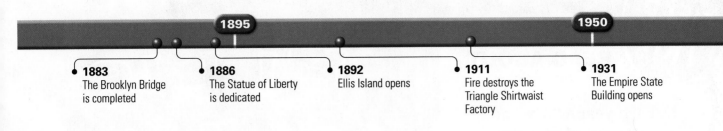

1895   1950

1883
The Brooklyn Bridge
is completed

1886
The Statue of Liberty
is dedicated

1892
Ellis Island opens

1911
Fire destroys the
Triangle Shirtwaist
Factory

1931
The Empire State
Building opens

USE THE TIME LINE

Use the chapter summary time line to answer these questions.

1 Did the Empire State Building open before or after the Statue of Liberty was dedicated?

2 How many years after the Brooklyn Bridge was completed did Ellis Island open?

USE VOCABULARY

Use these terms to write a story about the challenges faced by immigrants to the United States in the early 1900s.

3 **discrimination** (p. 257)

4 **tenement** (p. 263)

5 **sweatshop** (p. 274)

6 **labor union** (p. 275)

7 **strike** (p. 275)

RECALL FACTS

Answer these questions.

8 How was the Great Migration different from the Great Irish Migration?

9 Why was New York able to become a center of new industries?

Write the letter of the best choice.

10 **TEST PREP** In the early 1900s, Buffalo became home to many immigrants from—
A Syria.
B China.
C Sweden.
D Poland.

11 **TEST PREP** Elisha Otis helped make skyscrapers practical by designing—
F aqueducts.
G the telegraph.
H safe elevators.
J suspension bridges.

THINK CRITICALLY

12 Why do you think the Statue of Liberty is still an important symbol today?

13 Why do you think many immigrants stayed in New York even though life was often difficult?

APPLY SKILLS

Make a Thoughtful Decision

14 Imagine you are a new immigrant. You must decide whether to settle in a place with people from your own country or in one that does not have many new immigrants. What would be the consequences of each choice?

Resolve Conflict

15 Describe the steps you could take to resolve a conflict with a friend. Explain how compromise is part of your solution and why it is fair to both sides.

Use a Road Map and Mileage Table
Use the New York mileage table on page 283 to answer the following question.

16 Is it farther to Buffalo or to Syracuse from Rochester?

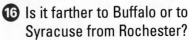

FIELD TRIP

READ ABOUT

Each year nearly one million people journey to the tiny island in New York Harbor called Ellis Island. They come to learn about the millions of immigrants who passed through the buildings here from 1892 to 1954.

Ellis Island lies in the shadow of the Statue of Liberty. The National Park Service began repairing the island's buildings in the 1980s. The main building reopened in 1990 and is now the Ellis Island Immigration Museum.

FIND

NEW YORK

Ellis Island

The Great Hall, or Registry Room, was where immigrants waited to answer questions.

This passport belonged to an immigrant who entered the United States through Ellis Island.

Visitors can see displays filled with photographs, clothing, toys, and other personal items that immigrants brought with them.

The American Immigrant Wall of Honor stands outside the museum. More than 500,000 names are carved into the wall.

A VIRTUAL TOUR

GO ONLINE For more resources, go to www.harcourtschool.com/ss1

VISUAL SUMMARY

Write a Letter Study the pictures and captions below to review Unit 4. Then choose one of the events shown and write a letter to a friend describing the event and how you think it will change New York.

USE VOCABULARY

Use a term from this list to complete each of the following sentences.

frontier (p. 228)   **locomotive** (p. 240)

draft (p. 250)   **human resources** (p. 270)

① During the Civil War, many New Yorkers believed the ____ was unfair.

② New York's many immigrant workers contributed to the state's ____.

③ After the American Revolution, people began moving to New York's western ____.

④ The invention of the ____ changed the way people traveled in New York.

RECALL FACTS

Answer these questions.

⑤ Why is the Erie Canal considered one of the greatest building projects in history?

⑥ What was the Underground Railroad?

⑦ Why did leaders in New York City build Central Park?

⑧ Why did many New Yorkers join labor unions in the early 1900s?

Write the letter of the best choice.

⑨ **TEST PREP** As a result of the Big Tree Treaty, the Senecas—
A gained much land in western New York.
B took control of Long Island.
C were forced to move to reservations.
D took control of Syracuse.

⑩ **TEST PREP** In the early 1900s, the Lower East Side area of New York City was home to many immigrants from—
F Sweden and Norway.
G the Netherlands.
H France.
J Russia and Poland.

Time

1800   1850

1803 Rochester is founded
p. 230

1825 The Erie Canal opens
p. 236

1848 The Seneca Falls Convention is held p. 248

288

11 TEST PREP One invention that changed New York in the late 1800s was the—

A windmill.
B electric lightbulb.
C funnel.
D compass.

THINK CRITICALLY

12 Why do you think Red Jacket was against the Big Tree Treaty?

13 Why do you think some people did not want women to have the right to vote?

14 Why do you think so many immigrants chose to live in ethnic neighborhoods? How did this make life easier for a new immigrant? How did it make life harder?

15 How would New York State be different if suburbs had never been built?

APPLY SKILLS

Use a Road Map and Mileage Table

Use the road map and mileage table on this page to answer the following questions.

16 If you wanted to travel from Buffalo to Niagara Falls, which highway would you use?

New York Mileage Table

	Buffalo	Niagara Falls	Rochester
Buffalo		19	75
Niagara Falls	19		81
Rochester	75	81	

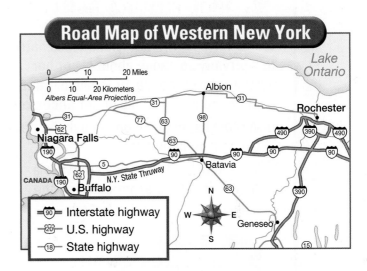

Road Map of Western New York

17 How many miles is it from Rochester to Niagara Falls?

18 What is the best route between Rochester and Buffalo?

19 In what city do State Highways 63 and 98 meet?

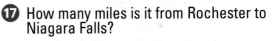

1900

1950

1904 New York City's first subway opens p. 279

1905 Buffalo's first steel mill is built p. 262

1931 The Empire State Building opens p. 280

289

Activities

Show What You Know

Unit Writing Activity

Write a Report Work with a classmate to interview someone about his or her immigrant experience, or the immigrant experience of one of his or her ancestors.

- Write a list of questions to ask the person you will be interviewing.
- Take notes, and use them to write a report about the experiences of the immigrant.

Unit Project

Create a 3-D Time Line Work with a group of classmates to finish the Unit Project described on page 225.

- Decide as a group which five events from the unit you will show on your time line.
- Write the dates and captions for the events on large cards.
- Tape the time line to the floor, and use art materials to build three-dimensional models to illustrate the events.

Read More

- *A Picnic in October* by Eve Bunting. Harcourt.

- *The Brooklyn Bridge: A Wonders of the World Book* by Elizabeth Mann. Mikaya Press.

- *Journey to Ellis Island* by Caroline Bierman. Hyperion/Madison.

For more resources, go to
www.harcourtschool.com/ss1

New York in the Modern World

The Big Idea

Challenge and Opportunity

The challenges and opportunities of the twentieth and twenty-first centuries have made New York the dynamic state that it is today.

What to Know

- How did important world events in the twentieth and twenty-first centuries affect New York?

- How do the many groups of people who live in New York today contribute to culture in the state?

- What are important industries in New York?

- How are New Yorkers preparing for the future?

New York City skyline

New York in the Modern World

Reading Social Studies

Focus Skill Draw Conclusions

Why It Matters Being able to draw a conclusion can help you better understand what you read.

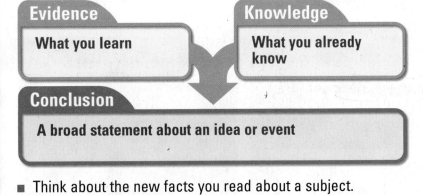

A **conclusion** is a broad statement about an idea or event. It is reached by using what you learn from reading, along with what you already know.

Evidence

What you learn

Knowledge

What you already know

Conclusion

A broad statement about an idea or event

- Think about the new facts you read about a subject.
- Think about the facts you already know about that subject.
- Combine the new facts with those you already know to draw a conclusion.

0   50   100 Miles
0   50   100 Kilometers
Albers Equal-Area Projection

St. Lawrence R.

Ogdensburg

11

Black Lake

Saranac Lakes

Saranac Lake

30

3

Lake Placid

Lake Champlain

VERMONT

73

9

Cranberry Lake

3

Adirondack Park

Long Lake

30

Lake George

Watertown

81

12

28

28

87

4

Lake Ontario

Oswego

104

Oneida Lake

Great Sacandaga Lake

30

7

104

Rochester

490

90

Syracuse

90

Utica

Mohawk River

90

Schenectady

Troy

Buffalo

62

20

Geneseo

Finger Lakes

81

96

Albany

MASSACHUSETTS

Lake Erie

90

62

Chautauqua Lake

219

Allegany State Park

Letchworth State Park

390

86

13

Ithaca

17

Binghamton

Elmira

12

Oneonta

88

28

87

Hudson River

90

Jamestown

86

417

15

81

Catskill Park

86

Kingston

209

CONNECTICUT

PENNSYLVANIA

Delaware River

Minnewaska State Park

Poughkeepsie

9

84

Newburgh

Port Jervis

Harriman State Park

684

Long Island Sound

★   State capital
•   City
✈   Major airport
⚓   Shipping port

90   Interstate highway
20   United States highway
3   State highway
Park

Yonkers

87

Port Jefferson

New York City

27

Fire Island National Seashore

NEW JERSEY

N W E S

Time

1900

1940

1901   The Pan-American Exposition is held in Buffalo   p. 300

1929   The stock market crashes   p. 309

1941   New York's workforce grows as the United States enters World War II   p. 312

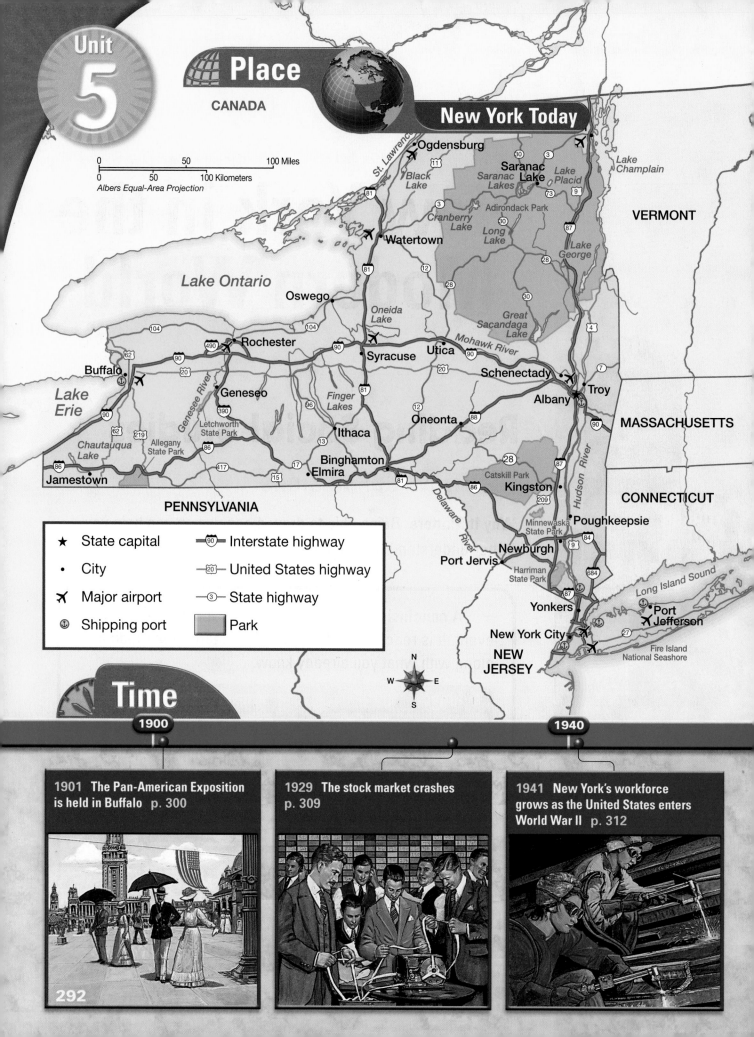

MAINE

RHODE
ISLAND

ATLANTIC OCEAN

Eleanor Roosevelt

1884–1962
- First Lady of the United States from 1933 to 1945
- Served as a delegate to the United Nations

Shirley Chisholm

1924–2005
- First African American woman to be elected to Congress
- Ran for President in 1972

Rudolph Giuliani

1944–
- Former mayor of New York City
- Helped New Yorkers after the terrorist attacks on September 11, 2001

1980

Present

2001 Terrorists attack sites in the United States   p. 315

Present New York continues to attract immigrants from around the world   p. 323

Present Tourism is a major industry in New York   p. 330

JOE and the Skyscraper:

The Empire State Building in New York City
by Dietrich Newman

The early 1900s brought many changes to New York State. None of these was more dramatic than the way skyscrapers were rising in cities across the state. Nowhere, however, were the skyscrapers as tall as those in New York City. Between 1929 and 1931, workers in New York City built what may be the most famous skyscraper in the world—the 102-story Empire State Building. One member of the construction team was 16-year-old Joe Carbonelli. His job was to take drinking water up to the workers. Read now about some of the amazing sights Joe saw.

EMPIRE STATE BUILDING · NEW YORK   (c) Wm. Franz

Joe liked to spend time with the workers who fixed the large steel girders together with rivets. They worked in teams of four. One man heated the steel rivets in a coal oven until they were glowing hot. Then he threw one of the rivets to another worker who caught it in a large metal funnel, picked it up with a pair of tongs, and placed it in one of the pre-drilled holes in the steel girder. The rivet was then pressed firmly from both sides with a pneumatic hammer. During the cooling process the rivet contracted, pulling the steel girders together. The workers used approximately 100,000 rivets to build the Empire State Building.

But Joe didn't have much time to watch. The work was dusty and the workers were thirsty. "This water isn't fresh; it doesn't taste good!" complained Vladimir Korloff, the brawny Russian man on the demolition team.

The next day Joe brought lemons and some salt from home. The water tasted better, and Joe got more tips. In some weeks he made more in tips than in his standard wages.

The structure grew and grew. The next step was to fill out the large, empty steel skeleton. Bricklayers, carpenters, and concrete workers came to make the ceilings. Stonemasons put up the limestone facings, and metal workers installed the decorated aluminum plates on top of the lime-stone. There were also electricians, plumbers, and many other workmen who did specialized jobs. Joe met many of them on his rounds, and some of them became his friends. . .

girder	a steel or iron beam used in building
rivet	a pin or bolt used to join metal parts
funnel	a cone-shaped utensil with an opening at the bottom
tongs	a tool, shaped like scissors, that is used to lift objects
pneumatic (noo•MA•tik) **hammer**	a tool that uses air pressure to drive rivets into girders

Steel Construction

Soon there were some water pipes on the upper floors, and Joe was able to concentrate on taking water to the top floors. How proud he was to be able to go up in the large freight elevators! On other construction sites the workers were carried up in cranes, which was much more dangerous. . . .

There were many Native Americans—Mohawks from Canada—among the steel workers. When they were talking to each other in their native language, Joe couldn't understand a word. They spoke English, too, in an unusual, singsong

way. They weren't afraid of heights—they walked around the steel girders on the fortieth floor as though they were taking a walk in Central Park. Joe wasn't so lucky, and he felt dizzy when he was up so high. The Mohawks taught him what to do. "Don't ever look down; look straight ahead at the end of the girder; never look down." One time Joe slipped on a little drop of oil. As he fell, he was able to catch hold of a girder in the last second. He was shaking all over when the Mohawks brought him to safety.

After he had come to his senses again, he went down to his boss on the ground floor. "I'm not going up there again today." "Then you're fired," was the reply. The foreman knew that this was the only way for Joe to overcome his fear. Later on in life Joe often recalled what he had learned from this experience: be cautious, but don't give up too soon!

Not everyone was so fortunate. There was one icy winter day that Joe would never forget. It was January 31, the day Giuseppe Tedeschi and Luis DeDominichi slipped and fell. Joe had known both of them. All in all, six workers lost their lives while working on the Empire State Building.

In April the building was finished, much earlier than expected. On May 1, 1931, there was a big opening day party, to which all the workers were invited . .

When Joe entered the building, he hardly recognized it. Everything was covered with marble. Metal plaques hung on the walls listing the most important roles of the construction workers: such as metal workers, elevator specialists, and electricians. Joe searched in vain for the water boys. He found one plaque which honored many of his friends for their exceptional work: Matthew McKean, who had built the wooden forms for the reinforced steel ceilings; Charlie Sexton, the merry mason; and Thomas Walsh, the thirsty crane operator. Today visitors can still read the names in the entry hall.

Response Corner

1 **Focus Skill** **Draw Conclusions** What kind of workers took the dangerous jobs on the construction sites of skyscrapers?

2 Why do you think Joe's boss made him go back to work after he almost fell?

3 **Make It Relevant** Like the workers on the Empire State Building, some people today face risks in their jobs. Think about some jobs you would like to do. Make a table that compares the rewards and the risks of those jobs.

START THE UNIT PROJECT

Plan a Website Think about what you might like to include in a website about New York today. As you read this unit, take notes about New York's people, culture, and economy. Your notes will help you decide what to include in your website.

USE TECHNOLOGY

GO ONLINE For more resources, go to www.harcourtschool.com/ss1

STUDY SKILLS

SKIM AND SCAN

Skimming and scanning are tools that help you quickly learn the main ideas of a lesson.

- **To skim, quickly read the lesson title and the section titles. Look at the visuals, or images, and read the captions. Use this information to identify the main topics.**

- **To scan, look quickly through the text for specific details, such as key words or facts.**

SKIM	SCAN
Lesson Title: Into a New Century	**Key Words and Facts:**
Main Idea: In the early part of the twentieth century, New York played an important role in national and world events.	• After President William McKinley was assassinated at the Pan-American Exposition, Theodore Roosevelt became President.
Section Titles: The Pan-American Exposition; A New President; A World War	• The United States began fighting in World War I in 1917.
Visuals: exposition pavilions; President Theodore Roosevelt; World War I soldiers	

Niagara Square, Buffalo

Continuing to Change

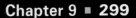

Into a New Century

1900 — 1920 | Present

WHAT TO KNOW
How were New York and the United States affected by major world events in the early 1900s?

VOCABULARY
exposition p. 300
war bond p. 302
interest p. 303

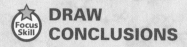

DRAW CONCLUSIONS

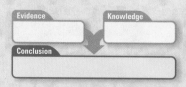

Evidence | Knowledge

Conclusion

YOU ARE THERE Buffalo has been a busy place since the Pan-American Exposition opened. People are flocking to this fair to see exciting new inventions, such as electric lights. You can't wait to see them for yourself. But the news you just heard is terrible. The President was shot at the exposition! You hope it isn't true.

The Pan-American Exposition

As the new century began, United States leaders planned an **exposition**, or fair. It was held in Buffalo to help build understanding between the countries of North America and South America.

To show the wonders of electricity, the buildings at the Pan-American Exposition were brightly lit at night.

People visited from all around the nation and the world. The exposition had rides, animal shows, and sports events. It also displayed new inventions for homes and businesses.

The exposition was supposed to be a celebration, but a terrible event changed that. On September 6, 1901, President William McKinley was visiting the exposition. As he shook hands with people, a man who was angry with the government shot him. McKinley died eight days later.

REVIEW Why did United States leaders want to hold the Pan-American Exposition?

A New President

After William McKinley died, Vice President Theodore Roosevelt became President. Roosevelt was born and raised in New York City. Later, he lived near Oyster Bay on Long Island.

Before Roosevelt became Vice President, he had worked for New York

· HERITAGE ·

The Teddy Bear

Many people think the teddy bear is named for President Theodore "Teddy" Roosevelt. While on a hunting trip in 1902, Roosevelt refused to shoot a small bear. After hearing about this, a toymaker in Brooklyn displayed two toy bears in his shop. A teddy bear craze soon swept the nation. Teddy bears have been among the most beloved toys of children all over the world ever since.

in many ways. He served as New York City's police commissioner, as a state representative, and as governor.

As President, Roosevelt started the National Forest Service to manage and protect the nation's wilderness areas.

FAST FACT The most famous building at the Pan-American Exposition was the Electric Tower. It stood 391 feet (119 m) tall and was covered with 11,000 lightbulbs.

The explorer and writer John Muir (right) helped convince President Roosevelt and Congress to create the first national parks.

He also supported building a canal across Panama in Central America. When the Panama Canal opened, ships no longer had to sail around South America to get from the Atlantic Ocean to the Pacific Ocean. The trip from New York City to San Francisco was shortened by more than 7,000 miles (11,265 km).

REVIEW What were some of Theodore Roosevelt's achievements as President?

A World War

Events outside the United States soon affected New Yorkers and all other Americans. In 1914 a war started in Europe. Britain, France, and Russia joined together to form the Allied Powers. They fought against the Central Powers. The Central Powers included Germany, Austria-Hungary, and the Ottoman Empire. The war spread to so much of the world that people called it the Great War, or the "war to end all wars." It later became known as World War I.

The United States joined the war on the Allied side in 1917. It was the first time that soldiers from the United States were sent to fight in Europe.

New York played an important part in helping the United States fight the war. About 370,000 New Yorkers served in the military—more soldiers than from any other state. Most troops and supplies were shipped overseas through New York ports. The state's factories made guns, uniforms, airplanes, and other equipment.

New Yorkers at home also did their part. Women took up many factory jobs that men had left behind. New Yorkers used less food and fuel so that more could be sent to the soldiers.

Many New Yorkers bought war bonds. A **war bond** is a piece of paper showing that

This group of World War I soldiers came from New York.

During World War I, many women worked in factories. Posters (right) encouraged people to buy war bonds, also called liberty bonds.

the buyer has lent money to a government to help pay for a war. After a certain amount of time, people could turn in their bonds and get back their money with interest. **Interest** is the money a bank or a borrower pays for the use of loaned money. Support from New York and other states helped the Allied Powers win World War I. The war finally ended on November 11, 1918.

REVIEW How did New Yorkers contribute to the war effort?

REVIEW

1. **WHAT TO KNOW** How were New York and the United States affected by major world events in the early 1900s?

2. **VOCABULARY** How is **interest** related to **war bonds**?

3. **CIVICS AND GOVERNMENT** How did Theodore Roosevelt serve New York?

4. **CRITICAL THINKING** Do you think the Panama Canal was good for New York? Explain.

5. **PLAN A DISPLAY** If an exposition were held in New York to show the technology of today, what item would you want to show? Write a letter to exposition leaders, describing your choice and the reasons you selected it.

6. **DRAW CONCLUSIONS** On a separate sheet of paper, copy and complete this graphic organizer.

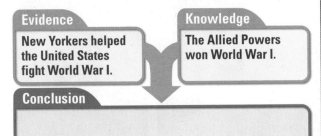

Evidence		Knowledge
New Yorkers helped the United States fight World War I.		The Allied Powers won World War I.

Conclusion

The Pan-American Exposition

Background In May 1901 Vice President Theodore Roosevelt announced the opening of the Pan-American Exposition. Over the next six months, the exposition drew about 8 million visitors to Buffalo. Many people came to see new inventions such as electric lighting.

DBQ **Document-Based Question** Study these primary sources and answer the questions.

MAP OF EXPOSITION GROUNDS

The Temple of Music (right) had daily music concerts. The Stadium (bottom right) hosted bicycle races and cowboy shows. The New York State Building (bottom left) is the only exposition building still standing.

DBQ **1** What appears to be the tallest structure?

TICKET

An exposition ticket cost visitors 50 cents.

DBQ ② When did the Pan-American Exposition start? When did it end?

POSTCARD

The Electric Tower was one of many lighted buildings at the exposition.

ELECTRIC TOWER.

DBQ ④ Buffalo was nicknamed the "City of Light." Why do you think this was so?

BUTTON

This button shows the logo of the Pan-American Exposition.

DBQ ③ What continents do the shapes of the female figures resemble?

SOUVENIR

In 1901, exposition souvenirs were very common, but today many are rare and valuable.

DBQ ⑤ Why do you think this souvenir is in the shape of a buffalo?

WRITE ABOUT IT

Imagine that you have been asked to plan a new public building, such as a school or post office. Draw your design, and then write a report to explain how the building will be used.

 GO ONLINE For more resources, go to www.harcourtschool.com/ss1

Lesson 2

Good Times and Bad

1900 ———— 1920–1940 ———— Present

WHAT TO KNOW

What was life like in New York during the Great Depression and the New Deal years?

VOCABULARY

consumer p. 307

consumer good p. 307

assembly line p. 307

aviation p. 307

depression p. 309

unemployment p. 309

DRAW CONCLUSIONS

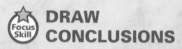

Evidence → Knowledge

Conclusion

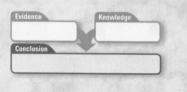

YOU ARE THERE

It is a fall day in New York City in 1918. You watch a parade make its way down the street. The marching women are holding signs that say "Let us vote." You remember that last year women in New York won the right to vote in state elections. But these women want to be allowed to vote in all elections. This is just one of the big changes that have been happening all over the country in recent years.

The Twenties in New York

In the years after World War I, people worked to change laws that they thought were unfair. Women's groups worked for an amendment to the United States Constitution that would give women the right to vote in

Women worked to gain support for suffrage, or the right to vote.

VOTES FOR WOMEN

all elections. Women won the right to vote in all elections when the Nineteenth Amendment was passed in 1920.

In the 1920s new products changed consumers' lives. A **consumer** is a person who buys a product or service. People had the chance to buy washing machines and vacuum cleaners. These **consumer goods**, or products made for personal use, shortened the time it took to do many jobs.

Many of New York's first radio stations were on the air by 1922. Movie theaters also became popular. The first movies had no sound, but by the late 1920s the movies had become "talkies."

Before World War I began, Henry Ford had started making low-cost cars. He did this by producing the cars on factory **assembly lines**. Instead of being built one at a time, Ford's cars were assembled, or put together, as they moved past a line of workers. This helped workers make more products in much less time.

Movie theaters were some of the first places in New York to have air-conditioning.

Progress was also made in **aviation**, the making and flying of airplanes. In 1927 Charles A. Lindbergh became the first person to fly alone across the Atlantic Ocean. Lindbergh's flight from New York to Paris, France, changed the way people thought about air travel. Soon commercial airlines were carrying passengers and goods.

REVIEW What changes took place in transportation in the 1920s?

In 1920 there were only 2,000 radios in homes in the United States.

Duke Ellington (right) was a famous band leader and jazz musician.

The Harlem Renaissance

The Great Migration of African Americans that began in the 1890s continued during and after World War I. Jobs in factories led many African Americans to move to New York and other northern states.

All through the 1920s, Harlem, in New York City, remained the largest African American community in the United States. It was the site of a new wave of African American culture and creativity. So many artists, musicians, and writers lived and worked in Harlem that this time was called the Harlem Renaissance (REH•nuh•sahns). A renaissance is a time of new ideas in art and culture. Renaissance is French for "rebirth."

A new kind of music called jazz became very popular during the Harlem Renaissance. Jazz blends West African rhythms and the spirituals once sung by slaves with other musical styles.

Many people went to Harlem to see performances by singers like Billie Holiday and Ethel Waters, band leaders like Duke Ellington, and dancers like Bill "Bojangles" Robinson. Others read the works of writers such as Countee Cullen, Zora Neale Hurston, and Langston Hughes. Like other writers of the Harlem Renaissance, they wrote about African American life in the United States.

REVIEW What was the Harlem Renaissance?

Zora Neale Hurston moved to New York City after traveling with a theater company.

The End of Good Times

In New York and across the United States, the 1920s brought good times for most people. Cities and businesses grew. Many people made money in the stock market.

For most of the 1920s, stocks went up in value. Many people borrowed from banks so they could buy more stocks. Then, in October 1929, stock prices began to fall. Thousands of people rushed to sell their stocks before the value fell even more. On October 29, stock prices fell so low that the drop was called a crash. Almost everyone who owned stocks lost money.

In New York and the rest of the country, the stock market crash of 1929 led to an economic depression (dih•PREH•shuhn). A **depression** is a time when there are few jobs and people have little money. The economic depression that began in 1929 was so bad that it became known as the Great Depression.

Many people had to sell their belongings to get money to buy food and other necessary items after 1929.

Many banks closed, and many of their customers lost all their money. Manufacturing slowed down, and many businesses closed. **Unemployment**, or the number of workers without jobs, was high. People lost their cars, homes, and other property when they could no longer make payments on them.

REVIEW What happened to the stock market in 1929?

These unemployed people in New York City are waiting for a free meal. What other kinds of help do you think people needed during the Great Depression?

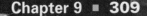

During the 1930s, the mayor of New York City, Fiorello La Guardia (left), and President Franklin D. Roosevelt worked to help people in New York City.

A New Deal

In 1932 New Yorker Franklin D. Roosevelt was elected President of the United States. He promised a New Deal for Americans. The New Deal was the name given to programs set up to help end the Great Depression.

New Deal programs put people to work building roads, bridges, and hospitals. They also paid artists, writers, actors, and musicians so that people could enjoy their works. Other projects built parks. In New York, several state parks, including Allegany State Park and Gilbert State Park, began as New Deal projects.

In New York City, Mayor Fiorello La Guardia (fee•uh•REH•loh luh•GWAR•dee•uh) approved projects to build houses that poor people could afford. Other projects improved police and fire protection and built new roads, bridges, and a modern airport.

REVIEW What was the New Deal?

REVIEW

1. **WHAT TO KNOW** What was life like in New York during the Great Depression and the New Deal years?

2. **VOCABULARY** Use **depression** and **unemployment** in a sentence about New York in the 1930s.

3. **HISTORY** What were some New Deal projects in New York?

4. **CRITICAL THINKING** What was the relationship between banks closing and people losing their jobs?

5. **CONDUCT AN INTERVIEW** Imagine that you are interviewing President Franklin D. Roosevelt, an artist from the Harlem Renaissance, or a supporter of women's right to vote. Write three questions you would ask that person.

Have a classmate write the answers that the person might have given.

6. **DRAW CONCLUSIONS** On a separate sheet of paper, copy and complete this graphic organizer.

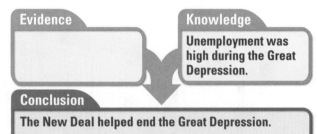

Evidence		Knowledge
		Unemployment was high during the Great Depression.

Conclusion
The New Deal helped end the Great Depression.

World War II and After

1941–Present

YOU ARE THERE Life has been different since the war started. Your mother now has a job helping build ships. Your family also cannot buy as much sugar, meat, and coffee as it used to. But you don't mind too much. Your father is one of the soldiers who will get that food. Still, you can't wait for the war to be over. Will life ever be the same afterward?

Another World War

On September 1, 1939, Germany invaded its neighbor Poland. Two days later Britain and France declared war on Germany. This marked the start of World War II. On one side were the Allies, made up of Britain, France, and later the Soviet Union. On the other side were the Axis Powers, made up of Germany, Italy, and Japan.

WHAT TO KNOW How did New York grow and change after World War II?

VOCABULARY
ration p. 312
civil rights p. 314
terrorism p. 315

DRAW CONCLUSIONS

Evidence	Knowledge

Conclusion

During World War II, workers at the Brooklyn Navy Yard built or repaired more than 15,000 ships.

A World War II Political Cartoon

Background A political cartoon uses symbols to express an opinion about politics or current events.

1 This list shows the nation's war-supply production for 1942.

2 Uncle Sam, who stands for the United States government, is making war supplies.

3 President Franklin D. Roosevelt is speaking to the American people.

DBQ Document-Based Question Why do you think Uncle Sam is sweating?

The United States did not enter the war at first. Only after Japan attacked the United States naval base at Pearl Harbor, Hawaii, on December 7, 1941, did the United States declare war.

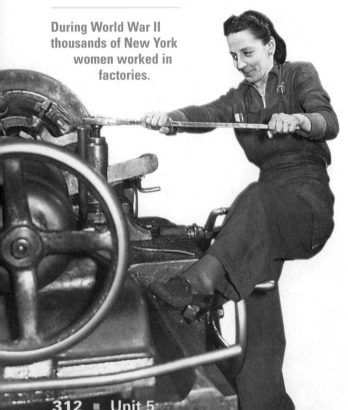

During World War II thousands of New York women worked in factories.

Once again, New York sent more people to serve in the war than any other state. New York factories made war supplies, from boots and tents to warplanes and battleships. New York military bases trained troops, and New York ports shipped soldiers and supplies overseas.

New Yorkers at home bought war bonds and worked in factories that produced war goods. As in World War I, many women took over men's factory jobs. Other women joined the armed forces.

To make sure that soldiers had enough supplies, the government rationed some products. To **ration** something is to limit the amount of it that a person may buy at one time. Gasoline, rubber, and sugar were rationed.

By the time the Allies finally won the war in 1945, millions of people had been killed. About 400,000 Americans had died. More than 30,000 of these were New Yorkers.

REVIEW How did New Yorkers contribute to the war effort?

· BIOGRAPHY ·

Eleanor Roosevelt
1884–1962

Character Trait: Compassion

During her time as First Lady and afterward, Eleanor Roosevelt had many opportunities to help people. During the Great Depression she wrote a newspaper column to let people know what the government was doing to help them. As a delegate to the United Nations, she helped write and pass the Universal Declaration of Human Rights. This document states the basic rights of all people to free speech, a fair trial, and an education.

GO ONLINE For more resources, go to
www.harcourtschool.com/ss1

Decades of Change

In order to keep another world war from happening, world leaders joined together to form the United Nations, or the UN. The UN was created to help member nations work together to solve problems. Each member nation sends a delegate to the UN. Former First Lady Eleanor Roosevelt was the first delegate to represent the United States. In 1952 the UN headquarters building opened in New York City.

During the 1950s and 1960s, people continued to move to New York in search of a better way of life. However, not everyone enjoyed the same opportunities. Across the country some groups, such as African Americans, Hispanic Americans, and Asian Americans, were often treated unfairly.

The UN headquarters in New York City.

In many places, members of these groups could not work in certain jobs or were not welcome in certain neighborhoods.

To protest this unfair treatment, many people began working for civil rights. **Civil rights** are the rights of all citizens to equal treatment. One early civil rights leader was W. E. B. Du Bois (doo•BOYS). In 1909 Du Bois and other leaders founded the National Association for the Advancement of Colored People, or NAACP, in New York City. One of its best-known leaders was Thurgood Marshall, who later became the first African American justice on the United States Supreme Court.

Other New Yorkers also helped the Civil Rights movement. Jackie Robinson played baseball for the Brooklyn Dodgers. In 1947 he became the first African American to play in the major leagues. In 1968 Shirley Chisholm from Brooklyn became the first African American woman elected to the United States Congress.

Other groups—including women, Hispanic Americans, and Asian Americans—also joined the struggle for equal rights. In 1971 New York City's Herman Badillo became the first Puerto Rican–born member of the United States Congress. In 1974 Asian Americans protesting unfair job laws founded Asian Americans for Equality.

The 1970s were a difficult time for New York. The state's economy was not doing well, and many people lost their jobs. New York City suffered increased crime and cuts in public services. New York leaders of the 1980s and 1990s had to work hard to make people feel good about New York again.

REVIEW How did New Yorkers help the Civil Rights movement?

Shirley Chisholm (below) often took part in civil rights protests in New York. This protest (right) took place in Queens in 1964.

Before their destruction, the World Trade Center towers were the tallest buildings in New York City. After the attacks Mayor Rudolph Giuliani (right) helped organize the cleanup effort (above).

New York United

In the 1990s New York faced a new crisis—terrorism. **Terrorism** is the use of violence to promote a cause. Terrorists first attacked the World Trade Center in New York City in 1993. At the time, the Trade Center's twin towers were among the tallest buildings in the world. That bomb attack killed six people and injured many more.

On September 11, 2001, the World Trade Center was attacked a second time. Terrorists hijacked (HY•jakt), or illegally took control of, four airplanes. They crashed one into each of the Trade Center's twin towers, causing them to collapse. The third plane crashed into

the Pentagon, near Washington, D.C. The fourth plane crashed in an empty field in Pennsylvania. In all, more than 3,000 people died in the attacks.

Rudolph Giuliani, who was mayor of New York City at the time, helped New Yorkers work together to recover from the attacks. Thousands of other New Yorkers—police, firefighters, and citizens—became heroes for trying to rescue people who were inside the towers.

After the attacks, President George W. Bush met with Vice President Dick Cheney (left) and Secretary of State Colin Powell. Powell is from New York.

Giuliani reminded everyone of the city's strong spirit, saying, "New York is still here. We've suffered terrible losses . . . but we will be here, tomorrow and forever."

The events of September 11, 2001, affected New York in different ways. Many people lost loved ones. New Yorkers also had to learn how to respond to terrorist alerts. At the same time, the state's economy suffered—which led to cuts in jobs and services. Today New Yorkers continue to work toward a better future. One example of this is the design for the new World Trade Center. Another way New Yorkers are trying to make a better future is by helping defend our country. Many people in the armed forces are from New York. These New Yorkers are making sure that the United States remains free.

REVIEW How did the terrorist attacks affect New York?

REVIEW

1. **WHAT TO KNOW** How did New York grow and change after World War II?

2. **VOCABULARY** Use the word **ration** to tell how New Yorkers helped the United States fight World War II.

3. **HISTORY** What event caused the United States to enter World War II?

4. **CRITICAL THINKING** How might the African Americans who were part of the Civil Rights movement have influenced others to work for equal rights?

5. **COMPARE AND CONTRAST** Ask a family member how life in New York in the 1960s and 1970s was different from life today. Then report your findings to the class.

6. **DRAW CONCLUSIONS** On a separate sheet of paper, copy and complete this graphic organizer.

Evidence

Knowledge
In the 1950s and 1960s some groups were treated unfairly.

Conclusion
African Americans, Hispanic Americans, Asian Americans, and women gained more rights.

Read a Circle Graph

VOCABULARY

circle graph

WHY IT MATTERS

Suppose you want to show in a simple, clear way how the production of war supplies during World War II was divided among some cities in New York. One way you could show this information is by making a circle graph. A **circle graph** is sometimes called a pie graph because it is round and is divided into pieces that look like slices of a pie.

WHAT YOU NEED TO KNOW

The circle graph on this page shows how the total amount of war supplies made in New York was divided among some cities and metropolitan areas. A percent, shown by the % symbol, is given to each part of the graph. One percent (1%) is one-hundredth of something. For example, if you cut a pie into 100 pieces, those 100 pieces together would equal the whole pie, or 100 percent (100%) of it. Fifty pieces would be one-half of the pie, or 50% of it.

PRACTICE THE SKILL

Use the circle graph to answer these questions.

1 What area contributed the most to New York State's total war-supply production during World War II?

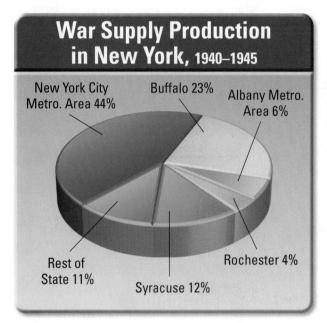

War Supply Production in New York, 1940–1945

New York City Metro. Area 44%

Buffalo 23%

Albany Metro. Area 6%

Rest of State 11%

Syracuse 12%

Rochester 4%

2 What percent of New York State's total war-supply production took place in Rochester?

3 How much more did Buffalo contribute to the state's total war-supply production than Syracuse?

APPLY WHAT YOU LEARNED

Use the circle graph to write a paragraph about the cities that produced war supplies during World War II. Think about each city's location to give possible reasons why some cities produced more war supplies than others. Compare your conclusions with those of a classmate.

Chapter Review

Summarize the Chapter

Focus Skill **Draw Conclusions** Complete this graphic organizer to show that you can draw conclusions about New York in the twentieth and twenty-first centuries.

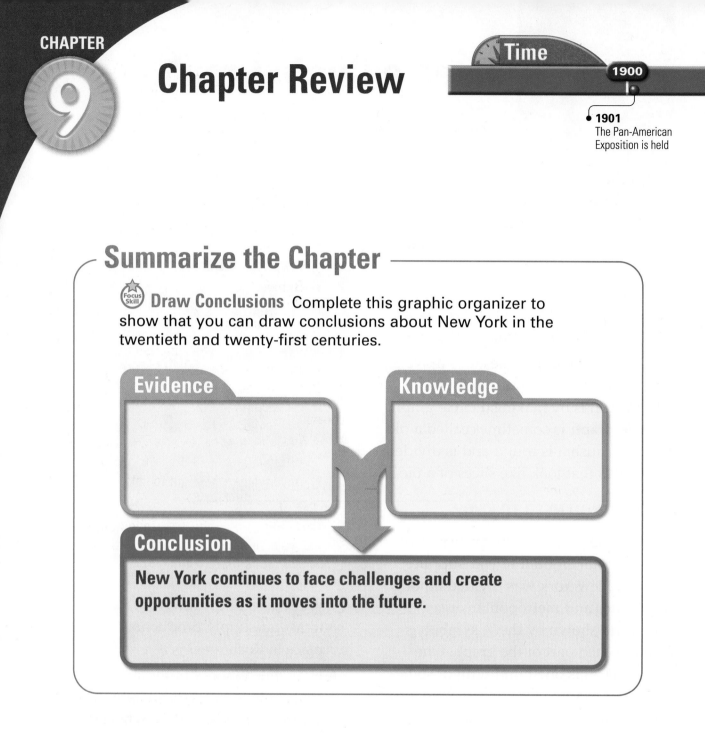

Evidence

Knowledge

Conclusion

New York continues to face challenges and create opportunities as it moves into the future.

THINK & WRITE

Write a Letter Imagine that you are working on a New Deal project in New York during the 1930s. Write a letter to a friend describing the project.

Write a Short Story Write a short story describing life in New York City after the stock market crash of 1929.

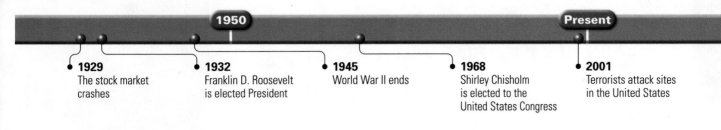

1950   **Present**

1929
The stock market
crashes

1932
Franklin D. Roosevelt
is elected President

1945
World War II ends

1968
Shirley Chisholm
is elected to the
United States Congress

2001
Terrorists attack sites
in the United States

USE THE TIME LINE

Use the chapter summary time line to answer these questions.

1 When did World War II end?

2 Was Franklin D. Roosevelt elected President before or after the stock market crash?

USE VOCABULARY

Identify the term that correctly matches each definition.

exposition (p. 300)
interest (p. 303)
consumer (p. 307)
aviation (p. 307)
ration (p. 312)

3 the money a borrower pays for the use of loaned money

4 to limit the amount of something that someone may buy at one time

5 a person who buys a product or service

6 a fair

7 the making and flying of airplanes

RECALL FACTS

Answer these questions.

8 Which United States President helped start the National Forest Service?

9 Who were Countee Cullen, Zora Neale Hurston, and Langston Hughes?

10 Which countries made up the Axis Powers during World War II?

Write the letter of the best choice.

11 **TEST PREP**   The Pan-American Exposition was held in—
A Brooklyn.
B Buffalo.
C Harlem.
D New York City.

12 **TEST PREP**   The Nineteenth Amendment to the United States Constitution—
F allowed American companies to produce automobiles and airplanes.
G provided funding for the New Deal programs.
H gave women the right to vote.
J created the NAACP.

13 **TEST PREP**   The first United States delegate to the United Nations was—
A Thurgood Marshall.
B Herman Badillo.
C Shirley Chisholm.
D Eleanor Roosevelt.

THINK CRITICALLY

14 Why do you think many women thought it was important to work for suffrage?

15 How do you think the Civil Rights movement changed life in New York?

APPLY SKILLS

Read a Circle Graph
Use the circle graph on page 317 to answer the following question.

16 How much of New York's war-supply production did Buffalo and Syracuse produce together?

STUDY SKILLS

MAKE AN OUTLINE

An outline can help you organize main ideas and details.

- Topics in an outline are shown by Roman numerals.

- Main ideas about each topic are shown by capital letters.

- Details about each main idea are shown by numbers.

New York Today and Tomorrow

I. Living in New York

  A. A Growing and Changing Population

    1. Third-largest state

    2. Most New Yorkers live in metropolitan areas

    3.

  B. Celebrating Different Cultures

    1.

    2.

New York Today and Tomorrow

Rockefeller Center, New York City

Lesson 1

Living in New York

WHAT TO KNOW
What makes New York an interesting place to live?

VOCABULARY
ethnic group p. 323
recreation p. 326

DRAW CONCLUSIONS

YOU ARE THERE "Are you new here?" a classmate asks. "Yes, we just moved to the United States." It's your first day at a big school in New York City. The students there come from many different cultures. You're excited. You wonder whom you'll meet next.

A Growing and Changing Population

Each year thousands of people move to New York from other places. Over time, those immigrant groups have helped shape our state's history and culture. They have made New York a more interesting place in which to live.

Today, more than 19 million people live in New York. That makes New York the third-largest state in population. However, the state's population is not spread out evenly. Most New Yorkers—about 92 out of every 100— live within one of the state's metropolitan areas.

With a population of about 8 million people, New York City is at the center of the state's largest metropolitan area. In fact, more than half of all New Yorkers live there. Other

FAST FACT About one out of every four people in New York is less than 18 years old.

large metropolitan areas in the state include Suffolk and Nassau Counties, on Long Island, and the areas around Albany, Syracuse, Rochester, and Buffalo.

Part of New York's growth is caused by the arrival of people from other countries. Today, more than 3 million people living in New York were born in another country. Almost 150,000 new immigrants arrive each year.

As they did in the past, people come to New York from all over the world. However, most immigrants now come from Asia and Latin America instead of from Europe. Latin America includes all the countries in the Western Hemisphere south of the United States. Many of the immigrants from Latin America come from island nations in the Caribbean Sea.

REVIEW Where do most New Yorkers live?

Celebrating Different Cultures

Because so many people in New York have come from other places, the state's population includes many different ethnic groups. An **ethnic group** is a group of people from the same country, of the same race, or with a shared culture. Each ethnic group has brought some of its own culture to New York.

Cultural differences among New Yorkers can be found in the kinds of music they listen to, the foods they eat,

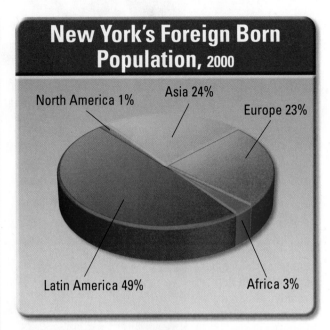

New York's Foreign Born Population, 2000

- North America 1%
- Asia 24%
- Europe 23%
- Latin America 49%
- Africa 3%

Analyze Graphs Immigrants from all over the world have made New York their home.
From where have the greatest number of recent immigrants to New York come?

the clothes they wear, the religious groups they belong to, and also the languages they speak. These differences have made New York a more interesting place and have given all New Yorkers a richer life.

Stores that sell Latin American foods provide New York with a taste of Hispanic culture.

Each year thousands of people visit the Brooklyn Botanic Garden to enjoy the blooming of the cherry blossoms.

Every year New Yorkers hold festivals to celebrate their different cultures. These festivals often include music, parades, games, and foods. For example, each June thousands of people gather to enjoy the Celebrate Brooklyn! Performing Arts Festival. Singers, dancers, and musicians from around the world perform at the festival.

Two other popular festivals take place near Whiteface Mountain in the Adirondacks. In August, people gather for the Native American Festival. Native Americans from across the country celebrate their cultures through dance, songs, and stories. In September, people of Scottish heritage celebrate their culture at the Scottish Highlands Festival.

REVIEW How are different cultures celebrated in New York?

The Arts in New York

Another way New Yorkers can learn about cultures is by visiting cultural centers, libraries, theaters, and museums. Most of New York's larger cities offer such places. For example, the Albright-Knox Art Gallery in Buffalo features a collection of modern art. The New York State Museum in Albany is the oldest state museum in the United States.

New York City is one of the world's leading centers of culture. It is home to the nation's largest public library—the New York Public Library. The Museum of Chinese in the Americas has

A bagpiper at the Scottish Highlands Festival

information about the history and the culture of Chinese Americans. The Hispanic Society of America has a museum and library for the study of Hispanic arts and cultures.

Famous works of art are displayed in New York City's many art museums, such as the Metropolitan Museum of Art. The city is also famous for its orchestras, ballets, television studios, and theaters. In Broadway theaters, audiences are treated to some of the best acting, singing, and dancing anywhere.

Grandma Moses

New York State has been and still is home to many famous writers, musicians, and artists. Artist Frederick Church lived much of his life in the Hudson River valley. In the 1820s he and other artists developed a style of painting known as the Hudson River School. Many of their paintings were of the Catskill Mountains. Other famous New York artists include Grandma Moses and Andy Warhol.

Among New York's best-known writers of the past were Washington Irving, Walt Whitman, and Edith Wharton. In the 1800s Walt Whitman, a Long Islander, was one of the country's best-loved poets. In the 1900s Edith Wharton wrote about life in New York City.

REVIEW **What makes New York a center for the arts?**

The Solomon R. Guggenheim (GOO•guhn•hym) Museum, in New York City, displays modern paintings and sculptures.

Other Favorite Pastimes

Enjoying the arts is a favorite pastime for many New Yorkers. However, New Yorkers can also take part in other kinds of recreation (reh•kree•AY•shuhn). **Recreation** is an activity that people do for fun. New York's varied climates and landforms allow for many kinds of outdoor activities. Popular summer sports include bicycling, swimming, and boating. In winter, some New Yorkers head to the mountains to ski and ride snowmobiles. Others get out their ice skates and find the nearest skating rink.

New Yorkers can also watch many sporting events. The United States Open, a major tennis tournament, is held each summer at the National Tennis Center in Flushing.

New Yorkers can watch sports teams in action, too. In addition to its many college teams, New York has professional basketball, football, and hockey teams. Many of these teams have winning records. In baseball, both the Mets and the Yankees have won World Series.

Other pastimes New Yorkers enjoy are seasonal events. The country's oldest winter festival, for example, takes place each year at Saranac Lake. The first Saranac Lake Winter Carnival was held in 1897. Today, people come to the

• GEOGRAPHY •

Cooperstown
Understanding Places and Regions

Baseball has a long tradition in New York. Many people believe that the game was invented in 1839 in Cooperstown. Some stories say that it began when Abner Doubleday made changes to a popular game called Town Ball.

To celebrate the one-hundredth anniversary of baseball, in 1939, New York leaders decided to build the National Baseball Hall of Fame in Cooperstown. Today visitors come to Cooperstown to learn more about the history of baseball. They also come to honor baseball's great players, including Babe Ruth, Jackie Robinson, and Willie Mays.

Christy Mathewson was one of the first players honored in the National Baseball Hall of Fame.

GIANTS

Mathewson
OF THE
NEW YORK NAT-ONALS

Otsego Lake

NATIONAL BASEBALL HALL OF FAME

Lake St.
80
Main St.
Church St.
Main St.
80
28 Glen Ave.
80
Grove St.
Maple St.
Chestnut St.
Elm St.
Pioneer St.
Fair St.
Susquehanna Ave.
River St.
Susquehanna R.
31
Estli Ave.
Beaver St.
28
Walnut St.
Mill St.

0   500   1,000 Feet
0   150   300 Meters

Ice sculptures are always a part of the Saranac Lake Winter Carnival.

carnival to watch and take part in winter sports such as snow volleyball, inner-tube races, and snowshoe softball.

Some communities also hold harvest festivals to celebrate different crops or products. Among these are the Apple Country Festival in Busti, the Central New York Maple Festival in Marathon, and the Oyster Festival in Oyster Bay.

New York also has many fairs. They often highlight different crafts and the importance of farming. The Lewis County Fair in Lowville is the oldest fair. The largest fair is the Great New York State Fair in Syracuse. More than 1 million people attend it.

REVIEW **What do New Yorkers do for recreation?**

REVIEW

1. **WHAT TO KNOW** What makes New York an interesting place to live?

2. **VOCABULARY** Use the term **ethnic group** in a sentence about New York.

3. **CULTURE** In what ways is New York City a world center for culture?

4. **CRITICAL THINKING** Why do you think so many people in New York live in and around New York City?

5. **MAKE A CALENDAR** Research other festivals in New York. On a calendar show the dates on which the festivals are held. Tell the locations of the festivals and describe the festivals' events.

6. **DRAW CONCLUSIONS** On a separate sheet of paper, copy and complete this graphic organizer.

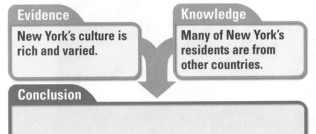

Evidence	Knowledge
New York's culture is rich and varied.	Many of New York's residents are from other countries.

Conclusion

Read a Population Map

VOCABULARY

population density

➡ WHY IT MATTERS

You may live in one of New York's large cities or in a suburb. Perhaps you live in a small town or in a rural area. Each kind of place has a different population density. **Population density** is the number of people who live in an area of a certain size. This size is usually 1 square mile or 1 square kilometer. A square mile is a square piece of land with sides that are each 1 mile long. A square kilometer is a square piece of land with sides that are each 1 kilometer long.

The population density of your area may affect the way you live. Suppose that 6 people live on each square mile of land. With only 6 people per square mile, there would be a lot of space for each person. Now suppose that 6,000 people live on each square mile. The area would be much more crowded.

➡ WHAT YOU NEED TO KNOW

People are spread unevenly across Earth the way resources are. More people live in some areas than in others. Would you expect to find the highest population density in a city, a small town, or a rural area? In which area would you expect to find the lowest population density?

Large cities like Buffalo (left) have many more residents than small communities like Roseboom (right).

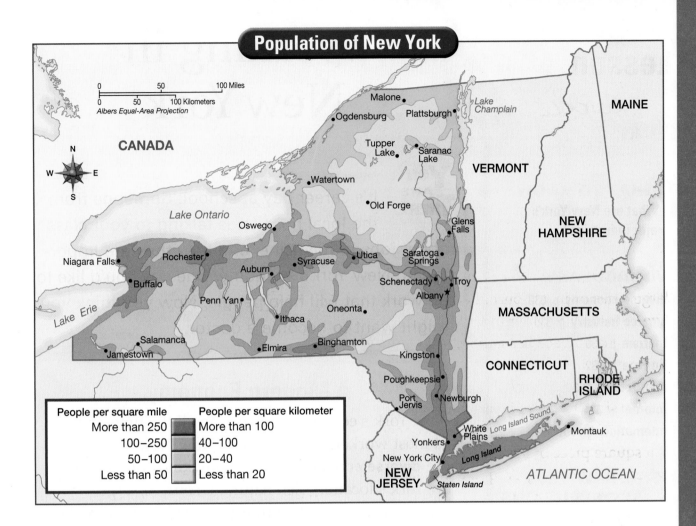

Population of New York

0   50   100 Miles
0   50   100 Kilometers
Albers Equal-Area Projection

CANADA

Lake Ontario

Lake Erie

MAINE

VERMONT

NEW HAMPSHIRE

MASSACHUSETTS

CONNECTICUT

RHODE ISLAND

NEW JERSEY

ATLANTIC OCEAN

Malone
Ogdensburg
Plattsburgh
Lake Champlain
Tupper Lake
Saranac Lake
Watertown
Old Forge
Glens Falls
Oswego
Rochester
Niagara Falls
Auburn
Syracuse
Utica
Saratoga Springs
Buffalo
Schenectady
Troy
Albany
Penn Yan
Oneonta
Ithaca
Salamanca
Elmira
Binghamton
Jamestown
Kingston
Poughkeepsie
Port Jervis
Newburgh
White Plains
Long Island Sound
Montauk
Yonkers
New York City
Long Island
Staten Island

People per square mile		People per square kilometer
More than 250		More than 100
100–250		40–100
50–100		20–40
Less than 50		Less than 20

The map on this page is a population map of New York. A population map shows where people live. It also shows the population densities of different areas.

▶ PRACTICE THE SKILL

❶ What is the lowest population density shown on the map? What color is used to show it?

❷ What is the highest population density on the map? What color is used to show it?

❸ Find Buffalo on the map. What is the population density of the area in which the city is located?

❹ Which city has the higher population density, Ithaca or Albany?

❺ Which city has the lower population density, Plattsburgh or Old Forge?

❻ How do you think population density affects the lives of people?

▶ APPLY WHAT YOU LEARNED

Choose five of the cities shown on the population map. List the population density of each city. Then make a bar graph comparing the population densities of the cities you chose.

Practice your map and globe skills with the **GeoSkills CD-ROM**.

MAP AND GLOBE SKILLS

Working in New York

WHAT TO KNOW
What are New York's major industries?

VOCABULARY
diverse economy p. 330
service industry p. 330
tourism p. 330
finance p. 332
high-tech p. 333
Internet p. 334
international trade p. 335

DRAW CONCLUSIONS

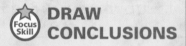

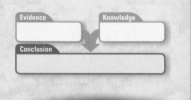

You Are There

It's career day at school. Someone from the local hospital is talking to your class about jobs in medicine, and how they are important to New York's economy. One day you'd like to do work that will help people. Now you think you might want to become a doctor.

A Modern Economy

New York's economy is changing all the time. In the past most workers were farmers. Now New York has a more **diverse economy**. It has many kinds of industries. New York's location, rich natural resources, large population, and excellent transportation systems make this possible.

Service industries make up the largest part of New York's economy. A **service industry** is made up of businesses that provide services rather than produce or sell goods. Nearly one-third of New York's workers have service jobs. They may work in hotels or stores or repair cars.

The fastest-growing service industry is tourism. **Tourism** is the selling of goods or services to visitors. Publishing also provides jobs for New Yorkers. New York City alone has more book and magazine publishers than any other city in the United States.

Doctors provide health services to people.

Analyze Graphs   This graph shows the number of New Yorkers who work in different kinds of industries.

❖ About how many people work in retail?

New York's Top Industries, 2001

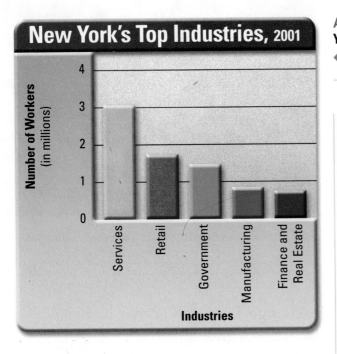

parts of the state. In Syracuse, workers build machines and electronic items. In Rochester, they make lenses and film. In Buffalo, they process food and make electronic items and chemicals.

Many New Yorkers also have jobs in construction, mining, fishing, and agriculture. The main farming activity is dairy farming. Most dairy farms are in the Hudson and Mohawk River valleys. The dairies that buy milk from these farms process it for market. They make cheese, ice cream, and other products. These products are then sold to stores so that people can buy them.

Other manufacturing industries provide jobs, too. Goods made include clothing, medicines, machinery, and toys. Much of the manufacturing takes place in the New York City metropolitan area and in the central and western

REVIEW In which kinds of industries do most New Yorkers work?

From Farm to Market

Analyze Diagrams   Grapes are one of the main crops grown in New York.

1 Grape vines are grown.
2 The grapes are picked for processing.
3 The grapes are pressed and bottled for market.
4 Consumers like you buy and drink grape juice.

❖ Are grapes pressed before or after they are picked?

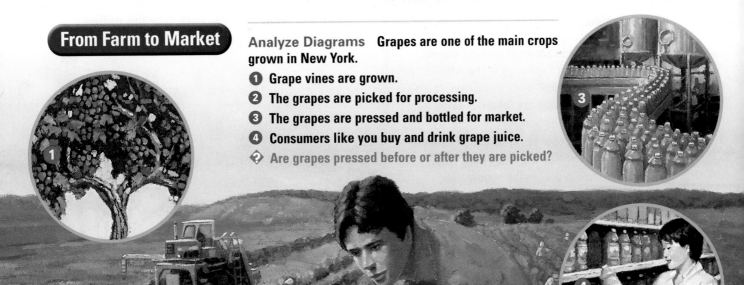

The Nation's Financial Capital

Albany, Rochester, and Buffalo are all important centers of finance in New York. **Finance** is the use or management of money. However, New York City is the state's leading financial center. It is also the leading financial center in the United States. New York City is home to many of the nation's largest banks and companies.

The New York Stock Exchange is a main reason why New York City became such an important financial center. The New York Stock Exchange, which opened in the early 1800s on Wall Street, was the country's first stock

Wall Street is the center of New York City's financial district.

exchange. Banks and other financial businesses grew up around it.

Today, the name *Wall Street* is used to describe the nation's overall financial market. About 3,000 companies trade their stock on the New York Stock Exchange. The American Stock Exchange, also in New York City, is the second-largest exchange.

REVIEW Why is New York City the nation's leading financial center?

A CLOSER LOOK
The New York Stock Exchange

A stock exchange is a place where stocks, or shares in a company, are bought and sold. People buy stocks in hopes of making money. The New York Stock Exchange is the world's leading stock exchange.

1. These broker booths are where brokers receive stock orders.
2. These trading posts are where floor brokers place orders to buy or sell stocks.
3. This platform is where the opening and closing bells are sounded.
4. These electronic message boards list a stock's most recent price.

❓ Where does a floor broker place an order to buy or sell a stock?

New Technologies

In recent years high-technology, or high-tech, industries have become more important to the economy of New York. **High-tech** industries invent, build, or use computers and other kinds of electronic equipment. Today, most high-tech industries work to make smaller and faster electronic items.

High-tech manufacturers in several cities build computer parts and microchips. Some microchips process information. Others store information. Microchips are used in computers, compact disc (CD) players, digital video disc (DVD) players, and other electronic items.

Workers in New York manufacture computer chips and other high-tech products.

Researchers in Rochester and other New York cities are developing new and better communication tools. Some of these tools make Internet connections much faster and much more reliable.

The **Internet** is a system that links computers around the world. People use the Internet to find and exchange information. People also use the Internet to send electronic mail, or e-mail.

High-tech tools and the Internet have made it easier for people to communicate, trade goods and services, and organize information. People use computers to communicate directly with people in other parts of the world.

High technology is also used to find treatments for diseases. There are more than 700 medical research companies in New York. Some companies develop new medicines. Others research ways to keep people from getting sick.

REVIEW What are some examples of high technology?

New York and the World

Many companies in New York sell their products to markets all over the world. Many companies from other countries also have businesses in New York. This makes New York part of a growing global economy, or worldwide marketplace.

In many ways New York has always been a part of a global economy. In colonial times settlers sent raw materials from New York to England. Then, in

· GEOGRAPHY ·

The St. Lawrence Seaway

Understanding Human Systems

The St. Lawrence Seaway was built by the United States and Canada in the 1950s. It allows ships to sail from the Great Lakes to the Atlantic Ocean. Before it was built, Niagara Falls and rapids on the St. Lawrence River stopped ships from sailing the whole distance.

The seaway stretches about 450 miles (724 km) from Lake Erie to Montreal. It includes the Welland Ship Canal, which connects Lake Erie and Lake Ontario. The seaway has helped make Buffalo and Rochester important manufacturing centers. It has also increased New York's role in international trade.

The St. Lawrence Seaway allows large ships to travel from the Great Lakes to the Atlantic Ocean.

Montreal
Cornwall
St. Lawrence R.
Ogdensburg
CANADA
Kingston
ST. LAWRENCE SEAWAY
Lake Ontario
Oswego
Welland Ship Canal
Lake Erie
Buffalo
NEW YORK

0 25 50 Miles
0 25 50 Kilometers

exchange, merchants in England sent goods to New York.

Today, New York is a leader in **international trade**, or trade with other countries. Through international trade, states and countries can get goods that they cannot make or grow themselves. Each year New York imports and exports millions of dollars' worth of goods. Among its exports are electronic and food products. Imported goods include foods and automobiles.

Because of its location, New York exports many goods to Canada. Goods exported to Canada include automobile engines, computers, books, and film.

New York also buys goods from Canada. Goods imported from Canada include natural gas, petroleum, and automobiles. In 2002, Canadians spent more than $9 billion on goods from New York. New York spent more than $18 billion on goods from Canada. New York's other leading trading partners include Japan, Israel, China, Mexico, and Belgium.

Before imported goods can be sold, however, they must pass through ports of entry. These are harbors or airports where imports can be inspected by government officials. The Port Authority of New York is the largest port of entry on the Atlantic coast of North America. At its center is New York Harbor.

REVIEW Why is international trade important?

REVIEW

1. **WHAT TO KNOW** What are New York's major industries?

2. **VOCABULARY** How is the **Internet** useful?

3. **ECONOMICS** How is the New York Stock Exchange important to New York's economy?

4. **CRITICAL THINKING** What might New York's economy be like if it had only one industry?

5. ✏️ **WRITE A BUSINESS PLAN** Is there a business or service that is missing in your community? Write a short paragraph describing a business that you could start in your community. Don't forget to give your business a name. Share your idea with the rest of the class.

6. ⭐ **DRAW CONCLUSIONS** On a separate sheet of paper, copy and complete this graphic organizer.
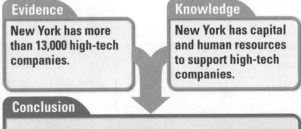

Evidence		Knowledge
New York has more than 13,000 high-tech companies.		New York has capital and human resources to support high-tech companies.

Conclusion

Read a Land Use and Product Map

VOCABULARY
land use

▶ WHY IT MATTERS

What do people in New York use their land for? What kinds of products are grown or made in the state? To find the answers to questions like these, you need a map that shows how the land is used and what products are made. This kind of map is called a land use and product map. **Land use** is the way in which the land in a place is used.

▶ WHAT YOU NEED TO KNOW

The map on page 337 is a land use and product map. It uses colors to show how land is used in New York. Look at the map key to see what each color stands for. The map also uses picture symbols to show where some of New York's leading products are raised or made. To learn what each picture symbol stands for, look at the map key.

These workers are some of the many people who work in manufacturing.

New York Land Use and Products

CANADA

Ogdensburg •
Plattsburgh •
Lake Champlain

VERMONT

• Watertown

Lake Ontario

NEW YORK

Oswego •
Rome •
Glens Falls •

Niagara Falls
Rochester •
Utica •
Saratoga Springs •

Buffalo
Syracuse •
Auburn •
Schenectady •
Troy •

Lake Erie
Bath •
Ithaca •
Albany ★

Jamestown •
Corning •
Binghamton •
Kingston •

PENNSYLVANIA
Poughkeepsie •
Newburgh •

MA

CT

0   50   100 Miles
0   50   100 Kilometers
Albers Equal-Area Projection

NEW JERSEY
New York City
Long Island
ATLANTIC OCEAN

Map Key

- Forest
- Farming and grazing
- Manufacturing
- Apples
- Beef cattle
- Garnets
- Crushed stone
- Electronics
- Fish
- Food products
- Grapes
- Hay
- Machinery
- Milk
- Poultry
- Printing
- Vegetables

PRACTICE THE SKILL

1. Which color shows areas where farming and grazing are the most important land uses?

2. How is most of the land in northern New York used?

3. What is the main land use for the New York City area?

4. If you visited Binghamton, what kinds of products might you see being made there?

5. What kinds of products are made near Buffalo?

APPLY WHAT YOU LEARNED

Draw a land use and product map of the area near your community. Use the map on this page, encyclopedias, library books, and the Internet to find out how people use the land. What products are grown or made in your area? Make a map key to explain the colors and symbols you used for your map. Compare your map with the maps drawn by your classmates.

Practice your map and globe skills with the **GeoSkills CD-ROM**.

WHAT TO KNOW
What are New Yorkers doing to make sure New York remains a great state?

VOCABULARY
urban sprawl p. 339
pollution p. 339
conservation p. 340

DRAW CONCLUSIONS
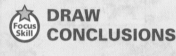

Evidence		Knowledge

Conclusion	

YOU ARE THERE You're visiting your grandparents in Cooperstown. Yesterday, they took you to the National Baseball Hall of Fame. Today, you're going to the Farmers' Museum. "Workers at the museum still farm by using methods from the 1800s," your grandmother explains. "You'll also see some of the farming and cooking tools we used when I was your age."

Remembering New York's Past

Many people from around the world have come to New York to find jobs and a better way of life. This growth has given New Yorkers many new challenges to face. They must work to prepare for the future.

One way New Yorkers plan for the future is by preserving the past. Many of the state's historic sites have been preserved as state and national parks. For example, volunteers have been working to preserve the Mills Mansion in the Hudson River valley. Today, the Mills Mansion is known as the Staatsburgh State Historic Site.

The Farmers' Museum in Cooperstown

The Little Red Lighthouse was first lit in 1921. Today the George Washington Bridge spans over it.

Many people visit the estate to learn about life in New York in the late 1800s and early 1900s.

New Yorkers also help preserve their state's heritage by taking part in various historical reenactments. In a historical reenactment people act out events that took place in the past. Each August, for example, reenactors at Long Lake set up a realistic Civil War camp. They wear Civil War costumes and reenact Civil War battles.

New Yorkers can also learn about their state's heritage in more traditional ways. The New York State Museum in Albany has exhibits that show life in New York from prehistoric times to modern times. The Farmers' Museum, near Cooperstown, shows early farming tools.

REVIEW Why do people work to preserve the state's heritage?

Meeting New Challenges

As the population of New York has increased, its cities have spread out over larger areas. Shopping malls and apartment buildings now stand on land that was once fields and forests. This **urban sprawl**, or the spread of urban areas and the growth of centers of business and shopping, has affected many parts of the state.

Population growth and urban sprawl have caused problems for many New Yorkers. This is especially true in urban areas. Highways and city streets there are often crowded with vehicles. These cars, trucks, and other machines—as well as many factories—put pollution into the air. **Pollution** is anything that makes a natural resource dirty or unsafe to use. Many New Yorkers live along the state's coast, lakes, and rivers.

Some of these waterways have also become polluted.

A growing population also means that more services are needed. For example, as the population increases, more electricity is needed for people to run their homes and businesses. More water is needed, too, and there is more trash to be collected. In addition, the need for schools and hospitals increases along with the population.

The people of New York are dealing with all these problems so that New Yorkers will have a good quality of life. The Department of Environmental Conservation works to control pollution and overcrowding. **Conservation** is the protection and careful use of natural resources. One program, called the Open Space Conservation Plan, works to save New York's open spaces, such as forests and parks. So far, the program has saved more than 394,000 acres of land.

Another program, the Watershed Stewardship, asks New Yorkers to help protect the state's rivers, lakes, and streams. Volunteers test water for quality and clean up garbage.

Areas that were once undeveloped are now home to large communities, such as this New York neighborhood.

POINTS OF VIEW
Urbanization

As more and more people move to cities and build suburbs, some people worry whether the development of the land will affect the environment.

NEW YORK CITY AUDUBON SOCIETY, a conservation group

66 Of the many reasons given to explain the decline [drop] in some bird species, . . . habitat loss seems to emerge [appear] as the primary cause. . . . But the damage has been done and developed land will not revert [return] to open fields and woodland. 99

DR. PETER HUBER, a lawyer and writer

66 It's true that we lose a little green space at the edge of cities as suburbs grow, but that loss is more than offset [canceled out] by all the wilderness gained from the farms abandoned farther away. 99

Analyze the Viewpoints

1. What two views on urbanization are shown above?

2. **Make It Relevant** Look at the Letters to the Editor section of your newspaper. Find two letters that express different viewpoints about the same issue. Then write a paragraph that summarizes the viewpoint of each letter.

New Yorkers are working to reduce pollution. Many cities have recycling programs so that people throw away less. Many New Yorkers also use public transportation systems and drive cars that put less pollution into the air.

REVIEW How are New Yorkers trying to protect their environment?

Education

At this very moment you and your classmates are sharing an important part of life in New York—education. By going to school and learning, you are becoming an important part of New York's future. New York was the first state to offer public elementary schools in every town. Today, New York has more than 5,000 public schools, private schools, colleges, and universities.

People who get a good education do better in what they choose to do, and this helps their state do better as well.

You and the education you receive are very important to New York's future.

Educated people think of ideas for improving the economy and environment. They also know how to express themselves. They can communicate with others to get things done. That helps them be more active citizens.

REVIEW Why is it important to get a good education?

REVIEW

1. **WHAT TO KNOW** What are New Yorkers doing to make sure New York remains a great state?

2. **VOCABULARY** Use the term **urban sprawl** in a sentence that explains its meaning.

3. **CIVICS AND GOVERNMENT** How does a growing population affect New York?

4. **CRITICAL THINKING** Why is preserving its past important to New York's future?

5. **CONDUCT AN INVESTIGATION** Have you ever wondered where your water comes from? Conduct an investigation to discover where the water supply for your home comes from. Also, find out where it goes once the water goes down your drain. Share your findings with the rest of the class.

6. **DRAW CONCLUSIONS** (Focus Skill) On a separate sheet of paper, copy and complete this graphic organizer.

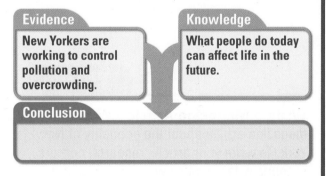

Evidence	Knowledge
New Yorkers are working to control pollution and overcrowding.	What people do today can affect life in the future.

Conclusion

Chapter Review

Summarize the Chapter

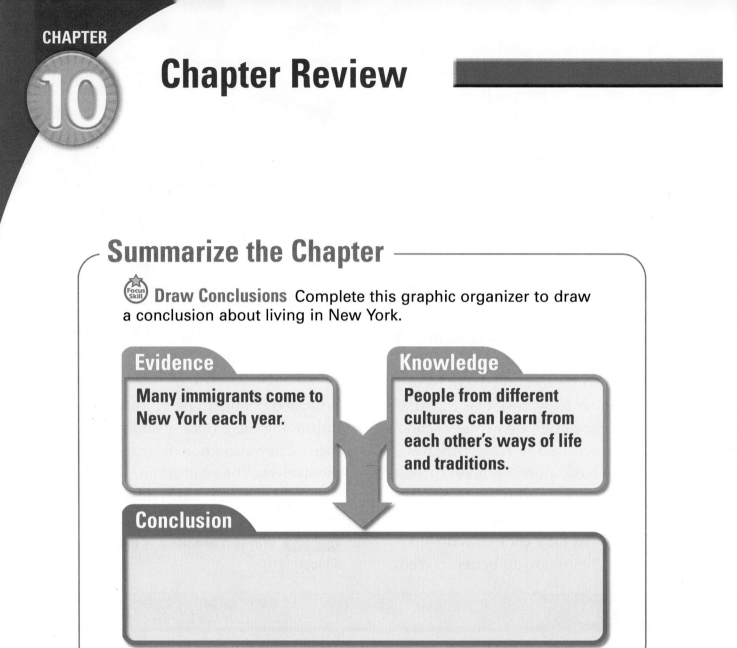

Focus Skill **Draw Conclusions** Complete this graphic organizer to draw a conclusion about living in New York.

Evidence

Many immigrants come to New York each year.

Knowledge

People from different cultures can learn from each other's ways of life and traditions.

Conclusion

THINK & WRITE

Write a Magazine Article Write a magazine article about the economy of New York. To write your article, research centers of tourism, large cities with factories, and high-tech industries.

Write a Persuasive Letter Think about all the reasons New York is a wonderful place to live. Write a persuasive letter to a friend or relative, explaining why he or she should move to this great state.

USE VOCABULARY

Write a term from the list to complete each sentence.

ethnic groups (p. 323)
diverse economy (p. 330)
international trade (p. 335)
urban sprawl (p. 339)
conservation (p. 340)

1 Many different industries make up New York's _____.

2 _____ programs help protect the natural resources of New York.

3 _____ allows New Yorkers to buy goods from other countries.

4 Hispanic people make up one of New York's _____.

5 The spread of urban areas and the growth of centers of business and shopping is called _____.

RECALL FACTS

Answer these questions.

6 In what ways do people show their cultural differences?

7 What is the main reason New York City has become such an important financial center?

8 What are some of the goods that New York exports to Canada?

Write the letter of the best choice.

9 **TEST PREP** Today most immigrants to New York come from—
  A eastern and central Europe.
  B Asia and Latin America.
  C Africa and Europe.
  D Canada and Mexico.

10 **TEST PREP** What industry makes up the largest part of New York's economy?
  F the tourism industry
  G the manufacturing industry
  H the service industry
  J the high-tech industry

THINK CRITICALLY

11 Why is it important for people in New York to work to protect the environment?

12 What do you think might happen if cities did not plan to manage urban sprawl?

APPLY SKILLS

Read a Population Map
Use the population map on page 329 to answer the following questions.

13 What is the population density of the area around Malone?

14 Which city has a higher population density, Yonkers or Glens Falls?

Read a Land Use and Product Map
Use the land use and product map on page 337 to answer these questions.

15 Which industry depends on coastal waters?

16 How is most of the land around Watertown used?

READ ABOUT

Every August nearly one million people visit the Great New York State Fair in Syracuse. The Great New York State Fair is the country's oldest fair. It started in 1841 as a way to promote the state's agriculture.

At the fair, you can enjoy music, rides, and cultural displays. You can try foods from different cultures, such as sukiyaki, beef Stroganoff, and hummus. You can also go to auto races, outdoor concerts, and a horse competition. There is so much to do that you might have to visit twice!

FIND

Syracuse

NEW YORK

THE GREAT NEW YORK STATE FAIR

The midway of the Great New York State Fair is filled with rides (above). These visitors (left) are riding the green caterpillar roller coaster.

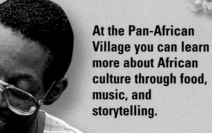

Visitors can have fun with science activities.

Every year a butter sculpture is made to honor New York's food processors and farmers.

At the Pan-African Village you can learn more about African culture through food, music, and storytelling.

There are many competitions at the fair in everything from painting to apple-pie making. If you enter a competition, you might win a ribbon!

A VIRTUAL TOUR

GO ONLINE
For more resources, go to
www.harcourtschool.com/ss1

Review and Test Prep

VISUAL SUMMARY

Write Sentences Use the pictures and captions below to help you review Unit 5. Write one or two sentences for each picture, explaining how the picture relates to New York.

USE VOCABULARY

Write one or two sentences to show how the terms in each pair are related.

1. **war bond** (p. 302)   **interest** (p. 303)

2. **depression** (p. 309)   **unemployment** (p. 309)

3. **service industry** (p. 330) **tourism** (p. 330)

4. **urban sprawl** (p. 339)   **pollution** (p. 339)

RECALL FACTS

Answer these questions.

5. How did New Yorkers at home help during World War I?

6. How did entertainment change in the 1920s?

7. What are some of the challenges that New Yorkers face today?

Write the letter of the best choice.

8. **TEST PREP** The New Deal was the name given to programs set up to—
   A work for women's suffrage.
   B help the war effort during World War II.
   C help end the Great Depression.
   D make advances in aviation.

9. **TEST PREP** The United States entered World War II right after—
   F Germany invaded Poland.
   G it began to make war supplies.
   H Japan attacked a United States naval base at Pearl Harbor, Hawaii.
   J Germany attacked the United States.

10. **TEST PREP** One of the early leaders of the Civil Rights movement was—
    A W. E. B. Du Bois.
    B Theodore Roosevelt.
    C William McKinley.
    D Henry Ford.

Time

1900

1940

1901 **The Pan-American Exposition is held in Buffalo** p. 300

1929 **The stock market crashes** p. 309

1941 **New York's workforce grows as the United States enters World War II** p. 312

11 TEST PREP What is the Internet?
F a system that links computers around the world
G a high-powered microchip
H a system that allows people to travel more quickly
J a computer

THINK CRITICALLY

12 How did World War II change life in New York?

13 How might people having more leisure time affect industries?

14 How have New Yorkers' jobs changed over the last 100 years?

15 What are some ways you can help preserve the past?

APPLY SKILLS

Read a Population Map
Use the population map on this page to answer the following questions.

MAP AND GLOBE SKILLS

16 Find Manhattan on the map. What is the population density of most of its area?

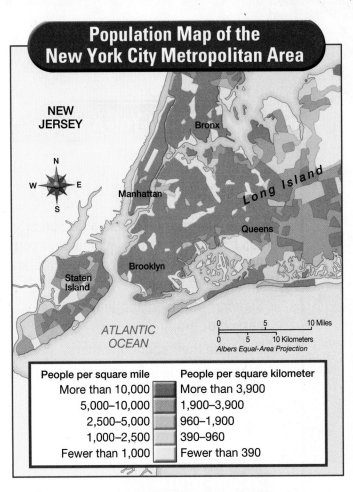

Population Map of the New York City Metropolitan Area

People per square mile		People per square kilometer
More than 10,000		More than 3,900
5,000–10,000		1,900–3,900
2,500–5,000		960–1,900
1,000–2,500		390–960
Fewer than 1,000		Fewer than 390

17 What part of Manhattan has a population density of fewer than 1,000 people per square mile?

18 Which has a higher population density, Brooklyn or Staten Island?

19 Which borough has the lowest population density?

1980 — Present

2001 Terrorists attack sites in the United States p. 315

Present New York continues to attract immigrants from around the world p. 323

Present Tourism is a major industry in New York p. 330

Show What You Know

✏️ Unit Writing Activity

Write a Summary Choose a person or group from the unit, and imagine that you have been chosen to write a speech about that person or group.

■ Summarize the contributions of the person or group.

■ Describe their effect on others.

■ Be sure to include important details, and express main ideas in your speech.

🖌️ Unit Project

Plan a Website Work in a group to plan a website about New York.

■ Organize information into categories, such as New York's people, the arts in New York, and the state's economy. These can be the pages to which a computer user can link from your home page.

■ Decide how to present the information. Include pictures and drawings of people, places, and events that are important to the state.

■ Show what each page will look like.

Read More

■ *Lookin' for Bird in the Big City* by Robert Burleigh. Silver Whistle.

■ *Eleanor* by Barbara Cooney. Puffin.

■ *Lily's Crossing* by Patricia Reilly Giff. Yearling Books.

GO ONLINE For more resources, go to www.harcourtschool.com/ss1

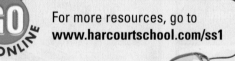

Discover Your Community's History

Become a Historian

●

Use the Library to Discover History

●

Write to or Visit Historical Societies, Museums, and Historic Sites

●

Find Photographs and Maps of Your Community

●

Interview Someone in Your Community

●

Share Your Information

Become a Historian

Imagine that you have been asked to discover the history of your community. How should you begin? First, think of yourself as a historian. Historians are history detectives. They put all of the information they gather together to form a picture of what life was like in a community in the past.

As you investigate the history of your community, you will study the people, places, and events that have shaped life there. You will learn what life was like when Native Americans lived at or near your present-day community, when the first Europeans settled the area, and how people in colonies lived. You will also discover Revolutionary War heroes and how local people from long ago took part in the Industrial Revolution and the development of New York State. This will help you connect the events that took place in your community to historical events in New York and in the United States.

Use the Library to Discover History

To discover the history of your community, start at the library. The library will have many reference works, or sources of facts. Ask a librarian to help you find what you need. Take notes when you find something useful at the library.

Reference works include books such as almanacs, atlases, dictionaries, and encyclopedias. They also include magazines and newspapers, which are known as periodicals. Reference materials are marked *R* or *REF* for *reference*. They are for use only in the library and may not be checked out. Libraries also have electronic reference materials on CD-ROM and the Internet.

Write to or Visit Historical Societies, Museums, and Historic Sites

To get more information about the history of your community, you can write to or visit historical societies, museums, and historic sites.

▶ HOW TO WRITE FOR INFORMATION

You can write a letter to ask for information about the history of your community. When you write, be sure to do the following.

- Tell who you are and why you are writing.
- Tell exactly what you want to know. For example, you might want to know how your community got its name or in what year it was started.

▶ HOW TO ASK QUESTIONS DURING A VISIT

If you have a chance to visit a museum or historic site, you can ask questions about your community's history. When you visit, remember the following tips.

- Take along a list of questions you want to ask.
- Tell who you are and why you are visiting.
- Listen carefully, and take notes when your questions are answered.
- Take any folders or booklets of information the place has for visitors.
- Before you leave, thank the person who answered your questions.

Find Photographs and Maps of Your Community

Looking at photographs and maps from different years can help you see changes in your community. It can also help you see places that have remained the same throughout the years. You can find photographs and maps at libraries, museums, and historic sites.

Interview Someone in Your Community

Asking people questions, or interviewing, is a good way to learn about the history of your community. There are many people you can interview. For example, if you want to know what life was like long ago, you can interview one of your grandparents or an older member of your community. If you want to know about your community's government or businesses, you can interview the mayor or a business leader. Here are some steps you can take to get a good interview.

1 PLAN THE INTERVIEW

- Make a list of the people you want to interview.

- Write to or call each person to ask for an interview. Tell the person who you are and why you would like to interview him or her.

- Ask the person to set a time and place to meet.

2 BEFORE THE INTERVIEW

- Read as much as you can about your topic. Also, try to find out a little about the person you will be interviewing.

- Make a list of questions to ask.

- Be on time for the interview.

3 DURING THE INTERVIEW

- Listen carefully. Do not interrupt the person.

- Take notes as you talk with the person. Write down the person's ideas and some of his or her exact words.

- If you want to use a tape recorder or a video camera, first ask the person if you may do so.

4 AFTER THE INTERVIEW

- Before you leave, thank the person you interviewed.

- Follow up by writing a thank-you note.

Thank You

Share Your Information

After you have gathered your facts and interviewed people, the next step is to show what you have learned.

WRITE A REPORT

One way to share what you have learned is to write a report about the history of your community. Follow these steps when you write a report.

▶ **1 GATHER AND ORGANIZE YOUR INFORMATION**

▶ **2 WRITE YOUR FIRST DRAFT**

▶ **3 REVISE YOUR DRAFT**

▶ **4 PROOFREAD AND PUBLISH**

OTHER WAYS TO SHARE INFORMATION

There are many ways to share what you have learned about the history of your community.

- Make maps
- Make time lines, charts, or other diagrams
- Give an oral presentation

For Your Reference

Almanac

Facts About New York

New York

LAND	SIZE	CLIMATE	POPULATION*	LEADING PRODUCTS
Highest Point: Mount Marcy in Essex County 5,344 feet (1,629 m)	**Area:** 53,989 square miles (139,831 sq km)	**Highest Recorded Temperature:** 108°F (42°C) at Troy on July 22, 1926	19,490,297	**Crops:** hay, corn, oats, cabbages, onions, snap beans, sweet corn, tomatoes, apples, grapes, potatoes
Lowest Point: Atlantic Coast sea level	**Greatest Distance North/South:** 310 miles (499 km)	**Lowest Recorded Temperature:** ⁻52°F (⁻47°C) at Old Forge on February 18, 1979	**Rank Among the States:** third	**Livestock:** milk cattle, beef cattle, poultry, hogs, sheep
	Greatest Distance East/West: 409 miles (658 km)	**Average Temperature:** 69°F (21°C) in July, 21°F (⁻6°C) in January	**Population Density:** 408 people per square mile (155 per sq km)	**Fishing:** clams, flounder, lobster, oysters, scallops, striped bass, eels, yellow perch, trout
	Rank Among the 50 United States: twenty-seventh	**Average Yearly Rainfall:** 36 inches (91 cm)	**Population Distribution:** urban, 92 percent rural, 8 percent	**Manufacturing:** chemicals, photographic and photocopying equipment, computer and electronic products, food products, transportation equipment, clothing, metal products, printed materials, paper products, medical supplies
				Mining: salt, sand, gravel, limestone, garnet, zinc, clay, lead, natural gas, peat, silver, talc

*latest available population figures

The Olympic facilities built for the 1932 and 1980 Olympic Winter Games in Lake Placid are still used today to train athletes.

The home of Harriet Tubman, the most famous "conductor" on the Underground Railroad, is now a museum in Auburn.

HARRIET TUBMAN HOME

The United States

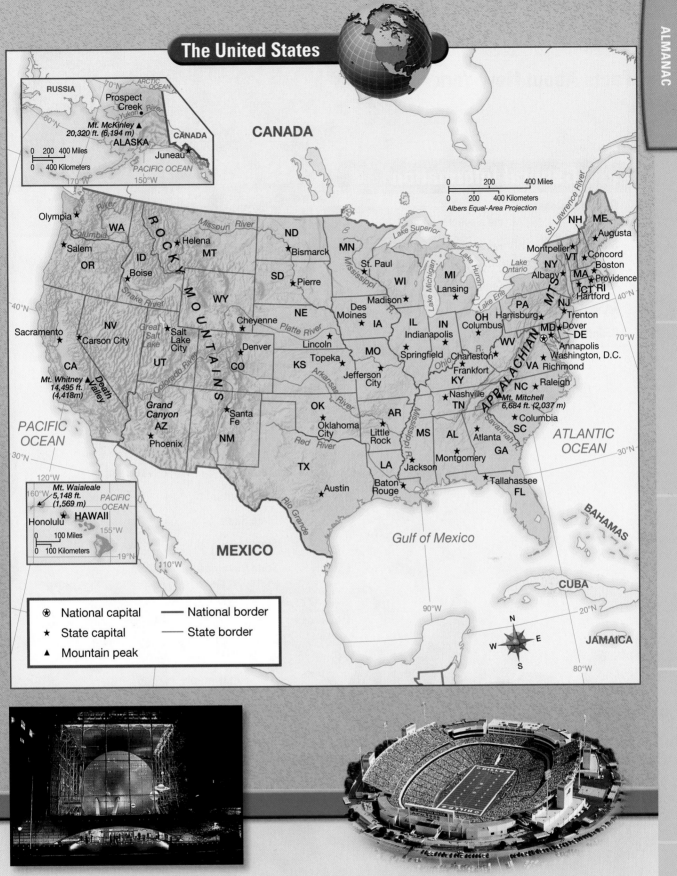

RUSSIA
ARCTIC OCEAN
70°N
60°N
Prospect Creek
Yukon River
Mt. McKinley ▲
20,320 ft. (6,194 m)
ALASKA
CANADA
Juneau ★
0   200   400 Miles
0   400 Kilometers
PACIFIC OCEAN
170°W   150°W

CANADA

0   200   400 Miles
0   200   400 Kilometers
Albers Equal-Area Projection

Olympia ★
Columbia River
WA
Salem ★
OR
Boise ★
ID
Helena ★
MT
Missouri River
ND
Bismarck ★
SD
Pierre ★
MN
St. Paul ★
Mississippi R.
WI
Madison ★
Lake Superior
Lake Michigan
MI
Lansing ★
Lake Huron
Lake Ontario
Lake Erie
NH Concord ★
ME Augusta ★
Montpelier ★ **VT**
NY Albany ★
Boston ★ **MA**
Providence ★
CT **RI**
Hartford ★
40°N
PA Harrisburg ★
Trenton ★ **NJ**
St. Lawrence River

ROCKY MOUNTAINS
40°N
WY
Cheyenne ★
NE
Platte River
Des Moines ★
IA
IL
Springfield ★
IN
Indianapolis ★
OH
Columbus ★
Ohio R.
WV
Charleston ★
APPALACHIAN MTS
MD Dover ★ **DE**
Annapolis ★
Washington, D.C. ⊛
70°W

Sacramento ★
NV
Carson City ★
Great Salt Lake
Salt Lake City ★
UT
Colorado River
Denver ★
CO
Topeka ★
KS
Lincoln ★
Arkansas River
MO
Jefferson City ★
KY
Frankfort ★
Nashville ★
TN
Mt. Mitchell
6,684 ft. (2,037 m)
VA Richmond ★
NC Raleigh ★

CA
Mt. Whitney
14,495 ft. (4,418 m)
Death Valley
Grand Canyon
AZ
Phoenix ★
Santa Fe ★
NM
OK
Oklahoma City ★
Red River
AR
Little Rock ★
Mississippi R.
MS
Jackson ★
AL
Montgomery ★
Atlanta ★
GA
Savannah R.
Columbia ★
SC

PACIFIC OCEAN
30°N

120°W
Mt. Waialeale
5,148 ft. (1,569 m)
160°W
Honolulu ★ **HAWAII**
PACIFIC OCEAN
155°W
0   100 Miles
0   100 Kilometers
19°N
110°W

MEXICO

TX
Austin ★
LA
Baton Rouge ★
Jackson
Tallahassee ★
FL

Rio Grande

ATLANTIC OCEAN
30°N

Gulf of Mexico

90°W

BAHAMAS

CUBA

20°N

N
W   E
S

JAMAICA
80°W

⊛ National capital   ── National border
★ State capital   ── State border
▲ Mountain peak

People from all over the world come to New York City to visit its many museums and admire its stunning architecture. The Rose Center for Earth and Space contains a spherical planetarium enclosed in a six-story glass cube.

The New York City area has two football teams, the New York Jets and the New York Giants. The Buffalo Bills play in Orchard Park's Ralph Wilson Stadium in Buffalo.

Almanac
Facts About New York

General Information

Date of Statehood	July 26, 1788; the eleventh state
State Motto	*Excelsior* (Latin, meaning "Ever Upward")
Nickname	The Empire State
Abbreviations	NY (postal); N.Y. (traditional)
Counties	62

Some State Symbols

State Bird	Bluebird
State Flower	Rose
State Tree	Sugar maple
State Song	"I Love New York" words and music by Steven Karmen
State Fruit	Apple
State Insect	Ladybug
State Animal	Beaver
State Fish	Brook trout
State Gem	Garnet
State Muffin	Apple muffin
State Shell	Bay scallop
State Fossil	Sea scorpion
State Beverage	Milk

Sugar maple

Apples

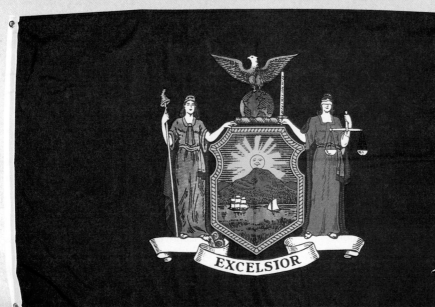

The current design for the New York flag was adopted in 1909. The flag features two women who represent the ideas of liberty and justice. The state motto, *Excelsior*, is also found on the flag. This same emblem is seen on the state seal of New York.

Bluebird

Beaver

Rose

Ladybugs

Sea scorpion

Almanac

Facts About New York Counties

County	Population*	County Seat	Year	Named For
Albany	297,414	Albany	1683	The Duke of York and Albany, who later became King James II of England
Allegany	50,602	Belmont	1806	A Delaware Indian word, applied by settlers of western New York to a trail that followed the Allegany River
Bronx	1,357,589	Bronx	1914	Joseph Bronck, first settler of the region north of the Harlem River (A peace treaty with the Indians was signed at his home in 1642.)
Broome	196,947	Binghamton	1806	John Broome, who was lieutenant governor when the county was established in 1806
Cattaraugus	82,502	Little Valley	1808	A Seneca Indian word meaning "bad-smelling banks," referring to the odor of natural gas leaking from rock seams
Cayuga	81,454	Auburn	1799	The name of the fourth tribe of the Iroquois League
Chautauqua	139,409	Mayville	1808	A contraction of a Seneca Indian word meaning "where the fish was taken out"
Chemung	89,512	Elmira	1836	The name of the Delaware Indian village signifying "big horn"
Chenango	51,755	Norwich	1798	The Onondaga Indian word meaning "large bull-thistle"
Clinton	82,047	Plattsburgh	1788	George Clinton, first governor of the state
Columbia	63,622	Hudson	1786	The Latin feminine form of Columbus, the name that was popular at the time as a proposed name for the United States of America

* latest available population figures

Gazetteer

The Gazetteer is a geographical dictionary that can help you locate many of the places discussed in this book. The page number tells you where each place appears on a map.

Adirondack Mountains (a•duh•RAHN•dak) A mountain range in northern New York. p. 31

Adirondack Park The largest park and forest preserve in the continental United States. It has an area of more than 5 million acres. p. 292

Adirondack Upland An upland region that stretches across much of northern New York. It includes the Adirondack Mountains. p. 31

Albany New York's state capital and the county seat of Albany County. (43°N, 74°W) p. 22

Albion The county seat of Orleans County. (43°N, 78°W) p. 203

Allegheny Plateau (a•luh•GAY•nee) See *Appalachian Plateau.*

Allegheny River A river that flows across southwestern New York before uniting with the Monongahela River in Pennsylvania to form the Ohio River. p. A18

Ancram A town in the Hudson River valley that was the site of New York's first ironworks. p. 129

Appalachian Mountains (a•puh•LAY•chuhn) The largest mountain system in the eastern United States. It stretches from northern Alabama through New York into southern Canada. p. A15

Appalachian Plateau New York's largest land region. Also called the Allegheny Plateau, this upland region covers most of southern New York. p. 31

Atlantic Coastal Plain A lowland region that lies along most of the Atlantic coast of the United States. Staten Island and Long Island are part of this land region. p. A15

Auburn The county seat of Cayuga County. (43°N, 77°W) p. 203

Ballston Spa The county seat of Saratoga County. It is a resort known for its mineral springs. (43°N, 74°W) p. 203

Batavia (buh•TAY•vee•uh) The county seat of Genesee County. (43°N, 78°W) p. 203

Bath The county seat of Steuben County. (42°N, 77°W) p. 203

Belmont The county seat of Allegany County. (42°N, 78°W) p. 203

Binghamton The county seat of Broome County. The first farm bureau in the United States was started there in 1911. (42°N, 76°W) p. 203

Black River A river in north-central New York that flows into Lake Ontario. p. A19

Bronx The county seat of Bronx County and one of New York City's five boroughs. It is the only borough located on the mainland. (41°N, 74°W) p. 203

Brooklyn The county seat of Kings County and one of New York City's five boroughs. (41°N, 74°W) p. 203

Brooklyn Heights The site of a Revolutionary War battle. It is now part of the borough of Brooklyn. (41°N, 74°W) p. 180

Buffalo A port city located on the Niagara River in western New York and the state's second-largest city. It is the county seat of Erie County. (43°N, 79°W) p. 22

Canandaigua (ka•nuhn•DAY•gwuh) The county seat of Ontario County. (43°N, 77°W) p. 203

Canandaigua Lake One of the 11 Finger Lakes. It is 15 miles (24 km) long and 2 miles (3 km) across at its widest point. p. A18

Canisteo River (ka•nuh•STEE•oh) A river in southwestern New York. It is a tributary of the Tioga River. p. A18

Canton The county seat of St. Lawrence County. (45°N, 75°W) p. 203

Carmel The county seat of Putnam County. (41°N, 74°W) p. 203

Catskill The county seat of Greene County. Settled by the Dutch in 1680, it is the gateway to the Catskill Mountains. (42°N, 74°W) p. 203

Catskill Mountains A mountain range in southeastern New York. It is part of the larger Appalachian Mountain range. p. 31

Cayuga and Seneca Canal A canal linking Cayuga and Seneca Lakes and the Erie Canal. It is part of the New York State Barge Canal System. p. A18

Cayuga Lake (kay•YOO•guh) One of the 11 Finger Lakes. It is 67 miles (108 km) long and 2 miles (3 km) wide. It is connected to Seneca Lake by the Cayuga and Seneca Canal. p. A18

Central Park An 843-acre park located in Manhattan. p. 247

Champlain Canal (sham•PLAYN) A canal in eastern New York that links Lake Champlain with the Erie Canal. It is part of the New York State Barge Canal System. p. A19

Chautauqua Lake (shuh•TAW•kwuh) A lake in western New York. It is 18 miles (29 km) long and more than 2 miles (3 km) wide in some places. p. 31

Chenango River (shuh•NANG•goh) A tributary of the Susquehanna River. p. 37

Cohocton River (kuh•HAHK•tuhn) A river in southern New York. It is about 60 miles (97 km) long. p. A18

Cooperstown The county seat of Otsego County and the site of the Baseball Hall of Fame. (43°N, 75°W) p. 326

Corning A city in Steuben County. The 200-inch (508-cm) lens for the observatory telescope at Mt. Palomar, in California, was manufactured in Corning in 1934. p. 337

Cortland The county seat of Cortland County. (43°N, 76°W) p. 203

Cranberry Lake A lake in northern New York. It is 6 miles (10 km) long. p. A19

Delaware River A river in southeastern New York that forms part of the New York–Pennsylvania border. p. 31

Delhi (DEL•hy) The county seat of Delaware County. (42°N, 75°W) p. 203

East River An estuary that connects the Harlem River, Upper New York Bay, and Long Island Sound. It serves as a major port. p. 205

Elizabethtown The county seat of Essex County. (44°N, 74°W) p. 203

Ellis Island An island in Upper New York Bay. Between 1892 and 1954, more than 12 million immigrants passed through the immigration station on Ellis Island. p. 286

Elmira The county seat of Chemung County. (42°N, 77°W) p. 203

equator An imaginary line that circles Earth halfway between the North Pole and the South Pole. It divides Earth into the Northern Hemisphere and the Southern Hemisphere. p. 24

Erie Canal A waterway that connects Lake Erie with the Hudson River and the Atlantic Ocean. Now part of the New York State Barge Canal System. pp. A18–A19

Erie-Ontario Lowland A lowland region that stretches inland from Lake Erie and Lake Ontario. p. 31

Finger Lakes Eleven narrow lakes in west-central New York. They include Conesus, Hemlock, Honeoye, Canadice, Canandaigua, Keuka, Seneca, Cayuga, Owasco, Skaneateles, and Otisco. p. A18

Finger Lakes National Forest New York's only national forest. It is located between two lakes, Seneca Lake and Cayuga Lake. p. A18

Fonda The county seat of Montgomery County. (43°N, 74°W) p. 203

Fort Niagara A fort in western New York that was built by the French and later used by British and American troops. p. 134

Fort Stanwix A fort in central New York that was used during the French and Indian War and the Revolutionary War. p. 173

Fort Ticonderoga (ty•kahn•duh•ROH•guh) A military post near Lake Champlain during the Revolutionary War and now a historic site in the town of Ticonderoga. It was the site of the first American victory of the Revolutionary War. (44°N, 73°W) p. 173

Fort William Henry A military post during the French and Indian War and the Revolutionary War and now a historic site. It is located at the southern end of Lake George in northeastern New York. (43°N, 74°W) p. 133

Genesee River A river in western New York that flows north through Rochester and into Lake Ontario. p. 31

Geneseo (jeh•nuh•SEE•oh) The county seat of Livingston County. (43°N, 78°W) p. 203

Goshen The county seat of Orange County. (41°N, 74°W) p. 203

Governors Island An island in Upper New York Bay, south of Manhattan. It was known as Nut Island until 1784. (41°N, 74°W) p. 180

Great Sacandaga Lake A reservoir in eastern New York, formed by Conklingville Dam. p. 22

Harlem River A river channel separating Manhattan Island and the Bronx. p. 205

Herkimer The county seat of Herkimer County. It is the site of Fort Dayton, from which General Nicholas Herkimer marched to the Battle of Oriskany during the Revolutionary War. (43°N, 75°W) p. 203

Howe Caverns A system of underground caves in east-central New York. Discovered by Lester Howe in 1842, it is now a popular tourist attraction. p. 33

Hudson The county seat of Columbia County. It is the home of the American Museum of Fire Fighting. (42°N, 74°W) p. 46, 203

Hudson Falls The county seat of Washington County. (43°N, 74°W) p. 203

Hudson-Mohawk Lowland A lowland region stretching alongside the Hudson and Mohawk Rivers. p. 31

Hudson River New York's largest river. It flows 306 miles (492 km) south from the Adirondack Mountains into Upper New York Bay. It is named for Henry Hudson, who explored the area in 1609. p. 31

Hyde Park A town in the Hudson River valley that is the home of the Franklin D. Roosevelt Presidential Site. p. 200

Ithaca The county seat of Tompkins County. (42°N, 76°W) p. 203

Jamaica The county seat of Queens County. It is now part of the borough of Queens. (41°N, 74°W) p. 203

Jamestown A city in Chautauqua County. It was settled in 1810 and chartered as a city in 1886. (42°N, 79°W) p. 12

GAZETTEER

Johnstown The county seat of Fulton County. (43°N, 74°W) p. 203

Keuka Lake (KYOO•kuh) One of the Finger Lakes. It is 18 miles (29 km) long. p. A18

Kingston The county seat of Ulster County. It was the meeting place of New York's first state government. (42°N, 74°W) p. 203

Lake Champlain A lake 125 miles (201 km) long in northeastern New York, forming a border between New York and Vermont. It is named for Samuel de Champlain, who explored the area in 1609. p. 22

Lake Erie The fourth-largest of the five Great Lakes. It borders New York. p. 22

Lake George A lake in eastern New York. p. 31

Lake George The county seat of Warren County. (43°N, 74°W) p. 203

Lake Ontario The smallest of the five Great Lakes. It borders New York. p. 22

Lake Placid A lake in northeastern New York. p. 31

Lake Pleasant The county seat of Hamilton County. (44°N, 74°W) p. 203

Letchworth Gorge A 17-mile (27-km) gorge on the Genesee River in western New York. Part of Letchworth State Park, the gorge is sometimes called the Grand Canyon of the East. p. 292

Little Valley The county seat of Cattaraugus County. (42°N, 79°W) p. 203

Lockport The county seat of Niagara County. (43°N, 79°W) p. 203

Long Island A large island in southeastern New York, lying between Long Island Sound and the Atlantic Ocean. p. 22

Long Island Sound A body of water located between Long Island and Connecticut. It is 110 miles (177 km) long and 25 miles (40 km) across at its widest point. p. 22

Long Lake A lake in northern New York. p. 22

Lowville The county seat of Lewis County. (44°N, 75°W) p. 203

Lyons The county seat of Wayne County. (43°N, 77°W) p. 203

Malone The county seat of Franklin County. (45°N, 74°W) p. 203

Manhattan An island at the northern end of New York Bay, lying between the Hudson and East Rivers, and one of New York City's five boroughs. p. 205

Mayville The county seat of Chautauqua County. (42°N, 79°W) p. 203

Mineola (mih•nee•OH•luh) The county seat of Nassau County. (41°N, 74°W) p. 203

Mohawk River A river 148 miles (238 km) long in east-central New York. It is the Hudson River's largest tributary. p. 31

Montauk Point (MAHN•tawk) New York's easternmost point. It has a lighthouse and a museum. (41°N, 72°W) p. 32

Monticello (mahn•tuh•SEH•loh) The county seat of Sullivan County. (42°N, 75°W) p. 203

Mount Marcy The highest point in New York, with an elevation of 5,344 feet (1,629 m). Located in the Adirondacks, in northern New York, it was named for Governor William Marcy. (44°N, 74°W) p. 37

Mount Vernon A city in Westchester County, near New York City. It is one of New York's largest cities. (41°N, 74°W) p. 45

New City The county seat of Rockland County. (41°N, 74°W) p. 203

New England Upland An upland region that covers much of southeastern New York, including Manhattan. p. 31

New Paltz A village in the Hudson River valley that was founded by French Huguenots in 1677. p. 84

New Rochelle A city in Westchester County. It is one of New York's largest cities. p. 45

New York Bay An inlet of the Atlantic Ocean in southeastern New York. It includes Upper New York Bay and Lower New York Bay. p. A19, 181

New York City The largest city in New York State and the United States and the county seat of New York County. (41°N, 74°W) p. 22

New York State Barge Canal System A canal system made up of the Erie, the Champlain, the Oswego, and the Cayuga and Seneca Canals. pp. A18–A19

Niagara Falls The falls of the Niagara River, on the United States–Canada border. Its two falls are the American Falls and the Canadian Falls. It is a major hydroelectric power source and tourist attraction. (43°N, 79°W) p. 31

Niagara Falls A city in Niagara County. It is located on the Niagara River, just below the falls. (43°N, 79°W) p. 282

Niagara River A river 35 miles (56 km) long in western New York that links Lake Erie to Lake Ontario. p. 31

Norwich The county seat of Chenango County. (43°N, 75°W) p. 203

Ogdensburg A city on the St. Lawrence River, in St. Lawrence County. (45°N, 75°W) p. 292

Oneida Lake A lake in central New York. It is the largest natural lake completely within the state's borders. It is 22 miles (35 km) long and 6 miles (10 km) across at its widest point. p. 31

Oriskany A town in central New York that was the site of a major battle during the Revolutionary War. p. 173

GAZETTEER

GAZETTEER

Oswegatchie River (ahs•wih•GAH•chee) A river in northern New York that flows into the St. Lawrence River. p. A19

Oswego One of Oswego County's two county seats. (43°N, 76°W) p. 203

Oswego Canal A canal linking the Erie Canal with Lake Ontario. It is part of the New York State Barge Canal System. p. A18

Otsego Lake A lake in central New York, 9 miles (14 km) long and 1 mile (2 km) wide. It is the source of the Susquehanna River. p. 326

Owasco Lake One of the 11 Finger Lakes. It is 11 miles (18 km) long and about 1 mile (2 km) wide. p. A18

Owego The county seat of Tioga County. (42°N, 76°W) p. 203

Penn Yan The county seat of Yates County. (43°N, 77°W) p. 203

Plattsburgh The county seat of Clinton County. (45°N, 73°W) p. 203

Poughkeepsie (puh•KIP•see) The county seat of Dutchess County. In 1777 it served as a temporary state capital. (42°N, 74°W) p. 203

Queens One of New York City's five boroughs. p. 205

Riverhead The county seat of Suffolk County. (41°N, 73°W) p. 203

Rochester The county seat of Monroe County and New York's third-largest city. It was a key location on the Underground Railroad and the home of Frederick Douglass. (43°N, 78°W) p. 203

St. George The county seat of Richmond County. (41°N, 74°W) p. 203

St. Lawrence Lowland A lowland region lying along the St. Lawrence River. p. 31

St. Lawrence River A river in northern New York that separates New York from Canada. p. 31

St. Lawrence Seaway An important shipping route that connects Lake Erie and Lake Ontario with the St. Lawrence River and the Atlantic Ocean. The seaway was completed in 1959. p. 334

Salmon River A river in central New York that flows into Lake Ontario at Mexico Bay. p. A18

Saranac Lake A village in northeastern New York that holds an annual winter carnival. p. 292

Saranac Lakes Three lakes in northeastern New York, including Upper Saranac Lake, Middle Saranac Lake, and Lower Saranac Lake. p. A19

Saranac River A river in northeastern New York that flows into Lake Champlain. p. A19

Saratoga A town in northeastern New York that was the site of two famous Revolutionary War battles. p. 173

Schenectady (skuh•NEK•tuh•dee) The county seat of Schenectady County. It was first settled in 1661 and was incorporated as a city in 1798. (43°N, 74°W) p. 203

Schoharie (skoh•HAR•ee) The county seat of Schoharie County. (43°N, 74°W) p. 203

Schroon River A river in northeastern New York that flows south into the Hudson River. p. A19

Seneca Falls A village in central New York that was the site of a women's rights convention in 1848. p. 25

Seneca Lake One of the 11 Finger Lakes. It is 35 miles (56 km) long. p. A18

Shawangunk Mountains (SHAHNG•guhnk) A mountain range in southeastern New York that is part of the larger Appalachian Mountain range. p. 31

Skaneateles Lake (ska•nee•AT•luhs) One of the 11 Finger Lakes. It is 16 miles (26 km) long. p. A18

Staten Island An island in New York Bay and one of New York City's five boroughs. p. 205

Susquehanna River (suhs•kwuh•HA•nuh) A river in south-central New York. p. 31

Syracuse The county seat of Onondaga County and once the site of the capital of the Iroquois Confederacy. It is New York's fifth-largest city. (43°N, 76°W) p. 203

Taconic Range A low mountain range in eastern New York that is part of the larger Appalachian Mountain range. It lies along New York's borders with Vermont, Massachusetts, and Connecticut. p. 31

Taughannock Falls (tuh•GA•nuhk) A waterfall in south-central New York, in Tompkins County. At 215 feet (66 m), it is one of the highest waterfalls in the eastern United States. (43°N, 77°W) p. A18

Thousand Islands An area of about 1,800 islands formed where Lake Ontario meets the St. Lawrence River. p. A18

Troy The county seat of Rensselaer County. The Erie Canal was built to link Troy, on the Hudson River, with Buffalo. (43°N, 74°W) p. 203

Tug Hill Plateau A high, flat, rocky area in the northern part of the Appalachian Plateau. It usually receives more snow than any other part of New York. p. 31

Utica The county seat of Oneida County. The city was built at the site of Old Fort Schuyler, which served as a fort during the French and Indian War. (43°N, 75°W) p. 203

Van Cortlandt Park A park in the Bronx that is also the site of an eighteenth century mansion. p. 131

Wallkill River A tributary of the Hudson River. p. A19

Wampsville The county seat of Madison County. (43°N, 76°W) p. 203

Warsaw The county seat of Wyoming County. (43°N, 78°W) p. 203

Waterloo One of Seneca County's two county seats. (43°N, 77°W) p. 203

Watertown The county seat of Jefferson County. It was settled about 1800. (44°N, 76°W) p. 203

Watkins Glen The county seat of Schuyler County. (42°N, 77°W) p. 203

Welland Ship Canal A waterway 27 miles (43 km) long in western New York, connecting Lake Ontario and Lake Erie. It is part of the St. Lawrence Seaway. p. 334

West Point A town in the Hudson River valley that is the site of the United States Military Academy. p. 179

White Plains The county seat of Westchester County. (41°N, 74°W) p. 203

Yonkers A city in Westchester County, near New York City. It is New York's fourth-largest city. (41°N, 74°W) p. 45

Glossary

The Glossary contains important social studies words and their definitions. Each word is respelled as it would be in a dictionary. When you see this mark ´ after a syllable, pronounce that syllable with more force than the other syllables. The page number at the end of the definition tells where to find the word in your book.

add, āce, câre, pälm; end, ēqual; it, īce; odd, ōpen, ôrder; tŏŏk, pōōl; up, bûrn; yōō as *u* in *fuse*; oil; pout; ə as *a* in *above*, *e* in *sicken*, *i* in *possible*, *o* in *melon*, *u* in *circus*; check; ring; thin; this; zh as in *vision*

abolish (ə•bäl´ish) To end. p. 249

abolitionist (a•bə•li´shən•ist) A person who worked to get the United States government to end slavery. p. 249

absolute location (ab´sə•lōōt lō•kā´shən) An exact position on Earth's surface, determined by latitude and longitude. p. 24

adapt (ə•dapt´) To change or adjust. p. 54

agriculture (a´grə•kul•chər) Farming. p. 54

alliance (ə•lī´əns) A formal agreement among nations, states, or individuals to cooperate. p. 135

ally (a´lī) A partner, especially in time of war. p. 135

amendment (ə•mend´mənt) An addition or change to the Constitution. p. 183

analyze (a´nəl•īz) To examine each part of something and relate the parts to one another. p. 3

ancestor (an´ses•tər) A family member who lived long ago. p. 53

appeal (ə•pēl´) To ask for another trial. p. 194

apprentice (ə•pren´təs) A person who worked for a skilled craftsperson for three years or more to learn a trade. p. 110

aqueduct (a´kwə•dəkt) A large pipe or structure built to carry water. p. 235

archaeologist (är•kē•ä´lə•jist) A person who studies artifacts to learn how people lived long ago. p. 55

artifact (är´tə•fakt) Any object made by people in the past. p. 55

assembly line (ə•sem´blē līn) A factory system in which a product, such as a car, is put together as it moves past a line of workers who each perform one task. p. 307

aviation (ā•vē•ā´shən) The making and flying of airplanes. p. 307

bar graph (bär graf) A graph that uses bars of different lengths to stand for different amounts. p. 168

bill (bil) A plan for a new law. p. 192

bill of rights (bil uv rīts) A list of rights and freedoms. p. 183

blizzard (bliz´ərd) A storm that combines heavy snow with high winds. p. 41

board of supervisors (bōrd uv sōō´pər•vī•zərz) A group of officials who govern a county. p. 203

borough (bûr´ō) A district. p. 205

bouwery (bou´ə•rē) A colonial Dutch farm that had both livestock and crops. p. 109

boycott (boi´kät) A refusal to buy goods or services in order to force the seller to change a rule. p. 158

budget (bu´jət) A written plan for spending money. p. 192

Cabinet (kab´nit) The group made up of the President's most important advisers. p. 199

canal (kə•nal´) A human-made waterway. p. 233

capital resource (ka´pə•təl rē´sôrs) A resource, such as money, a building, a machine, or a tool, needed to run a business. p. 271

cardinal direction (kär´dən•əl də•rek´shən) One of the four main directions—*north*, *south*, *east*, and *west*. p. A3

cause (kôz) An event or action that makes something else happen. p. 121

century (sen´chə•rē) A period of 100 years. p. 105

ceremony (ser´ə•mō•nē) A series of actions performed during a special event. p. 69

chronology (krə•nä´lə•jē) The order in which events take place. p. 2

circle graph (sûr´kəl graf) A round chart that is divided into parts to show information; often called a pie graph. p. 317

civics (si´viks) The study of citizenship. p. 9

civil rights (si´vəl rīts) The rights of all citizens to equal treatment. p. 314

civil war (si´vəl wôr) A war between two groups in the same country. p. 250

claim (klām) To say that one owns something. p. 93

clan (klan) A group made up of families that are related to one another. p. 60

classify (kla´sə•fī) To group items or ideas. p. 70

climate (klī´mət) The kind of weather a place has most often, year after year. p. 38

coastal plain (kōs'təl plān) Low, mostly flat land next to an ocean. p. 32

colonist (kä'lə•nist) A person who lives in a colony. p. 99

colony (kä'lə•nē) A settlement started by people who leave their own country to live in another land. p. 98

Columbian Exchange (kə•ləm'bē•ən iks•chānj') The exchange of goods, plants, animals, and ideas that took place between Europeans and Native Americans after Columbus's voyages. p. 95

commander in chief (kə•man'dər in chēf) The highest leader of an armed force. p. 172

commute (kə•myoot') To travel back and forth. p. 280

comparison (kəm•par'ə•sən) A statement of how two or more things are the same and how they are different. p. 70

compass rose (kəm'pəs rōz) A direction marker on a map. p. A3

confederacy (kən•fe'də•rə•sē) A loose group of governments that work together. p. 62

congress (kän'grəs) A formal meeting attended by representatives. p. 135

consequence (kän'sə•kwens) The result of a decision or an action. p. 261

conservation (kän•sər•vā'shən) The protection and careful use of natural resources. p. 340

constitution (kän•stə•too'shən) A plan of government. p. 166

consumer (kən•soo'mər) A person who buys a product or service. p. 307

consumer good (kən•soo'mər good) A product made for personal use. p. 307

continent (kän'tən•ənt) One of the seven main land areas of Earth. p. 20

convention (kən•ven'shən) A meeting where people discuss issues that affect them as a group. p. 183

council (koun'səl) A group that makes laws. p. 63

county seat (koun'tē sēt) The city or town in which a county's government meets. p. 202

cultural region (kul'chə•rəl rē'jən) An area in which people share a similar language or some other cultural trait. p. 56

culture (kul'chər) A way of life. pp. 10, 54

decade (de'kād) A period of ten years. p. 105

delegate (de'li•gət) A representative. p. 135

demand (di•mand') A desire for a good or a service by people who are willing to pay for it. p. 272

democracy (di•mä'krə•sē) A form of government in which the people rule by making decisions themselves or by electing leaders to make decisions for them. p. 190

depression (di•pre'shən) A time when there are few jobs and people have little money. p. 309

discrimination (dis•kri•mə•nā'shən) The unfair treatment of people because of their background, religion, or race. p. 257

diverse economy (də•vərs' i•kä'nə•mē) An economy that is based on many kinds of industries. p. 330

division of labor (də•vi'zhən əv lā'bər) The dividing of jobs among workers. p. 68

double-bar graph (də•bəl•bär'graf) A graph that compares two sets of numbers. p. 238

draft (draft) A way to force people into the military. p. 250

drought (drout) A time of little or no rain. p. 40

drumlin (drum'lin) An oval-shaped hill created by a glacier. p. 34

economics (e•kə•nä'miks) The study of how people use resources to meet their needs. p. 8

economy (i•kä'nə•mē) The way the people use resources to meet their needs. pp. 8, 128

effect (i•fekt') The result of an event or an action. p. 121

elevation (e•lə•vā'shən) The height of the land above sea level. p. 36

entrepreneur (än•trə•prə•nûr') A person who starts and runs a business. p. 265

environment (in•vī'rən•mənt) The surroundings in which a person, an animal, or a plant lives. p. 44

equator (i•kwā'tər) The imaginary line that circles Earth halfway between the North Pole and the South Pole. The line divides Earth into the Northern Hemisphere and the Southern Hemisphere. p. 21

estuary (es'chə•wer•ē) A body of water where fresh water from a river or lake mixes with salt water from the ocean. p. 33

ethnic group (eth'nik groop) A group of people from the same country, of the same race, or with a shared culture. p. 323

evidence (e'və•dəns) Proof. p. 2

executive branch (ig•ze'kyə•tiv branch) The branch of the government that makes sure that laws are carried out. p. 166

expedition (ek•spə•di'shən) A journey into an area to learn more about it. p. 93

export (ek'spôrt) A good sent from one country to another, usually to be sold. p. 157

exposition (ek•spə•zi'shən) A fair. p. 300

extinct (ik•stingt') Having died out completely, as of a kind of animal. p. 54

fact (fakt) A statement that can be checked and proved to be true. p. 47

famine (fa′mən) A period of time when food is limited and people starve. p. 257

federal government (fe′də•rəl gu′vərn•mənt) The government of the entire United States. p. 198

finance (fī′nants) The use or management of money. p. 332

flow chart (flō chärt) A drawing that shows the order in which things happen. p. 196

frontier (frun•tir′) The land that lies beyond a settled area. p. 228

garment (gär′mənt) A piece of clothing. p. 246

generation (je•nə•rā′shən) The average time between the birth of parents and the birth of their children. p. 75

geographer (jē•ä′grə•fər) A person who studies geography. p. 6

geography (jē•ä′grə•fē) The study of Earth and the people who live on it. p. 6

glacier (glā′shər) A huge, slow-moving mass of ice. p. 28

government (gu′vərn•mənt) A system of leaders and laws that helps people live safely together in a community, a state, or a country. p. 9

governor (gu′vər•nər) The leader of a colony or a state. p. 122

grid (grid) An arrangement of lines that divides a drawing, such as a map, into sections. p. A2

harbor (här′bər) A part of a body of water where ships can dock safely. p. 32

hemisphere (he′mə•sfir) Half of a sphere, such as a ball or a globe; a half of Earth. p. 21

heritage (her′ə•tij) A way of life that has been passed down from one's ancestors. pp. 10, 73

high-tech (hī•tek′) Involving the use of computers or other kinds of electronic equipment. p. 333

historian (hi•stôr′ē•ən) A person who studies the past. p. 2

historical map (hi•stôr′i•kəl map) A map that shows a place as it was at a certain time in history. p. 138

history (hi′stə•rē) The study of people, places, and events in the past. p. 2

human feature (hyōō′mən fē′chər) A feature created by humans, such as a building or a road. p. 6

human resource (hyōō′mən rē′sôrs) A person who is a worker. p. 270

hurricane (hûr′ə•kān) A powerful storm that has heavy rains and high winds; near its center, wind speeds may reach 74 miles (119 km) or more per hour. p. 41

hydroelectric power (hī•drō•i•lek′trik pou′ər) Electricity made by machines that are turned by running water. p. 272

immigrant (i′mi•grənt) A person who comes from some other place to live in a country. p. 207

immigration (i•mi•grā′shən) The movement of people into one country from another. p. 256

import (im′pôrt) A good brought into one country or place from another, most often to be sold. p. 157

impress (im•pres′) To force into military service. p. 232

inauguration (i•nô•gyə•rā′shən) A ceremony in which a leader takes office. p. 184

indentured servant (in•dent′shərd sûr′vənt) A person who agrees to work without pay for a set time in exchange for some benefit. p. 107

independence (in•di•pen′dənts) Freedom of a country to govern itself. p. 164

Industrial Revolution (in•dus′trē•əl re•və•lōō′shən) The period of time during the 1700s and 1800s in which machines took the place of hand tools in the manufacturing of goods. p. 246

industrialization (in•dəs•trē•ə•lə•zā′shən) The growth of industries. p. 270

industry (in′dəs•trē) All the businesses that make one kind of product or provide one kind of service. p. 129

inset map (in′set map) A smaller map within a larger one. p. A3

interact (in•tə•rakt′) To act upon one another. p. 6

interdependence (in•tər•di•pen′dəns) The depending on one another for resources and products. p. 281

interest (in′trəst) The money a bank or borrower pays for the use of loaned money. p. 303

intermediate direction (in•tər•mē′dē•ət də•rek′shən) A direction between two cardinal directions. p. A3

international trade (in•tər•na′shən•əl trād) Trade among nations. p. 335

Internet (in′tər•net) A system that links computers around the world for the exchange of information. p. 334

investor (in•ves′tər) A person who spends money on a project with the hope of earning back more money in return. p. 273

GLOSSARY

judicial branch (jŏŏ•di′shəl branch) The branch of the government made up of courts and judges that decides if laws are fair. p. 166

jury (jŏŏr′ē) A group of citizens that decides a case in court. p. 125

justice (jəs′təs) A judge. p. 195

labor union (lā′bər yŏŏn′yən) A group of workers who act together to improve their working conditions. p. 275

land speculator (land spe′kyə•lā•tər) A person who buys land at a low price with the hope of selling it later for a higher price. p. 229

land use (land yŏŏs) The way in which the land in a place is used. p. 336

language group (lang′gwij grŏŏp) A group of two or more languages that are alike in some way. p. 55

legend (le′jənd) A story handed down by a group of people over time. p. 61

legislative branch (le′jəs•lā•tiv branch) The branch of government that makes laws. p. 166

legislature (le′jəs•lā•chər) The group of people responsible for making laws. p. 122

liberty (li′bər•tē) Freedom. p. 158

line graph (līn graf) A graph that uses a line to show change over time. p. 168

line of latitude (līn uv la′tə•tŏŏd) A line on a globe or a map that runs east and west. It is used to tell how far north or south of the equator a place is. p. 24

line of longitude (līn uv län′jə•tŏŏd) A line on a globe or a map that runs north and south. It is used to tell how far east or west of the prime meridian a place is. p. 24

location (lō•kā′shən) The place where something is found. p. 6

locator (lō′kā•tər) A small map or picture of a globe that shows where the place shown on the main map is located. p. A2

lock (läk) A part of a canal in which the water level can be raised or lowered to bring ships to the level of the next part of the canal. p. 233

locomotive (lō•kə•mō′tiv) A train engine used to move railroad cars. p. 240

longhouse (lông′hous) A long, narrow Iroquois home made of wooden poles covered with bark or grass mats. p. 59

Loyalist (loi′ə•list) A colonist who remained loyal to the British king and did not support independence. p. 159

manor (ma′nər) A large farm. p. 131

manufacturing (man•yə•fak′chə•ring) The making of products. p. 129

map key (map kē) The part of a map that explains the symbols used on the map. p. A2

map scale (map skāl) The part of a map that shows how to use distance on the map to find out the distance in the real world. p. A3

map title (map tī′təl) Words on a map that tell the subject of the map. p. A2

metropolitan area (me•trə•pä′lə•tən âr′ē•ə) A large city and the suburbs that surround it. p. 280

migration (mī•grā′shən) A large movement of people. p. 228

mileage table (mī′lij tā′bəl) A chart that lists the distances between cities. p. 283

militia (mə•li′shə) A volunteer army. p. 174

mountain range (moun′tən rānj) A group of connected mountains. p. 30

natural resource (na′chə•rəl rē′sôrs) Something found in nature that people can use. p. 42

naturalized citizen (na′chə•rə•līzd si′tə•zən) An immigrant who has become a citizen of the United States by taking certain steps described in the law. p. 207

neutral (nŏŏ′trəl) Not taking a side in a conflict. p. 159

nomad (nō′mad) A person who has no permanent home but keeps moving from place to place. p. 53

nonrenewable (nän•ri•nŏŏ′ə•bəl) Not able to be made again by nature or people. p. 43

nor′easter (nôr•ēs′tər) A storm that has strong winds that blow from the north and the east. p. 41

Northwest Passage (nôrth′west pa′sij) A hoped-for waterway through North America that explorers thought would connect the Atlantic Ocean and the Pacific Ocean. p. 93

opinion (ə•pin′yən) A statement that tells what the person who makes it thinks or believes. p. 47

opportunity cost (ä•pər•tŏŏ′nə•tē kôst) What you give up in order to buy something. p. 206

oral history (ôr′əl his′tə•rē) A story told aloud about an event. p. 2

GLOSSARY

palisade (pa•lə•sād′) A wall made of tall wooden poles. p. 59

Parliament (pär′lə•mənt) The part of the British government that makes laws for the British people. p. 156

Patriot (pā′trē•ət) A colonist who was against British rule and who supported independence. p. 158

patriotism (pā′trē•ə•ti•zəm) Love of one's country. p. 211

patroon (pə•trōōn′) A landowner in the Dutch colonies. p. 102

permanent (pûr′mə•nənt) Long-lasting. p. 99

physical feature (fi′zi•kəl fē′chər) A feature that was made by nature. p. 6

plantation (plan•tā′shən) A large farm. p. 109

plateau (pla•tō′) An area of high, level land. p. 29

point of view (point uv vyōō) A person's beliefs and ideas. p. 3

pollution (pə•lōō′shən) Anything that makes a natural resource dirty or unsafe to use. p. 339

population density (po•pyə•lā′shən den′sə•tē) The number of people who live in an area of a certain size. p. 328

precipitation (pri•si′pə•tā′shən) Water in the form of rain, sleet, hail, or snow that falls to Earth's surface. p. 38

primary source (prī′mâr•ē sôrs) A record made by someone who saw or took part in an event. p. 4

prime meridian (prīm mə•rid′ē•ən) An imaginary line that divides Earth into the Eastern Hemisphere and the Western Hemisphere. p. 24

proclamation (prä•klə•mā′shən) An order from a leader to the citizens. p. 137

product (prä′dəkt) Something that people make, grow, or raise, usually to sell. p. 43

profit (prä′fət) The money left over after all costs have been paid. p. 229

quarry (kwôr′ē) A place where stone is cut or blasted out of the ground. p. 43

ratify (ra′tə•fī) To approve. p. 183

ration (ra′shən) To limit the amount of something that a person can buy at one time. p. 312

raw material (rô mə•tir′ē•əl) A resource in its natural state, such as wood, that can be used to make a product. p. 93

recreation (re•krē•ā′shən) An activity that people do for fun. p. 326

reform (ri•fôrm′) To change for the better. p. 247

region (rē′jən) An area on Earth whose features make it different from other areas. pp. 6, 23

register (re′jə•stər) To sign up. p. 209

relative location (re′lə•tiv lō•kā′shən) The position of a place in relation to other places on Earth. p. 22

relief (ri•lēf′) The use of color or shadow to show differences in elevation on a globe or a map. p. 36

renewable (ri•nōō′ə•bəl) Able to be made again by nature or people. p. 43

repeal (ri•pēl′) To cancel. p. 158.

representation (re•pri•zen•tā′shən) The act of speaking for someone else. p. 157

representative (re•pri•zen′tə•tiv) A person chosen by a group and given power to make decisions for the group's members. p. 122

republic (ri•pub′lik) A form of government in which people elect representatives to govern the country. p. 182

reservation (re•zər•vā′shən) Land set aside by a government for use by Native Americans. p. 74

reservoir (re′zûr•vwär) A human-made lake that stores water held back by a dam. p. 44

responsibility (ri•spän•sə•bil′ə•tē) A duty; something a person should do because it is right and important. p. 207

revolution (re•və•lōō′shən) A sudden, complete change, such as the overthrow of a government. p. 161

riot (rī′ət) A violent protest. p. 250

rural (rōōr′əl) Having to do with the countryside. p. 46

sachem (sā′chəm) A chief of a clan. p. 61

scarce (skârs) Hard to find. p. 68

sea level (sē le′vəl) The level of the surface of the ocean. p. 29

secede (si•sēd′) To separate from. p. 250

secondary source (se′kən•der•ē sôrs) A record of an event made by someone who did not see it. p. 5

self-government (self•gu′vərn•mənt) Control of one's own government. p. 117

service industry (sûr′vəs in′dəs•trē) An industry made up of businesses that provide services rather than produce or sell goods. p. 330

slave (slāv) A person held against his or her will and forced to work without pay. p. 108

slave trade (slāv trād) The buying and selling of enslaved people. p. 108

society (sə•sī′ə•tē) A human group. p. 10

sound (sound) A narrow body of water that lies between a mainland and an island. p. 33

special district (spe'shəl dis'trikt) A form of local government that handles one problem or one service. p. 205

specialize (spe'shə•līz) To work at one kind of job that a person can do well. p. 68

stock (stäk) A share of ownership in a company. p. 184

stock exchange (stäk iks•chānj') A place where people can buy and sell stocks. p. 185

strike (strīk) A refusal to work until requested changes are made. p. 275

suburb (su'bərb) A town or small city near a larger city. p. 46

supply (sə•plī') The amount of a good or service offered for sale by a business. p. 272

sweatshop (swet shäp) A factory that had dangerous working conditions and where people had to work long hours for little pay. p. 274

technology (tek•nä'lə•jē) The use of new ideas or knowledge to do things. p. 239

telegraph (te'lə•graf) A machine that uses electricity to send messages over wires. p. 242

temperature (tem'pər•chûr) The measure of how hot or cold the air is. p. 38

tenant farmer (te'nənt fär'mər) A person who farmed land belonging to a manor owner. p. 132

tenement (te'nə•mənt) A run-down apartment building. p. 263

terrorism (ter'ər•i•zəm) The use of violence to promote a cause. p. 315

textile (tek'stīl) Cloth. p. 246

time line (tīm līn) A diagram that shows the important events that took place during a certain period of time. p. 104

time zone (tīm zōn) A region in which people use the same time. p. 244

tourism (toor'i•zəm) The selling of goods and services to visitors. p. 330

trade (trād) The buying and selling of goods. p. 60

trade-off (trād'ôf) The giving up of a chance to buy one thing in order to buy something else. p. 206

tradition (trə•di'shən) An idea, a belief, or a way of doing something that has been handed down from the past. p. 69

traitor (trā'tər) A person who works to harm his or her own country. p. 177

treaty (trē'tē) An official agreement between groups or countries. p. 178

tribe (trīb) A group of Native Americans united under one leader or sharing a culture or land. p. 54

tributary (tri'byoo•târ•ē) A stream or river that flows into a larger stream or river. p. 32

trustee (trəs•tē') An elected official who makes laws for a village. p. 204

turning point (tûr'ning point) An event that causes important changes. p. 176

turnpike (tûrn'pīk) A road that people must pay to use. p. 231

tyrant (tī'rənt) A leader who rules harshly. p. 117

unemployment (un•im•ploi'mənt) The number of workers without jobs. p. 309

urban (ûr'bən) Having to do with a city area. p. 45

urban sprawl (ûr'bən sprôl) The spread of urban areas and the growth of centers of business and shopping. p. 339

urbanization (ûr•bə•nə•zā'shən) The spread of city life. p. 277

veto (vē'tō) To refuse to give permission for a bill to become law. p. 193

wampum (wäm'pəm) Beads made from shells that were used by Native Americans as money and to mark agreements. p. 60

war bond (wôr bänd) A paper showing that the buyer has loaned money to the government to help pay the cost of a war. p. 302

wigwam (wig'wäm) A round, bark-covered shelter used by the Algonquians. p. 66

Index

Page references for illustrations are set in italic type. An italic *m* indicates a map. Page references set in boldface type indicate the pages on which vocabulary terms are defined.

Abolish, 249
Abolitionists, *248*, **249**, *249*, *m249*, *R2*
Absolute location, 24
Adams, John, 172, R13
Adapt, 54
Adirondack Mountains, 14–17, 29, *29*, 30, *m31*, 39
Adirondack Park, 29, *m292*
Adirondack Upland region, 29–31, *m31*, 39
Advertisements, 111, 275
Africa, *m24*
African Americans
abolitionists, *248*, 249, *249*, *R2*
in American Revolution, 150–153, 177
civil rights of, 314, *314*
during Civil War, 250–251
in Congress, 314
discrimination against, 313–314
education of, 124
in Harlem Renaissance, 308, *308*
inventions by, 272, *272*
literature of, 124, 308, *308*
migration of, 257, *257*, 308
music of, 308, *308*
in New York City, 257
in sports, 314
on Supreme Court, 314
women, *248*, 249, 308, *308*, 314, *314*, *347*, *R2*, *R15*
Africans, in colonies, 108, *108*, 123–124, 130 *See also* Slaves and slavery
Agriculture (farming), 42–43, *42*, 44, **54**, 331, *331*, *m337*
cities and, 281
dairy, 30, 42–43, *43*, 331, *m337*
of early people, *13*, 54, *54*, *81*
Farmers' Museum (Cooperstown) and, *338*, 339
manors in, 131–132
among Native Americans, 59, 66, 68, *81*
in New Netherland, 102–103, 109–110
in New York Colony, 131–132
plantations in, 109
regions for, 28, 32, 34

slash-and-burn, 59, *59*
soil for, 28, 32, 34, 44, 45, 59
tenant farmers in, 132
tools used in, *54*, 58
in upland regions, 28, 30
See also Crops
Airplanes, 307
Albany, *m12*, 13, *m22*, *m25*, 45, *m45*, 231
in American Revolution, 174–175, 176
buildings in, *116*, 130, 192, *192*
daily life in, 130
distance to other cities, 283
Empire State Plaza in, *188–189*
Erie Canal and, 233, *238*
as financial center, 332
immigrants in, 263
as metropolitan area, 325
New York state capitol building in, 192, *192*, 214, *m214*, *214–215*
New York State Museum in, 2, 324, 339
population in 1800s, *238*
population in 1700s, 130
See also Fort Orange
Albany Congress, 135
Albany County, 203, *m203*, R6
Albany Plan of Union, 135
Albion, *m25*, *m203*
Albright-Knox Art Gallery (Buffalo), 324
Alexandria Bay, 34
Algonquian languages, 13, 55, *m57*, 71
Algonquian tribes, 13, 65–69, *67*, *81*, 103
areas lived in, 65
birchbark canoes of, *66–67*, 68
division of labor in, 68, *68*
in French and Indian War, 134
villages of, 66
ways of life of, 65, 67–69, *68*, *69*
Allegany County, *m203*, R6
Allegany State Park, *m292*, 310
Allegheny Plateau, 30–31, *m31*
Allen, Ethan, 164, R13
Allen, Thomas S., 235
Alliance, 135
Allied Powers, 302–303
Allies, 135
in World War II, 311
Amendments, 183, 306

American Falls, 34, 35
American Federation of Labor (AFL), 275
American Indians. *See* Native American(s)
American Revolution, 163–179, *m164*, *172*, *m173*, *174*, *175*, *176*, *177*
African Americans in, 150–153, 177
battles in New York, *166*, 173–174, *m173*
beginning of, 162–167, *162*, *m164*, *165*
British surrender following, *149*, 178, 217
effects of, 178–179
France in, 176
importance of New York in, 172, 174–176
Native Americans in, 175, *175*, 177, 179
turning point of, 176
women in, 150–153, *174*, 178
Analyzing, 3
Ancestor, 53
Ancram, ironworks in, 129, *129*
Animals
bones of, as tools, 58
early people and, *52*, 53, *53*
extinction of, 54
hunting of, *12*, *52*, 53, *53*, 54, 58, 60, 65, 66, 68, *80*
introduced into the Americas, 96
skins for clothing, 53, 58, *58*, 59, *59*, 66
state, R4, *R5*
wildlife, *29*, *52*, *53*, 96, 99, R4
See also Livestock
Antarctica, *m24*
Anthony, Susan B., *248*, *248*, R13
Appalachian Mountains, A15, 30, *m31*
Appalachian Plateau, 30–31, *m31*, 46
Appeal, 194
Apple (state fruit), R4, *R4*
Apple Country Festival, 327
Apprentices, 110–111
Aqueducts, 235
Archaeologists, 55, *55*
Architecture, colonial, *106*, 110, *116*, 119, *120*, 130, *130*
Arnold, Benedict, 164, 175, 177, R13

Art(s)
centers for, 322.
Native American, *74*
in New York, 324–325, *325*
Arthur, Chester A., 200, *200*, R13
Articles of Confederation, 182
Artifacts, 55, *55*, 126–127, *126*, *127*
Asia, *m24*, 52, 325
Asian Americans
in civil rights movement, 314
discrimination against, 313–314
museum about, 325
Asian Americans for Equality, 314
Assembly, *85*, 145, 192, *192*, *196*
Assembly line, 307
Astor, John, R13
Atlantic Coastal Plain, A15, *m31*, 32
Atlantic Ocean, 21, 23, 39
Atlas, A1–A21
Auburn, *m203*, 231
Austria-Hungary, 302
Automobiles, 307, 335, 341
Aviation, 307
Axis Powers, 311

Badillo, Herman, 314, R13
Ball, Lucille, R13
Banking, 330, 332
Bar graph, 168–169, *169*, 187
double, **238,** *238*, 253
Bartholdi, Frédéric-Auguste, 258, *258*, R13
Baseball, 326, *326*
Basin, A20, *A20*
Basketball, 326
Bath, New York, *m25*, 231
Battle of Bemis Heights, 177
Battle of Concord, 163
Battle of Fort Necessity, 134
Battle of Fort William Henry, 136
Battle of Golden Hill, 163, *163*
Battle of Lexington, 163
Battle of Long Island, *148*, 178, *m180*, *m181*, 216
Battle of Oriskany, 175, *175*
Battle of Saratoga, 154, 176, *176–177*

INDEX

INDEX

INDEX

INDEX

INDEX

For permission to reprint copyrighted material, grateful acknowledgment is made to the following sources:

Atheneum Books for Young Readers, an imprint of Simon & Schuster Children's Publishing Division: Cover illustration from *The Big Tree* by Bruce Hiscock. Copyright © 1991 by Bruce Hiscock.

Betty J. Beam: From "World Wonder" by Betty J. Beam.

Candlewick Press Inc., Cambridge, MA: From *When Jessie Came Across the Sea* by Amy Hest, illustrated by P.J. Lynch. Text copyright © 1997 by Amy Hest; illustrations copyright © 1997 by P.J. Lynch.

Caroline House/Boyds Mills Press, Inc.: Cover photograph from *Hudson River: An Adventure From the Mountains to the Sea* by Peter Lourie. Photograph copyright © 1992 by Boyds Mills Press.

Chelsea House Publishers, a division of Main Line Book Co.: Cover illustration from *Peter Stuyvesant: Dutch Military Leader* by Joan Banks. © 2000 by Chelsea House Publishers, a division of Main Line Book Co.

Clarion Books/Houghton Mifflin Company: Cover illustration by Margot Tomes from *Anna, Grandpa, and the Big Storm* by Carla Stevens. Illustration copyright © 1982 by Margot Tomes.

Coward – McCann, a division of Penguin Young Readers Group, A Member of Penguin Group USA, Inc., 345 Hudson Street, New York, NY 10014: From *Phoebe and the General* by Judith Berry Griffin. Text copyright © 1977 by Judith Berry Griffin.

Delacorte Press, a division of Random House, Inc.: Cover illustration from *Lily's Crossing* by Patricia Reilly Giff. Copyright © 1997 by Patricia Reilly Giff.

Elsmere Music Inc.: From "I Love New York" by Steve Karmen. Lyrics copyright © by Steve Karmen.

Peggy Eyres: "Esther" by Sandra Weber and Peggy Eyres. Lyrics copyright © 1994 by Peggy Eyres/BMI.

Harcourt, Inc.: Cover illustration by Nancy Carpenter from *A Picnic in October* by Eve Bunting. Illustration copyright © 1999 by Nancy Carpenter. Cover illustration by Marek Los from *Lookin' for Bird in the Big City* by Robert Burleigh. Illustration copyright © 2001 by Marek Los.

HarperCollins Publishers: Cover illustration from *A More Perfect Union: The Story of Our Constitution* by Betsy and Giulio Maestro. Illustration copyright © 1987 by Giulio Maestro.

Historical Society of Rockland County: From "Marretje Haring April, 1687 Arrival" from *Adventures From the Past: True Stories of Children Who Lived Long Ago in Orangetown* by Alice Gerard. Text copyright © 1997 by The Historical Society of Rockland County.

Madison Press Books: Cover illustration by Laurie McGaw from *Journey to Ellis Island: How My Father Came to America* by Carol Bierman. Illustration copyright © 1998 by Laurie McGaw.

Mikaya Press Inc.: Cover illustration by Fernando Rangel from *Beyond the Sea of Ice: The Voyages of Henry Hudson* by Joan Elizabeth Goodman. Illustration copyright © by Fernando Rangel. Cover illustration by Alan Witschonke from *The Brooklyn Bridge* by Elizabeth Mann. Illustration copyright © by Alan Witschonke.

Prestel Verlag: From *Joe and the Skyscraper* by Dietrich Neumann, translated by Anne Heritage, illustrated by Andrea Madeleine Büdinger. Copyright © 1999 by Prestel Verlag.

G. P. Putnam's Sons, a division of Penguin Young Readers Group, A Member of Penguin Group (USA) Inc., 345 Hudson Street, New York, NY 10014: Cover illustration by David Shannon from *The Rough-Face Girl* by Rafe Martin. Illustration copyright © 1992 by David Shannon.

Tundra Books, McClelland & Stewart Young Readers: Cover illustration by Brian Deines from *Charlotte* by Janet Lunn. Illustration copyright © 1998 by Brian Deines.

Viking Penguin, a division of Penguin Young Readers Group, A Member of Penguin Group (USA) Inc., 345 Hudson Street, New York, NY 10014: Cover illustration from *Eleanor* by Barbara Cooney. Copyright © 1996 by Barbara Cooney.

All maps by MAPQUEST.COM

PHOTO CREDITS

Cover: Corbis (statue, flag); Maps.com (map); Nancie Battaglia (skaters); Bruce Coleman, Inc. (waterfall).

KEY: (t)=top, (c)=center, (b)=bottom, (l)=left, (r)=right.

INTRODUCTION

Page i, ii, iv, Museum of the City of New York; v, Museum of Civilization, Canada; vi, Mariners Museum, Newport News, Virginia; vii, Politicalbadges.com; viii, Beryl Goldberg; facing page 1, ChromoSohm/Photo Researchers, Inc.; 1, Museum of the City of New York; 2(t), Library of Congress; 2(c), Corbis; 2(b), Rafael Macia/Photo Researchers, Inc.; 3(t to b), Tom & Dee Ann McCarthy/Corbis, Anthony Redpath/Corbis, Richard T. Nowitz/Photo Researchers, Inc., Catherine Karnow/Woodfin Camp & Associates, Marilyn "Angel" Wynn/Nativestock.com; 4(l), National Archives and Records Administration; 4(c), (r), Museum of the City of New York; 5(t), Pictures, Inc.; 5(b), Joseph Sohm/Corbis; 7(cl), Getty Images; 7(b), Johann Schumacher; (tr), Stephen Varone/Grace Davies Photography; 8, HSP; 9(t), Reprinted with the permission of the New York State Secretary of State; 9(b), E.R. Degginger/Color-Pic; 10(t), Bruce Coleman, Inc.; 10(c), Beryl Goldberg; 10(b), Michael P. Gadomski/Photo Researchers, Inc.

UNIT 1

Opener, Fotoconcept/Bertsch/Bruce Coleman, Inc.; 11(t), Canadian Museum of Civilization, 18-19, Ted Spiegel/The Image Works; 21, Phil Norton/Fraser Photos; 23(l), NASA; 23(r), Ken M. Johns/Photo Researchers, Inc.; 28-29, Michael P. Gadomski/Superstock; 29(t), Hardie Truesdale; 29(inset), Tom Murphy/Superstock; 30(t), Adirondack Research Library; 30(b), Nancie Battaglia; 32(t), New York Stock Photo/Ambient Images; 32(b), Paul Rezendes; 33, courtesy of Howe Caverns; 34(t), photo courtesy of Cornell University; 34(b), E.R. Degginger/Color-Pic; 35, Superstock; 36, Mark Turner/Turner Photographics; 38, Nancie Battaglia; 40, Reuters NewMedia/Corbis; 41, Getty Images; 42, New York Photo/Ambient Images; 43(t), J. Meuser/Photolink Image & Design; 44, Robert Holmes/Corbis; 45, Corbis; 46, Panoramic Images; 47, Nancie Battaglia; 50-51, Andy Olenick/Fotowerks; 53, Abbe Museum; 54, Marilyn "Angel" Wynn/Nativestock.com; 55, State University of New York, Albany & New York State Museum; 60(t), The Mariners Museum, Newport News, VA; 60(b), Museum of Civilization, Canada; 61(t), Shako: wi Cultural Center; 61(b), The New-York Historical Society/Bridgeman Art Library International; 63, The Granger Collection, New York; 64, Library of Congress; 65, Detroit Institute of Art; 67, Museum of Civilization, Canada; 68, Haffenreffer Museum; 69, Marilyn "Angel" Wynn/Nativestock.com; 70, Corbis; 71, Eugene & Clare Thaw Collection, New York State Historical Association, Cooperstown, NY; 72, Nathan Benn/Corbis; 73(b), Darlene Bordwell, Ambient Light Photography; 74(t), Stonedust.com; 74(b), courtesy, Joann Shenandoah; 75(l); Shako: wi Cultural Center; 75(r), Marilyn "Angel" Wynn/Nativestock.com; 78-79(background) Andy Olenick/Fotowerks; 78-79(all others), Shako: wi Cultural Center.

UNIT 2

Opener, Lee Snider/The Image Works; 83(t), The Mariners Museum, Newport News, Virginia; 90-91, Peter Gridley; 92(both), The Granger Collection, New York; 93, Tony Falhouse; 94, The Granger Collection, New York; 96, Bettmann/Corbis; 98, L.F. Tantillo; 99(t), Museum of the City of New York; 99(b), 100, The Granger Collection, New York; 102(both) The New-York Historical Society; 103, North Wind Picture Archive; 104(l), The New-York Historical Society/Bridgeman Art Library International; 104(r), 105(both), The Granger Collection, New York; 106-107, Yale Center for British Art, Paul Mellon Collection; 107(t), Stock Montage; 108(t), The Granger Collection, New York; 108(b), Brooklyn Historical Society; 109(t); The New-York Historical Society/Bridgeman Art Library International; 109(b), Duncan William Strong Museum, Columbia University; 110(t), Albany Institute of History & Art; 110(bl), The New-York Historical Society/Bridgeman Art Library International; (bc), Museum of the City of New York; (br), The New-York Historical Society; 111(l), The Granger Collection, New York; (r), The New-York Historical Society; 114-115, Lee Snider Photo Images; 116, Albany Institute of History & Art; 117, James C. Johnson, Jr., photo by Steven Vater; 118(t), The Granger Collection, New York; 118(b), Getty Images; 119, Darlene Bordwell/Ambient Light Photography; 120(l), Corbis; (r), Jeff Greenberg/Photo Researchers, Inc.; 122 National Portrait Gallery, London; 124, The Granger Collection, New York; 125, The Historical Society of the Courts of the State of New York; 126(both), The New-York Historical Society/Bridgeman Art Library International; 127(all), The New-York Historical Society; 128, The Mariners Museum, Newport News, VA; 128(inset), New Bedford Whaling Museum; 129(bl), Darlene Bordwell/Ambient Light Photography; 129(r), 130(t), The Granger Collection, New York; 130(c), The Blackwell Education Museum; 130(b), Albany Institute of History & Art; 131, Grace Davies Photography; 132, Bridgeman Art Library International; 133, Thomas R. Fletcher; 135(l), The Corcoran Gallery of Art/Corbis; 135(r), Corbis; 136(t), Syracuse Newspapers/The Image Works; 136(bl), McCord Museum; 136(br), JLG Ferris; 138, Nancy Rotenberg; 142-143, Angelart Fine Photography. Used with permission.; 142(inset), Photolink Image & Design; 143(tl), Old fort Niagara; 143(tr), Angelart Fine Photography. Used with permission.; 143(b), Corbis, 146, Harcourt.

EXCELSIOR